A History of Rice University

A Rice University Studies Special Publication

A HISTORY OF

Rice University

The Institute Years, 1907–1963

FREDERICKA MEINERS

Published in cooperation with the Rice University Historical Commission

Rice University Studies · Houston, Texas

To the memory of
William Marsh Rice, Edgar Odell Lovett,
and all the men and women who
have contributed to the building of
Rice University

CONTENTS

ILLUSTRATIONS

FOREWORD

This history of Rice University during its first fifty years is largely the product of the inspiration and hard work of a Rice alumnus, Willoughby Williams (Rice '39). Willoughby, a long-time staunch supporter of Rice, was one of the primary forces in an earlier project that brought to publication *William Marsh Rice and His Institute*, a volume based on the work of historian Andrew Forest Muir and edited by Sylvia Morris. That book derived to a considerable extent from an existing manuscript that had been prepared by Muir before his death. Work on a history of the university loomed as a much larger project, since materials and oral histories would have to be compiled from scratch. To Willoughby, ably seconded by Ray Watkin Hoagland (Rice '36) and a group of other interested individuals, time was critical. Many of the early records of the university had already been lost beyond recovery, and much that was available only in the memories of early faculty and graduates would soon be gone. If a history of the early years of the university was to be written, it had to be done without delay.

Willoughby began to organize support, and the Rice University Historical Commission was formed in 1975 with H. Malcolm Lovett (Rice '21) as chairman. I agreed to direct the project with the advice of historian and provost Frank E. Vandiver and archivist Nancy Boothe Parker (Rice '52). Willoughby Williams, aided by Malcolm Lovett and Ray Hoagland (and later by E. Joe Shimek, Rice '29, and John B. Coffee, Rice '34), spearheaded the money-raising aspects of the work, and a three-year project was organized to survey the existing records, recover what was possible of the early material, interview key figures, and write the history of Rice from its founding through 1962–63, the year of the semicentennial celebrating the opening of Rice in 1912. This work would not have been possible without Willoughby Williams, Joe Shimek, and all those individuals who contributed money and time in support of our effort.

This history has been written in order to recapture as accurately as possible the story of the planning and dedication, as well as the working out in practice, of the ideas of a group of men devoted to creating an educational institution worthy of the trust evinced by William Marsh Rice when in 1891 he drew up an indenture containing the outlines for the institution he intended to endow. The goals of William Marsh Rice himself, of the members of the first Board of Trustees, and of Edgar Odell Lovett, the first president of the university, provided the guidelines by which the institution gradually worked out its organization and plans for the future.

Although Rice University (officially Rice Institute throughout most of the time covered by this history) is the central focus of this book, Rice cannot be regarded as standing in isolation from the rest of the world of university education. If in these pages it sometimes appears that Rice faced unusual financial problems during the Great Depression, we should remember that those problems were different only in detail from problems facing every institution of higher learning at the time; if Rice faced problems reestablishing its educational image following the conclusion of World War II, so also did every other university worthy of the name. The world of education is not static. William Marsh Rice himself had experienced some feeling of this in the gradual shift of his goal from endowing an orphans' technical school to endowing an institution of higher learning for the advancement of science, literature, and art. Likewise the ideas of the members of the Board of Trustees expanded and developed through their years of grappling with the problems of freeing the endowment of entanglements, of searching for a president for the new institution, and of working with a series of notable university presidents, beginning with the first, Edgar Odell Lovett, in setting goals for the university and striving to attain those goals in practice.

Our author, Fredericka Meiners (Rice '63), who holds the Ph.D. in history, is well trained for her task, and she has worked long and hard to portray this history of Rice as accurately as possible. Of course, since she is a Rice alumna, she cannot be unbiased—no alumnus is. The great majority of students who have attended Rice have loved the place—for its weaknesses as well as for its strengths. Miss Meiners is no exception. Hers is an honest representation based on a great deal of work and a careful sifting of the source material available. I hope that you like it—I too am an alum.

Katherine Fischer Drew '44

PREFACE

Students at Rice learn slowly about the history of the university. During freshman orientation they hear the story of the founder's murder. They tour the campus and begin to appreciate the buildings and their often whimsical decorations. Tales of professors or past events are passed down through the student grapevine, and traditions are maintained, although even those change with time. A professor may relate a story from the "good old days" some fifteen or twenty years ago; the student newspaper, the *Thresher*, may reprint an item from an early edition, explain the evolution of the college court system, or describe the development of the spring festival, Rondelet, and its component Beer-Bike Race. An alumnus may ask a current student how things are going and then start reminiscing with the ominous words, "Now, when I was at Rice, it was really hard." Through these sources students gain a piecemeal knowledge of the past, lore that often has little meaning for present residents of Rice, who are naturally more interested in the university as they experience it. It is the view of Rice that one absorbs as a student that tends to stick in the mind and that often leads to the assumption that Rice is unchanging. Only by active, prolonged involvement with the university, its faculty, and its students does an alumnus really see changes taking place within the structure.

My original view of Rice was as an undergraduate coming to the campus in 1959 (when it was still the Rice Institute). After staying for an additional year beyond my B.A. in 1963 to earn a teaching certificate, I left to teach in public school. I retained some of my ties on campus and read about events there, and when I returned to Rice in 1970 for graduate work, I did not expect much difficulty in adapting myself.

What I found, however, was a university much changed. It was bigger: more buildings, more students, more professors, more courses. There was an administrative bureaucracy. The feeling was more impersonal; gone were the days when everyone knew almost everyone else on campus. There was also somehow a different atmosphere, a more relaxed, less pressure-filled existence for the undergraduates. Perhaps this was due to the changed curriculum. Every other undergraduate seemed to be a "double major," a difficult status to obtain in my previous student days because of all the specific courses required. There were also many smaller changes. No longer were women plagued with the regulation against wearing pants in the library. The Chemistry Lecture Hall was air-conditioned and sported upholstered seats. Freshmen were downright pampered during orientation week, and liquor could be served on campus.

Even with the changes, however, Rice was recognizable to a graduate of 1963. Some of the old student irreverence toward the place lingered, much softened and showing up hilariously in the performances of the MOB (Marching Owl Band). A great deal of pressure remained. Students still found it difficult to explain what Rice was really like to their friends who had gone to other schools. That particular brand of self-deprecating arrogance and snobbishness was still manifest, now in T-shirt inscriptions: "I go to Rice, I must be smart." The college system was stronger than ever, as were the perennial complaints about the college food service. And even without a speaker at commencement, Rice managed a satisfying spectacle with flags flying, the traditional simple ceremony, and attention where it belonged: on the graduates.

When I returned to Rice in 1976 to write its history, I knew that change and development would be one of my major themes, as it is for almost any history. At the same time I knew that there were several different perceptions of that change that I would have to explore. The Board of Governors had one perspective on the Institute, the faculty another, the students still another, and the outside world yet a different one. My main areas for concern would be the board's actions, usually involving finances, construction, and presidential searches; the university administration's decisions and actions relating to a wide range of subjects; and faculty actions and changes. Curriculum developments would be important because they would show what kind of education Rice offered its students and hence what kind of university program its presidents and faculty envisioned. I would also want to report on student life, from student associations to hazing, from special campus events to routine occurrences, from the trials of athletic teams to student attitudes toward Rice in general.

Since it is impossible to name every person of prominence on campus and to tell every story, I knew I would have to limit my coverage of this area to firsts (such as the first May Fete queen and king), to stories involving many people, and to ongoing events and traditions, hoping to evoke memories in the minds of alumni while describing student life sufficiently for nonalumni to understand.

As I began to explore the sources it became clear that I could not organize the story around a series of chapters dealing with single topics, such as one chapter on all the board decisions and another on curriculum development. Each topic was tied to the others, so interlocked that telling each separately would make the story incomprehensible. So I have told the story chronologically. After a synopsis of the events leading to the founding of the Institute, William Marsh Rice's murder, and actions settling the murder case and Rice's will, this history begins with receipt of the endowment by the board in 1907. It ends with the semicentennial year, 1962–63. This is a convenient stopping point for a variety of reasons. Up to that time, even considering the growth of the Institute after World War II and perhaps despite the change in student attitudes in the 1950s, Rice history seems a coherent fabric. During the 1960s, partly through President Pitzer's expansion program, partly because of the turmoil and changes in American society as a whole, the Rice that emerged was not the same, in real and in subtle ways.

To tell the later story would greatly lengthen the time needed for research and writing and would involve events too recent for us to have developed a historical perspective. Furthermore, it was a problem to decide where to stop if I continued past 1963. I did not find it sensible to end with Kenneth Pitzer's departure, or Frank E. Vandiver's acting presidency, or Norman Hackerman's arrival; either too much was still unsettled at each of these points, or my history would seem just to meander to a close. By stopping in 1963 I could include the name change from Institute to University, introduce the new president and his plans, use the formal opening and the semicentennial as stylistic bookends, and finish optimistically.

Sources for the history up to 1963 were not as plentiful as I had hoped. The most important were the collection of Presidents' Papers, other collections such as the Watkin Papers, copies of Rice publications, and various artifacts in the Woodson Research Center of Fondren Library, where the archives of the university are located. These documents did not satisfy my historian's curiosity. As a private institution in a time of little regulation by any outside entity, the Institute was not obliged to keep many records. The only office that could be counted on to have its records intact was that of the registrar. The Presidents' Papers are full of lacunae: in some instances no memoranda were kept (if they were ever written), papers were lost in floods or were simply cleaned out of the files and thrown away when the relevant matters were settled. Rice was a small community, and much of its business was transacted by one person who consulted another, arrived at a decision, and implemented it without recording it. No Deans' Papers exist for the first fifty years, except for a few letters and some other information from Dean Cameron's tenure in the 1950s. The minutes of the faculty have been preserved and were quite valuable in tracing curriculum development. The minutes of the Board of Governors are complete in the treasurer's office, but the correspondence files are nearly empty for the years before 1940. Departmental records simply do not exist before the fifties. I was surprised to find that for many matters I had more information on the early days than I did for the beginning of Pitzer's administration. Much of the Pitzer collection has not yet been carefully inventoried; I expect that more detailed information from the first years of that administration will be found in it.

Fortunately, there are still a number of people living who remember the beginnings of the school. Or to put it another way, as Allie Mae Autry Kelley did at the reunion of the fifty-year classes in 1976, "Isn't it wonderful that so many of us are still vertical!" I am indebted to the alumni and faculty members who were kind enough to share their memories. Interviews with them were extremely helpful, giving me information for which there was no other source. Since memories are notoriously tricky,

I have tried not to use information from an interview unless I had corroborating evidence from another informant or in a written source. The tapes and transcripts from these interviews will be placed in the Woodson Research Center after the project is completed.

I have enjoyed looking into the past of Rice University. There were many outstanding personalities to consider, a few mysteries to unravel, and a number of things to learn. Most of my preconceptions were confirmed, but not all. (For example, although excellence has always been its standard, Rice was never as wealthy as legend had painted it.) I have met a number of Rice graduates and found that, even though we are of different generations, we speak the same language concerning the university—most of the time. Some of my opinions, formed after the change I perceive in student attitudes in the 1950s, are closer to those of present students than to those of students who graduated fifteen years before me.

I do not envy whoever picks up the story from here and has the task of describing and explaining the 1960s, but I wish that person well. I know that he or she will enjoy, as I have, being the first on the scene to work with all the sources, trying to decide what really happened and why, while attempting to maintain a balance between a professional history and what might be called a popular one. I hope that whoever carries on the story will be a Rice

graduate. Rice is not like other universities. And all of its alumni should rejoice in that fact.

Fredericka Meiners
July 1982

ACKNOWLEDGMENTS

I have many people to thank for their help with this history. The members of the Rice Historical Commission gave both financial and moral support. Their interest made it considerably easier to get the job done. Katherine Drew let me work with a minimum of interference and a maximum of aid. Frank Vandiver answered many questions about the past and the present, and Nancy Parker guided me through the archives in the Woodson Research Center. The staff of the center gave much of their time and energy to the project and put up with me and my assistants at the same time. Moira Sullivan, a graduate assistant, was indispensable for her interest and observations and for her exhaustive inventory of the Presidents' Papers. Holly Leitz had to decipher my scribblings and produce a clean typed copy of the manuscript. Elizabeth Williams, Bryan Pedeaux, and Ray Watkin Hoagland began the interviews before I arrived; they asked all the right questions. My editors at Rice University Studies, first Kathleen Much and then Barbara Burnham, must be especially commended for their excellent and professional aid. I wish to thank especially all the alumni and friends of Rice who gave generously of their time to be interviewed. Without them the history would have been impossible. To the many readers of the manuscript versions, especially Ray Hoagland, Eula Goss Wintermann, and H. Malcolm Lovett, I wish also to express my appreciation for their careful reading and valuable suggestions.

F.M.

CHAPTER 1

The Opening

Emblazoned with a silver seal and blue ribbon, invitations went out in wooden cylinders to the leading universities and learned societies of the world: the president and trustees of the Rice Institute request a representative at the formal opening of the new university in Houston, Texas, on October 10, 11, and 12, 1912. Replies came from the University of Paris, the Royal Society of London, the American Philosophical Society, Harvard, Yale, and Princeton, the American Society of Civil Engineers, the National Geographic Society, the South African School of Mines and Technology, the University of the Philippines, and from scores of others. They were happy to send delegates to the ceremonies and wished the Institute well in its endeavors.[1]

So gathered in Houston a group such as few Texans had ever seen: mathematicians, biologists, physicists, philosophers, poets, historians, engineers—illustrious scholars, preeminent representatives of their fields, leaders of their own institutions, all arriving to celebrate the Institute's opening.

Situated on a low-lying coastal plain fifty miles inland from the Gulf of Mexico, Houston was a fast-growing adolescent city of 109,000 in 1912.[2] Except for the port of Galveston, there were no large towns for miles around. Coming from the northeast, many of the visitors might have looked upon their trip as something of an adventure: Houston was not known for its cultural attractions in 1912, and the very word "Texas" conjured visions of the wild western frontier. The city did offer opportunities, although they were more financial than aesthetic or intellectual. The old money came from southern staples—cotton, cattle, and lumber—but recent big oil discoveries in East Texas and production of sulfur in Brazoria County to the south augured well for the future.

At the time of the opening, Houston was a commercial town, seemingly more interested in the advantages of dredging a ship channel to the Gulf than in the higher aspects of the mind. Official Houston was not blind, however, to the attractions that might derive from a university. One newspaper editor was so bold as to declare that the Rice Institute would be more valuable to Houston than two Panama Canals and would add thousands to the city's population.[3] Whether Houstonians viewed the addition as offering intellectual benefits or monetary ones, they turned out to give the Institute a rousing send-off. City dignitaries attended all the functions, and several clubs opened their doors to guests of the Institute. The Chamber of Commerce hosted one of the breakfasts for the delegates. Many Houstonians saw some part of the ceremonies. There was much to see and hear.

President Edgar Odell Lovett and the Board of Trustees under the chairmanship of Captain

1. *Main Street, downtown Houston, 1915.*

2. *Delegates and visitors to the formal opening ceremonies of the William Marsh Rice Institute, Saturday, October 12, 1912.*

James A. Baker had invited and assembled an outstanding group of scholars. University of London professor Sir William Ramsay, a Nobel laureate knighted for his contributions in chemistry, came to speak on the transmutation of matter; the eminent botanist Hugo de Vries of the University of Amsterdam on the biological form of transmutation in hered-ity; and the historian Rafael Altamira y Crevea of the University of Oviedo, Spain, on the history of human progress. The celebrated Emile Borel from the University of Paris lectured on mathematics, Sir Henry Jones from Glasgow discussed philosophy, and Vito Volterra, a senator of Italy, spoke on mathematics and the work of Henri Poincaré, who had been invited to speak but died after preparing his lectures for the opening.

Another group of invited lecturers presented their work by title at the ceremonies, with the actual papers being published later. Sir John William Mackail of London discussed poetry in modern life, and Frederik Carl Störmer from Christiania, Norway, wrote on cosmic physics and magnetic storms. From Tokyo came a paper by Privy Councilor Baron Dairoku Kikuchi on the introduction of western learning into Japan. The noted Italian philosopher and statesman Benedetto Croce wrote on art, and Privy Councilor Wilhelm Ostwald from Leipzig, Germany, discussed the theory of education.

Speakers at luncheons, dinners, and other gatherings included Dean William Francis Magie and Professor Edwin Grant Conklin of Princeton, President Harry Pratt Judson of the University of Chicago, Chancellor James Hampton Kirkland of Vanderbilt, Dean George Cary Comstock of the University of Wisconsin, and President Samuel Palmer Brooks of Baylor University. David Starr Jordan of Stanford, Ira Remsen of Johns Hopkins, Sidney Edward Mezes of the University of Texas, David Ross Boyd of the University of New Mexico, and William Trufant Foster of Reed College were only a few of the university presidents representing their institutions.

In the words of former Rice bursar John T. McCants, a "rather elaborate" schedule was arranged for the guests. His characterization was something of an understatement. President Lovett and the board had devised a program requiring stamina but also offering much entertainment. Thursday, October 10, and Friday the eleventh began with breakfast at the best hotel in town, the eleven-story Bender. Lectures followed at 10:30 in the Faculty Chamber of the Administration

Building at the Rice Institute. On Thursday the mayor and commissioners of Houston invited the delegates to lunch at the City Auditorium's banquet hall; afterwards all returned to the Institute for more lectures and an informal garden party. Thursday evening Hugo de Vries gave a popular illustrated lecture entitled "The Ideal of a Naturalist" at the Majestic Theater, and Captain and Mrs. Baker hosted a reception at their home.

Photographs and written accounts record the celebration. Those who knew many of the delegates in person or by reputation found it striking to see Ramsay, de Vries, Borel, and the others in the middle of a Texas prairie, or even in the banquet room of the Hotel Bender. The English biologist Julian Huxley, soon to be an instructor at the Institute, was not impressed with the speeches of some of the Texas politicians, especially that of Governor Oscar B. Colquitt, who spoke extemporaneously about the wonders of Texas. But a graceful little address by Dean Comstock of Wisconsin more than compensated for the governor's boasting.[4] Colquitt's luncheon address was one of the first in a long line of speeches and lectures to be heard in the next two days.

After the next morning's talks, Friday afternoon was filled by a luncheon at the Thalian Club given by Mr. and Mrs. Jonas Shearn Rice at one o'clock, a concert by the Kneisel Quartet of New York at the Majestic at three, a garden party given by Mr.

and Mrs. Edwin Brewington Parker at five o'clock, and another concert by the Kneisel Quartet in the Faculty Chamber at eight-thirty. Dinner in the Commons of the residential hall on campus rounded out a busy day.

By Friday night's dinner, which started much later than scheduled, some of the guests were feeling the effects of the constant activities. The first course, a grapefruit filled with a combination of potent liquors,[5] brightened the guests' outlook and provided some amusement; but afterwards the speeches continued. This round consisted of responses by the principal speakers, toasting the new institution in the name of various disciplines such as mathematics and philosophy.

After eight such addresses, cut short in some cases by the responder as he remarked on the lateness of the hour, Boston architect Ralph Adams Cram was called upon to speak about art. Julian Huxley, who was sitting next to Lady Ramsay, reported that "Cram rose to his feet, produced an enormous roll of typescript from his pocket and proceeded to read implacably on. After twenty minutes, the lady could stand no more: 'Oh, I am so tired! . . . ' she said, and let her head fall forward on to her hands on the table."[6]

Saturday was different; Saturday was special. Tired or not, at 9:30 A.M. the delegates and guests assembled in academic regalia at the residential hall and proceeded to the cloisters of the Administration Building for the formal dedication of the Insti-

3. *The academic procession at the formal opening ceremonies. The grounds were still under construction, with debris scattered in the background.*

tute. A band led the way. Upon reaching the Academic Court, speakers and board members mounted the platform, while delegates took their seats in the semicircle of chairs arranged in front.

First came a reading from the Bible and the singing of "Veni Creator Spiritus." Then Henry Van Dyke of Princeton read the inaugural poem, "Texas, A Democratic Ode," followed by Chief Justice Thomas Jefferson Brown of the Texas Supreme Court speaking on education and the state. Thomas Frank Gailor, the Episcopal bishop of Tennessee, discoursed on education and the church. President Lovett then had his opportunity to expound on the new university's source in the legacy of William Marsh Rice; its site in the South, in Texas, and in Houston; the scope of its activity; and its spirit of inquiry, inspiration, and progress.

A glimpse of the high purpose and enthusiastic spirit of adventure shared by the small group of students and faculty at the inauguration could be seen in the address. It reflected the idealistic and hopeful attitude of the early years of the Rice Institute and contained the germ of many ideas that, combined, were to make Rice unique. In the actual address and its expanded version published in Volume I, Number 1 of the *Rice Institute Pamphlet*, Lovett spoke of educating an intellectual elite, of community service, an honor system, a collegiate residential system, a broad liberal education, and of recognizing outstanding scholarship by awards and financial assistance. No less important were a spirit of independent judgment and initiative in scholarly re-

4. *Delegates and guests proceeding past the new dormitory, South Hall, and the Commons, both still under construction.*

search. The ceremony closed with the choir singing the "One Hundredth Psalm"; the Reverend Dr. Charles Frederic Aked, pastor of the First Congregational Church of San Francisco, pronounced the benediction.

After more speeches lunch was served in the Commons, and there were more congratulatory addresses. Another reception followed, this one given by Dr. and Mrs. Lovett at the young but elegant Houston Country Club. Then the delegates boarded a special train to Galveston for a sea-food supper and overnight accommodations at the Hotel Galvez, without speeches, for a change. The special train brought everyone back to Houston on Sunday for a religious service in the City Auditorium with a sermon by the Reverend Dr. Aked. Many Protestant churches in Houston omitted their morning services so their members could join in the dedication.[7]

The formal opening ceremonies caused a certain amount of disruption in class schedules, but for the most part the stu-dents were on the outskirts of the festivities. They heard some of the lectures in the Faculty Chamber from the small balcony above the entrance and were much impressed by the dignitaries there. A number of young men also found themselves invited to the dinner in the Commons when so many tired guests did not come that several tables were empty. These students devoured everything from the punch-filled grapefruit to dessert—quite a meal for brand-new freshmen.[8]

Photographs of the events

5. *Professor Henry Van Dyke of Princeton University reading the inaugural poem, "Texas, A Democratic Ode," which he wrote as part of the formal dedication ceremonies. October 12, 1912.*

show a physical plant in an imperfect state. No building was finished. Although exteriors were presentable, interiors were another matter. The Faculty Chamber, a high-ceilinged room approximately twenty-seven feet wide by eighty feet long, did have churchlike pews installed along each side facing the center aisle in the collegiate style; and the stage where the lecturers stood was in place. The lighting, however, consisted of bare bulbs dangling at the end of long wires extending from holes in the ceiling. Neither the chamber nor the Commons was large enough for the Saturday convocation, so a platform for the speakers was erected outside, on the west side of the Administration Building.

The new university's grounds look bleak in the black-and-white photographs. Construction equipment is strewn about in the background, and only the large-gravel beds for the roads had been laid, not the fine-gravel top. Although trees had been planted to line the roadways, one notices the street lights first because they are considerably taller than the trees. Shrubs and hedges had also been planted, but their slight size and the lack of landscaping around the Administration Building seem accentuated by potted palms and other movable shrubbery placed about the building and platform at regular intervals for the ceremonies. The view from the Administration Building was still prairie, and the distance between buildings looks greater than it actually was because of the open spaces.

6. *Interior of the Faculty Chamber in the Administration Building, 1912.*

7. *Approach to the Administration Building from Main Street, showing the Mechanical Laboratory on the right and new trees and shrubbery planted along the fence. October 12, 1912.*

Unfinished buildings and grounds did not deter either the speakers or the academic procession. Even the weather cooperated to welcome the new Institute with benevolence. Thursday and Friday were warm, with the temperature about ninety degrees; but a breeze helped cool the visitors. Evening temperatures in the low seventies made the days bearable. Saturday morning's procession also had a breeze to help it along, and in the photographs some of the delegates appear to be in full sail as they approach the Administration Building.[9]

On Sunday afternoon the delegates, guests, and other participants began their trip home, leaving the institution of higher learning to the members of its faculty, who had been much in evidence at the exercises, and to its first students, who had not.[10]

Indeed, delegates outnumbered the stalwart little band of young men and women who came to the untried school; those guests probably thought that the adventure in Texas was over. But that did not matter. The president, faculty, and students would have the real adventure—beginning the William M. Rice Institute.

CHAPTER 2

The Beginnings

The Rice Institute had an eventful beginning by any definition. Its story opened with William Marsh Rice—Massachusetts-born merchant, cotton trader, businessman—who had made a great deal of money in Texas. Rice was interested in education (his father's interest in it may have influenced him) and in somehow returning part of his wealth to society. By 1880, at the age of sixty-three, he was considering the establishment of some philanthropic enterprise to be the beneficiary of his millions. His first wife, Margaret Bremond Rice, had died in 1863, and in 1867 Rice had married a young widow, Julia Elizabeth Baldwin Brown. Both marriages were childless. Influenced by the example of Stephen Girard (who had established Girard College in Philadelphia) and Peter Cooper (of Cooper Union for the Advancement of Science and Art in New York City), Rice first intended to build an orphans' institute in Somerset County, New Jersey. In 1882 he made a will leaving the bulk of his estate to such an institution, hoping that he might help those without family or influence to secure training for a skilled job.

Before the orphans' home was set up, however, Rice changed his mind. While in Houston on business in 1886 or 1887, Rice visited his old friend Cesar M. Lombardi, who was president of the Houston School Board. Lombardi was looking for money with which to build a municipal high school. Since Rice had made a large part of his fortune in Houston, Lombardi suggested that Rice leave some of it to the city in the form of a school. Rice made no immediate decision, but by the spring of 1891, he had decided what he would do with his money. He informed Lombardi that he wanted to endow an "institution of learning" similar to Cooper Union but separate from the public school system, to be called the William M. Rice Institute of Literature, Science and Art. Provisions were to be made for financing, including a $200,000 note to be held as endowment; but beyond that Rice did not want anything to be done during his lifetime toward the establishment of the Institute.[1]

On May 13, 1891, Rice and the six trustees whom he had picked signed a deed of indenture for "a Public Library and Institute for the Advancement of Literature, Science and Art." On May 19 the charter for the William M. Rice Institute was registered in Austin, and the deed of indenture was included in the charter. The six trustees were Lombardi; Emanuel Raphael, president of the Houston Electric Light and Power Company and trustee of the Houston public school system; Rice's brother Frederick, a banker and treasurer of the Houston and Texas Central Railroad; James E. McAshan, a banker; Alfred S. Richardson, a director of the Houston and Texas Central Railroad; and James A. Baker, Jr., Rice's attorney.

8. *William Marsh Rice as an older man. This engraving was the frontispiece of B. H. Carroll's* Standard History of Houston, Texas *(Knoxville, Tenn.: H. W. Crew & Co., 1912).*

In 1892 Rice drew up four deeds of gift with his second wife Elizabeth as cosigner and gave the recently incorporated Institute a sizable amount of land in several parcels. The most important for the school would be almost 50,000 acres of timberland in Beauregard Parish, Louisiana. The Institute also received nearly 10,000 acres in Jones County, Texas, seven acres in Houston fronting on Louisiana Street (listed in the deed as "Site of the Institute"), and the Capitol Hotel at Main Street and Texas Avenue. After his second wife's death in 1896, Rice made a new will leaving the bulk of his estate to the Institute.

From 1896 to 1904 the proposed endowment of the Institute was in jeopardy. Mrs. Rice died in Houston on July 24, 1896, having made an extraordinary will on her deathbed without her husband's knowledge, disposing of one-half of all assets acquired by Mr. Rice during their marriage. This will included a repudiation of the deeds for the Institute, and it named as executor Houston attorney Orren Holt, the husband of a woman who had attended Mrs. Rice constantly in her last illness. Mrs. Rice's will was in accordance with Texas community property laws; but since the Rices were not actually Texas residents at the time, William Marsh Rice was confident that the will was not valid. He contested it. The case had not yet been resolved when on September 23, 1900, Rice himself died under mysterious circumstances in New York City. To the consternation of James A. Baker, Jr., and the other Institute trustees, one Albert T. Patrick, lawyer and colleague of Orren Holt, materialized with a new will purporting to supersede Mr. Rice's will of 1896. Patrick also produced a general assignment under which he assumed control of all of Rice's property. Under the new documents the Institute would get nothing.

Baker rushed to New York and, with Rice's New York lawyers and the cooperation of the district attorney's office, investigated the sudden death and suspect legal instruments. As a result Patrick and Rice's young valet, Charles Jones, were indicted on October 4, 1900, for forgery of the will and other documents. Soon after that the coroner reported that he had found a fatal quantity of bichloride of mercury in Rice's vital organs.

The manservant Jones confessed that he and Patrick had murdered the elderly gentleman. Jones claimed that Patrick had held a towel containing chloroform over Rice's nose and mouth until he had ceased to breathe. In addition, he admitted that the two of them had been administering mercury pills to Rice before the successful murder. After this confession Jones twice tried to commit suicide in prison and was confined to Bellevue Hospital. Patrick, who had been released on bail from the forgery charge, was arrested again in March 1901 and charged with the murder of William M. Rice. A sensational trial followed, during which Jones admitted that he

9. *The last page of the will forged by Albert T. Patrick in William Marsh Rice's name. This document was later discredited.*

had actually administered the chloroform at Patrick's suggestion. Patrick was convicted of responsibility for planning the deed and was sentenced to die. (The sentence was commuted to life imprisonment, and Patrick was pardoned in 1912.) Jones, who had given evidence, was set free and allowed to return to Texas, where he committed suicide in 1954.[2]

Even after the fraudulent Patrick will had been discredited, Baker had to worry about Elizabeth Rice's last testament. Her executor Orren Holt knew that there was little chance of proving his claims of Texas residence in court in light of all the information that had surfaced in the Patrick trial. He eventually settled out of court with Baker and the other executors for $200,000 for Mrs. Rice's legatees. Lawyers' fees, executors' commissions, and Rice's own bequests to his relatives took more than a million dollars out of the estate as well; but when matters were settled in 1904, the Institute had a beginning endowment of $4,631,259.08.[3]

The Board of Trustees

The original members of the Institute's Board of Trustees were William M. Rice's friends, and all were prominent in Houston affairs. They were an interesting group of men. The chairman of the board was James Addison Baker, Jr., a lawyer with his father's firm of Baker, Botts, & Baker, known to most people as

10. *First Board of Trustees of the Rice Institute, 1911.* Back row, left to right: *Benjamin Botts Rice, Edgar Odell Lovett, Emanuel Raphael, William Marsh Rice, Jr.* Front row: *James Everett McAshan, Cesar Maurice Lombardi, James Addison Baker, Jr.*

"Captain Baker" because of his captaincy of the Houston Light Guard, a drill team and social association. Baker had graduated from the Texas Military Academy but never attended college. He had been chairman of the Rice Board of Trustees at Rice's request since 1891 and would continue to serve as chairman until his own death in 1941. His quick action at the time of Rice's murder had in large measure saved the endowment. A businessman as well as a lawyer, Baker was also a director of the Merchants and Planters Oil Company, the Houston Gas and Light Company, the Guardian Trust Company, and the South Texas Commercial National Bank.[4]

The first secretary of the board was Emanuel Raphael. In addition to being president of the Houston Electric Light and Power Company, he was president of the Southern Bridge and Construction Company and an organizer of the Houston Clearing House Association. Swiss-born Cesar M. Lombardi had been associated with William D. Cleveland and Company, wholesale grocers and cotton factors, until 1899 when he moved to Portland, Oregon. Lombardi returned to Texas in 1907 as vice-president and acting president of the A. H. Belo Company, publishers of the *Dallas News* and the *Galveston News.* Although the charter specified that the trustees should be residents of Houston, that provision was not applied to the original group. Lombardi remained an active member of the board while living in Dallas. James E. McAshan, in the banking business since his youth, was one of the organizers and a charter director of the South Texas National Bank, which later merged with the Commercial National Bank to become the South Texas Commercial National Bank, with which Baker was affiliated. McAshan was also connected with the Union Compress and Warehouse Company and the American Surety Company of New York. At the time of his death in 1916 he was vice-chairman of the Institute's board.[5] In addition to his directorship of the Houston and Texas Central Railroad, Alfred S. Richardson had been city secretary of Houston. After Richardson's death in 1899, the board appointed a nephew of the founder, William M. Rice, Jr., to Richardson's place. (Rice the founder had very much wanted this nephew on the board in the first available vacant position.) The founder's namesake was a director of the Union National Bank, the Guardian Trust Company, and the Houston Land and Trust Company and was president of the Merchants and Planters Oil Company. After the founder's murder in 1900, the board had appointed another nephew, Benjamin Botts Rice, to take his place. This third Rice was president of the Rice Land Lumber Company, vice-president and general manager of the Mer-

chants and Planters Oil Company, and vice-president of the Grant Locomotive Works. When original member of the board Frederick Allyn Rice (brother of the founder) died in 1901, the board left his position open.[6]

The Board of Trustees, as established by the charter, was a self-perpetuating group of seven members. After the estate was settled, full control and management of the endowment passed to the hands of these men. The trustees continued to have the final decision-making power over the Institute and the endowment and its increase. They were not, however, without limitations on their actions; William M. Rice was too shrewd a businessman not to protect his investments. The Institute was subject to visitation by any court to prevent and redress "any mismanagement, waste, or breach of trust." Furthermore, the trustees were forbidden to go into debt with Institute funds. For all their work the trustees were to receive no salary or other compensation.[7]

Much of the endowment as received in 1904 consisted of railroad, city, and miscellaneous bonds, and bank, trust company, and other stocks. There were also about $370,000 in promissory notes. The trustees made changes in some of these investments and organized the Rice Land Lumber Company to handle the Louisiana holdings. By judicious investment, mostly in bonds, first mortgage notes, and stocks, the trustees increased the endowment to more than $7 million by 1910, with gross revenues per an-

num in excess of $200,000 and net revenues of more than $140,000.[8]

Defining the Institute

Once the trustees felt that the endowment was prudently invested, they could turn to their primary purpose: establishment of the Rice Institute. The charter was both explicit and vague. It directed the establishment and maintenance of "a Public Library, and the maintenance of an Institution for the Advancement of Literature, Science, Art, Philosophy and Letters; and establishment and maintenance of a Polytechnic school; for procuring and maintaining scientific collections; collections of chemical and philosophical apparatus, mechanical and artistic models, drawings, pictures and statues; and for cultivating other means of instruction for the white inhabitants of the City of Houston, and State of Texas." The indenture within the charter further stated that the library and Institute were to be free and open to all,[9] that the "thorough polytechnic school" was to admit women as well as men, and that it should be designed "to give instructions on the application of science and Art to the useful occupations of life." Furthermore, all the subdivisions were to be nonsectarian and nonpartisan, subject only to such restrictions as the board thought necessary to preserve the good order and honor of the Institute.[10]

Some of the ideas inherent in

these instructions can be traced to Rice's interest in the Cooper Union and Girard College. Cooper's school admitted female students and was the first important trade school for women in the United States. Both Cooper and Girard wanted practical subjects taught at their institutions, and both wanted to help those who could not afford to help themselves. Rice had never gone to college, but he had helped his nephew William Marsh Rice, Jr., finance his education at Princeton, an experience that may also have added to his determination to make attendance at the Institute free. Girard had directed that his college be nonsectarian, and so had Rice, although Rice was not as insistent on this point as Girard was. Rice's reason for the stipulation of nonsectarianism may be found in the 1882 will that would have established an orphans' home:

All the instructors and teachers shall take pains to instill into the minds of the scholars the purest principles of morality so that on their entrance into active life they may from inclination and habit evince benevolence toward their fellow creatures and a love of truth, sobriety and industry, and I further direct and require that no sectarianism shall be permitted in the Institution, so that the pupils may be left free to adopt such religious views as their matured reason may dictate.[11]

Even though as friends they had had many conversations with the founder about the Rice Insti-

tute, and though they held written instructions, the trustees still had many decisions to make in order to put Rice's ideas into practice. The major decision to be made, before almost anything else could be done, was exactly what kind of school they were going to build. "We think," trustees Raphael and McAshan wrote, "it was the intention of the founder to give manual training, applied science and liberal arts preference in the organization. It is our desire to realize his wishes if possible and at the same time be affiliated with the school system of the country." The bylaws for the board adopted in 1905 speak of "a school for instruction in the arts of design, and in such other branches of knowledge as in their [the trustees'] judgment will tend to the elevation and employment of intelligent labor." Students were to be amateur and industrial pupils, and the courses they were to take included chemistry, physics, mechanics, electricity, and mechanical drawing. "This instruction shall be adapted to the comprehension and improvement of the mechanics and mechanic's apprentices of Houston and its vicinity being intended to bridge over the gap which now exists between science and the practical occupation of life."[12]

Before making any further decisions regarding the school, the trustees studied other institutions of learning. On a trip east in 1906 Raphael visited several schools of technology, manual training, and art. He investigated Girard College, Drexel Institute,

the Academy of Fine Arts, and the Memorial Hall and Museum, all in Philadelphia, and Pratt Institute in Brooklyn. He had seen Cooper Union on a previous visit. On his return to Houston he wrote a report, and it is clear that Raphael had done a thorough job. He had examined endowments, revenues, expenditures, courses of study, tuition, makeup of the student body, types of laboratories and machine shops and equipment, the size of each campus, cost of the buildings, and the need for dormitories and a gymnasium. The report closed with a plea to the other trustees to visit several of these types of schools themselves to get "a much better idea of what our Institute ought to be." Clearly at that time the trustees had in mind an institution more along the lines of Pratt Institute or Cooper Union than the university that they finally created.[13]

The Search for a President

It was January 1907 before the board acted formally to find someone to head the school, although they had been receiving recommendations since 1905. One man from Florida had recommended himself and had sent in copies of seventeen testimonials, each on a separate small strip of paper. Of more importance were the recommendations for Arthur Lefevre, former professor of mathematics at the University of Texas and state superintendent for public instruction in Texas. Letters praising Lefevre came from all over the state and from outside of Texas. The board, however, preferred more order in their search. Chairman Baker appointed Raphael and McAshan to compose a letter asking for recommendations and to send it to the leading universities and institutes in the United States. Other recipients of the letter were such prominent Americans as Theodore Roosevelt, Grover Cleveland, and William Jennings Bryan.[14]

The letter inviting recommendations gave some indication of the problems that the board was having both in deciding on the nature of the school and finding a "superintendent" for it. The only hard facts mentioned in the letter were that the school had an endowment of $5 million or more, that it would be nonsectarian and nonpolitical, that it would have free tuition and be open to whites, and that it would be located in Houston. Otherwise, the trustees could speak only in generalities about the type of institution they wanted and ask for a recommendation of the very best man who could help make some of the decisions and hasten the work. "We need a young man, a broad man, and we need him at once."[15]

This method produced a number of prospects, although some of the advisers echoed the trustees' uncertainty about what the Institute was to be. David F. Houston, president of the University of Texas, was anxious to help but wrote that it would aid his recommendation if he knew more definitely what the board wanted—an institute like Drexel or Girard, a technical college like the Massachusetts Institute of Technology, or a combination like Cornell. J. E. Pursons of Cooper Union answered the query with the news that his institution was also looking for its own president and so could not help.[16]

The board wrote to twenty-five individuals and institutions and compiled a list of thirty-nine names, from which it appears that four were chosen for closer scrutiny. Albert Ross Hill, dean of the Teachers College at Missouri State University, had been recommended by both President David Starr Jordan of Stanford and President Jacob Gould Schurman of Cornell. Howard McClenahan, professor of electrical engineering at Princeton, was Grover Cleveland's suggestion. President Henry S. Pritchett of the Boston School of Technology had recommended Charles R. Richards of Columbia. And Edgar Odell Lovett, professor of mathematics at Princeton, had been recommended by Woodrow Wilson, president of that university.[17]

In the early stages of the search, Hill was the most favored candidate and McClenahan second. Raphael went to Missouri to see Hill and returned much impressed by him. Only thirty-eight, Hill had had considerable experience in university administration and was at that time in charge of the administrative work of his institution. He was in line for the presidency of Missouri State and could expect a salary of $6,000 a year. Raphael liked the recommendations, Hill's present work, his youth, his ambition. Hill said that he was willing to visit Houston before accepting the position at the Institute, "(provided that position were tendered to him at $6,000 per annum, including a home)," so that both board and prospect could know each other before further steps were taken.[18]

Through Grover Cleveland the board communicated with McClenahan, who wanted to know what the salary would be before committing himself in any way. The question of salary had probably already come up with the board. President Houston from the University of Texas had mentioned in his letter that it would be difficult to get "one of the really strong, sane educators" from out of state for less than $5,000 or $6,000 and a house. The board told McClenahan that compensation would be "$6,000 per annum and dwelling free."[19]

Certainly none of the four seemed eager to become the first president of the Rice Institute. Hill was interested but wrote that the main defect he saw in the charter was the provision for free tuition. McClenahan had reservations about the salary because he was "so totally ignorant of the character of the Institute and of the work involved." He was willing, however, to hold the matter of compensation in abeyance until he and the board had time to learn about each other. In spite of his reservations McClenahan was enthusiastic about the possibilities as he imagined them. "My mind glows when I think of the enormous amount such an institution may be made to do for the further development of the whole great Southwest." The board invited both Hill and McClenahan to come to Houston. They also invited Richards and Lovett; but in the case of these latter two, there seems to have been little preliminary correspondence.[20]

Hill came to Houston on March 18, McClenahan on April 8, Lovett on April 11, and Richards on April 22. Edgar Odell Lovett wrote an account of his experiences, which were probably similar to the other candidates'. He was shown around the city and taken to see several possible sites for the Institute. The trustees were obviously not convinced of the desirability of the location on Louisiana Street, which had been designated as the school site by William Marsh Rice. The trustees and presidential candidates looked at the Louisiana Street lot, the old Rice ranch in what is now Bellaire, a wooded site "down the channel," and another location far out Main Street. That night Lovett and the board had an intensive discussion. Lovett reported later that the trustees' examination "was the most trying ordeal I have as yet passed through. Question after question about things I knew nothing about and had never thought out."[21]

Choosing a president was not an easy task, and Lovett had great sympathy for the members of the board. "They were successful men of business, and facing as difficult a problem in trying to

select a college president as a group of college professors would be if they had to set about to find a railroad president. Indeed I think the chances might have been in favor of the college professors' group."[22]

The trustees' examination elicited a number of opinions from Lovett that he thought significant. He thought it would be well to build and maintain the Institute out of the income from the endowment alone. He anticipated a fall in interest rates and related that Princeton funds were being invested in local enterprises. Concerning the site, Lovett advocated an extensive area outside the city on the side to which industries would never come: he liked the Main Street location. He also spoke of the necessity of developing a comprehensive architectural plan before breaking ground for any buildings. On the salary question, he thought it would take $10,000 to get the right man. Finally he said that the trustees ought to get Woodrow Wilson to do the job.[23]

There was one other problem that the board might not have noticed but that spoke volumes to academics: the matter of the word "institute." "The very designation 'institute', if it did not mean a female seminary, or one for defectives, or one for the colored race, meant an institute of technology," Lovett wrote in 1944. "There was some hint of this that night, so I told them that I could not be a party for any such undertaking that would not assure as large a place for pure science as for applied science. It

was an entering wedge away from technology and towards the university idea. I have always thought it bore fruit in the future."[24]

When he got back to Missouri, A. Ross Hill had some second thoughts about the situation in Houston. He wrote Raphael on March 25 that he thought the board had "a fine opportunity to either make a great success or a stupendous failure in administering its affairs." Eleven days later he asked to be removed from consideration.[25]

Other advisers whom the board consulted included Arthur Lefevre, R. S. Heyer of Georgetown, Texas, President Houston from Austin, President H. H. Harrington of the Agricultural and Mechanical College of Texas (Texas A&M), Dr. A. E. Turner of Trinity University in Waxahachie, and Professor J. H. Dillard of Tulane. The visits continued into June and did not go unnoticed. The *Houston Post* reported the comings and goings, and its editor expressed his pleasure that the Rice board was taking action to appoint a president and organize the Institute.[26]

After all their haste in securing recommendations, choosing candidates, and arranging visits, the trustees made no decision until November, although the board minutes indicate no reason for this delay. Then at the regular meeting of November 20, 1907, the trustees unanimously elected Edgar Odell Lovett as their choice for the first president of the Rice Institute. William M. Rice, Jr., was appointed to go to Princeton and call Dr. Lovett "to take charge as educational head of the Institute"; Rice was empowered to offer a salary of up to $7,500 and a contract for five years.[27]

Rice went to Princeton and returned to report to the board on December 18. Lovett, he stated, could not say at that time whether he would accept or not, as he had just started a new project. When Lovett indicated that the $6,000 that Rice had tendered was insufficient, Rice had offered $7,000 and a home. Although Lovett was not particular about a contract, he could not seem to come to a decision; Rice finally suggested that Lovett take thirty days to decline or accept the offer.[28]

To help persuade Lovett to come, chairman Baker wrote a strong letter the next day. Baker expressed his disappointment that Lovett had not given them a definite answer and wrote *"to urge upon you to cast your lot with us."* The trustees had proceeded quite deliberately in making a selection, Baker said. They had talked to many people from Texas and elsewhere in the search, but the position had been offered to no one except Lovett. Lovett had made a fine impression upon the trustees; they liked his manner and his candor, and they believed him to be eminently qualified for the presidency.

One paragraph presented the real selling point.

Our institution is well endowed—more so than any institution I know of in the South; the Trustees are practically without any experience in educational matters and they will be disposed to give you a very free hand. As a rule they are broad minded and liberal, and desire in establishing the new institution to lay its foundations broad and deep, and to employ at all times the best talent that can be had anywhere. The opportunity offered you is an unusual one, and however promising may be your prospects at Princeton, you ought to be slow in declining. Such an opportunity rarely comes to one so young in life [Lovett was thirty-six].[29]

Raphael added his inducements a couple of days later and indicated certain decisions that the board had made in the past year. He said that the board had agreed that Lovett would not be called upon to teach; filling the position of president with its executive duties would be sufficient service. The trustees also agreed with Lovett that the faculty should be "high class men, nominated by yourself, because it is our express aim to make the Wm. M. Rice Institute a high class institution patterned—in great measure—after the Massachusetts School [sic] of Technology." More important, the board was "free and untrammeled to make our institute as broad and as progressive as the heart of any ambitious educator could desire." Raphael called Lovett to be the leader of an institution that (quoting Lovett's own words back to him) "shall contribute powerfully to the sustaining sources of the life of the nation—where by the Nation I mean the life, the thought, the conscience, the authority, of all the people of all the land. . . . Can you imagine that any work appeals to you more powerfully than this great work in our Southland?"[30]

About the same time, Lovett wrote William Rice, Jr., that he did want to come to the Institute. He had seen Woodrow Wilson, Rice's old classmate from Princeton, and discussed when he could leave the university. Wilson had asked him to hold his professorship until the end of that academic year but said he could drop his duties in February and come to Houston in March. The only problem that Lovett saw was in the matter of salary. He wanted $8,000 and a house. He said he had not been able, while Rice was there, to think clearly about salary and was unwilling "to seem to hold up an honest man in my own house."[31]

The board read and discussed Lovett's letter on December 28, and they unanimously accepted his terms. Raphael sent Lovett a telegram followed by a letter announcing his official election as the educational head of the Rice Institute. Since Lovett had not particularly wanted a five-year contract as originally offered and had not mentioned it in his acceptance letter, a contract was not part of the terms.[32]

Lovett's informal reply on January 2, 1908, indicated his enthusiasm. He wrote that he was "almost arrogant in my hopefulness. I believe that we are going to have the patience and the power to do the thing right, and by all the demons dancing in the Dog-star we will make the thing go." His formal reply on January 18 expressed his delight more soberly but nonetheless powerfully.

He pledged his strength and training to the task and was relying confidently on the cooperation of all friends of education in Texas. He had a large vision of purpose for the Institute:

I promise to serve The Rice Institute of Houston in patiently seeking with them [the trustees] the lines of its development; in persistently pressing with them the plans for its usefulness; in striving with their help to combine in its personality those elements—largeness of mind, strength of character, determined purpose, fire of genius, devoted loyalty—which make for leadership in institutions as in men; in blazing with the brands and torches they shall hand me a trail down which we may hope to find a time when from its walls shall go forth a continuous column of men trained in the highest degree, equipped in the largest way, for positions of trust in the public service, for commanding careers in the affairs of the world.[33]

The Rice Institute had its first president.

Edgar Odell Lovett

Edgar Odell Lovett was born in Shreve, Ohio, on April 14, 1871. At the age of fifteen he enrolled at Bethany College in West Virginia, a school of the Christian Church, to which his parents belonged. (They had hesitated to send him so young to one of the bigger universities.) He graduated in 1890 from Bethany with a

11. *The first president of the William Marsh Rice Institute, Edgar Odell Lovett, 1911.*

Bachelor of Arts degree and by 1892 had both Bachelor of Science and Master of Arts degrees. While at Bethany Lovett had tutored in Greek, and he never lost his love of classical literature. From 1890 to 1892 he taught mathematics at West Kentucky College, another Christian Church school. Lovett was too ambitious and too good in mathematics to stay in small, isolated towns, however, so in 1892 he went to the University of Virginia for graduate study. While he was a student there he also taught astronomy. He graduated three years later with another master's degree and a doctorate.

In those days a career in mathematics demanded study in Europe. From Virginia, Lovett went to Leipzig to study under Sophus Lie, one of the leading mathematicians on the continent. He also attended lectures in Rome and in Christiania, Norway, and on his way home through France he heard the famous lecturers of that country. He returned home with two more degrees, another M.A. and another Ph.D. Every one of his seven degrees, "none of which I attach to my name," had been taken with honors. With Lie's help he secured positions at both the Johns Hopkins University and the University of Virginia for the spring term in 1897 and commuted between them with a pass on the B&O Railroad. That summer he lectured at the University of Chicago.

Lovett was not without offers for the fall. Drake University had him in mind for its presidency, and the University of Minnesota wanted him to teach mathematics. He turned them both down to take an assistant professorship at Princeton. Twenty-six when he went to Princeton, he had already published at least six articles in the *American Astronomical Journal*, *Annals of Mathematics*, *Astronomische Nachrichten*, *Astro-Physics*, and the *Bulletin of the American Mathematical Society*. He had also read a number of papers before the Mathematical Club of the University of Virginia and the American Mathematical Society. From all who had worked with him, he had garnered high recommendations as an excellent teacher and a man of unspotted character. He described himself then as "in mathematics for the sake of the science and its use as a powerful educational implement and [I] enjoy text-book teaching and formal lecturing equally well. I am in no hurry to settle and propose to be thoroughly satisfied that a place is the one for me and I the man for the place before I attach myself permanently anywhere." In 1897 he married Mary Ellen Hale, who had been a student at West Kentucky College when he was teaching there.[34]

Lovett rose quickly in the academic hierarchy at Princeton. By 1900 he was a full professor, and in 1905 he succeeded Charles A. Young as professor of astronomy. Princeton, however, was more than just a place to work for Lovett. He made friends there, and the one he most cherished was Woodrow Wilson. The feeling was evidently reciprocal. When Wilson told Lovett that he had recommended him to the trustees at Rice, he said that there was no one on the faculty whom he had counted on more to remain; but he felt bound to present the chance to the best man and let the man decide for himself. Lovett had some trouble framing his letter of resignation to Wilson.

I am leaving Princeton a Princeton man firmly believing that whatever training I may have achieved here can be devoted to the interests of the University in no better way than in an effort to bring to realization in another environment those spiritual and intellectual ideals and traditions which have made Princeton conspicuous in the Nation's service, and which, in terms of your far-reaching plans for the development of the University, are now making Princeton the most interesting educational center on the continent. . . . I am unwilling to bring it [the letter] to a close without saying to you again that my roots here are long and deep; I cannot tell you how hard it is for me to break them.[35]

But break them he did, and in March 1908 Lovett arrived in Houston with a number of ideas for the organization of the Rice Institute. He wanted to open the Institute in 1910 and to hold two formal ceremonies connected with the opening—the laying of the cornerstone of the first building and the installation of the first president. Local and state dignitaries would be invited to the first, and for the second the guest list would be increased to include representatives of foreign and domestic universities and a group of distinguished scholars and scientists who would deliver lectures. The seeds of the formal opening were thus planted early. Lovett wanted to make the scope of the new institution broad, to realize the full meaning of the objectives as stated in its title and charter, not only for the individual or society but also to advance the body of human knowledge. For the present, the Rice Institute would look to the organization of a faculty of sciences of undisputed distinction. An embryonic faculty of letters would be developed at first only as far as necessary to complement the courses in technical subjects. Lovett especially wanted the Institute to be a university that could award doctorates.

Structuring the Institute

Before the faculty was recruited, a more detailed plan of general organization had to be developed. To that end Lovett asked the board to send him on a journey of inspection to investigate the leading educational institutions of the United States and Europe. He wanted to see what other schools were doing in all aspects of university life and to confer with the educators who were responsible. The board agreed.[36]

While in Houston Lovett was entertained by the mayor and the Houston Business League and met with many prominent men of the city. The press duly reported his visit and for the most part seemed pleased with his appointment. An editorial in the *Houston Chronicle*, however, voiced an opinion on a situation that Lovett might have to deal with when he returned; the board seemed to be ignoring it. Many citizens held the view that William Marsh Rice had given the Institute to the people of Houston, and some of them were impatient to learn something definite about the school. Only the "high character, business ability and honesty of purpose of the trustees" had prevented criticism of them for withholding information to which the public felt entitled, the editorial claimed. It is interesting to note that the editor seemed more interested in the size of the endowment and its investment than in the educational plan. "There are not perhaps ten men in Houston," the editor said, "who, if asked what the resources of the institute are or will likely be, either for building or for endowment, could give an answer which would be more than a hazardous guess. . . . Of what the fund consists and how it is invested, and what are the returns upon the investment is known only to the trustees." The editorial concluded with the faint praise, "The highest tribute that could have been paid the trustees is the patience and confidence with which the people have so long waited in ignorance for information which they feel they ought to have."[37]

In May Lovett hired F. Carrington Weems to be his private secretary and in June sent the board an itinerary; the trustees voted him $1,625 for the trip. Lovett, Mrs. Lovett, and Weems sailed for Liverpool and landed about August 1, not to return to the United States until April of the following year. It was an extensive trip. The party traveled through Great Britain, Ireland, Scandinavia, Germany, Switzerland, Italy, France, Belgium, the Netherlands, Spain, Portugal, Greece, Austria-Hungary, Poland, and across Russia by the Trans-Siberian Express to Japan. They returned to Houston on May 7, 1909.[38]

President Lovett visited a large number of the major universities in Europe and many of the minor ones, as well as technical schools, laboratories, and even "public school" Eton. His interests were eclectic: architecture, building plans, laboratory arrangements, faculty organization, administration, museums, and regulations. More important than his investigation of the physical establishments were the people with whom Lovett discussed his new institution. Besides prominent members of the various schools, he visited the king of Norway and consulted many Americans such as Woodrow Wilson and poet and professor Henry Van Dyke of Princeton who were traveling or lecturing in Europe at that time. All were quite willing to give the new president advice.

Vice-chancellor A. W. W. Dale of the University of Liverpool told him to consider men and equipment rather than expensive buildings. "Students do not observe and there are no architects." He also urged large salaries for the faculty and would not require science students to study the classics. J. Theodore Merz, author of a history of nineteenth-century European thought, advised a larger place for theoretical than for practical science. Progress would be slower, but he thought that it would reap rewards in the long run. Merz also said that women should be admitted to the institution because "the woman question will not be solved as long as the women wish to have the same education as men." Professor J. A. Gibson of Glasgow told Lovett that entrance requirements should include English, mathematics, one foreign language (classical or modern), and a course in science. He recommended constructing the institution with the need for later additions in mind. Furthermore, "Academic scope and content [are] conditioned by two things: what the students are prepared for on entrance; what they should be prepared for on leaving."

In London Lovett encountered Professor Simon Newcomb of Johns Hopkins, who thought that America already had enough universities. He was, however, willing to pass along some recommendations. He advised high standards for degrees but a standard of admission that would permit the student body to grow rapidly. He also recommended a small beginning at the earliest date possible and the hiring of Americans as instructors, preferably southerners; he warned that

it would be difficult to interest other men in the undertaking because the Institute bore an individual's name and was local. Six English educators whom Lovett met in Dublin, including J. J. Thomson, D. W. W. Shaw, and W. E. Shipley, were considerably more helpful than Newcomb. They said that the Texans "should consider men before mortar and brains before bricks" and pay good salaries, especially to the junior members of the staff. They all agreed that the best teachers were researchers who had time and facilities for their own investigations.

Recommendations for the new faculty proliferated. Early in his trip, Lovett laid out in his journal a plan for the faculty that would have required at least 135 members. He knew what he wanted in a faculty of sciences, which "should be of larger scope in subject and function than any similar body heretofore organized. It must be prepared to *make science, teach science,* and *apply science . . . .* The work must be threefold:—Constructive in creating the new, educative in teaching the old, immediately utilitarian in application of new and old to the common good."[39]

While in Europe, Lovett took time to do more than ask questions. He read papers at the Association for the Advancement of Science meeting in Dublin and to mathematicians of Stockholm and Uppsala at a dinner in Stockholm—the first papers presented from the Rice Institute. He took advantage of opportunities to work in the outstanding libraries

of universities that he visited. On a side trip he climbed to the highest edge of the crater of Vesuvius, and he remarked from Tokyo that the censors' vigilance had made it impossible to send reports by mail from Russia.[40]

All in all, Lovett's trip was extremely important. The fledgling president had met almost everyone of importance in education, including people from India and South Africa, and had made many friends for Rice. The guest list for the formal opening is eloquent testimony to the scope of his acquaintance. Furthermore, he had studied and discussed every facet of university organization, administration, and equipment with experts in the field. Without this trip, it is doubtful whether the Institute could have attracted an initial faculty of the caliber it did. Lovett knew that the people of Houston and the trustees were impatient for construction to begin; his own impatience was at times "almost uncontrollable." He was determined, however, not to rush but to get the maximum return from the trip and to do justice to the endowment. And he did.

When Lovett returned from Europe, he and the trustees made several formal decisions that were to set the tone and scope for the Institute for years to come. The recommendations originated with Lovett and answered several of the questions with which the board had been wrestling since 1904. The first decision was to build and maintain the institution out of annual income alone, keeping intact not only funds designated by the founder as endowment, but also those that might have been spent outright under the terms of the charter. Because of the prohibition on debts, this decision meant that growth would be slow.[41]

Second, and equally important, the Rice Institute would aspire to university standing of the highest level, seeking "to attain that high place through the research work of its early professors, setting no upper limit to its educational endeavor and the lower limit no lower than the level reached by its prospective students on graduation from the better public and private high schools preparing for college." This decision removed the institution from the purely "technical school" category that some of the trustees had first contemplated. It also meant that Lovett, who was cognizant of changes that had occurred in the preceding thirty years in higher education and of the connotations already mentioned for the word "institute," proclaimed an intention and a design larger than the trustees might have realized at the time.

The idea of a "university," what one was and what it did, had gone through a number of definitions and redefinitions in the United States after the Civil War. Originally higher education in America had meant the establishment of colleges that were schools of rather narrow scope. Their aims were to build character and instill moral and mental discipline, and they concentrated on teaching a superficial kind of knowledge in a fixed, four-year course of study with no specialization in any subject. Those few students who planned to continue their educations beyond college were destined for "professional" schools of law, medicine, and divinity. From Germany came a different concept, that of the university, where the methods and goals were quite different. The heart of the German system was research, the disinterested pursuit of truth through original investigation with the goal of advancing knowledge. Furthermore, German professors and their students specialized in narrow areas, and German universities became famous for their success in joining teaching and research and in producing creative, inquiring, scholarly minds. Before the Civil War, American scholars began to go to Germany to study and came back highly enthusiastic about changing the system of higher education at home to fit the German mode. By the 1870s and 1880s, it was absolutely necessary for scholars to study in Germany and earn a doctorate there before they could advance in an academic career.

As with other concepts imported from the Old World, the idea of a university was modified by American viewpoints, needs, opinions, and realities. Questions had to be answered concerning its shape, governance, curriculum, students, and social purposes, as well as the place and role of the old undergraduate colleges. What finally emerged as the American university reflected a period of experimentation.

Different universities tried different organizational schemes. State universities in the Midwest and West discarded the traditional classical curriculum and organized around a series of specialized undergraduate departments. They added a number of strictly vocational subjects to the normal letters, arts, and sciences. New universities like Johns Hopkins and Clark concentrated on graduate teaching and research, trying to do without an undergraduate college entirely or subordinating it as much as possible to the graduate division. Harvard president Charles Eliot introduced the elective system and tried to convert the college itself into a university, with research and scholarship also on the undergraduate level. Yale, which in 1861 awarded the first earned doctorates in America, tried to build a university around Yale College by adding schools such as Sheffield Scientific School to those of medicine, law, and theology, while at the same time retaining the collegiate aspects of fellowship, general studies, and a prescribed curriculum in the college. Problems arose, however, in trying to keep Yale College from becoming subordinate to the university schools. As new American universities were founded and old colleges reorganized, they tended to develop along departmental lines, with a college of arts and letters as one among several equivalent schools or departments.

Unlike the Germans, whose philosophy called for the pursuit of knowledge for its own sake, Americans talked about utility in education. A university was to be useful to society by providing various services to the community, and it was to offer a utilitarian education for its students by providing them with an occupation for life. Vocational subjects, such as engineering and other applied sciences that were formerly learned on the job, joined the humanities and pure sciences as university subjects; the distinctions between professional and vocational careers began to blur. American pragmatism and the growing need for experts in the rapidly developing technological fields of industry further promoted the vocational side of higher education.

This did not mean, however, that the university became a trade school. Entrenched in many schools were the departments of classical studies and humanities, and these often waged fierce battles to maintain their places. Even though they had no visible relation to a "useful occupation," humanistic studies remained in the new university, at times in very powerful positions. Students could still earn a Bachelor of Arts degree carrying the connotation of a "good liberal education."

By the early 1900s, most of the arguments concerning the nature of a university had been settled. Universities would be characterized by specialization in studies, professional training, graduate and undergraduate programs, ongoing research by the faculty, and a balanced, comprehensive mixture of the humanities, the pure sciences, and the more vocational applied sciences.

The elective system came under attack after 1900 for leaving many graduates with only a smattering of knowledge in a number of fields and faulty preparation for specialization. Even so, this system had done a great deal toward bringing science and the new disciplines into equality with the classical collegiate subjects. What to put in its place, how to arrange the curriculum to blend the new subjects with the old, and how to reorganize the undergraduate course of study, were a few questions that had not been decided with any degree of unanimity.

Rice, neither so old as the eastern schools nor so large as the western ones, had the chance to choose its entry point into the university world and to determine its own emphasis. It was not an easy decision. On one hand, the Institute was dedicated to the advancement of literature, science, and art. On the other, there was simply not enough money immediately to establish really strong departments in every category. It would be possible, however, to have the backbone of a university program— faculty research and graduate training—in one area in the beginning and then to expand as circumstances permitted.[42]

Hence the board arrived at its third decision. The Rice Institute would first enter into a university program in the sciences. This course of instruction would also benefit the community. (There was no school of applied and pure science in the rapidly developing Houston area, and technical ex-

pertise was at a premium.) Even at the start there would be a basic core of "liberal education" courses considered essential to a university degree, but humanities departments would be added later, as resources became available. Graduate doctoral programs would concentrate on mathematics, physics, and chemistry. With respect to art, the trustees decided to "take architecture seriously" and provide a physical setting of great beauty as well as utility.[43]

The Site and the Physical Plan

The last decision made selection of an architect critical. When he returned to Houston, President Lovett wrote and then visited many architects throughout the North and East, soliciting their ideas for the Institute. The visits allowed reduction of the list of possible architects to three or four men. After much thought, Lovett picked and the board approved Ralph Adams Cram of Cram, Goodhue and Ferguson of Boston. Lovett later said that his choice was in the end more intuitive than reasoned, as he was more impressed by Cram's imaginative grasp of the elements of the problem than he was by the other candidates'. Nevertheless, he made the recommendation somewhat reluctantly, because Cram was Princeton's supervising architect and Lovett wanted to establish some reputation for independence of judgment in his new home.[44]

12. *Ralph Adams Cram, of the Boston architectural firm of Cram, Godhue and Ferguson, which designed the plan and early buildings of the Rice Institute. Drawn by F. M. Rines from a photograph.*

To ensure that the best possible laboratories would be built, Lovett organized an advisory committee of eminent scientists to help plan the structures. The group was composed of Joseph S. Ames, director of the physical laboratory at Johns Hopkins, Edwin G. Conklin, director of the new biological laboratory at Princeton, Theodore W. Richards, head of the department of chemistry at Harvard, and Samuel W. Stratton, director of the National Bureau of Standards in Washington. All had considerable experience in the construction of laboratories and were knowledgeable about the essential equipment.[45]

While Lovett was on his trip around the world, the trustees had bought land for the site of the Institute. They chose the acreage on Main Street that Lovett had suggested, about three miles from the city center. In June 1908 the board decided to purchase about 300 acres, and they began negotiations to acquire them. Altogether there were purchases of ten parcels of land ranging in size from under an acre to over 95 acres. Almost one-third of the acreage was purchased from George W. Hermann, who later gave the city of Houston much of the adjoining land for a park. The board had completed the major purchases, with one notable exception, by May 1909, in time for Lovett's return from abroad. The total cost was almost $250,000 for approximately 290 acres.[46]

The exception was an eight-acre farm that cut into the grounds from Main Street. It belonged to Charles F. Weber, who claimed that he had no desire to sell any part of his land. Nonetheless he finally agreed in 1910 to sell at a price of more than $7,000 per acre. At the time of the sale, the trustees made an agreement with Weber that allowed him to remain on the land for three-and-a-half years. The board soon regretted its concession. As the plans for the site developed, Weber's farm rested next to the location of the Administration Building, with, some remember, a pigsty at the south corner of the building. In addition, for a time Weber had extended his fence onto Institute property. After much effort Weber was persuaded to move off the land, and the fence and other farm appurtenances were removed only a few days before the academic procession leading to the formal dedication would have been forced to change its intended route to the platform.[47]

Completed, the site had five sides, bounded by what are today Main Street, Sunset and Rice Boulevards, Greenbriar Street, and University Boulevard. There was a bayou, Harris Gully, to be known by students as "the Blue Danube," cutting across the western end; today this waterway is channeled through a conduit under the parking lot of the football stadium. The site was flat, marshy, and subject to flooding. Trees and shrubs lined the bayou, and there was a small grove of trees near the intersection of Main and Sunset. Otherwise, the site was bare prairie land.

Architect Cram seems to have been both intrigued and appalled by this site, which he called "level and stupid." With no historical or stylistic precedent in the vicinity and no ideas imposed by the president or trustees, however, the possibilities for invention were boundless. Cram's favorite Gothic style simply would not suit this site, but then neither would colonial or Georgian or Spanish-Indian-Baroque. In his search for a style that was beautiful, southern in spirit, and continuous with the historic and cultural past, Cram invented a new style based on elements from Mediterranean architecture. Venice and the Dalmatian coast offered the most promising inspirations. The result has been called "a combination of the twelfth and thirteenth century Byzantine, Romanesque, and Venetian Gothic."[48]

In addition to deciding on a style, Cram had to plan at once for both the present and the distant future. The school needed adequate and economical buildings immediately; but in order to expand efficiently in the future and avoid an unorganized hodgepodge, it also needed a flexible scheme. It did not take long for Cram to invent three possible plans, all very ambitious and rather cluttered. The quadrangle system of organization was perhaps the one idea that survived all the various planning stages. (There were thirty-five or forty preliminary studies.) In the trial plans as well as in the final one, Cram proposed quadrangles for science, fine arts, student residences, law, medicine, and a graduate college. Cloisters—roofed colonnades open on the sides— connected buildings within quadrangles and sometimes the quadrangles themselves. Since Rice was to be "aggressively nonsectarian" (as Cram put it),[49] there was no provision for a chapel. One tentative plan shows a Greek amphitheater with an artificial lake constructed along the bayou, and the final one called for reflecting pools in the first quadrangle to heighten the Venetian effect. These pools were never built, possibly because of Lovett's misgivings, although the president did consider lining them with concrete and stocking them with small fish to deal with mosquito larvae.[50]

In spite of Cram's multitudes of ideas, or perhaps because of them, it took months to arrive at a mutually agreeable general plan. What Cram suggested, the board or Lovett changed, and vice versa. Buildings were moved on paper and moved again. A trip to Houston by Cram and Goodhue at the end of November 1909 helped to clarify some items and resulted in cost estimates, but it left many problems unsolved. The architects were hardly back in Boston before Lovett wrote that the preliminary floor plan for the Administration Building allotted too much space to activities of secondary importance, such as a museum and a trustees' room. Lovett wanted a practical, purely academic arrangement with space for classrooms, conference areas, lecture rooms, and a library. He was also dissatisfied with the placement of the physical laboratory group and the powerhouse.[51]

Linchpin to the entire arrangement was the location of the Administration Building, and that proved especially difficult to settle. Part of the difficulty was created by the Weber farm, not yet purchased, but part was due to the aesthetics of the plot. To one of Lovett's arrangements Cram replied that there were "no distinguished architectural compositions," and in fact, he called it "a catastrophe from an architectural standpoint."[52]

The location of the Administration Building on a line oriented east-west or north-south also determined its floor plan and its exterior appearance. As the building was moved about, so the ground-floor arcades were moved from one side of the building to the other. By March 1910, Cram was moved to ask,

How can you not place some reliance in us as your chosen architects when it comes to a matter that, like this, is one almost wholly of design? It seems to us that it is really our function to determine more or less questions of this nature. Where cost, practical considerations, or the sacrifice of valuable space is concerned, it is, of course your duty to pass upon everything we suggest, but while we welcome every particle of assistance you can give us from an artistic standpoint, we must admit that this case of the Rice Institute is the only one we have ever had in our experience where the highest authorities were so exceedingly conscientious as to strictly architectural considerations.[53]

Where cost was concerned, the trustees certainly knew their duty, to Cram's exasperation. Because of some confusion over the cost of the buildings—Cram estimated forty cents per cubic foot, but the trustees thought twenty-five cents adequate—the trustees had not signed a formal contract or begun to pay the commission. The architects were understandably upset. Producing plans, sketches, and specifications cost them money. They pointed out to Lovett that every one of their other clients paid for estimates, even the United States government. This was the first time in their twenty-two years of experience that a client had demanded that they wait until contracts

were assigned before paying. Lovett later commented that "team work was not always easy with trustees sitting tight on the money bags and an architect's imagination soaring to the stars."[54]

On April 27, 1910, the Board of Trustees formally approved the architect's plans. Bids were invited, and on June 27, 1910, a contract was signed with the firm of William Miller & Sons Company of Pittsburgh for the construction of the Administration Building. In September the same firm also won contracts for the Mechanical Laboratory and powerhouse combination. Approximate costs, exclusive of contents, were $400,000 for the Administration Building, $235,000 for the power plant and Mechanical Laboratory, and $420,000 for the first residential group.[55]

As finally accepted, the general plan provided for every contingency of expansion. From the Institute's main entrance at the corner nearest the city, the road to the Administration Building branched off at a thirty-degree angle. This approach led to the central axis of the plan: a clear view through the Sallyport in the Administration Building westward to the far edge of the campus, a distance of approximately one mile. Before the quadrangle was closed by construction of Fondren Library in 1949, the Sallyport framed the setting sun during the summer months. To be lined with oak trees, the road from the entrance to the Administration Building stretched about

a quarter of a mile, ending in a forecourt. On one side of the court (according to the plan) was to be built the School of Fine Arts and on the other a residential college for women. The road divided at the Administration Building and rounded each end of the building to continue in two oak-lined drives parallel to the main axis, about 700 feet apart. Passing through the Sallyport, one entered the court of the first academic group. Cram envisioned this court surrounded on three sides by five buildings with cloisters facing the court. Measuring 300 by 500 feet, the garden within was to be planted in cypresses. Beyond this group opened a larger court planted with live oaks and surrounded by more academic buildings. At the extreme west end of the second court was to be a pool and Greek amphitheater.

Secondary axes lay perpendicular to the main axis. The first of these began on Main Street and ran north past the dormitories, through the first academic court to the Mechanical Laboratory and powerhouse. Those buildings were the first in the engineering quadrangle. The first north-south axis lay east of the student dormitories. The second ran through the middle of the dormitory group, across the larger academic court, and was intended to end in another quadrangle containing the Graduate School and its professional departments.

The residential quadrangle was to have its own east-west axis, parallel to the main axis, with dormitories on two sides, a stu-

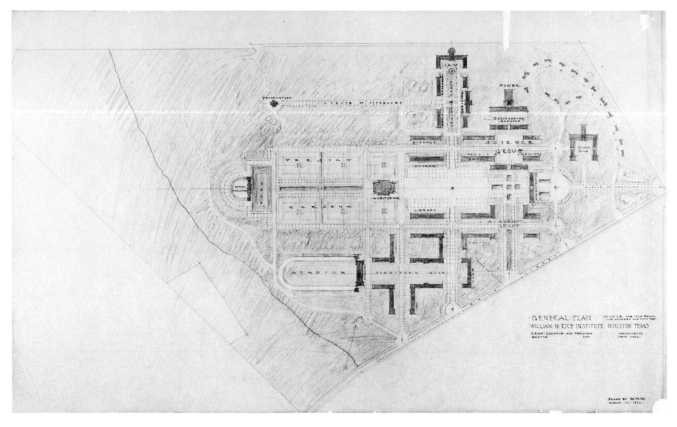

13. *Final plan for the Institute, drawn by the firm of Cram, Goodhue and Ferguson.*

dent union at the eastern end, and a gymnasium and athletic stadium at the west end. The architects provided for faculty residences, including a president's house on the east side of the campus off Sunset Boulevard. If all these proposed structures were built, there would still be room for professional schools such as law and medicine in the third of the campus that was left untouched. Cram's spacious plan would allow pleasing vistas through the campus and would avoid crowding buildings meanly together in a muddle in the way that several of the older eastern schools had done. Cram's plan also oriented buildings to take advantage of the prevailing southerly breezes, a necessity in the days before air conditioning. Open spaces, high ceilings, large windows, and one-room-thick buildings would help counteract the oppressive Houston heat. Considering the semitropical climate, one understands why Rice would have no summer session (until 1977) and why the faculty, more often than not from cooler climates, would abandon the city for the mountains and other more temperate locales during the summer months.[56]

The First Buildings

Gem of the campus, then and now, was the Administration Building, now called Lovett Hall. Ralph Adams Cram, who left the actual construction supervision to a representative from the Boston office (architect William Ward Watkin, who would later

14. *Early stages of construction of the Administration Building, now called Lovett Hall. The flat and marshy site made it necessary to construct gangplanks in order to avoid the standing water.*

15. *William Ward Watkin, who supervised construction of the early buildings for Cram, Goodhue and Ferguson and stayed at Rice to establish the architecture department.*

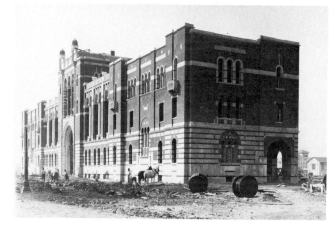

16. *Construction of the Administration Building, May 1912.*

17. *The nearly completed Administration Building.*

18. *The finished building, showing the Mechanical Laboratory to the right.*

found the university's architecture program), is said to have exclaimed in surprise and delight when he first saw the completed structure. In this building can be seen all the elements that Cram drew together—vaulted Byzantine cloisters, Dalmatian brickwork, marbled columns, sculptured capitals. Cram used all the color he could command. A special rose-hued brick contrasts harmoniously with gray mortar. Marble for the columns and sheathing came from the Ozark Mountains, Greece, Italy, Switzerland, Vermont, and Tennessee. A frieze of blue tile runs under the marble cornice, and glazed tile decorates the tower facades. Carved column capitals embody caricatures of ancient and modern scientists and humanists, football players, women students, and a few strange beasts frolicking beneath the arches. At the

four corners of the Sallyport muse representatives of the freshman through senior classes, the freshman looking hilariously happy, the senior studiously serious.[57]

The building itself is 300 feet long and 50 feet deep. Its three stories are deceptive. Because of the high ceilings, each flight of stairs seems a story and a half to the climber. A sallyport thirty feet high runs through the center of the building; above it was located President Lovett's office. It is said that Lovett wanted his office to be placed over a sallyport as was Woodrow Wilson's at Princeton, but he had not reckoned on the height of the one in his new building. Two flights of stairs, one on either side of the Sallyport, led to the office; Lovett told a student later that there were seventy-seven steps on the south side and seventy-eight on

the north, but that they came out to the same height. Hubert Bray of the mathematics department immortalized Lovett's location in a limerick:

A great man is Edgar O. Lovett.
His office has nothing above it.
It is four stories high,
As close to the sky,
As William Ward Watkin
could shove it.[58]

Because of the Sallyport and the need for cross ventilation, the floor plan of the building eliminated interior halls, except for the stairwells. Most rooms stretched completely across the building. The Administration Building did double and triple duty, especially in the early days of the Institute, containing administrative offices, professors' offices, classrooms, seminar rooms, the library, a lounge and study room for women, and a

19. *View through the completed Sallyport, October 6, 1912.*

20. *The completed Faculty Chamber, with light fixtures and other details in place.*

21. *President Lovett's office on the fourth floor of the Administration Building.*

22. *Boys' study in the Administration Building.*

23. *Classroom on the third floor of the Administration Building.*

24. *Construction photograph of the Mechanical Engineering Laboratory and powerhouse, probably 1912.*

study for men. The two-storied Faculty Chamber took the place of an auditorium until the physics amphitheater was added in 1914.

The Mechanical Laboratory, machine shop, and powerhouse complex sat at the head of the second major axis. Similar to the Administration Building but by no means as intricate, the complex had a facade that echoed the cloisters of the other buildings and repeated the color scheme. The smokestack for the powerhouse boiler was disguised as a campanile, which historian Andrew Forest Muir called an "unfortunate piece of architectural hypocrisy." As originally constructed, the campanile had "a hideous shingled skirt" near the top that repeated the roof line of the building beneath it. (It was removed when lightning struck it in the 1930s.) Heat, light, and water were delivered from the powerhouse to the other buildings through a tunnel network of considerable size and length. Central heating would eliminate the need for fireplaces, although there would be a few in the Administration Building.[59]

For the men students, one residential hall and the Commons were to open in 1912. The general plan for South Hall (now known as Will Rice College), a three-story structure with a tower of five stories, would be repeated in East and West Halls (Baker and Hanszen Colleges) within a few years. East and South Halls connected with the Commons (now the Baker College commons) by cloisters; West

25. *The completed Mechanical Engineering Laboratory with landscaping. "Mr. Dennis" is in the foreground.*

Hall stood across the road. The Commons was the dining hall for all residents and had its own tower where a few single faculty members and graduate students lived.

No university is complete without a touch of heraldry, and the Rice Institute would have its colors, shield, and patron saints. Pierre de Chaignon la Rose of Cambridge, Massachusetts, designed the shield, combining elements of the arms of several families having the names Rice and Houston. Some of these coats of arms had both chevrons and three avian charges, and la Rose adapted these for the Institute. In the official shield a double chevron divides the field, and the charges are the owls of Athena as they appear on a small Greek coin, the silver tetradrachmenon of the fifth century B.C. Choosing colors was more difficult than designing the shield, because it was not proper to duplicate the colors of another institution. At the same time, the designer wanted to harmonize the appearance of the new shield with state and national colors. The colors also needed to be easily procurable and appropriate to the climate: colorful but not hot, delicate but

26. *Dining room of the Commons, now Baker College commons.*

27. *The Commons kitchen.*

28–30. *Figures carved into the Administration Building capitals by sculptor Oswald J. Lassig. 28. Darwin. 29. DeLesseps. 30. Thucydides.*

28

29

31–32. *Exterior plaques on the Administration Building. 31. Plaque dedicated to science. 32. Plaque dedicated to art.*

30

31

32

33. *Ceremony laying the cornerstone of the Administration Building, March 2, 1911.*

34. *The cornerstone of the Administration Building. Translated, the inscription reads, "'Rather,' said Democritus, 'would I discover the cause of one fact than become King of the Persians.'"*

not lifeless. The final choices were Confederate gray enlivened by a tinge of lavender and a blue deeper than the Oxford blue.[60]

Into the capitals of the Administration Building's cloister were carved effigies of the "patron saints" of the new Institute. Sixteen men represented the university's various disciplines. For example, Thucydides symbolized history, Ferdinand de Lesseps engineering, Charles Darwin biology, and Pierre Curie studies in radioactivity. An Austrian sculptor, Oswald Lassig, carved the capitals after they had been put in place. He and his workers were also responsible for the other carvings on the building. The exterior walls of the Faculty Chamber displayed tablets carved with inscriptions to the concepts of letters, science, and art, selected from the writings of Homer, Isaac Newton, and Leonardo da Vinci. Flanking the Sallyport on the cloister side were two more tablets—dedicated to science and art—with life-sized, draped symbolic female figures and appropriate dicta from the writings of Aristotle and Plotinus.

Construction Begins

In a simple ceremony the cornerstone for the Administration Building was laid March 2, 1911, the seventy-fifth anniversary of Texas's independence from Mexico. (Lovett had hoped to lay it on Washington's birthday, but those plans went awry.) On dedication day the trustees were present, and Captain James Baker wielded the trowel. Deposited in the stone was a sealed copper box containing a copy of the King James version of the Bible, the charter of the Institute transcribed on parchment, a brief biography of William Marsh Rice, short sketches of the careers of the trustees, a photograph of the general site plan and buildings, a copy of the *Houston Chronicle* of January 12, 1911, and a copy of the *Houston Daily Post* of January 18, 1911. The stone itself, Ozark marble, is on the forecourt side of the Sallyport. On it are the shield of the Institute, the date, and the shield of the state of Texas. The inscription below is a Greek quotation in Byzantine lettering from the *Praeparatio Evangelica* of Eusebius Pamphili, which reads in English, " 'Rather,' said Democritus, 'would I discover the cause of one fact than become King of the Persians.'"[61]

Construction continued throughout 1911 and into 1912. Workmen excavated tunnels and laid drains, buildings sprang up above ground, and the Teas Nursery Company under the direction of Edward Teas, Sr., planted trees and shrubs along the new gravel walks and roads. Gravel was chosen instead of asphalt or concrete for both walkways and roads because it harmonized with the architecture, although some people would later claim that Lovett wanted it because Princeton University had gravel walks. The construction did not proceed fast enough to suit some of the citizens of Houston. The *Houston Post* declared in November 1911, " 'Some tremendous event is going to mark the end of time and the beginning of eternity,' says a Richmond divine. If he is alluding to the anticipated completion of the Rice Institute, we desire to state it would be too late to be of service to the boys of today." And again in December, "Time may be divided into four grand periods, viz., past, present, future, and the twilight zone which may or may not mark the completion of the Rice Institute."[62]

By May 1912 the board had decided to set the opening of the school for September 23 of that year, the twelfth anniversary of the founder's death. They were worried that the buildings would not be completed and called upon supervising architect Watkin and representatives of the construction companies to state firm dates for completion. The trustees instructed Watkin to put extra men on the job if it became necessary.[63] They were determined to open the Institute on time.

CHAPTER 3

The Formative Years

Completed buildings were undoubtedly important to the Institute, but its ultimate success would depend on two other factors: the faculty and the student body. President Lovett wanted to obtain an outstanding faculty because he knew that without one, good students would not come. The trustees, aware of the importance of a first-rate faculty, agreed. Upon returning from an inspection trip of European schools in 1908, trustee J. E. McAshan reported, "My interviews with educators lead me to believe that the only way we can command patronage is to have men and apparatus that will challenge the appreciation of the earnest students of the world, who desire to achieve success, and not cater too much to those students who only go to college as a matter of good form."[1]

Selecting the Faculty

While one purpose of Lovett's own long trip in 1908–09 was to seek recommendations for faculty members, he could not actually hire anyone until the opening date had been set. During 1910 and 1911, hopeful candidates from all over the United States sent letters of inquiry along with their credentials and recommendations; it appears, however, that their efforts were in vain. Lovett wanted faculty members who were found through his own endeavors instead of those who found him. He was particularly interested in securing a good physicist and a good mathematician. He was able to hire both.

From Sir John Joseph Thomson, world-renowned physicist of the Cavendish Laboratory at Cambridge, Lovett received a list of outstanding men in physics. Of the five on the list, he talked seriously with two, P. V. Bevan

and H. A. Wilson, both former Fellows of Trinity College, Cambridge. In 1912 Bevan was professor of physics at the Royal Halloway College for Women, University of London, and Wilson was professor of physics at McGill University in Montreal. Some of the difficulties that Lovett had in hiring faculty members were evident in negotiations with these two men.

Everyone mentioned the infamous Houston climate at some point in his discussions. Besides the city's reputation for debilitating heat and humidity, there were old fears of yellow fever and malaria that had not yet been laid to rest. Wilson thought that it would be undesirable to attempt any summer work: "I have been very healthy all my life but I confess very hot weather makes me very limp and unable to do much," he wrote.[2]

Prospective members of the faculty considered isolation from other centers of learning to be another drawback. Scholars engaged in research wanted to be able to discuss their findings with others in their fields, and as yet Texas had few such colleagues to offer. Bevan expressed an interest in participating in the launching of a new school with fine propects, but the advantages of his post in London were too great. When Bevan finally turned Lovett down, the only reasons he gave were "fear for the health of my children and doubts as to their education." Texas still seemed part of the frontier to many Europeans.[3]

It appears that Lovett tried to hire at salaries on the low side, but the market was unusual. He had to sell the idea of the new Institute to prospective candidates as much as they had to sell their qualifications to him. Bevan spoke of outside sources of income that were available in England but not in Texas; he did not think that Lovett offered enough inducement to leave the old associations. Wilson negotiated not only for a higher salary than the one offered but also for a research assistant and, at times during the discussions, a house.

In the end, Lovett had to pay well to attract good men from abroad. He wrote later that the trustees adopted uniformity of neither compensation nor rank, and that is evident in the final salary schedules. For the first few years professors earned between $4,000 and $6,000 a year, assistant professors between $1,200 and $3,600, and instructors between $900 and $1,500. This was not out of line with what Har-

vard was paying its faculty at that time, although the bottom range of the assistant professors' salary was low. President Lovett received $10,000 in 1912, plus lodging for himself and his family, which included Mrs. Lovett and three children, Adelaide, Henry Malcolm, and Laurence Alexander, who had moved to Houston early in 1909.[4]

Research-minded men like Wilson were somewhat concerned that they would not have enough time to devote to research in a new school. Wilson expected a lot of work connected with organization and establishment but thought that a year or two would be sufficient to get his department properly started. The teaching load was also bound to be heavy until more professors were hired, although some faculty members were even more annoyed at having to teach lower-division courses. Teaching beginning students had its special problems, among them boredom for the professor. A few teachers had other prejudices as well. For example, mathematician Griffith C. Evans, recommended by Italian mathematician Volterra, did not particularly look forward to teaching engineering students.[5]

Despite these difficulties, President Lovett managed to assemble a faculty of considerable promise. Present for duty the first year as professor of physics was Harold A. Wilson, Fellow of the Royal Society, Fellow of Trinity College, Cambridge, former professor at King's College, London, and research professor of physics at McGill. Besides Lov-

ett, who was listed as professor of mathematics, there was one other full professor, Thomas Lindsey Blayney, who had earned his Ph.D. at Heidelberg University and was professor of European literature and the history of European art at Central University in Kentucky. Blayney would teach German at Rice.

Lovett's only assistant professor was Griffith C. Evans, Sheldon Fellow at Harvard University. His field was mathematics, and his Harvard professors had given him excellent recommendations. He wrote that he hoped to get a position at a "respectable" university but did not have any good offers until two came at once, one from Rice and one from Yale. He chose Rice.[6]

Instructors included Philip H. Arbuckle, former director of athletics at Southwestern University, who was to develop an athletic program and teach English if necessary; electrical engineer Francis E. Johnson, previously with the British Columbia Electric Railway Company; John T. McCants, a Yale graduate who had been Lovett's private secretary since 1910 and who would teach English; and William Ward Watkin, with his degree in architecture from the University of Pennsylvania, who stayed to establish the architecture department after supervising construction of the first buildings for Cram, Goodhue and Ferguson. William F. Edwards was named lecturer in chemistry; he had been president of the University of Washington.

Listed as members of the faculty but not present for the first

35. *The first faculty with board members, 1912.* **Left to right:** *William F. Edwards, Francis E. Johnson, Thomas Lindsey Blayney, Philip H. Arbuckle, Edgar Odell Lovett, Benjamin Botts Rice, William Ward Watkin, Emanuel Raphael, Griffith C. Evans, James E. McAshan, John T. McCants, James Addison Baker, Jr., Harold A. Wilson.*

year were Percy J. Daniell and Julian S. Huxley. J. J. Thomson had recommended Daniell for applied mathematics; Daniell had been the last senior Wrangler (for special first class honors in mathematics) at Cambridge. Huxley, a biologist, was the grandson of Thomas H. Huxley, the well-known defender of the Darwinian theory. Julian Huxley was also a scholar of Balliol College and university lecturer at Oxford. Daniell and Huxley were listed as research associates in 1912 and received traveling fellow-ships of $1,000 each from the Institute for that school year. They also had three-year appointments as assistant professors with the Institute; specific appointments appear to have been given only to them.[7]

The Classes Begin

That other necessity of a university—students—appeared on the day of matriculation, September 23, 1912. Fifty-nine young men and women made their way out to the end of Main Street to register at the new school. President Lovett turned matriculation into another ceremony. After registration, the students, faculty, trustees, and many visitors who had come to see the first day of the Institute gathered in the Faculty Chamber of the Administration Building to hear an address by Lovett.

The president's matriculation address in 1912 was the beginning of a Rice tradition. Lovett said later that he thought it only appropriate to address the new first class, and he prepared his remarks with great care. In 1913 he thought it just as well to repeat the performance, and by 1914 the matriculation address had become a custom. So also was the handshake with each student at the conclusion of the address. Lovett missed only one matriculation address, in 1937, when he did not return in time from a trip to Europe; he had to be content with mailing it to the school

newspaper for publication. The speech became famous for its high idealism and classical allusions and for Lovett's felicity with words, an ability recognized by all who heard him or who read his written prose. Trustee A. S. Cleveland later remarked that when the board needed to write a memorial or another announcement, they always asked Lovett to compose it, and "concern for adequate expression vanishe[d]." The matriculation address, however, did not always come easily to Lovett. He wrote in 1935 that the thought of another speech gave him "a sickening jolt, for in

36. *Registration day for the first Rice Institute students, September 23, 1912.*

June I am utterly bankrupt in ideas and always in despair of ever being able to think out a twenty-minute matriculation address again."[8]

Classes began the next day, September 24. The students in the first class soon numbered seventy-seven, and approximately one-third of them were women. Most of the students had come from the Houston area, but there were a few from such places as Weatherford, San Angelo, Cisco, and Crockett, Texas, one from Lake Charles, Louisiana, and, according to the 1915 catalog, even one from San Diego, California. Admission requirements were not stringent by the standards of the 1980s, but they were difficult enough to meet in 1912. A certificate of graduation from an accredited public or private high school or successful examination in the entrance subjects was only the beginning. In addition to character references, a student also needed fourteen high school units (a unit representing a course of study pursued five hours a week for an academic year). Three units were to be in English, two-and-a-half in mathematics, two in history, and three in one foreign language or two in each of two modern languages. Applicants who did not have the required units could be admitted, on condition that they remove the deficiency by course work or tests before they could be accepted as candidates for a degree.[9]

Since there were so few faculty members, all freshmen took the same subjects, with the exception of engineering students, who took an extra course in engineering drawing, and architects, who took architectural work in place of chemistry. With these exceptions, everyone took English, German, physics, mathematics, and chemistry. It was a full load. Here began the infamous Math 100, required of all students no matter what their majors. In 1915 Math 100 consisted of trigonometry, analytic geometry, and advanced algebra; but by the 1920s, at the latest, calculus had been added (some said it took over), and the tales of taking Math 100 three or four times became well known.

Physics 100 under H. A. Wilson was no easy subject, either. Wilson did not really have that special quality needed to teach beginners, although he was excellent with upper-level students. One alumna of the class of 1918 reports that Wilson lectured twice a week; on Fridays instructor Claude Heaps came in and taught the physics on which Wilson had lectured the other two days.[10]

President Lovett was determined to make Rice a true university and to uphold generally accepted university standards. Therefore, the instruction and work required may have been somewhat more difficult than many freshmen expected. The school year consisted of three terms, the first ending before Christmas, the second about the middle of March, and the third in June. By the end of the first term, about twenty percent of the first freshman class had failed so many of their subjects that they were asked to withdraw. One explanation for so many failures was that in many high schools students could be exempted from examinations if their average grades were high. All students coming to Rice were highly ranked in their former schools and thus not accustomed to taking examinations. Since they did not know how to study for them, many failed.

One irate father, who had received one of Lovett's letters explaining that his son would not be permitted to continue that year, protested the school's action. He complained of the "incalculable injury" done to the "boys" who failed, to their parents, and to the community; he claimed that his son's ambitions had been crushed. When Lovett replied that the Institute's aspirations of service and scholarship demanded maintenance of high standards and that he believed the student would persist in his academic plans, the father was not satisfied. He wanted a second chance for those who had failed an "exceptionally and unexpectedly severe" examination coming after such a brief experimental period, part of which was "largely devoted to football." He did not think that William Marsh Rice would have been so strict. Lovett, however, stuck by his standards; the students were not readmitted until the next school year, when they had to begin the course of study all over.[11]

Those students who survived their first year and those who came in later years had to contend with other difficulties. Simply getting to the Institute for class could be arduous for men who lived off campus and for the women, all of whom lived off campus. Main Street was paved out to Eagle Street (where a Sears store is now located); a dirt and shell road ran from there to the Institute and beyond. Two cattle gates barred the path, and passengers could make themselves useful to the driver of a car by opening and shutting the gates. Passengers might also be of help if the car got stuck in a hole or in the frequent mud. A possibly apocryphal story is told about a farmer who used to water the road from time to time so he could make a little extra money pulling cars out of the mud.

For those with no transportation of their own, there was a trolley line. The South End streetcar came out Fannin Street to Eagle, where those bound for the Institute had to change to a shuttle car known by students as the "Toonerville trolley." It ran every hour on a projection of Fannin Street to Bellaire Boulevard (now Holcombe Boulevard) and turned west there to the isolated village of Bellaire. Once passengers had disembarked at the Institute, they faced another obstacle if it had been raining. Mud and standing water often stretched from the raised track to the entrance gate. A wooden walkway was built over the water, but getting to the Administration Building could still be messy. If students missed the trolley, their only recourse was to walk out the track. The first yearbook paid tribute to the weary marchers with a car-

toon in which the motorman cried, "Doggone it! There's always a cow or a professor on the track."

Those with early classes sometimes had trouble getting to Eagle in time to catch the trolley. Once, an alumna relates, she and three or four others were standing there late wondering what to do, when Dr. Lovett, also late, came up. He arranged to get a jitney and invited the students to ride with him. Lovett was often on the trolley with the students, but this jitney ride was somewhat more exciting for them than the usual shuttle.[12]

— The Position of Women

Women had special problems at the Institute. In the first place, some were not so sure that they were wanted. The charter called for "a thorough polytechnic school, for males and females," so women had to be admitted; but no particular provisions were made for them. Lovett later proclaimed his pride in the "unusually fine group of young women" who bore "their full share in making and maintaining the good name of the Rice Institute," but he also thought the best form of academic organization was found in places such as Harvard and Oxford where separate women's undergraduate colleges existed. If Lovett and some of the other faculty members were disinclined to teach women, their attitude might be traced to their own careers in all-male institutions, as both students and

teachers. Some women noticed a certain amount of nervousness in their male instructors who had to face a room full of female students not much younger than they were.[13]

The curriculum certainly provided no "women's" courses. The absence of such courses as home economics drew some criticism around town, the *Chronicle* claiming that an institution that did not take into account the "inclinations" and "leanings" of women for courses in the domestic sciences, art, and pedagogy was not truly coeducational. President Lovett is reported to have considered such courses to be fads and out of keeping with the aims of the Institute. Lel Red '16 tells the story that when her mother called the school to find out what the course offerings would be and heard about all the science and mathematics, she commented that they did not sound like what a girl would like to take. The person on the phone at the Institute replied, "No, it really doesn't. We don't encourage girls to come." Her mother answered that they could come if they wanted to, and Miss Red's father took her out to the campus on the day it opened.[14]

Whatever the *Chronicle*'s claims about inclinations and leanings, it appears that few women, if any, felt deprived because there were no "women's" courses. And despite the attitude of some of the professors, all courses were open to any student who could pass muster. Everyone took the same subjects, at the same speed and with the same intensity. Women may not have felt over-welcome on first arrival, and at the first registration some did not sign up for a full schedule. But any woman, or man, who wanted a thorough education could find it at the Institute.[15]

At any rate, the women were there. No dormitories were built for them, and therefore they had to live off campus; but so did many of the men. A large room was set aside at the north end of the second floor of the Administration Building (where the provost's office is now located), and there the women could study, relax, or eat lunch. They could also go to the Commons to lunch with the men; but Sara Stratford, stenographer in the president's office, went along to chaperone. Mrs. Stratford also made certain that all women were off campus by 5:00 P.M., when she left to go home. Young ladies simply did not stay on campus by themselves. Neither were any benches placed invitingly under shade trees—for fear that two students of opposite sexes might sit together on them.

For reasons unspoken but easily conjectured, classes were divided by gender that first year. When the women came out of class, the men would line up on both sides of the hall or cloister to watch, to the great excitement of all. But the second year saw an end to this practice of segregation, probably because of the increased enrollment and small faculty but also possibly because the women had proved that they could keep up with the men academically. (However, there would

continue to be some sections of Math 100 only for women.) That second year saw a continuation of what became known as "cloister courses," or "Sallyport 100" (when students gathered in the cloisters for conversation), and the cloisters and the Sallyport of the Administration Building became and remained the center of campus student life. In 1915 Mrs. Stratford was appointed adviser to women, but the duties of her office were unclear; she seems to have been more of a chaperone than anything else.[16]

Early Campus Life

The first occupants of on-campus residential halls must have felt to some extent that they were camping out. When classes started, the dormitory building was still unfinished; the young men were only able to move in as rooms were completed. The first meals were prepared on kerosene stoves and were served in kitchen staff quarters on the second floor of the Commons, because the floor had not yet been laid on the main level. Tables were made by spreading planks across sawhorses. The dining room floor was completed in time for the formal opening banquet, however; tired of creamed chipped beef, the boys were happy to see the real kitchen in operation.[17]

The first four classes began many traditions at Rice. President Lovett seemed anxious that the school have the right traditions, that no practice start that anyone would later regret. One of

the first traditions established was the honor system for examinations. Each student had to sign the pledge, "On my honor, I have neither given nor received any aid on this examination," at the end of each test. The student-elected Honor Council decided cases of infractions as proclaimed in the Honor Council constitution. The most extreme penalty available to the council was a recommendation that the offender be expelled. Final disposition was in the hands of the president. This system, only slightly modified, is still in use today.[18]

In the residential halls, men had a great deal of freedom for the first two years. President Lovett referred to the halls as gentlemen's clubs, regulated by no other code than "the common understanding by which gentlefolk determine their conduct of life." Numbers, however, made a difference; and some of the more obstreperous students, tasting freedom from home for the first time, necessitated establishment of the Hall Committee. Theoretically the Honor Council had general authority over the students, but in practice it confined itself to violations of the honor code as applied to papers and examinations. The Hall Committee ran the dormitories, making and enforcing rules by which the "gentlemen's clubs" were to run.[19]

Lovett had seen the honor system in practice at both the University of Virginia and Princeton University. He had also observed Woodrow Wilson's attempt to abolish exclusive student clubs at

Princeton. Perhaps because of this experience, along with the divisiveness caused on some campuses by the rivalries between fraternities and independents, and the democratic tenor of the times, Lovett outlawed social fraternities and sororities at Rice. The big national organizations would never come; instead, the students formed organizations of their own. The first were the Young Men's Christian Association and the Young Women's Christian Association, followed by the Menorah Society for Jewish students. To challenge the mind, the students established three "literary societies," the Owl Literary Society and the Riceonian Literary and Debating Society for men, and the Elizabeth Baldwin Literary Society—named for the founder's second wife—for women. In the beginning, these were true debating and literary societies, holding intersociety contests, reviewing books, and reading essays. Elizabeth Kalb, class of 1916, won the state oratorical contest in 1915.

While the men's literary societies did not survive long, the women's did, and the EBLS split in 1919 to form another "lit," as these organizations came to be known: the Pallas Athene Literary Society (PALS). In 1924 another group of women formed the OWLS, the Owen Wister Literary Society—named for the popular author of *The Virginian*. Until 1915–16 any woman who wanted to join the EBLS could do so, on her own initiative. New membership was closed to seniors that year, on the grounds that if a

37. *The Owl Literary Society, 1916.*

38. *The Elizabeth Baldwin Literary Society, 1916.*

39. *The Rice Institute Engineering Society, 1916.*

40. *The Women's Tennis Club, 1916.*

woman had been at Rice and had not participated in the society before her senior year, she must not be genuinely interested.[20] Before long, the organizations began to invite women to join during their freshman year and became more sorority-like. What had begun as a literary group would end as an almost totally social organization.

By 1916 there were a number of clubs and organizations on campus, some academic, some social. Rice engineering students had formed the Engineering Society in 1914, and the architects and biologists soon organized groups in their own disciplines. German students founded the Goethe Verein, and French students formed Les Hiboux. For women there were the Choral Club and the Tennis Club. An early addition to the Rice scene was the Rice Band, twenty-one members strong in 1916. On January 15, 1916, the *Thresher* began publication as the official student newspaper. Established through the literary societies, the paper secured enough support from students and city merchants to be published biweekly. William M. Standish was the first editor-in-chief and James P. Markham the first business manager. In 1916 the first graduating class published the first yearbook, edited by Ervin F. Kalb, with Hildegarde Elizabeth Kalb as assistant editor and William Max Nathan as business manager. The seniors chose the name *Campanile* for the yearbook, from the landmark campanile/smokestack of the Mechanical Laboratory.[21]

Although Dr. Lovett wanted

the residential halls to become individual social units similar to Oxford's colleges (without taking over the university's academic role), the Institute's dormitories did not develop an organization beyond the Hall Committee. The only associations unique to one hall or another were some intramural sports teams, but these were plebeian compared with Lovett's noble vision of college debating or musical organizations. Instead, the student body split horizontally by classes. The classes received the loyalty and energy that Lovett had hoped to see in the separate halls; and with the arrival of the class of 1917 in 1913, a tradition began that later brought turmoil. The newly turned sophomores found it great fun to haze freshmen.

Hazing consisted of pranks played on male freshmen or "slimes." The term "slime" had several possible origins. Some have suggested that it was a synonym for "fish," by which sobriquet the Texas A&M Aggies called their freshmen. Others say that freshmen were thought just to have emerged from the primordial ooze on the way to being civilized. Whatever its derivation, the name "slime" stuck. Sophomores greeted freshmen as they emerged from registration and subjected them to a number of indignities, such as having their faces painted, pushing a mothball in a race across the gravel walks, and other similar foolishness. Freshmen had to run errands for sophomores and clean their rooms. In the practice known as "running the gauntlet," a fresh-

man ran through a lane formed by sophomores, each of whom had a leather strap or broom handle with which he gave the slime a swat. This trick resulted in a broken collar bone on one occasion, but the sophomores paid the medical bills. The administration did not take any action to curb hazing until after World War I. There was no hazing of women students in the beginning.[22]

Athletic activities were just as much a part of the college scene as were classes, examinations, and social clubs, and the Institute's students were quick to go out for various teams. Rice athletics had started in 1912 with the first class under the direction of Philip H. Arbuckle, who taught English and occasionally a history course in addition to his coaching duties. During the first season Rice played football games against Houston and Orange high schools, Sam Houston Normal Institute, Southwestern University, and Austin College. The team finished the season with three victories and two defeats. In the process it acquired the name "the Owls." A suggestion in the Houston Post that the name be "the Grays" for one of the school colors did not bear fruit, and the team was named instead for the bird on the Institute seal.

In that first season the Rice football team held its own against the high schools and Sam Houston but lost badly to the bigger schools. The next year Rice had its revenge against Southwestern and finished the season of four

games undefeated. In 1914 the Owls began playing a full schedule in football as an original member of the newly organized Southwest Conference,[23] and the University of Texas and Texas A&M quickly became primary rivals. Rice beat the Aggies in 1915 and 1916, but it was 1916 before the Owls managed even to score against Texas, and then the final score was 16–2. That same year the Owls also ran up the highest score in their history: they beat brand-new Southern Methodist University 146–3.[24]

As a symbol for the team, students constructed a large canvas owl, which they carried to the games. It was a tempting target for those irrepressible mascot rustlers, the Aggies, who kidnapped it in 1917 and took it home to College Station. Rice students sent a private detective to find out the owl's location. When he sent a telegram saying, "Sammy is fairly well and would like to see his parents at eleven o'clock," the Rice mascot had a name. Students organized the Owl Protective Society to rescue Sammy and set off for College Station, breaking into the A&M Armory and starting back for Houston with the bird as quickly as they could. Their deed did not go undiscovered, however, and practically the whole Aggie Cadet Corps rose in pursuit. The Rice students had only a couple of cars for transportation; the Aggies got a train, caught up with the Rice men, and captured all except four. Those four managed to cut up Sammy's canvas covering and smuggle the skin back to

41. *Football team, 1912.* Back row, left to right: *Oliver R. Garnett, (Louis J. ?) Smith, R. Wyllys Taylor, William M. Standish, Wesley G. Mims, Joe Brigham, George Journeay, Philip H. Arbuckle (coach);* middle row: *George K. Wilkinson, George I. Goodwin, Robert E. Cummings (captain), Clinton H. Wooten, Wilson T. Betts;* front row: *Rex Graham Aten, Louis L. Farr.*

42. *Football team, 1913.*

43. *Sammy.*

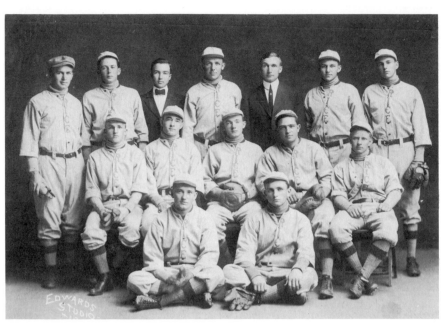

44. *Baseball team, 1913.* Back row, left to right: *Harry M. Bulbrook, Louis L. Farr, Elmer E. Shutts (manager), William M. Standish, Philip H. Arbuckle (coach), Clinton H. Wooten, Gordon S. Mayo;* middle row: *J. B. Spiller, Robert E. Cummings, Oliver R. Garnett (captain), (Brantly C. ?) Harris, Wilson Betts;* front row: *Harry Lee Harless, George I. Goodwin.*

Houston. Sammy was home once again, but that was not to be his last run-in with the Aggies.

Other sports also began early in the history of the Institute. In the spring of 1913 the first baseball team played a variety of opponents from local high schools, the Southern Pacific Railroad, and Houston National Bank. In 1914 Rice men participated in a track meet. Basketball began in 1915, and the Owls won the conference in 1918.[25]

Further Faculty Appointments

As the student body grew in numbers, so did the faculty. The second year, 1913–14, Percy

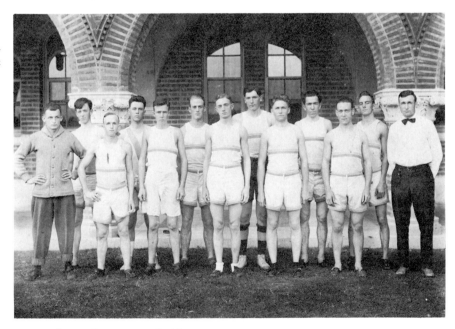

45. *Early track team, probably 1916 or 1917.*

Daniell and Julian Huxley arrived to assume their positions as assistant professors. Professor Wilson had been helping President Lovett find good faculty members in several fields, emphasizing that "unless we get some really first rate men, the Institute will get a poor reputation which will take years to live down." He suggested to Lovett that advertising positions at better salaries than were paid elsewhere (or at least equivalent ones) was an efficient method of establishing the Institute's reputation. Wilson also lobbied hard for a second physicist, and Lovett hired one that year. The new assistant professor was another scholar recommended by J. J. Thomson: Arthur Llewelyn Hughes.[26]

President Lovett also added two full professors to the staff in humanities: Albert L. Guérard from Stanford to establish the French department, and Stockton Axson from Princeton to head English, which up to this time had consisted of McCants, Coach

47. *Percy John Daniell, assistant professor of applied mathematics.*

Arbuckle for a term, and Roy P. Lingle, an instructor. Axson was Woodrow Wilson's brother-in-law and was known and loved at Princeton as an ideal professor. His lectures at Rice soon became famous, especially those on Shakespeare with Axson reciting the various parts. Those who saw him said that he veritably became Falstaff. Axson had an unusual arrangement with the Institute whereby he remained in the Northeast for the first term each year but taught the second and third terms at Rice.[27]

The 1913–14 budget gave some indication of the faculty situation, and a letter from Professor Wilson to Lovett echoed the needs of the Institute. Listed in the budget in a special column marked "imperative" were the fields and ranks that had to be filled. Lovett wanted professors for chemistry and education, instructors in physics and English, and lecturers in history and politics. Engineering appears to have had special problems. Although

46. *Harold Albert Wilson, professor of physics.*

48. *Julian Sorell Huxley, assistant professor of biology.*

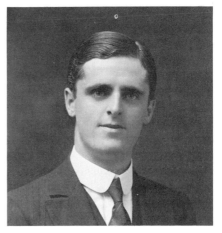

49. *Arthur Llewelyn Hughes, assistant professor of physics.*

50. *Stockton Axson, professor of English literature.*

51. *Albert Léon Guérard, professor of French.*

52. *Radoslav Andrea Tsanoff, assistant professor of philosophy.*

engineering was becoming recognized as a valid college subject, not just a vocational one, there were many academics who claimed that it was more a trade than a profession and as such should be taught on the job instead of in the classroom. Whatever Lovett personally may have thought about this claim, he had a firm grasp of local demands, which called for an engineering course at the Institute. He said later that because of these considerations, he had to introduce engineering courses somewhat earlier than he had originally planned. Since students who wanted to be engineers were admitted with the first class, the Institute would need an engineering faculty for the third year. In 1913 Wilson indicated the need for a good engineer to take charge of outfitting the Mechanical Laboratory, and he forecast failure for the engineering course if an engineer was not hired soon.[28]

For the third year, President Lovett was able to make some important appointments to the faculty but still did not have all the professors that he needed. Radoslav A. Tsanoff, beloved by many generations of Rice students for his idealism and intellect, came from Clark University to be assistant professor of philosophy. Claude W. Heaps, a Princeton Phi Beta Kappa with a "tremenjous" (his favorite word) sense of humor,[29] was added to the physics department. Clyde C. Glascock became assistant professor of modern languages, Rolf F. Weber of Berlin was appointed to instruct in German, and William C. Graustein joined the mathematicians as an instructor. Lovett finally found a historian, Robert G. Caldwell, who held a Ph.D. from Princeton, and also hired two engineers: Herbert K. Humphrey, instructor in electrical engineering, and Joseph H. Pound, instructor in mechanical

engineering. Edwin E. Reinke was to join Huxley in biology as an instructor; and Joseph Ilott Davies, a glassblower and research assistant for Huxley, was brought from England. (After 1940, Davies's theatrical Biology 100 classes would be fondly remembered by many Rice graduates.)

During 1915 Lovett hired a number of new faculty members, among them Hermann J. Muller, who would later win a Nobel Prize in biology (although not at Rice), and cheerful Harry B. Weiser, who would do important work in colloidal chemistry.[30] That same year Samuel G. McCann, noted for his "pink" hair, became a fellow in history. (He would later become an instructor after he received his M.A. in 1917 and a year later would become registrar as well.) One of Rice's most unusual fellows, William J. Sidis, also arrived in 1915. A child prodigy from Harvard, Sidis

53. *Claude William Heaps, instructor in physics.*

54. *Henry Boyer Weiser, instructor in chemistry.*

55. *Samuel Glenn McCann, instructor in history.*

had to teach students older than he was in his mathematics class, and the women teased him a great deal. He fled back to the East in 1916 and in a newspaper interview complained of his treatment at the hands of Texas girls.[31] Lovett continued to add to the faculty until World War I disrupted the university and the country.

Life for the new faculty members could be an adventure in its own way. Most of the men were new to Texas and found the cultural and climatological shocks memorable, although some were happy to be away from northern winters. The faculty socialized as well as studied. Belle Heaps remembers that she and her husband, Claude Heaps, exchanged dinner parties with other young faculty couples and attended a spate of elaborate teas. Mrs. Lovett was mindful of the advantages of good community relations and gave elegant receptions for Hous-

tonians so they could meet faculty families. The faculty and students got together for parties at the bay or for trips down the ship channel. Faculty bachelors did not neglect their social life, either. They dated some of the women students, and several young professors married women out of the first classes.

Faculty bachelors were invited to live on campus in the tower above the Commons; Griffith Evans was the first inhabitant. He occasionally invited students to his rooms for conversation and coffee—he had the first instant coffee some had ever seen—or offered them his tickets to concerts and plays when he could not attend. Huxley, Hughes, and several graduate students, including the shy but courtly Hubert E. Bray (who would later become a math professor at Rice), soon joined Evans in the faculty tower.

The British contingent often congregated behind a curtain in

the biology laboratory for four o'clock tea, and some of their conversations could well have revolved around the differences between English and American college life. Huxley and Hughes wrote Lovett in August 1914 to suggest some improvements in the American form. First, the food in the Commons was "very monotonous and often ill cooked." They suggested minimizing the use of canned fruits and vegetables and serving better quality bread and meat. Not long after the professorial complaint, some students staged a food riot to make the point more forcefully. Huxley and Hughes's second suggestion concerned living accommodations. English colleges had janitors and special arrangements for faculty meals. The two professors found much of their time being spent not on research and private work but on "petty duties" that they thought could be more quickly and more properly performed by an attendant. Third, they asked for a high table for the faculty in the Commons. Huxley added a fourth to these requests in November when he asked for a common room for the faculty, a place to get away from the students and relax. He understood America's preoccupation with democracy, but he thought that the lack of a faculty room discriminated against the faculty. He wanted Rice to recognize what Oxford and Cambridge already understood—that "faculty were adults and due some privileges which students did not merit." Huxley, Hughes, and Evans soon moved off campus and built a house, nicknamed the "Bach," about three-quarters of a mile away. Evans invited another bachelor to stay, and this housekeeping arrangement seemed to meet their needs for a while.[32]

Other Changes

As student enrollment increased and the faculty grew in numbers, more buildings were added to the campus. The handsome turreted Physics Building with its adjoining amphitheater was completed in 1914, and two more dormitory buildings were constructed: East Hall in 1914 and West Hall in 1916.

Thanks to the efforts of a man who became a Rice institution, the grounds also began to look like more than prairie. Salvatore Martino, or "Tony," as everybody called him, had been Captain Baker's gardener, and Baker "lent" him to Rice in 1915. Tony never

returned to the Baker garden. He planted trees, the quadrangle hedges, cape jasmine, crape myrtle, and vegetables (the last for the Commons table), and guarded his flowers zealously from casual pluckers. Flattery or cajolery did aspirants for the blooms no good, and anyone whom Tony caught in the act of picking even a single blossom was ostracized. For his student and faculty favorites, however, he always produced a flower, usually from the cape jasmine bushes. Tony became one of the biggest boosters of Rice's athletic teams and was famous for his bonfire speeches. While the content was not always expressed in standard English, the intent was clear. Tony also helped faculty members with their own gardens, and some of those new to Texas learned that the area was fine for growing "lee-voka" trees and "boka-da-veeya" vines (live oak trees and bougainvillea vines).[33]

Administration and Curriculum

In those days Rice had a minimum of what is today called administration. At the top was the board. The trustees did not interfere with President Lovett's running of the school, but they certainly knew what was going on. They had made Lovett a member of the board in 1910 to fill the place vacated by Frederick Rice's death in 1901. Their primary job was to invest the endowment and see that the income was spent wisely. For the fiscal year ending

April 29, 1916, the books showed expenditures on the "educational department" of almost $168,000 and revenues in excess of expenditures of more than $281,000. The board listed more than $11.3 million in assets, most in first mortgage notes and interest-bearing securities, bonds, and the buildings and grounds of the school.[34]

Out at the Institute—the "general offices and financial department" were downtown in the Scanlan Building—the administration consisted of President Lovett and his secretary, John T. McCants. McCants was an unofficial second-in-command, much like an executive assistant, who handled requests and complaints before they got to the president. He made both friends and enemies in the process. To many he was a likable man; to others, he was known as "Mr. McCan-not." Mrs. Stratford seems to have had no voice in policy-making, although she had the title "adviser to women." The only real secretary handling correspondence, files, and office matters was Anne Wheeler, Lovett's secretary, who came to Rice in 1919.

For the departments and faculty, President Lovett believed in the German type of organization, where there was one professor per department. That professor was, in effect if not in title, the chairman or head of the department. The rest consisted of assistant professors, instructors, and lecturers, and possibly some teaching fellows. There were no associate professors. Occasionally in a large and important department like mathematics or physics there might be two professors, but not often. As a result of this arrangement, promotions were slow in coming. In later years it was not unusual for a Rice assistant professor to be offered a chairmanship and a full professorship at another institution, circumventing the normal progression of assistant professor-associate professor-full professor. There was no tenure policy at Rice, but this did not seem to arouse the same feeling of insecurity that it does today. There was also no pension or retirement plan, and sabbaticals were rare.

It is difficult to determine exactly when the faculty organized into a formal body. Professor Wilson complained at least twice in March 1913 about the lack of a definite plan for course work and for filling staff needs. Lovett remarked in 1950 that the first committee on curriculum and degrees was appointed in the spring of 1913 with Wilson as chairman, but no minutes or reports of the committee remain. The committee consisted of Wilson, Evans, Guérard, Huxley, and Axson; if they did anything, it was only to plan for the coming year. There is no evidence that the faculty met in an organized manner to hear about the appointment of the committee or the committee's recommendations.[35]

The small size of the faculty leads one to believe that there was no formal organization until the spring of 1914. Until then, decisions had usually been made by one man (professor or president) or one department. Since these decisions involved equipment or faculty, opinions and conclusions were easy to gather without a formal meeting. By March 1914, however, more formal planning was necessary. The sophomores would enter into upper-class specialized work in the fall, and they needed a coherent course of study. Policy on such matters as admission, attendance, probation, and promotion had to be promulgated as well. The earliest minutes existing for the faculty sitting as a formal body are dated March 27, 1914.

In May 1914 another committee was appointed to draw up a tentative plan of studies for the next and succeeding years. It consisted of the same members as the 1913 committee, and they filed their report in June. Their recommendations were the basis for programs leading to the Bachelor of Arts degree and fifth-year engineering and architecture degrees. They also reiterated Lovett's goal that the Institute be a university. Although the program was concentrated in the sciences, advanced courses would be available in the "so-called humanities . . . to offer both the advantages of a liberal general education and those of special and professional training." In addition to bachelor's degrees, Rice would offer graduate degrees, although the committee had not yet spelled out the requirements for these. Furthermore, the work would be at "a high university standard." (The committee report said "moderately-high," but in the completed catalog the word "moderately" was omitted.)[36]

The plan divided the Bachelor of Arts curriculum into a general course and an honors course. The general course did not involve highly detailed, specialized study, as did the honors course, but either could be the path to graduate study. The first two years' work were the same for both curricula, covering five courses each year. In the freshman year each student took mathematics, English, a modern language, a science, and an elective; in the sophomore year, mathematics or a science, English, a language, and two electives. At that point, students had to decide whether to take the general or the honors course; they also had more latitude in choice of subjects than in the first two years. For the general course, subjects were divided into Group A (the humanities) and Group B (the sciences, engineering, and mathematics). In the junior year, students took four subjects: two that had been taken in the second year, one that had been taken in both freshman and sophomore years, and an elective. At least one subject had to be from Group A and one from Group B. The senior year provided for four subjects: two continuing from the third year, one from either the second and third years or the first and third years, and an elective. Again, one subject from each group was necessary.[37]

Honors students, on the other hand, were considered to be entering rigorous professional training; they concentrated in one subject area with no requirement to take a course from the other group. Juniors took five subjects, seniors four (later five), all of which could be in their chosen disciplines or closely related ones. Each program was devised by the department concerned, but not all departments offered honors courses. At first these were available only in pure and applied mathematics, theoretical and experimental physics, modern languages and literatures, biology, and chemistry. Others were slowly added to the list over the next thirty years.

The general B.A. student who performed at a very high level was honored by the designation "with distinction" at commencement, and the successful honors student graduated "with honors in" his or her special field. (Only with the graduating class of 1959 did the common academic distinctions "cum laude," "magna cum laude," and "summa cum laude" appear on Rice sheepskins.)

B.A. students in either curriculum were allowed a certain amount of flexibility in their courses of study. Engineering students had none at all, except sometimes to pick their foreign languages. Engineers took five subjects each year and in some cases more in their fourth and fifth years. To meet the requirements of the engineering profession and become a "well-rounded" graduate, students who could "afford the time" were encouraged to spend three or four years on preliminary work, take the B.A. at the end of four years, and receive an engineering degree

at the end of six or seven years. It appears, however, that few followed the recommendation. Most elected to stay for five years, receiving a B.S. after the fourth year and an engineering degree after the fifth. Degrees were offered in mechanical, civil, electrical, and chemical engineering. Architects were in a similar category, but they were allowed more electives. At the same time, they were obliged to study the "indispensable elements of a liberal education" as well as the engineering and technical subjects that were becoming mandatory for a practicing architect.[38]

All courses offered at Rice ran for a full year. Remedying a failure in a course meant taking it over the next year. Exceptions to this rule were a few courses in engineering and philosophy offered as term courses and later as semester courses when the two-semester year replaced the three-term year.

It appears from the faculty minutes that these curricula were adopted without much controversy, perhaps because the courses of study were similar to other schools'. There had been many experiments in higher education in the first decade of the century, and Rice was able to take advantage of the experience of others. The Institute was probably more fortunate in its curriculum development than anyone realized at the time. Rice was a school without tradition and had a new faculty drawn from many places. There was no entrenched course of study with adherents unwilling to give up their "em-

pircs," no opposition on the basis of habit, no large constituency of alumni, no meddling trustees to satisfy. At the same time, it could tolerate both a course of study for the engineer and one for the humanist, and strive to maintain intellectual quality, discipline, and community interest in each.[39]

There were still curricular matters to be worked out and some regulations to be defined after the original plan was adopted. In December 1914 the faculty regularized the grading system. Students were to be divided into five categories, but instead of As and Bs, Rice students received numerical grades: I signified very high standing, II high standing, III medium standing, IV low standing, and V failure. There were no percentages attached formally to these numbers, such as 85 equals a II. In May 1915 the faculty decided on regulations for graduation, promotion, probation, and withdrawal. Students needed to pass at least half their course work to remain at the Institute. To graduate, they needed passing grades in eighteen courses, of which eight had to be grades of III or better. In 1917 the faculty spelled out exactly what kinds of courses those eighteen had to be: five freshman courses (courses listed in the 100s in the catalog), five at the sophomore level (200s), four at the junior level (300s), and four senior courses (400s). (Graduate courses were numbered 500 and above.) The faculty was interested in continuity of learning, and they emphasized that each year's learning was intended to build on the previous one. In his book, *Memories*, Julian Huxley recalled the difficulty of convincing students that his two-year advanced course was a unity. "They clung to the idea that all they had to do was to pass their exams at the end of each semester, and if I asked any questions concerning earlier work, would protest: 'But, Prof, we've *done* all that.'" He persisted and thought he had some success in establishing biology as a unitary study, "not to be chopped into unrelated chunks of knowledge."[40]

The first two years passed with few regulations. By 1915, however, enrollment had passed 200, and some rules became necessary. Up to that time there had been no penalty for absenteeism or tardiness beyond a caustic remark from the instructor. In January 1915, the faculty approved a new system of mandatory class attendance. The professors were determined that students should attend classes "with absolute regularity." They also expressed their displeasure with a system that allowed a definite number of cuts, for students then always took the full number allowed. Therefore, no cuts were to be permitted, and any student who missed class had to bring a written excuse from parents, physician, or adviser accounting for the absence—and in addition pay twenty-five cents for clerical expenses to process the file. At the same meeting the faculty voted to require thirteen freshmen and one sophomore to leave school because of excessive absences. With a small student body, the

faculty could and did consider each student's problem individually and vote a solution. At the same time, faculty members were not insensitive to the confusion and needs of the students. An adviser system was established in 1914 so that faculty members could assist students with personal problems and counsel them in choosing courses.[41]

Admission requirements also worried the faculty. In the spring of 1916 they recorded several discussions and reports on entrance examinations. Tests took seven or eight days to administer, and the faculty wanted to shorten the exams without lowering standards. These were Rice-originated tests, not the tests of the College Entrance Examination Board. It was not until 1919 that the Institute accepted CEEB scores for entrance purposes, and even then the test was only for students who had not attended accredited high schools.

In 1917, for the first but by no means the last time, the faculty discussed the problem of enrolling well-prepared freshmen. They considered several alternatives: limiting the number of students, raising the number of units required, prescribing certain subjects as prerequisites for admission, and admitting from only the upper two-thirds of a high school class. One possibility that they raised was to select only applicants with certified high school records and to require examinations for all. None of these procedures seemed acceptable at the time, especially since some of the requirements would exclude good

graduates from the state's very small schools, which did not offer the city schools' variety of courses.[42]

Except for very general statements permitting a master's degree (after one year's graduate work and a thesis in a principal subject) or a doctorate (after three years' work, a dissertation, and a public examination), the faculty did not concern itself with graduate requirements until October 1916, after Walter W. Marshall had obtained the first Master of Arts degree at the Institute's first commencement the previous June. In November the master's requirements were set. The graduate student would have to take and pass four advanced courses with high credit, at least two of which had to be at the 400 level or above and one at the 500 level. The course work included research in the student's principal subject, and the student had to submit a thesis and pass a public oral examination. The Ph.D. requirements did not state a specific number of courses but did call for a "distinctly original contribution to the subject" in the thesis and for its publication in an accredited journal or series. The last requirement had evidently been discussed since at least 1914, because in that year Professor Blayney complained about the problems faced by candidates for literary or philosophical doctorates in publishing their long theses in journals. Blayney also pointed out that if this provision were adopted, the judges of the student's work would not be the specialists of the Institute but the journal editors, who had their own interests. He believed that the sugestion was unsound in theory and would prove even worse in practice. Nevertheless, the requirement was adopted and continued until 1950.[43] Since the Ph.D. degrees earned at Rice until 1955 were all in mathematics and science (with the lone exception of a Ph.D. in history awarded to Albert Grant Mallison in 1933), the publication requirement does not appear to have been a hardship for graduate students in the early years.

Although the president issued a list of dates for faculty meetings each year, it appears that after 1916 the faculty met only when a problem arose or new regulations or course requirements were needed. To take care of routine matters, Lovett appointed a small number of committees. By 1916 the committees and their chairmen were Examinations and Standing, Caldwell; Course of Study and Schedules, Wilson; Entrance Examinations, Daniell; Library, Evans; Outdoor Sports, Watkin; Non-Athletic Organizations, Axson; Recommendations, Graustein; and Student Advisors, Guérard.[44]

The committees brought their reports to the full faculty for discussion and adoption, but not every committee recommendation was accepted. For example, Wilson's 1914 committee on the curriculum had suggested that the six-day school week (there were Saturday morning classes) be divided so that classes met not every other day but on three consecutive days, each day con-

sisting of four periods in the morning beginning at 8:30, with labs in the afternoon. This may have pleased the scientists, but at least one humanist objected. German professor Blayney protested against crowding work in literary subjects into three days followed by four without instruction. Such a schedule would also allow students "too much" leisure time at the beginning or end of the week, if they could arrange their schedules carefully. The committee's suggestion was not adopted.[45]

The First Library

One of the pivotal components of any institution of higher learning is its library. No matter what their disciplines, scholars need a collection of sources and information about their fields. The charter of the Rice Institute called specifically for a free public library and reading room, but that was not easy to establish. Lovett wrote to his friend T. J. J. See, a noted astronomer at the Naval Observatory, that he was

56. *Alice Crowell Dean '16, assistant librarian, and Sara Stratford, adviser to women.*

working on a plan whereby the Houston Public Library would confine itself to "things literary and popular" and leave the Institute's library fund free to purchase scientific and technical publications.[46] Nothing appears to have been done to develop a library until the school had been in operation for a while. In 1915 Lovett appointed a faculty Library Committee with Griffith Evans as chairman. Evans, however, did not run the library alone. Whenever the library is mentioned, the first person who comes to mind is Alice Crowell Dean.

Miss Dean had been superintendent of high schools in Victoria, Texas, but she did not have a college degree; she came to Rice in 1913 to finish her work. She graduated in 1916 with honors in mathematics and remained to work on a master's degree. She also stayed to help build the library. As an undergraduate, she wanted to contribute to her support by working; possibly because she was a little older than most of the undergraduate and graduate students, the school hired her to manage the library under the committee's direction. She also taught a section of Math 100 for years and was listed in the budgets as a fellow in mathematics. One of her students was Howard Hughes, the multimillionaire entrepreneur. When asked why she had given him a failing grade, she replied, "He flunked himself by frittering away his time." Miss Dean was not one to fritter.

Named acting librarian in 1914, Alice Dean never obtained a library degree. Her training in the field consisted of one summer at Columbia University and one day at Harvard; nonetheless, she proved to be an excellent librarian. She and Evans used the new faculty's specialized knowledge to build a working library where books were bought because there was a need for them, not just to add to the collection. High on the list of priorities were scientific, literary, and technical journals. The Institute purchased journals and other publications in series, including their complete back files, on the theory that there was no school or institution in the area with a large collection of back issues of periodicals. Miss Dean also put the library on the Library of Congress cataloging system, an action that saved a great deal of expense later when the Dewey Decimal system lost favor.[47]

The size of the library depended, of course, on the budget. In 1913–14 and 1914–15, $10,000 was allotted each year for books. By 1915–16, Evans and Miss Dean had established a system of units to allocate the money among the various departments. The science, engineering, and architecture departments got ten units each, some of the humanities were allotted six, and fine arts, Spanish, education, and Latin and Greek got four each, with an extra eight units left over for special purchases. Any new course received an extra credit, as did new members of the faculty. That year the amount in the budget was raised to $16,000 and the next to $18,000. The war years

brought substantial reductions, but by 1920 the library allotment was up to $15,000 again.[48]

The physical size of the library determined its location. In the beginning it was housed on the second floor of the Administration Building, in what is today the president's office. As the collection grew, it spread into rooms on the first floor, then took over the basement, and finally colonized branches in other buildings as well. As might be expected, problems arose from using the basement of the Administration Building. During heavy rains the basement flooded so badly that the bottom shelf was unusable. Librarian Sarah Lane remembered going down one day to check on the state of the current flood only to find a large snake swimming in the waters. She left the basement library to the snake that day.[49]

Public Lectures

In addition to class lectures, laboratories, research, and committee work, the faculty had another task: lecturing to the public. In an attempt to foster harmonious ties with the city, Lovett established in 1913 what were called the University Extension Lectures, realizing his inaugural aspiration "to support the intellectual and spiritual welfare of the community."[50] They had a twofold purpose: to expose the people of the community (especially the "several hundred college men and women") to Rice's scholars and vice versa, and to extend the

57. *The first library, in the Administration Building.*

influence of the university's academic life beyond the Institute's walls. Given free of charge, the lectures were delivered three afternoons a week in series of thirty-six. They were drawn from all aspects of work at Rice. While they were as nontechnical and popular in treatment as their subjects permitted, some of the lecture series amounted to short university courses. Stockton Axson gave the first addresses and proved to be one of the most popular speakers. In the first five years, he presented sixty talks, half again as many as the next most prolific speaker, Professor Guérard.[51] For some of Axson's lectures, and for some of the others by faculty and guest speakers, it was necessary to move to the City Auditorium to accommodate all who wished to attend. For the most part, however, the

lectures were held in the physics amphitheater on campus.[52]

The extension lectures received wide publicity, many being abstracted in newspapers throughout the state. To publicize the extension lectures and other talks by faculty and visitors, Lovett established the *Rice Institute Pamphlet,* a quarterly serial (known as *Rice University Studies* since 1960). The *Pamphlet* began in 1915 by publishing the inaugural lectures and soon included extension lectures, commencement addresses, and scholarly papers.[53]

Early Achievements and Problems

Rice held its first commencement in June 1916. The festivities lasted several days and

included dances, a play, a tennis tournament, and a garden party given by the Lovetts in honor of the graduates. The baccalaureate and commencement ceremonies were held out of doors, on the west or court side of the Administration Building to take advantage of the morning cool and the building's shade. The Reverend Dr. Peter Gray Sears of Christ Church Cathedral, Houston, preached the baccalaureate sermon, and Dr. David Starr Jordan, chancellor of Stanford University, addressed the commencement audience on the subject "Is War Eternal?" The proud graduates received diplomas that were unlike any others. Designed by Dr. Lovett and presented by him along with a firm handshake, the Rice diploma was, and is still, a large sheepskin with the seal of the school at the top and the words positioned in such a way that the margins form the outline of a Grecian urn. Of the original seventy-seven matriculants, twenty-seven remained to graduate in 1916. The class of 1916 numbered thirty-five—twenty men and fifteen women, including eight students who had entered after 1912. Of the thirty-five, twenty-seven received Bachelor of Arts degrees and eight Bachelor of Science degrees (signifying that they were engineers or architects.)[54]

President Lovett was somewhat disappointed that he had no real prizes for scholarship to give at that first commencement, but he could be proud of the Institute and its graduates. In 1915 Rice had qualified for admission to the

58. *The academic procession at the first commencement, 1916.*

Southern Association of Colleges and Secondary Schools and was certified as a Class A college by the Texas Department of Education. Lovett did have his critics, who complained that Rice was not democratic enough in its faculty, that the "dominant part" of the faculty was made up of foreigners, that Lovett and the trustees had wasted money on fancy buildings instead of purchasing good equipment, and that the president was developing in the students "a snobbish intellectual aristocracy."[55] But there were also those like Albert Guérard who understood what Lovett was trying to make of the Rice Institute. Guérard thought that Rice had a "special mission." Texas already had a large, many-sided state university and a number of small colleges. In 1918 he wrote Lovett:

What Rice, with its splendid plant, and its complete independence should stand for, is not numbers, nor is it purely local service. Our part should be to establish a standard. Let us have few buildings, few departments, few professors, few students, but each the best that can be secured. It would be false democracy to attempt to provide an all-round course for all comers, without limitations. We cannot do that on our present endowment without a decided lowering of our ideals. If we were alone in the field, it would be our obvious duty to accept conditions as we find them, and work up slowly to the desired standard. But the South can afford to have one at least of its numerous institutions

59. *The conferring of degrees at the first commencement.*

of learning kept on the highest possible level, irrespective of numbers and cost, as an example to the rest. I would rather see 300 picked students at Rice than a thousand indifferent ones. If the Trustees should boldly announce a policy of strict limitation of numbers, there would be an outcry, no doubt, but in a few years, the result would justify the new departure and your opponents themselves would be proud of what Rice had become in the life of the City and the state.[56]

Lovett could hardly have said it better.

Criticism or praise aside, the Institute had some problems. The faculty was understaffed, and if the student body kept growing as it had been—the number in 1916 was about six hundred—the physical plant would soon be overcrowded and need enlarging. Furthermore, the library was woefully in need of books and other resources in the humanities. How much money the board could invest in these improvements and expansions was an unanswerable question at that time.

There was also no end to little vexing problems. One of the most troublesome to President Lovett must have been convincing others of his vision for the Institute: that it be a real university. A friend of Lovett's, Hopson O. Murfee, twitted the president in 1909 and suggested that Lovett change the letterhead, which read "The Rice Institute," either to omit "The" or to insert "Only" after it. In 1916, physics professor Hughes wrote Lovett that one of the new Rice graduates, Norman Hurd Ricker, was having difficulty being accepted by Princeton's graduate school. The quarrel was not with Ricker, an honors physics student, but with the Rice courses. Dean David Magie of Princeton had told Hughes that Princeton regarded the Institute as a technical institution and not of university standing. Furthermore, he said, its courses were not sufficiently broad and liberal to serve as a foundation for graduate work there. Princeton dean Andrew F. West had informed Hughes that he thought a science student at Rice concentrated entirely on science. In rebuttal, Hughes pointed out that a B.A. course at Rice required two years of English, two years of a modern language, and other humanities courses; still, West was not impressed. To him, English and modern languages (even two years of each) did not equal the cultural value of Latin (only one year of which was required at Princeton), and he was not even sure that they should be considered as part of a university education. Rice could do nothing in the face of this sort of opposition but wait until Princeton, Yale, and other institutions like them should drop Latin from their graduate entrance requirements. Ricker stayed at the Institute for both his M.A. and Ph.D. degrees and went on to make a name for himself as a physicist; Princeton's loss was Rice's gain.[57]

The difficulty over what Rice actually was—institute, college, or university—lingered, however. The title pages of the *Pamphlet* and the catalog, as well as formal announcements of lectures and other matter sent out by the Institute, proclaimed it to be "The Rice Institute, A University of Liberal and Technical Learning Founded in the City of Houston Texas by William Marsh Rice and Dedicated by Him to the Advancement of Letters, Science and Art." When asked in 1926 why "The Rice Institute" was not sufficient, Lovett replied that the combination was a compromise. "We might have said once for all 'Rice University'. Standing alone, 'The Rice Institute' fails, on the one hand of giving the founder explicitly and fully such recognition as apparently was desired, and, on the other, to record with sufficient completeness what his trustees set out to do in their own generation." There were still connotations of an institute of technology or of an eleemosynary institution, and this particular problem would not go away until the name was changed.[58]

Beside the problem of the Great War in Europe, however, all smaller difficulties paled. The United States and Rice had managed, for the most part, to stay out of the momentous events taking place across the Atlantic; but as the nation moved closer to war, the university did also. The war would bring difficult times to the Rice Institute.

CHAPTER 4

Rice and the Great War

When World War I broke out in Europe in August 1914, the Rice Institute took little notice of it. Julian Huxley went back to England to join the army, and A. L. Hughes reported the impossibility of getting vacuum pumps and induction coils from Germany. The college rhythm, however, was maintained: there were still lectures, tests, labs, sports, dances. When in 1916 President Wilson spoke of the need for American preparedness, Rice students formed a voluntary cadet corps eighty strong, directed by Herbert N. Roe, an instructor of physical education. Two companies organized and began drilling in March. The corps, called "a battalion," continued in the fall of 1916, and by 1917 there were one hundred men enrolled.[1]

Declaration of war in April 1917 changed the situation considerably; the Institute immediately faced decreases in student and faculty numbers as men volunteered for the army. For those

faculty members who enlisted, the board voted to continue their full salaries until they were accepted by the army, and then to make up any difference between their military pay and their Institute salaries until the war ended. In addition, they would be reinstated in their university positions when they were mustered out.[2]

Rice students were prime candidates for officers' training school, and before graduation in June 1917 thirty-five of them had been admitted to the training camp at Camp Funston, Leon Springs, north of San Antonio. The regular commencement ceremony was held on campus, although it was somewhat subdued. For those graduating seniors who were already at Leon Springs, President Lovett went to the camp and conferred their degrees in a special ceremony held on the drill field.[3] Altogether, fifty-two degrees were awarded.

Twenty-five members of the

faculty served with the armed forces in some capacity during World War I. Lindsey Blayney, professor of German, participated in campaigns in France and Macedonia and received several citations. Mathematics professor Griffith Evans worked on high-altitude bombing in France, England, and Italy. Julian Huxley served with military intelligence in the British Army and physicist Arthur Hughes with the antisubmarine division of the British Admiralty. Harold A. Wilson served on the National Research Council's committee investigating antisubmarine devices and worked both at the Naval Experimental Station in New London, Connecticut, and independently at the Rice Institute. Woodrow Wilson tapped his brother-in-law Stockton Axson to be national secretary of the American Red Cross; Axson served in the United States, France, and Italy. Of the students who served, eight died during the war: Joseph W. Ay-

60–61. *The cadet corps of the Rice Institute, 1916–17. 60. Company A. 61. Company B.*

cock, Otta L. Cain, Thomas L. Coates, Lee Haltom, Roy E. Lillard, Fred P. Manaker, Charles H. Patterson, and Ira South.[4]

Military Life on Campus

The students who remained at Rice found a different Institute when they returned in the fall of 1917. Pressed by both students and staff, the administration had applied for and been granted a unit of the Reserve Officers' Training Corps under terms of the National Defense Act of June 3, 1916. The War Department assigned Philippine-campaign veteran Major Joseph Frazier, United States Army, Retired, as professor of military science and tactics. He and the university administration "effected a military organization of the students," as the catalog put it. The object seems to have been to train the students as though they were at a camp such as Leon Springs, so that upon completion of the course they would be eligible to take examinations to become commissioned officers. All students,

62. *Snapshots from infantry life at the Institute, 1917.*

women included, were required to belong to the corps. All men were required to take courses in the theory and practice of military science and tactics; women were to have modified courses including physical training, hygiene, and first aid. All had to wear uniforms. "It thus appears," the 1917 catalog stated, "that as far as may be consistent with the university programme of the Rice Institute, the conduct of the life of the place, including that of the campus and the residential halls, will be under military regulations, certainly as long as the war continues."[5]

What this meant was almost a complete reversal of life at Rice for men in the residential halls. Gone were the "gentlemen's club" rules, the freedom to go and come at will, the option of living in a perpetually chaotic dormitory room, and the liberty of keeping whatever hours they pleased. Instead, the new regimen began with reveille at 5:45 A.M. Cadets were to dress and come to assembly. Roll was usually called at assembly before each meal. At 6:15 rooms were inspected, and at 6:30 breakfast was served. Drill started at 7:30 and lasted for an hour, after which classes ran from 8:30 to 12:30. Lunch came at 12:45, and labs filled the afternoon until 4:30. On days without morning drill, there was an afternoon drill from 4:40 to 5:40. After dinner at 6:00 the cadet was allowed a brief time for relaxation, but he had to be in his room twenty minutes after the meal was over. He was then required to stay in his room until release from quarters at 9:30, and a guard was mounted to enforce the regulations. Any movement outside the rooms before release from quarters required a permit. Taps sounded at 11:00, signaling lights out. The only really free time was Saturday night, when the cadets could go wherever they pleased; but they still had to wear uniforms and be back at the dorms for taps. Students who lived off campus had considerably more freedom, although they followed the schedule when they were on campus and drilled with the rest, both morning and afternoon.[6]

Four companies, one for each residential hall and one for the town students, made up the corps. The women had their own four companies. Officers from major down to sergeant were appointed, and the students went about trying to pass as soldiers. This was not always easy, especially at first, because some had difficulty procuring uniforms (they purchased their own). Soldierly life was not without humor, either. A maverick company called Company BVD or Company B?D "formed" for "drill" and even had the effrontery to perform at a football game using brooms and other assorted oddities for weapons. The male cadets also thought it great fun to watch the women drilling.[7]

The women's corps was a special case. The hybrid uniform included a man's hat and an army nurse's shoes. There were some women like Sarah Lane who had to have their uniforms individually tailored, because they were

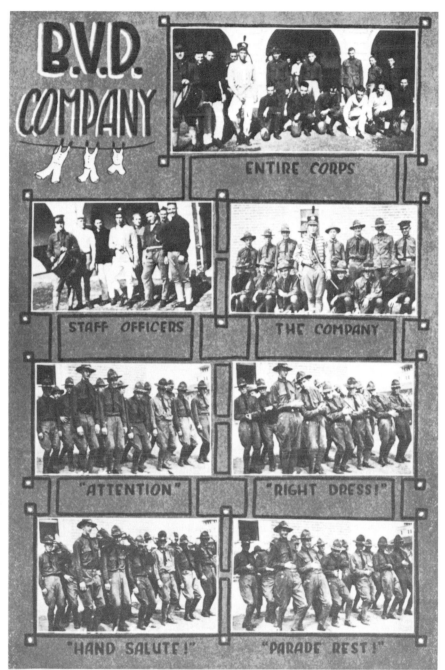

63. *Snapshots of the "B.V.D. Co.," 1917.*

64. *The women's cadet corps, 1917. (Panoramic photograph by F. J. Schlueter of Houston.)*

too tall for the ready-made versions. Women officers wore the same braid on their hats as did regular officers, causing confusion and consternation among the soldiers from Ellington Field and Camp Logan, who felt that they had to salute when they met the student officers on the streets in downtown Houston. Eventually women were allowed to wear civilian clothing when not on campus for drills. Training for the women was not as rigorous as the men's: they drilled only three times a week instead of five.[8]

At the start of the program, students were enthusiastic despite the disruption of their normal schedules. The *Thresher* came out foursquare behind the military regime and spoke of "the glory to the annals of Rice traditions" that would follow the war. The editors also hoped that the good features of the old Rice life would be retained. They

wanted to see literary societies and other organizations flourish and pledged that columns of the *Thresher* would be open to anyone wanting to voice an opinion on any subject.[9]

Handled differently, the military system might have been a success. As it was, several circumstances combined to bring the students to vigorous protest. Major Frazier was transferred almost as soon as the new school year started, leaving behind a set of strict military regulations to be put into effect. In his place, the War Department sent Captain Taylor M. Reagan, United States Army, Retired. Reagan proved to be an unfortunate commandant. At his first drill, he marched his men through a hedge, causing some of the cadets to wonder about his capability. To help the captain administer the rules, Lovett appointed a Military Committee under chairman William

Caspar Graustein, assistant professor of mathematics. J. T. McCants also helped enforce regulations in his capacity as bookkeeper and executive assistant.

Tape and the Student Rebellion

Dissatisfaction with the system was evident by December. Men in the dormitories did not appreciate having every minute of their days planned by someone else. A book of 220 regulations set forth actions for every contingency, and the cadets soon learned that every action had to have a corresponding permit—or so it seemed. Especially irksome was incarceration every night from around seven to half-past nine with no chance to consult with classmates about homework or leave campus without a permit. The poor quality of food in the mess hall added to their

discontent.[10] (The Commons became "the mess hall" as the campus adopted military nomenclature for the duration of the war.)

More serious than those curtailments to freedom was the students' dissatisfaction with the ROTC program itself. Army General Order No. 49, dated September 20, 1916, described the phases of the program; nowhere did it call for the radical transformation of the campus that had occurred. The order specified military subjects as part of normal school work and only three hours of drill a week instead of the five required by the Institute. The cadets claimed to be eager for real military training in history, tactics, ordnance, signaling, entrenchments, and other subjects an officer needed to know; but they were not receiving it. Nor did female cadets believe that they were receiving correct training, certainly not in first aid or Red Cross work or in drill. Like the men, they chafed at the regulations and the veritable sea of permits required for the slightest move. Furthermore, appeals to the Military Committee brought no relief.[11]

In November the *Thresher* began to print students' statements of protest. That brought the editor into conflict with the authorities, who, the editor claimed, accused the paper of "directing these articles against the good of the Institution, of 'agging on' the dissatisfaction . . . and even of proceeding in an unpatriotic manner." According to the editor, the real dissatisfaction lay in the fact that students could not see why they should be deprived of their freedom, due them by right of American birth and by precedents in college life. Drill was a duty, but the other petty restrictions were not.[12]

When the Christmas break was over, students found that some changes had been made in the system. Drill would take place only in the mornings, three days a week. The other three drill times would be given over to physical training, theory as well as practice. Little objection to this substitution surfaced, but Commandant Reagan also announced that instruction in drill would have to start at the very beginning because the students had not received proper training. The students blamed Reagan's teaching. Roll would be called only at reveille, and students could miss the other two meals on campus if they wished. But taps was moved up to 10:30 and release from quarters pushed back to 10:15, leaving only fifteen minutes free instead of the hour and a half the cadets had enjoyed before. Guard duty routine was also changed slightly. On the

DEDICATED TO "HIS HONOR"

Ride a cock-horse to Banbury Cross
To see Bradley manage a cavalry horse,
With glue on his fingers and nitrated nose,
He'll be a leader wherever he goes.

65. *Cartoon and poem of cavalry life, 1917.*

academic side, two new "war courses" were offered: "wireless telegraphy," to be taught by engineer Nicholas Diamant, and "gas engines" by A. H. Aagaard.[13]

Unfortunately, disgruntlement had already emerged, more than such cosmetic changes could mollify. The same day that the modifications were published in the *Thresher*, students found at their hall doors and at other points on campus a publication entitled *Tape* in large red letters. An anonymous author set forth in vitriolic style the conditions as seen by students and a lampoon of the authorities in charge. The situation had worsened over the holidays, as a number of students had either flunked out or gone on probation on the basis of Christmas grades, and a number had left to join the army. The paper repeated all the causes of discontent, dwelling especially on the punishments meted out for violating regulations. "Edgar Ideal," "Johnny T. McCan-not," and "Zeus Graustein" came in for particular abuse. The author called on students to unite and to decline to answer any questions about the source of the paper. He also asked them to send the paper home to acquaint their parents with the situation.[14]

The authorities reacted quickly. A letter went out from the board to parents over J. T. McCants's signature, claiming that the students had made no formal complaint of their troubles before publishing *Tape*, and that the board had been called in because of the students' "rebellious attitude" and "their apparent determination to enforce their own demands without consultation with anyone and irrespective of the opinions of the faculty and trustees." It said that military regulations were in the students' interest and had been adopted after careful consideration. The students' primary complaint, according to the letter, was confinement to rooms on weeknights. The board was not, however, going to take summary action in the face of troubles but would meet with the students and endeavor to show them the error of their ways. Those refusing to obey the rules and regulations would be expelled. The letter said that the faculty and trustees believed that parents would endorse this action, and it asked parents to wire their children to urge cheerful submission and obedience to the rules.[15]

Tape came out on Saturday, January 19. McCants's letter went out a few days later. After some disturbances in the dormitories (mostly pranks such as turning lights off suddenly in the wings, although a few sports poked a firehose down the chimney and flooded Captain Reagan's quarters in South Hall), the trustees intervened in person. On Saturday, January 26, they met with cadet officers and called a student meeting for Monday, the twenty-eighth. At 10:30 in the morning of the twenty-eighth a committee from the trustees met with all the students in the physics amphitheater. The cadets presenting grievances were Cadet Major Alston Duggan '18, Jay Alexander '20, James Markham '18, Pickens

Coleman '18, and Emmet Niland '17. Camille Waggaman '18 and Elsbeth Rowe '18 represented the women.

As the students saw the situation, confinement to rooms was not their primary grievance, as McCants's letter had alleged. They believed that there had been a basic impairment of their rights that was almost impossible to correct because of the authorities' attitude. Application to the administration (Lovett, McCants, and the Military Committee) had produced no results; the students met only delay, equivocation, or outright rejection, often without explanation. Since attempts by the *Thresher* to voice dissatisfaction resulted in threats of censorship or suspension and formal complaints were ignored, *Tape* seemed to some the only way to be heard. The students felt that the charges in McCants's letter were misleading or absurd. They did not see themselves as insurrectionists but as advocates for the bettering of the Institute, and they asked the trustees for just and wise consideration of their case.

After all the student speakers had expressed their opinions, Captain Baker said that the board would remedy conditions as soon as possible if they were presented with a formal petition and if the cadets would pledge to abide by the old rules until then. In response, the students adopted resolutions agreeing to stand by the rules and disassociating themselves from the authors of *Tape* (but not its charges). They also established a committee to draw

up a formal petition of complaints for the board.[16]

A formal petition addressed to the Military Committee was ready two days after the meeting. The male students asked for abolition of the requirements they disliked the most: call to quarters, guard duty, taps, roll call at every meal, punishment tours and confinements, and all rules and regulations that would not exist at a university maintaining only a unit of the ROTC. They also wanted the power to start a students' organization. The women requested consultation concerning their uniforms, abolition of military drill (with the substitution of competent instruction in physical training and Red Cross work), availability of tennis courts in the cooler hours of the day, and reintroduction of or support for those social activities that had been "hampered or repressed."[17]

On February 9 the trustees came to campus again to meet with the students. They brought with them new regulations acceding to many of the students' requests. Abolished were the call to quarters, guard duty, taps, roll call at meals, and women's drill. Women would receive Red Cross training and physical instruction and would have to wear their uniforms only on the days on which physical exercises were scheduled. The trustees approved formation of a student association and announced a new set of regulations. The students did not get everything they wanted; they still had to walk tours and suffer confinement to their rooms for infractions of the regulations.

Baker proclaimed the changes and new regulations and then spoke to the assembled students. He agreed with them that "Rice is not a military school," and that it was hard to convert an academic institution into a military academy in a few months. But, he said, "Rules not properly enforced cause disrespect for military rule." The board would not have granted the changes if the students' requests had not been reasonable or if calm on campus had not been restored. The chairman told the students that the new rules had to be enforced or "things will go back to the old conditions." President Lovett also responded and closed by extending his hand to the students as he did at the end of each matriculation address, saying, "May I not ask you to take the hand I extend and ask you to help me bridge the gulf?" The students thanked the board for the changes and closed the meeting with a standing ovation and the college yell, "Yea, Rice!" Then they filed out, shaking the president's hand as they went.[18]

In some ways the "rebellion" and its causes and results were peculiar. From the existing records it is impossible to discover exactly who ordered the first set of regulations to which the students objected so strongly. Why it was thought necessary to transform the Institute in such a manner is also unknown. Other schools established ROTC units without such radical changes, and General Order No. 49 did not call for them. Since the object

TAPE

Published in the hope of calling interested attention to evil conditions existing at Rice, in order that wise judgment and devoted energy may be incited to bring about improvements that are promotive of the welfare of an institution that is capable of noble work in "the advancement of Letters, Science and Art."

JANUARY, 1918

"MILITARY SYSTEM A RANK FAILURE"

PRESIDENT ADMITS IT IN SPEECH TO COMMISSIONED OFFICERS. COMMANDANT REAGAN SO ABSOLUTELY INEFFICIENT LOVETT INSISTS THAT WASHINGTON OUST HIM. SOME FACTS AND FIGURES ON THIS INSTITUTION OF HIGHER LEARNING.

NOTE: The author wishes to extend thanks to the university office for the records of our scholarship they have kept so carefully throughout the years; and to the office of the Commandant for the use of the official copy of General Army Orders No. 49, and for the privilege of perusing the battalion reports and rosters. Without their aid it would have been impossible to obtain the information for this article. He also wishes to say that the statistics given below have appeared over the signature of the Committee on Examinations and Standing, and are therefore authentic.

The military regime of Rice Institute is a most thorough failure.

The President of this institution has frankly admitted it—in fact, he is the man who made the statement. He recently called all the commissioned officers of our cadet corps before him and informed them that he realized the organization is a failure; that he had noted the total absence of discipline, and remarked that our Commandant is not as good as we should have (a very charitable way of expressing the idea), but that he is the best we can obtain. He told this assemblage of "permissioned personages" that he had made repeated visits to Washington in the past weeks endeavoring to secure another Commandant, expressed his chagrin at his inability to do so, and informed his hearers that Captain Reagan is fully aware of the attempts to shelve him. All of this doubtless causes the heart of our Commandant to swell with love and interest for our alma mater. He deplored the mistake that had been made in trying to transform at one fell stroke an academic student body, which had never previously been hampered by a single restriction, into a military camp.

After unburdening his heart in this fashion, Edgar Ideal leaned back in his chair, gazed at his favorite star, and implored the men before him to help him get away with the blunder that had been wished off on us for the balance of the year! Called on them to help him to continue a system that is killing Rice Institute.

* * * * *

A military reorganization began at the same time. All the companies were split up into squads, and instruction begun in the "school of the soldier"—the identical work we began with the first day we stepped onto our drill grounds, the Commandant explaining that he feared he had failed to teach us the rudiments of drill as thoroughly as he should have.

We did not need either the President or the Commandant to tell us these things. We have already gotten our education—with a brick. It was rather nice of them to make the admission, however, for their action saved us the trouble of gaining an audience with them and doing the talking ourselves. Perhaps we could have made a slightly more complete exposition of the case than did they.

We know that of the 422 men, who began the year at Rice, only 268 remain (information obtained from the consolidated morning reports of the battalion); that 51 men and 9 women failed to pass the Christmas exams, and were requested not to return to Rice; that 60 men in addition are on probation for unsatisfactory work, and that the chances are against them in weathering the next examinations; that 74 men and 15 women left Rice last term to enter the army, to enter some other school, or to go to work (this information is obtained from a report bearing the signature of the Committee on Examinations and Standing); that there are remaining in Rice very few more than 208 men who are not on probation; that more than half of these remaining 200 men have failed in some one of their courses; and that the grades of the handful of men who still remain in good standing, are 25 per cent lower than they were at this time last year. In all, 91 Freshmen, 35 Sophomores, 13

UNITED WE STAND!

THE ONLY LOGICAL, LOYAL, TRULY-RICE THING TO DO IS TO SAY: "I REGRET THAT I MUST DECLINE TO ANSWER THE QUESTION," AND THEN STICK TO IT LIKE A MAN.

The men who engaged in this work, individual student, did it to foster a cause that is vitally your own; they did it, individual student, because they conscientiously believe it may aid in correcting undoubted injuries that have been done to each and every one of you, and to your university. And now, individual fellow student, they need, and ask, and feel entitled to, your co-operation and protection, for the good of your mutual cause, and for the prosperity of Rice.

You will give them this support and protection.

The way will not be the easiest or the most selfish way for the individual student; nevertheless, he will adopt the following plan, even if at a personal sacrifice, to further a cause that certainly deserves the support of every loyal, real man of the student body.

If you are asked, individual student, whether you had anything to do with this paper, or whether you know anything about its source, there are three courses that you might follow: (1) give some information; (2) deny having any information, and (3) respectfully decline to answer the question, because it is directed against a just cause that is your very own. To follow course (1) would directly entangle yourself or another student—you will not do that. To follow course (2) would be the easy, selfish thing to do, and you might be cleared; this, however, as a process of elimination, would tend to draw the net more closely about those who have tried to serve your cause by publishing this paper, and continued, might lead to their misfortune. As you are a Rice man, you will not follow course (2). What you will do will be to follow course (3): when you are asked any questions, you will reply very respectfully: "I regret that I must decline to answer the question"; if you are prodded as to the grounds for your attitude, merely call the attention of the questioner to the fact that your reasons for respectfully declining to answer are certainly obvious to both of you.

For the sake of a cause that is your own, let the individuals of a welded student body harmonize their voices in a respectful, but firmly immovable, "I regret that I must decline to answer the question." True, this may violate one of the "regulations"—but was ever an arbitrary, autocratic, repressive, unjust, foolish dictum ever violated for a more worthy cause?

No harm can come to a justly firm and justifiably united student body that is unquestionably in the right.

Juniors, 7 Seniors and 3 special students have departed from our midst. The careful reader will note that this total from the university office does not check with the total from the office of the Commandant—worry not, gentle reader, for these two institutions seldom check so closely as this.

We know that the whole school is behind in its academic schedule; that we have not completed as much work as we accomplished within the same period last year; that the whole student body is discouraged; that this same feeling has crept into the hearts of our instructors, who realize that we cannot do our best work under existing conditions. We know this because many of the instructors, after first looking north, east, south and west, have expressed their disgust to us in language anything but parliamentary.

The President and Commandant have now come in, plead guilty to their failure, owned up that you cannot combine an academic student body and a military camp into one organization, for the reason that the two will not operate together; and have sought the support of the students, through their

66. *The first issue of* Tape, *in which students complained about military life on campus.*

A TRAGICAL JOKE— DRILL FOR GIRLS

BURDENED WITH THE WEARING OF AN UNGODLY UNIFORM AND THE OBSERVANCE OF A THOUSAND REGULATIONS, THE WOMEN ARE PROMISED RED CROSS TRAINING, BUT THEY GET SQUAD MANEUVERS FROM INFANTRY DRILL REGULATIONS.

Among all the iniquitous ramifications of the domineering, farcical militaristic system now obtaining at the Rice Institute, those applying to the women students are probably the worst.

What is the situation? Here we have it· A few hundred girls entering college in the fall of 1917 with the hope and expectation of broadening themselves by free and congenial converse with their college mates, and fitting themselves to fill better their stations in life by the acquisition of valuable knowledge. As they entered school, some, for they had been here in past years, had bright remembrances of the Rice of old, and some coming into their freshman year, had rosy anticipation of the benefit and pleasure that they were sure awaited them. But what did await them? We can speak only of the past, yet this past may well be taken as an index to the future, for the year is now almost half gone.

First, they are confronted with the mandate that all women students must wear uniforms of a certain prescribed cloth and pattern. And such cloth and such a pattern! A thin, rough, twill, of an uncertain color, between a grass green and a tobacco brown; the skirt cut with some regard for economy (being so narrow, in fact, that buttons go flying from the gaping front when a reasonably long step is taken); but with the coat cut with no regard for anything. We are told that the wife of the President planned these things. If so, the good wife is about equally as good in designing clothes as her husband is in planning an intelligent military regime. And the girls are forced to wear these unspeakably ugly costumes every day to and from school. It is a matter of record that no longer than ten days ago a young lady appeared on the campus dressed in clothes other than her uniform, that the "Little President," the so-called Dean of Women, who offices next the girls' rest room, seeing the young lady, ordered her to go home. Returning in a short while in an automobile to get her chum, the "Little President" again spies her, and summarily suspends her for five days.

The uniform is not the only evil. The catalog states that first aid and Red Cross work will be given the girls, with occasional periods of simple calisthenics. This would probably have been quite acceptable to the young women as training for their part of the war's work, and yet after four months of school not a class has been held in first aid or Red Cross work. They have had their Major, their Captains, Lieutenants and non-coms appointed, and have been given close order military drill, a thing for which they will never have use, though they lived for a hundred years, the coming triumphs of woman suffrage and feminism notwithstanding.

Military drill for girls! The authorities here hailed with acclaim, publishing the fact broadcast, even going so far as to have moving pictures taken of the young women in battalion formations. The first school in the United States to have real military drill for girls! Prideful and vainglorious over the fact, it would behoove our superiors rather to be shamefaced and conscience stricken for this unpardonable injustice.

Red Cross work and calisthenics—that is what we were promised, and what did we receive? A tri-weekly period of "squads right" and "squads left," offering above all an opportunity for our graceful and charming Commandant to pirouet in front of a couple of hundred young women, exercising his well known arts as a lady-killer, regardless of the rumor that has gone abroad concerning a certain Georgia helpmeet.

There we have it. A community of young ladies eager to learn something of value, and to do their part in the work of the war, forced to execute by the hour squad movements from the Infantry Drill Regulations. Surely a more nonsensical, absurd and altogether disgusting program could not have been devised.

SEND THIS SHEET HOME!

Your parents should be made acquainted with conditions at this place of Liberal and Technical Learning, to which they sent you.

Students' parents are entitled to a complete knowledge of the conditions surrounding their sons and daughters; the university office consistently deprives them of any opportunity of getting that knowledge this year; this paper presents the real facts, deplorable though they are—mail it to your parents, let them bring pressure to bear.

Rice Students:

This university, in its true, permanent form, is entitled—as your "Alma Mater"—to a devotion on your part that should set aside all individual, personal sacrifices; any personal considerations; any personal sacrifices that you may have to offer, any time and effort that it may become your lot, yes, and your privilege, to give to any cause that is truly in the interest of the enduring welfare of your university, should be given freely and eagerly.

Words and logic are not needed to convince you, who have lived some four months in "Rice, the military camp," that the glaringly inefficient, pitifully cumbersome, destructively inapplicable militaristic "system" which dominates, or rather, suffocates, life at Rice, is a proven menace to the progress and the prospects of "Rice, the university of liberal and technical learning, founded in the City of Houston, Texas, for the advancement of Letters, Science and Art."

This, as any other, factor that minimizes or destroys the potentiality for the good of higher education, that exists in the Rice Institute, should be zealously (though ever broadly and rationally and fairly) combated and opposed until the menace is removed, that this and succeeding generations may receive the intended benefit from the realization of the inspired ideal of a broad, worthy man, who was a noble, and a consistently practical, dreamer—the honored William Marsh Rice, cherished in loving memory!

No one, better than the students, can know the real conditions existing at a university, and no one—no, not even Trustees, President, or Faculty—can feel more deeply than those self-same students, any injury that comes to the welfare of their university.

You know, students, the truth of the conditions herein presented; you know, only too well, the evils that are products of the "system" at Rice; you know that all the evils of that system could be removed without sacrificing any of the really beneficial phases that are a part of the "system"; you know that exactly this should be done.

Therefore, endorse this paper, students, and mail it to your parents, in order that, with the true understanding of the situation, to which they are entitled, they may write to the President or Trustees, and thus, perhaps, be a stimulus in bringing about better conditions in Rice Institute.

HERE HE IS, "THE EDUCATOR."

Say, who is the guy with the browlet high?
Friend of the festive worm?
Who can bisect an arc in a room that is dark
And hog-tie a comma germ?
Yes, who knows the sky like you or like I
Are acquaint with a boiled egg?
Who's kink of a school with 10,000,000 cool?
A prexy that doesn't beg?
Who never knew how to milk a cow
Or wake up a mule with the reins;
Yet draws down the cash in a way that is rash
For admixing science and brains?
Whose heroes have sped with the days that are dead?
Whose manners are nifty and nice?
Yea, who is inclined to a double-deck mind?
Why, Lovett of old Puffed Rice!

* * *

T. M. R.

We've nothing but jeers for the gink who steers
Our corps through its troubled sea;
So there's nothing but grief for the little tin chief
As long as that chief is he!
Whatever he does he'll hear the buzz
Of critics as thick as flies,
And all of his aims are sins and shames,
And nothing he does is wise.

We've nothing but kicks for the wop who sticks
All day behind Caspar's chair,
And his weak heart aches, and his wishbone breaks,
And he's losing most of his hair!
We've nothing but howls and knocker's growls,
And deserved slings and slams,
And vile cartoons and a dish of prunes
And a chorus of students' damns.

Oh! You "humble Caps," with your simple "maps,"
Who fuss with the Sergeant sass,
Just view the woes of the simp who rose
Above and beyond the mass?
And be glad today that you go your way
'Mid quiet and peaceful scenes,
And spend more thought as you know you ought
In cramming your silly beans!

WHERE DID SERGEANT JERUS'LEM GO WITH HIS SATCHEL ON SATURDAY NIGHT?

Dedicated to Our "Serg." (with Apologies to the writer of "Where Did Robinson Crusoe Go With Friday on Saturday Night?").

Two months or more ago, I think that's when
Rice Institute had a Sergeant blow in.
Sergeant Jerus'lem, of horseman's fame,
Had a big name, but was there all the same.
He came to teach us of the Infantry,
Because he knew the cavalry;
He was a little mutt; he had an office, BUT
Saturday night it was shut. So:

CHORUS:
Where did Sergeant Jerus'lem go with his satchel on Saturday night?
Every Saturday night he would start out to roam.
And on Sunday morning he'd come staggering home.
In the City of Houston the beer's always foaming,
And where there is beer, there the Sergeant is roaming;
So where did Sergeant Jerus'lem go with his satchel on Saturday night?

Sergeant Jerus'lem was a good old scout,
Sergeant Jerus'lem knew his way about,
Citizen's clothes he would don now and then—
He knew just when he would like to have gin—
He told the rest of us we couldn't go.
All of our citz in the attic stow,
Now, we must stay behind, learn to be very kind,
Bringing the Sergeant home blind. So:

Where did Sergeant Jerus'lem go with his satchel on Saturday night?
Every Saturday night he would start out to roam,
And on Sunday morning hed come staggering home.
In the City of Houston the beer's always foaming,
And where there is beer, there the Sergeant is roaming;
So where did Sergeant Jerus'lem go with his satchel on Saturday night?

---

was to graduate men who were trained in both military and academic subjects and ready to become officers, perhaps someone thought that the military organization would prepare young men more thoroughly for the army than would a civilian structure.

There is some evidence that Major Frazier was the guiding force in the plan; had he stayed, he might have been able to carry out the program successfully. For overseeing the metamorphosis of civilian students into cadets, however, Captain Reagan was an inappropriate choice. Lovett wrote later that Reagan was not only inadequately prepared for instruction and the maintenance of discipline as commandant, but he also failed to develop the necessary skills while he held the position.[19] In December 1917 Lovett had tried to have Reagan replaced, but the army needed all its other officers elsewhere. His appeal was in vain. In December or early January Lovett admitted to the student officers that he regarded Captain Reagan as unsuitable, and they discussed the difficulty of trying to turn Rice into a military institution. He asked the young men to carry on patiently, but their discontent was too deep. Whoever published *Tape* took matters out of the hands of either the president or the student officers. *Tape* charged that the president's request called on students "to help him continue a system that is killing Rice Institute."[20]

Professor Graustein, who received much criticism as head of the Military Committee, said

67. *The Students' Army Training Corps, 1918.*

later that he thought the students had protested because they had "no conception of the necessity of individual discipline as part of preparation for war service." The situation could also have arisen from the difference between playing soldier, as the students had done the previous year, and actually becoming one.[21]

But there also seems to have been faulty communication between the administration and the student body. Student committees attempting to lodge formal protests claimed that they received no satisfaction, not even a decent hearing; it appears that Lovett, Graustein, and McCants made no attempt to talk with student leaders before sending the defensive letter to parents. Yet it is curious that the requests the students made of the board were, with one exception, not concerned with the arbitrariness

of the Military Committee or the poor food, as emphasized in the campus meetings and in *Tape.* Instead, they concerned more immediate matters; they impress today's reader as being rather minor grievances. The trustees' answers and new regulations certainly took no power from the Military Committee.[22]

The one exception and the request with the most enduring consequences was the desire for a students' association. This idea had surfaced the preceding spring and had provoked considerable discussion among the students. The first letter to the *Thresher* that had proposed such an organization introduced a notion of students' having a voice in athletic affairs, but that idea was quickly vetoed by the students themselves. Student opinion was divided on the real need for an association. Some saw no reason

to elect the managers of various student activities; others advocated a formal organization to encourage a spirit of unity and intelligent interest in the affairs of the student body. Why President Lovett should have opposed the idea of an organization, as spokesman Jay Alexander told the meeting, is something of a mystery. It is possible that he thought it unnecessary, since the classes and the Honor Council were already established and there was no overwhelming student interest. In any event, the students were granted their association; they soon devised a constitution and elected officers.[23]

The impression left by the *Thresher* accounts of this confrontation is that the board recognized the truth of the students' assertions and changed the regulations. However, no formal vote was taken at the board meeting on February 6, the only one on record between the two sessions with the students. It is more likely that the trustees allowed Lovett, McCants, and the Military Committee to change the regulations themselves, in the same way that McCants' letter to parents had been sent "by order of the board of trustees." The administration knew much better than the trustees which regulations were important; but considering the temper of the students, it was more discreet to announce the new rules as issuing from the board. It appears that the trustees were polled at least informally for their opinions of the regulations; chairman Baker stated that the board unanimously opposed women's drill. School authorities also kept control over the new Student Association. The faculty approved the association's constitution with the distinct understanding that measures passed by the association concerning the academic or general policies of the school would be regarded merely as petitions and recommendations to the proper authorities.[24]

By the time school ended in the spring of 1918, a student committee chaired by J. P. Coleman had written the first Student Association constitution, and students had elected officers for the Student Council, the governing body of the association. Officers elected in May were H. T. Dodge, president, Marguerite John, vice-president, H. Le Roy Bell, treasurer, and Jay Alexander, councilman-at-large. There was no secretary under the first con-

stitution. Officers for 1918–19 were H. L. Bell, president, Marguerite John, vice-president, J. Frank Jungman, treasurer, and Maurine Mills, secretary. The association was to organize and oversee interclass and intercollegiate relations, class customs and privileges, and matters that came within the province of the student body. Membership was open to all students of the Institute through payment of a blanket tax, which also covered subscriptions to the *Thresher* and the *Campanile* and admission to all Rice athletic contests. Editors-in-chief, assistant editors, and business managers for both campus student publications were also elected under this constitution. Women wrote into the constitution an organization of their own to deal with matters pertaining to their interests on campus: the Women's Council supervised the women's clubs and any other campus-wide activity directed by the women students. The constitution of the Women's Council excluded only that which fell under Honor Council jurisdiction.[25]

For commencement in 1918 Dr. Lovett had his own good news—several scholarships and a lectureship to announce. Captain and Mrs. James A. Baker had founded a studentship named for their eldest son, the late Frank Graham Baker. It would be awarded for high academic standing and would be open to both male and female undergraduates. The Graham Baker Student would hold the scholarship for a year and receive a stipend of $360. (The amount has been

raised from time to time, to $950 in 1981.) The second set of scholarships was given by the late Lionel Hohenthal, a Houston businessman, as a memorial to his parents and brother. Six Hohenthal Scholars would receive stipends of $200 each, and like the Graham Baker Studentship, the Hohenthal was based on high scholastic standing and was open to men and women. The lectureship and four additional scholarships were the gifts of Estelle B. Sharp, widow of oilman Walter B. Sharp. The Sharp Lectureship in Civics and Philanthropy established a new department for the training of social workers for the South. The scholarships were open to graduates of Rice and other institutions and were to be awarded for graduate training in social work.[26]

The Students' Army Training Corps

By the summer of 1918, January's uproar over the ROTC turned out to be pointless. The federal government stepped into the college military situation and changed procedures considerably. Great German offensives, the perilous situation of the Allies, the lowering of the draft age to eighteen, and America's effort to send as many recruits as possible to Europe combined to put an enormous amount of pressure on colleges. If war continued for long, the draft might actually empty the colleges and universities of students and faculty, causing the collapse of the entire system of higher education in the United States. On the other hand, the college student body was an important military asset as a source of potential officers. Furthermore, the students were already situated in places with good training facilities; new camps would not be needed. A well-planned system of military instruction for college men would foster patriotic participation in the war effort while justifying their studies, and would aid the colleges in surviving the war. To this end Congress authorized the establishment of the Students' Army Training Corps, the SATC. Units were established on at least four hundred academic campuses in 1918. Competent army officers were sent to run the programs, and the schools became armed camps. The Rice Institute joined the rest.[27]

When classes convened in the fall of 1918, many changes had been made. First, the student body was severely depleted by enlistments and the draft and by what was supposed to have been a practice training camp at Fort Sheridan, Illinois. A contingent of Rice students had attended the ROTC camp there in the summer, assuming they would be back at the Institute in the fall. At the last moment, however, they were commissioned and sent to the army. The students who returned to school found a real army camp and many newcomers who had arrived for military training. All able-bodied students who were United States citizens became soldiers in the SATC and subject to military discipline. In charge was another retired army officer, Colonel Charles J. Crane. The army sent a staff with him, and this time the unit ran smoothly.[28]

Under the SATC, the students' new schedule was more rigorous than it had been under the ROTC. Drill occupied two hours each morning; the period from 7:30 to 9:30 at night was given over to "supervised study." In addition to everything else, students had to attend a special war issues course that combined English composition, history, political science, and philosophy. All of this left little time for more normal college pursuits. Football games did continue (the Owls played a 5th Division Army team as well as teams from Kelly Field in San Antonio and the University of Texas), but other extracurricular activities dwindled. The *Thresher*, like student newspapers all over the country, suspended publication.

The Campus Returns to Normal

Fortunately the war ended in November, and the SATC began to demobilize and discharge that very month.[29] Both students and faculty were glad to be rid of it. In faculty meetings the question of retaining any military features on campus was unanimously answered with a resounding no. All forms of the military regime should vanish as soon as practicable. President Lovett notified the army that the school did not even want an ROTC unit on campus. The experiment had been interesting in some ways, but everyone wanted to get back to business as usual in the spring of 1919. The *Thresher* started publishing again, class and Student Council officers were elected, students resumed their regular studies, and many former classmates came home from the war.[30]

Rice was not, however, unaffected by the experiences of the war and its aftermath. The most lasting change was in the Institute's administration. It had become clear, partly because of the *Tape* episode and partly because of the growth of the school, that Rice needed formal administrators, with specific duties and jurisdictions. Dr. Lovett traveled a good deal in his role as president, and the university needed someone explicitly in charge when he was out of town. One of the students' major complaints had been the difficulty and impersonality of bringing grievances to and obtaining redress from McCants or the Military Committee. During the summer of 1918 Lovett and James Baker had begun to discuss with members of the board and the faculty the idea of appointing a dean as their liaison with the students. Stockton Axson favored having a dean as a "shock-absorber" to deal with the students, learn their views, and help them when needed. Raymond P. Hawes, instructor in education, testified that the procedure of applying to committees and faculty advisers seemed "arbitrary" to the students: "irrational, autocratic, mechanical, and coldly inhuman." But installation of the SATC in the fall had precluded any immediate action by the board.[31]

As soon as the SATC had disbanded, Lovett brought the matter of the dean and two other offices before the board. He recommended authorizing a dean to oversee student attendance, conduct, and discipline; a registrar to keep all records of registrations, attendance, examinations, and academic standing of the students; and a bursar to have responsibility for business and material equipment and to act as purchasing agent for all departments. On February 26, 1919, the trustees appointed Robert G. Caldwell, assistant professor of history, as dean; Samuel G. McCann, instructor of history, as registrar; and John T. McCants, secretary to the president, as bursar. Caldwell remained a history professor, while McCann became an instructor in jurisprudence and McCants an instructor in business administration. (It appears that the decision to include a course in business administration in the university program was connected with increasing pressure for some degree of commercial instruction in the regular liberal arts plan. "By entrusting this work to Mr. McCants, these pressures could be controlled and confined within limits as little harmful to the goals and purposes of the humanities as could be expected from this intrusion of vocational instruction," historian Floyd Seyward Lear later remarked.)[32]

There is some indication that the position of dean was intended to be temporary and strictly separate from professional duties— temporary because many circumstances might make it necessary to resign the office, and separate so that the officeholder had neither to give up his academic activities (as professor of history in this case) nor to prejudice his academic salary or position. In the first few years Caldwell received two salary checks, one for each position. This was not the day of highly paid administrators at Rice: Caldwell received only $1,000 for his deanship, and his entire salary for the school year 1919–20 was $4,000. As it evolved, the deanship remained neither temporary nor separate. Caldwell found that the separate spheres merged and that his own work as a historian suffered. Hardly temporary, Caldwell was dean, *the* dean of the Rice Institute, for fifteen years, until he left to become ambassador to Portugal in 1933.[33]

Public Reaction to Rice Professors

Besides hastening the organization of a formal administration, the Great War and its aftermath had another, less salutary effect on the Rice Institute: off-campus opinion about professors' views. From the earliest days, Houstonians and other Texans had paid close attention to Rice lectures on history, philosophy, religion, and biology. Julian Huxley, speaking in 1916 on biology and man, sex, the state, and religion, had stirred up a controversy when he advocated equal rights for women and introduced the idea of human evolution from a tailless ape. One Huxley lecture on the development of religion provoked a letter to the editor of the *Chronicle* asking if Rice students were not being misled and prejudiced against Christianity by a professor "obsessed by the idea of evolution" and determined to apply that unproven theory to religion. A local citizen who had seen a newspaper article on *Tape* had written Captain James Baker to state his support for the students' right of petition and, incidentally, his opposition to the teaching of "Infidelity, Agnosticism and Evolution."[34]

A potentially more serious matter involved the Houston Ministers' Alliance, an organization of some of the city's Protestant clergy. In 1918 the alliance requested a statement from President Lovett on two points: did the president and board "endorse and approve the teaching of atheism, agnosticism or infidelity" by the teachers at the Institute, and did the president and board interpret academic freedom as guaranteeing teachers "the privilege of publishing and declaring as truth, certain individual views which ignore the being of God, discredit the belief in the inspiration of the Bible and repudiate the thought of faith in the Divinity of Jesus Christ"? While the ministers said that they recognized they had no just cause in asking that the faculty declare their religious convictions—or lack of them—and that the board had the right to hire whomever they pleased—

"Mohammedan, Buddhist, pagan, or Christian"—the ministers still thought themselves "in the bounds of courtesy, fairness and right" in asking for a statement.

President Lovett suggested to the board that he respond to the questions first by pointing out how Rice had sought to give expression to the religious aspect of the university. Members of the clergy had participated in an important way in the formal opening and dedication in 1912 and had continued to take part in commencement convocations. Nor were the students without religious guidance. The YMCA, YWCA, and Menorah Society were official organizations, and each year the school sent to appropriate clergy of every denomination the names and addresses of students who had indicated a religious preference. Furthermore, the trustees as individuals were known to support religious enterprises in the city, state, and nation. Concerning the questions raised by the Ministers' Alliance, however, Lovett did not want to take a position. He suggested answering that the board neither approved nor disapproved the teaching of atheism or theism, agnosticism or gnosticism, infidelity or fidelity. Neither did the trustees interpret academic freedom as guaranteeing or denying the religious convictions of the faculty. In other words, "The Trustees in their corporate capacity cannot commit the university to the advocacy of either side of controversial theological questions." Lovett also doubted that any group of theologians would

agree unanimously on the controversial points in the ministers' questions.

Lovett did not think that he was dodging the questions with these answers; rather, he thought that he was facing the issue squarely. "We are building a university," he wrote, "not a school of Hebrew theology, nor of Christian theism, nor a school of rationalistic philosophy, nor of mechanistic interpretation of the universe, nor of any one of a hundred other special systems of thought or speculation or knowledge or faith." A university sought the truth, and a university that imposed its trustees' individual views (no matter what kind) on its students was a contradiction in terms to Lovett. The search for truth could flourish only in an atmosphere of responsible freedom in which people looked at all sides of an issue. Lovett thought that the strength of the Rice foundation lay in its freedom; neither partisan, sectarian, nor educational prejudices stood in the way of the trustees, faculty, and students. He did not believe that the university existed in a vacuum; quite to the contrary, he knew that the relationships of university to state and university to church were as important as freedom from control. He saw all three institutions not as fixed and final but as fluid and forming, constantly changing, each helping the other. (The president was an optimist; he thought that change was usually for the better.) At the same time, he believed that the spirit of science in universities and the con-

cepts of duty, conduct, and deity in religion led to a better life and civilization. While the religious and scientific aspects of this universe were separate, they could blend. Lovett believed that a comprehension of modern science combined easily with a profound and reverent faith. One did not exclude the other, as the Ministers' Alliance evidently feared.[35]

Politics, not religion, caused the next occasion for disharmony between the people at Rice and Houstonians. In May 1919 Russia was much on people's minds. Its Communist leaders were talking of worldwide revolution, and some fighting was still going on in northern Russia and Siberia, where Americans had joined the British and others in intervening in the Russian civil war. It would not be long before the United States would go through a period of internal suspicion called "the Red Scare."

The controversy started innocuously. Lyford P. Edwards, instructor in sociology, spoke to the adult Sunday school class of the First Congregational Church on Russia and the Soviet government during a series of lectures entitled "Ideals of Social Justice." The theme of this series was the forms of government maintained in European countries and their adaptability to modern society. In the course of his lecture, Edwards remarked that if the Soviet system was successful and became permanently established, then in a hundred years Lenin would be considered in Russia in the same way that George Washington was regarded in the United States. Edwards thought that Lenin was a greater idealist than Washington—that he was, in fact, one of the greatest idealists of all times and that the Soviet form of government would prove to be superior in efficiency to all others. He also referred to Washington's legendary honesty, saying something to the effect (his exact words cannot be reconstructed) that that integrity was not above question. J. W. Hawley, a guest of one of the Sunday school members, took exception to Edwards's remarks. After an argument that included other members of the class, Hawley and his host walked out rather than hear Washington and the country "maligned."

These facts seem clear; but soon the situation became more complicated. First, the *Houston Post* reported the episode with headlines claiming that Edwards had praised the Soviets and Lenin (spelled "Lenine" in the papers). Four days after the event, an editorial in that paper called Edwards "an incubator of bolshevism" and "a morbid intellectual" and labeled his remarks "utterances that smack of treason." Next A. E. Amerman, the mayor of Houston, ordered an investigation of the lecture by the city attorney, Kenneth Krahl. The major sent the affidavits and statements gathered in the investigation to the Rice trustees and told them that he regarded Edwards's remarks as only "an intemperate effervescence of an over-specialized mentality." He said, however, that the time had come to choose sides: "pure

old-fashioned Americanism" or the new "freak" doctrines. The mayor thought that Rice students' minds were being "warped in pursuit of these intellectual 'isms.'" Captain Baker responded that the trustees would conduct their own investigation as soon as they all returned to Houston. (Almost all of them had been out of town when the story first appeared in the papers.) Baker was not particularly happy with what he called the newspaper's "hue and cry." He and trustee John T. Scott called for calm and a suspension of judgment until the facts could be ascertained.

While the board tried to determine the true story, both sides gathered their support. Thirty-one members of the Sunday school class sided with Edwards. Dean Caldwell of Rice pointed to Edwards's war work and subscription to Liberty Bonds, even though Edwards was a Canadian citizen. Rice students supported the sociology instructor but fanned the flames of controversy with a demonstration waving red banners and a statement by one student that Edwards had misjudged his audience, thinking he was "talking to a group composed entirely of intelligent persons and it turned out he wasn't." For the other side, the Axson Club, a group of women interested in literature but not formally affiliated with the Institute, called for Edwards's dismissal. The *Post* continued to publish editorial statements on the matter: "Still, if there are fibroid-brained fools in this community who think that Rice

Institute ought to develop its technological courses before instituting a Chair of Bolshevism, we reckon it would be better to humor their ignorance and prejudice. Bolshevism is just a little too intellectual for the most of us." And, "Of course, if Dr. L. P. Edwards doesn't like George Washington, he might find a character that would suit him better in the late Benedict Arnold, John Wilkes or Aaron Burr." (The commentator seems to have forgotten John Wilkes Booth's last name.)

Two weeks after Edwards's eventful lecture, the Board of Trustees reported their decision. They had found it impossible to determine whether or not the views Edwards expressed in his lecture were unpatriotic; of the members of his audience, only the two who walked out had taken exception to what he had said. Statements gathered from witnesses were variant and contradictory. From everything the board knew of Edwards, he was loyal and patriotic and had proved those qualities during the war. Nevertheless, they asked for his resignation, because "he possesses certain views in respect to the political conditions in Russia, the character of Lenine, and some of the prevailing sentiment of the people of this and the Allied countries, and so contrary to the fundamental principles of our government, as, in the opinion of the Trustees, to utterly destroy his further usefulness to the Institute." The trustees went on to express their belief in academic freedom but noted that, "in times likc these," indiscreet persons might impair their influence or destroy their usefulness by word or deed. The board pledged to hire no one who did not measure up to the highest standard of American citizenship.

Edwards tendered his resignation and left town, a bit more abruptly than he had planned. Several friends came to his rooms and warned that a mob was forming downtown to come out and "get" him. Edwards hurriedly packed his belongings into a suitcase and boarded a train for Chicago "at a subordinate station at an uncomfortable hour."

Both the *Post* and the *Chronicle* congratulated the trustees for a fair-minded and unprejudiced investigation and congratulated

RICE INSTITUTE PROFESSOR LAUDS BOLSHEVIK HEAD

Dr. F. C. Edwards Declares in Lecture That Lenine Is Greater Idealist Than George Washington

PRAISES SOVIET GOVERNMENT

J. H. Hawley Takes Issue With Speaker When the Honesty of U. S.'s First President Questioned

RICE'S TRUSTEES WILL INVESTIGATE LENINE EULOGIST

President Lovett of Institute Announces That Dr. Edwards' Preachments Will Be Sifted

STUDENTS DEFEND STRANGE DOCTRINE

H. H. Robinson Makes Affidavit That Rice Instructor Asserted Lenine Superior to Wilson

SOCIAL JUSTICE TALKATCHURCH STIRS COMMENT

Rice Institute Instructor on Sociology Declares He Was Grossly Misquoted in His Russian References.

Harry W. Freeman, Attorney, Also Comes Forward With Statement on Study Circle at Congregational Church.

RICE INSTITUTE HOME OF "ISMS" IS REPORT MADE BY THE MAYOR, AFTER READING OF AFFIDAVITS

In Letter City's Executive Transmits Testimony Taken in Developing "Social Justice" Utterances of Dr. Lyford Edwards in Sociological Lecture.

Captain James A. Baker, Chairman of the Board of Trustees of the Institute, Announces a Thorough Investigation and Invites the Public To Join Therein.

68. *Headlines from the* Houston Post *and* Houston Chronicle *about the speech of sociology instructor Lyford P. Edwards, May 14–19, 1919.*

the public and themselves for inspiring the trustees to decide the matter in a manner favorable to their views. The trustees, however, were unhappy about the uproar and expressed their displeasure in the second half of their statement concerning Edwards's resignation. They spoke of the possible damage done to the Institute by the discontented members of the Sunday school class, by the local press, the mayor, the complaining organizations, and some citizens at large. The Institute could do its best only when it won the devotion of its students and the respect and confidence of their parents. Charges against the loyalty of any faculty member, charges broadcast by press and pulpit, charges made without the chance for responsible investigation did "incalculable harm" to the Institute. The trustees would have preferred that the original complainer, Hawley, had laid the matter before the president or the board first and that the press had pursued the same course. They deplored the melodrama of the episode and the demand for sensationalism shown by all parties. They even compared that demand to "the depraved taste of the populace" in the "decadent days" of Rome. The trustees closed their statement by expressing their hope that the Houston public would be helpful and cooperative; they pledged their receptiveness to suggestion and advice on any matter affecting the Institute.

The students indicated their displeasure with the board's ac-

tions by holding a short demonstration for Edwards in the Commons, but they could do little else. The faculty, who had refrained from comment during the week's events, passed a resolution on academic freedom. It stated their position that every instructor should be responsible for ability, character, and conduct, not for personal beliefs. It argued further that actions that limited freedom of thought and cast doubt on the honesty of teaching seriously compromised the independence of the university. However, the faculty did not condemn the board but promised its cooperation in service to the community and to the broader cause of education. There were rumors that several faculty members were going to resign, even that President Lovett was considering that measure himself; but no one did.

The Evans episode points to a public relations problem that Rice, its trustees, and its president faced from the beginning. Often the view of the institution held by its board, administration, and faculty contrasted with the public's estimate. During the time when the first buildings were being constructed, Houstonians wanted to know what was happening at "their" Institute. The board members, on the other hand, saw the Institute as their personal concern, as indeed legally it was. To such businessmen, who were accustomed to handling their own affairs with no aid and certainly without divulging the reasons for their actions, an intrusion into their

domain by the mayor and the press was unwelcome. The public outcry was exacerbated by the widespread ignorance that most Houstonians had about what actually went on at Rice. Almost all they saw or heard or read about the school concerned sports results or the scheduled public lectures. With the exception of a few professors such as Lovett, Axson, and Tsanoff, Rice faculty seldom ventured off campus; they were not widely known or connected with events noticed by the general public. Both Houston newspapers noted the aloofness—to some, snobbery—of the people at the Institute; the *Chronicle* called for information on the university's good works, "instead of hearing of it only when some freak discussion has taken place." One writer called for more statements of Dr. Lovett's views and asked the president to "identify himself more with the student life and the everyday life of the town."

Except for Edwards's departure, very little changed as a result of the imbroglio over his lecture. The board continued to conduct its affairs without advice from outside, and the Institute authorities returned to dealing with normal problems involving students, grades, lectures, and research.[36]

CHAPTER 5

Consolidation: The 1920s

In 1921 two Rice students, Elisha D. Embree and Thomas B. Easton, veterans of the war, published a little picture book called *The Flying Owls: Rice Institute from the Air*. The photographs taken from high above the campus reveal a Rice Institute in a serene setting, almost afloat in a seemingly boundless prairie. Closer shots show manicured hedges; today's large oaks are only raw saplings; vintage autos are parked with a fine disregard for order or egress in front of the Administration Building; an eerie forest looms in Hermann Park on the other side of a newly paved Main Street; and a few Rice people loiter around the Sallyport. Downtown Houston appears in the remote background in some of the shots, but the Institute seems removed from the bustle, almost unpopulated. In some ways, however, the opposite was true, and the pictures of 10,000 fans filling the stands for the Rice-A&M football game on Armistice Day might be a better

representation of the situation in 1921, for Rice was becoming overcrowded.[1]

Enrollment had been increasing since the war ended, and in the 1920s it continued to rise. In 1921 approximately 860 students were attending the Institute; in 1922 the number was over 900, and in 1923 it was about 1,050. The existing buildings could not accommodate such numbers; laboratories were especially crowded. In 1920 there were more registrations in chemistry classes than there were desks. The senior lab was held at night, and seven professors and graduate students were attempting to conduct research in a space built for four. By 1923 the biology department had to turn down prospective graduate students because there was simply no room to put any more.[2]

Two Solutions to Overcrowding

Two solutions were discussed and put into action. First was an expansion of facilities. The charter had established a sinking fund of one-tenth of the increase of the endowment, to be used for betterments and improvements. The fund had accumulated sufficient value to finance a new building, and in 1923 the Board of Trustees laid the cornerstone for the Chemistry Building. Designed in a simplified Mediterranean style that blended with the existing architecture, the building was completed in 1925. The Field House had opened in 1921 to house physical training classes and intramural and intercollegiate sports, and it had been the first new structure on campus since the original academic buildings and residential halls had been completed. Opening the Chemistry Building allowed classroom and laboratory facilities to expand and alleviate over-

crowding, but there was little
room to spare.

The administrators of the Institute therefore had to implement
the second remedy: limiting the
number admitted to each freshman class. The faculty had begun
to scrutinize admission requirements after the war, and in 1919
they raised the required number
of high school credits from fourteen to fourteen-and-a-half. In
1920 the number was raised
again, to fifteen. Entrance with
only thirteen credits was still allowed in special cases, but some
faculty members opposed this relaxation of standards. In 1921 the
Admissions Committee recommended that admission with
fewer than fifteen units be treated
distinctly as an exception but
that henceforth two units of
Latin be acceptable, instead of
three or more. These changes did
not diminish the numbers seeking admission to Rice, however,
and in the spring of 1923 the faculty first considered numerical
limits to the freshman class.[3]

At this point the Committee
on Examinations and Standing
took over the planning of admissions. Its report, subsequently
adopted by the faculty, called
for refusing admission to those
who had fewer than fifteen high
school units; it also recommended denying freshmen permission to enroll in fewer than
five courses except in special circumstances. The committee
stressed raising the quality of the
entering class, a goal that was as
strong a motivation for limitation
as were the overcrowded classrooms. The faculty did not vote

69–71. *Aerial photographs from* The Flying Owls. 69. *The Administration
Building, Physics Laboratory, and dormitory group.* 70. *Autry House, "The
Owl," and Main Street Boulevard.* 71. *The residential halls and Commons,
looking east across Main Street Boulevard. Autry House is across the street.*

71

to set a specific number for the new class entering in the fall of 1923, but it appears that the committee took matters into its own hands and closed enrollment in the freshman class at 400.[4]

In November 1923 the faculty began specific discussions about how to restrict the number of undergraduates, and they quickly arrived at a two-part plan. The philosophy behind the plan was based on three ideas. First, the faculty wanted to meet the increased demand for college training while maintaining the highest standards of instruction. Second, they wanted to admit students on a competitive basis in order to get the very best freshmen. To cause no injustice to well-qualified applicants, the number admitted was to be flexible, determined both by the demand and by the facilities. Third,

the faculty was deeply interested in reducing the size of classes in the required courses. They wanted a limit of thirty in each section of Math 100 and in the 100 and 200 sections of English, Spanish, and French.

Specifically, the plan called for admitting 400 freshmen direct from high school for the year 1924–25. That would mean a freshman class of about 490, counting transfers and those not promoted from the previous year. Total enrollment would be approximately 1,100. Sections in the required courses would be limited to 30 students. When the faculty determined admission, they would give preference to those who had the maximum number of units in English, mathematics, foreign languages, science, and history, to those in the upper half of their high school

classes who showed special promise and capacity for leadership, to those who were not in the first two groups but who proved their fitness by high performance on entrance examinations, and to those who applied early. No candidate would be accepted with fewer than fifteen units, but once chosen, applicants would be received without conditions. The faculty also decided to maintain the existing ratio of men to women of two to one. The freshman class of 1923 comprised 266 men and 134 women.[5]

The committee, the faculty, and the administration all realized that the plan might be criticized in public, and the committee's report and a subsequent notice to the faculty rehearsed some arguments in favor of limitation. One advantage was that the Institute could plan carefully before increasing the number of students and could ensure that there would be enough faculty and facilities for them. The desirability of early application was obvious: "People prize what they have to make a definite effort to secure." The plan would weed out those applicants less well fitted for academic life and would create "a body of students carefully selected to take full advantage of the opportunity which they have before them." Finally, the committee emphasized that in presenting the plan to the public, the Institute should leave the impression not of a rigid scheme, but of a flexible one: practical, workable, and just. Rice should not seem to be shutting "the door

72. *Exterior view of the new Chemistry Building, April 28, 1926.*

of opportunity permanently to well qualified students," or so the faculty thought.[6]

The trustees voted in March 1924 to endorse and authorize the plan, and that autumn the Rice Institute began to limit enrollment. But overcrowding continued despite restricted admissions. Fewer students left than in previous years, and as a result nearly 1,300 students were enrolled in 1926. To accommodate the greater numbers, there was a shift in the class schedules; classes began on the hour instead of the half hour (they started at 8:00 A.M. instead of 8:30 and continued until 1:00 P.M. instead of 12:30) to provide another period each day.

73. *One of the carvings on the capitals of the Chemistry Building columns. Dean Weiser is the dragon holding down a chemistry student.*

Other Solutions

In 1927 both faculty and trustees considered other ways to limit enrollment. Registrar S. G. Mc-Cann suggested in May that admission requirements be raised again, that only those in the top half of their high school classes be accepted, that a tuition fee of $100 to $200 be charged for out-of-state students, and that equal numbers of men and women be admitted to all departments, including engineering. (Up to this point women and men had been admitted in equal numbers only to the academic course.) Mc-Cann's proposal did not carry the faculty. In June the board stepped in and voted not to accept any more out-of-state students. (Eighteen had already been accepted.)[7]

Some members of the faculty found this ruling disturbing. The following December Dean Caldwell, speaking for the Committee on Examinations and Standing, wrote to President Lovett to recommend two changes in policy. First, the committee suggested that preference be given to state residents and that only students of special promise be accepted from elsewhere. The committee opposed a rigid rule excluding out-of-state students. Although cognizant of the spirit of William Marsh Rice's original gift and of the charter provisions, the committee also believed that the admission of a small number of non-Texas residents would directly benefit the other students and help the Rice Institute maintain its standing as a national in-

74

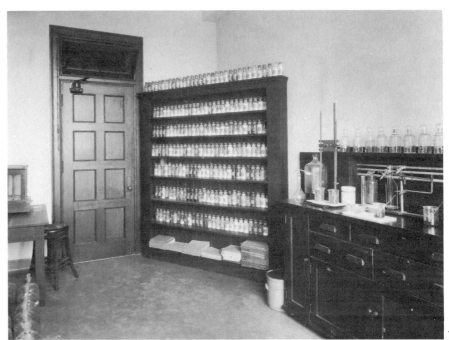

75

74–77. Interior views of the Chemistry Building, ca. 1925. 74. Industrial laboratory. 75. Individual laboratory.

76

76. *Main dispensing room. 77. Lecture hall.*

stitution. Besides, in the preceding five years, the largest number of nonresident students admitted in any one year had been 36. Such a small number would hardly cause the rejection of any well-prepared Houston student. Furthermore, Rice had to draw on a wide area for two desirable kinds of students: graduate students and athletes. To maintain both programs in the face of competition with other universities in the state, the Institute needed to admit applicants from out of state. Second, the committee recommended limiting the number of transfers from other colleges to 75 per year. Otherwise, admitting students from the growing junior college system might circumvent the limit of 400 freshmen. Students who had been rejected as freshmen could reappear as transfers to the sophomore class and thus increase enrollment to an undesirable level.[8]

It appears that President Lovett asked the committee to reconsider its requests, because eleven days after the first letter, Caldwell wrote again. The committee now recommended that the maximum number of transfer students be only 50, maintaining that accepting 400 new admissions and 50 transfers would in practice result in about 425 new students. The committee did not believe that such numbers would add substantially to costs, because no significant changes would be necessary to handle such a small increase.[9]

Evidently nothing came of either of these communications,

because Caldwell wrote to Lovett again in May 1928 on the matter of admissions. The committee "cheerfully" accepted the trustees' proposal to limit admission to 400 new students, including transfers. It again suggested a specific number for transfers, this time a maximum of 30. Caldwell said the committee was skeptical that limiting only the freshman class would hold down total enrollment. The professors expected that in the future a larger proportion of students would remain for the whole four-year course, a likelihood they saw as wholly desirable. The committee reiterated their belief that admitting a small number of out-of-state students was desirable, because this group usually contributed far beyond its numbers to the best graduate students and athletes. Although no formal record exists on the issue, it appears that the board changed its mind about non-Texans; subsequent lists of students show several each year from outside the state.[10]

Caldwell's committee also made a financial suggestion. They pointed out that a large number of Rice students could afford to pay a "substantial tuition fee to help meet a part of the cost of their training." The faculty members thought that such a payment, with exemptions and scholarships for deserving students, would provide for "a larger appreciation of the educational advantages of the Rice Institute." They realized that such a charge was impossible under the charter, but they wanted nevertheless to record their opinion.[11]

The Institute's Financial Condition

As the committee's suggestion indicated, the Institute's financial situation was much on the minds of the trustees, administration, and faculty throughout the 1920s. By 1919 inflation had hit faculty members hard. The cost of living was going up rapidly, while salaries remained the same. One professor, the physicist A. L. Hughes, estimated that the cost of living had risen eighty-five percent since his appointment in 1913, and his ten percent raise in 1916 had done little to alleviate the financial pinch. Hughes was making $2,750 a year in 1919. The board raised Hughes's salary by $500 for the year 1919–20 and began raising salaries of other faculty members as well. In 1920 Professor Harold Wilson, the highest-paid faculty member, pointed out that universities all over the country were raising salaries; he thought it reasonable to ask for an increase also.

Before going to the board with more requests, President Lovett surveyed the major universities to find out how they were compensating their faculty members. He discovered that full professors had made between $3,000 and $6,000 before the war, while after it they earned between $5,000 and $8,000. Corresponding increases were given to those in the lower ranks, with teachers at some schools receiving almost a one hundred percent jump in pay. The Rice board followed the action of other administrations

and raised its faculty salaries. In 1920–21 professors at Rice received from $4,500 to $7,500, assistant professors from $2,500 to $3,750, and instructors from $1,500 to $2,750. These raises increased the faculty salary budget from about $110,000 in 1918–19 to approximately $156,000 in 1920-21. The total Institute budget expanded from $260,000 to $336,000, an increase of almost thirty percent. From 1919 to 1921, however, net excess revenue declined from $208,000 to $176,000 per year.[12]

In 1923 and 1925 the Institute brought in more than $725,000 in gross revenues, but the usual annual income was closer to $690,000. The budget for university expenditures rose to $398,000 in 1924, $491,000 in 1926, and $518,000 in 1929. Using accounting techniques customary in business, the board took a depreciation allowance; as expenses rose, net income even after allowing for depreciation declined precipitously. The low point for the decade was $36,000 in net revenues in 1926. Rice's endowment increased from $12.8 million in 1921 to $14.8 million in 1929, with most of this amount (about $10 million) invested in mortgage and collateral loans and in bonds.[13]

In a note to James Baker in 1923, President Lovett mentioned monetary difficulties. It must have hurt this man, who yearned to build a university of recognized status, to say, "The university's immediate and prospective revenues are inadequate to the realization of the programme of instruction and research on which it has entered."[14]

In the spring of 1924 editorials appeared in the *Post* discussing Rice's financial needs. The writer speculated that Rice did not receive many gifts of money because of its fabled endowment: prospective donors thought that the Institute was too rich to need help. He pointed out the financial demands on Rice and applauded its decision to limit enrollment. While he did not make a straightforward request for funds, the editor suggested that "it has not been the policy of those responsible for the institution to solicit or invite financial assistance from outside, but it probably could be accepted."[15]

So serious was Rice's economic plight that even the board's usual reticence to discuss the Institute's money disappeared for a while. At commencement that June, after the awarding of degrees, Baker made the first public plea for donations. He disabused the audience of the popular impression that Rice was blessed with a rich endowment. Because the institution spent only its interest and not its principal, and because the size of the student body and the cost of upkeep were both increasing, its income was insufficient for growth. Baker urged citizens of wealth to donate funds to improve the Institute's financial position. In December before the Rotary Club, Baker said again that it was impossible to expand with the funds available and asked Rotarians to "stop to think a moment and then bequeath a portion of your money to Rice Institute." No evidence remains of any campaign to follow up Baker's requests, however, and the Institute struggled on as before.[16]

Throughout the rest of the 1920s, Houston newspapers continued to refer to the Institute's need for money, and a number of people developed schemes for raising it. The year after Caldwell suggested that tuition be charged, Lovett wrote to Stanford University to ask how Stanford had changed its charter to allow the charging of tuition. Beyond this inquiry, Lovett did not explore revising the Rice charter. It may have been wishful thinking considering Rice's straits, but Lovett also spoke in 1928 of establishing a law department at Rice in the near future and a medical school later.

John W. Slaughter, who became the Sharp Lecturer of Civics and Philanthropy, appealed independently to Houstonians for donations and also suggested to Captain Baker that it might be possible for the city to provide the Institute with funds through taxation. That idea did not seem feasible or legal to Baker; not, that is, until Will Hogg appeared. Hogg, son of a former governor and one of the enterprising founders of The Texas Company, was active in supporting higher learning throughout the state. He presented a plan for raising funds from the city, "in view of the benefits conferred by the Institute upon the City of Houston." The proposal was brought before the board in May and June of 1929 but got lost during the depression that followed.[17]

Rice Faculty in the 1920s

A large part of the rise in operating expenses was due to growth in the faculty to coincide with expansion of the student body. In 1920 the faculty numbered approximately forty; in 1924 it was up to fifty, and by 1927 there were seventy professors, assistant professors, instructors, and lecturers. Some of the most enduring and endurable teachers joined the Institute after the war and in the 1920s. In history there was Floyd S. Lear, an authority on Roman and Barbarian law; in biology, Edgar Altenburg and Asa C. Chandler; in English, eighteenth-century scholar Alan D. McKillop, George G. Williams (nurturer of Rice's creative writers for two generations), George Whiting, and Joseph Gallegly. The French department welcomed Marcel Moraud, André Bourgeois, and Fred Shelton, while Max Freund joined German and Lester Ford went to mathematics. Arthur J. Hartsook taught chemical engineering and later founded the department; Henry Nicholas taught chemistry; and Robert Crookston came to teach mechanical engineering. Frank A. Pattie, Jr., soon to be well known for his "hypnotic" lectures, established the Department of Psychology.

There were also some notable

departures. After a short stay at Rice, Asa Chandler went to India to become head of the Department of Helminthology at the School of Tropical Medicine in Calcutta. German professor Lindsey Blayney moved to Denton, Texas, to become president of the College of Industrial Arts (later Texas Women's University). Architect John Clark Tidden resigned after eleven years; the math department lost Percy Daniell, and French lost Albert Guérard. The heaviest blow came in 1924, when Harold A. Wilson, the professor of the physics department, decided to take the Kelvin Chair of Physics at Glasgow University. Lovett tried hard to keep Wilson, and he made an arrangement with William S. Farish, president of the Humble Oil and Refining Company, whereby Wilson would do consulting work with Humble to add to his salary. In the end, however, the Kelvin Chair was too important for Wilson to turn down. He had already agreed to go before the Humble plan was approved. At that news the general atmosphere in the physics department became one of gloom.[18]

There were also some notable returns. Less than eight months after Wilson left, Lovett had occasion to visit the Wilsons in Glasgow and found that they were not particularly happy there. "The honor and glory here may be all right," Wilson wrote to the president later, "but the salary is not enough for comfort." He would prefer to be back at Rice "with its better laboratory. I do not like to think of the Rice

Physics Building without a first class physicist to keep up the traditions we established there." Lovett moved quickly and by the end of the next month had worked out an arrangement for salary, the Humble consulting position, and a pension. The next fall Wilson was back in the laboratory he had built, there to remain. To make matters even better, Asa Chandler returned from India in 1926, at which the overworked biology department must have rejoiced.[19]

Wilson returned to a combined salary of $12,000 ($8,000 from Rice, $4,000 from Humble Oil), and Chandler to a professorship (he had been an assistant professor when he left) and $6,000. Faculty salaries rose for other individual faculty members through the 1920s, and that added to the cost of running the university, as did the growth in faculty numbers. But automatic raises were not built into the system. The more a man was wanted by another university, the better his chances were for an increase in salary at Rice. It appears that those who did not ask did not receive increases. When given, salary raises could be rather spectacular. In 1926 when Harvard approached G. C. Evans, the board approved a salary of $9,000 if he would remain at Rice. (He had been making $6,000.) Radoslav Tsanoff's offer from the University of Southern California brought him a salary increase at Rice, from $5,250 to $7,500. In the case of Evans's raise, the board was careful to place in its minutes the statement, "it being

understood that in taking this action, the amount of increase authorized shall, if possible, not be construed as a precedent for similarly increasing the compensation of other professors at the Institute, with the idea, however, that the salaries of such other professors shall be increased from time to time as may be considered advisable."[20]

The lack of a definite policy with regard to promotion and raises, plus lack of money for expansion, led to confusion for department heads trying to work out a program for their departments. Harry Weiser of chemistry remarked to Lovett in 1927 that it was difficult to plan very far ahead when he did not know if future policy would be expansion or retrenchment. At the same time, it seemed impossible that the department would stand still with a group of promising men. Said Weiser, "I cannot urge the appointment of another man, however much I feel the need of him, if I know ahead of time that such an addition is likely to interfere with the advancement or salary of the present members of the staff."[21]

Life for the Rice faculty in general remained as it had been during the first years of the school. There were always classes to teach, students to help, research and writing to do, and public lectures to give—more than enough to keep busy. Indeed, Edgar Altenburg complained in August 1924 that his teaching and administrative duties left him little time for intensive research and no time for public lectures. Per-

78. *The visit of the official French Mission, December 9, 1918.* **Left to right:** *M. Charles Koechlin (a composer and music critic), Mme M. L. Cazamian, Mrs. Edgar O. Lovett, Professor L. Cazamian, and President Lovett.*

79. *Guests arriving for "Pershing Day," the visit of General John J. Pershing to the Rice Institute, February 5, 1920.*

haps Altenburg was overworked; the *Thresher* reported that he had a nervous breakdown the following spring.[22]

On the matter of public lectures, the newspapers continued to take note of Rice speakers, but somewhat more benignly than before. A talk by physicist Wilson on the conflict between science and religion elicited an editorial saying that "the intellectual leadership which the Rice men offer, for Houston in particular, is illustrated once again." After one of Tsanoff's lectures on

democracy, the *Chronicle* noted that members of the Rice faculty were willing to serve the community and that Houston should take more advantage of what they had to give. "Incidentally," the article continued, "why not more Rice men on our public boards? Why not, as the first Rice 'man' to be named by Mayor Monteith, Miss Alice Dean, librarian of Rice, to be a member of the Houston Library Board? A better selection could not be made."[23]

Visiting Lecturers

In addition to lectures by Rice faculty members, the Institute community benefited from a procession of visiting lecturers from other institutions. The first, in 1919, were the British educational mission and the French mission to universities of the United States. General John J. Pershing came in February 1920 for a tour of the Institute; he planted a pecan tree in front of the Administration Building. In April of that year, former Presi-

80. *General Pershing autographing a parchment commemorating his visit. President Lovett is in the background.*

dent William Howard Taft inaugurated the newly endowed Godwin Lectureship on Public Affairs. The second Godwin lecturer was Sir Auckland Geddes, British ambassador to the United States, who in 1921 himself endowed a prize in writing in honor of his wife. (The Lady Geddes Prize is still a coveted honor among undergraduates.) Other visitors included Belgian poet and playwright Maurice Maeterlinck; Sir Arthur Shipley, biologist and vice-chancellor of Cambridge University; Jacques Hadamard of the Department of Mathematics of the French Institute, Collège de France, and Ecole Polytechnique; astronomer Henry N. Russell of Princeton; educator and philosopher John Dewey; historian William E. Dodd of the University of Michigan; and E. C. C. Baly, Grant Professor of Inorganic Chemistry at the University of Liverpool. Old Rice friends such as Julian Huxley and Edwin Grant Conklin returned to lecture, as did Louis Cazamian, a professor of English literature at the University of Paris, and Szolem Mandelbrojt, the Paris mathematician. Sir Henry Jones, professor of moral philosophy at the University of Glasgow, inaugurated the Sharp Lectureship in Civics and Philanthropy. An anonymously donated music lectureship brought the respected American composer John Powell to campus to inaugurate the series in 1923, and in 1928 the illustrious Maurice Ravel visited Rice. There was no lack of intellectual stimulus from the outside.

These personages received various honoraria for their lectures, and written versions of their lectures often were published in the *Rice Institute Pamphlet;* but the Institute did not grant honorary degrees to the speakers. In 1920 Lovett raised with the faculty the question of granting such degrees. However, there was no general sentiment in favor of doing so then, and evidently none developed thereafter. Rice still awards no honorary degrees, and avoiding this sort of recognition has become a strong tradition.[24]

During this decade two other events affected the faculty of the Institute. In 1920 several professors were instrumental in forming the Houston Philosophical Society, a town-and-gown group whose purpose was "to stimulate interest in modern developments in science and philosophy." Faculty families led active social lives together, and during the twenties a place was built on campus for faculty gatherings of all kinds. George S. Cohen, a Houston businessman and owner of Foley's department store, gave $125,000 to the Institute for a faculty club in honor of his parents, Robert I. and Agnes Cohen. The younger Cohen had become interested in Rice through his support of Rice athletics and through his assistance to many students who desired careers in business and professional life. William Ward Watkin designed the building, and Cohen House opened officially at homecoming in November 1927.[25]

81. *Sir Henry Jones of Glasgow, a member of the British Educational Mission to the United States, inaugurating the Sharp Lectureship in Civics and Philanthropy, November 1918.*

82. *Ceremony laying the cornerstone for Cohen House (the faculty club), July 26, 1927.* Left to right: *William Ward Watkin, Robert I. Cohen, Mrs. George S. Cohen, Mrs. Robert I. Cohen, Benjamin Botts Rice, President Lovett, E. A. Peden, Rabbi Henry Cohen, Thomas T. Hopper (contractor).*

83. *William Ward Watkin's rendering of the south elevation of the Robert and Agnes Cohen House.*

Curriculum

One of the continuing concerns of the faculty was the curriculum. Except for the normal tinkering with the curriculum—adding new courses and dropping old ones, tightening rules for scholastic probation, forced withdrawal, readmission, the system of grading—the faculty made few changes in the overall course of study. Professors continued to emphasize that the work was designed for a four-year course, built up year by year, and their primary worry was that some freshmen were unable to do college-level work. In 1922 a new course called English Zero was adopted for those with poor language skills. Freshmen were to take this course on recommendation of the English department, and upperclassmen on recommendation of two of their professors. English Zero carried no credit but had to be passed, and it was taught by regular members of the English department.

In 1925 the faculty changed the school calendar. They decided that freshmen needed a longer adjustment period to college work before taking final examinations, so they abolished the old three-term system. "Preliminary examinations" for freshmen and for students on probation replaced the first term examinations in December; examinations similar to term exams were scheduled for February; spring examinations were eliminated; and final exams were placed at the end of the school year. There was no reference to any sort of semester system; the faculty wished to reemphasize that courses were designed to last a full year. It was impossible to flunk out on the basis of the December preliminary examinations. February tests were to cover the year's work to that point for all students, but the final examinations covered only the work from February to May for freshmen and sophomores; juniors and seniors were to be tested over the entire year's work.[26]

Students continued to dread Math 100, which was described in the catalog as "elementary analysis of the elementary functions, algebraic, trigonometric and exponential; their differentiation and integration." In practice, Math 100 concentrated on the calculus, since professors reviewed algebra and trigonometry only in the first three or four class periods. One probable cause of Math 100 phobia was that students had usually taken no math courses during their last year or two of high school and were rusty in mathematical thinking by the time they got to college. An insert in the catalog advised high school students to take mathematics during their senior year but did little to help the situation.

By 1926 the mathematics department was determined to help prevent failures. The math professors thought that students who were failing were capable of doing the work but lost courage when they encountered some difficulty—even a trivial one. Perhaps personal instruction would restore their confidence and carry them through. The professors intended not to diminish the students' sense of responsibility but to develop initiative. Their plan called for changes in the basic Math 100 course, which was to meet for two-hour periods three times a week. Much of the work was to be done in class instead of as homework, so that each student could obtain individual assistance and supervision. Those who were still having trouble at the end of the first term would be placed in a new course called Math Zero. Like English Zero, it carried no credit but had to be passed before the student could reregister in Math 100, which was still required for graduation. Under this plan, Math 100 was redefined as elementary analysis in trigonometry, analytic geometry, and introduction to calculus; but as before it remained mostly calculus. The results of the experiment were so successful that the next year the two-hour-period, three-times-a-week schedule was extended to Math 200 and 210.[27]

A Change in Athletics

Perhaps the largest addition to the curriculum in the 1920s came in 1929 with the creation of the Department of Physical Education. When the Field House was completed in 1921, classes in physical training began for freshman men as a compulsory one-hour-a-week class. Intramural games were also established for upperclassmen. (The women had to fend for themselves at the Rice tennis courts or the YWCA.) Although students had proposed more supervised athletics and organized intramural sports, they appear to have sparked little interest in a separate department of physical education, much less a degree in the subject. The impetus for that came from Rice's fortunes—or misfortunes—on intercollegiate sports fields.[28]

Although there were a few individual standouts in Southwest Conference play from 1920 to 1923—players like Marion Lindsey, Eddie Dyer, Bert Hinckley, Edwin De Prato, and John Underwood—the Institute's teams did not distinguish themselves during that time. Philip H. Arbuckle's football team went from a high of second place in the conference in 1919 to fourth in 1920 and sixth in 1921. In 1922 Arbuckle retained his position as director of athletics but turned over the coaching position to Howard F. Yerges, who had been an instructor in engineering drawing. The Owls finished seventh in 1922 and remained in that position in 1923 when Arbuckle resumed coaching. The basketball team, under a different coach every year (Leslie Mann in 1920, Pete Cawthon in 1921, Yerges in 1922, and Arbuckle in 1923), did somewhat better, finishing fourth, fourth, sixth, and third in those years. Arbuckle resigned in December 1923. At that point the Committee on Outdoor Sports under the chairmanship of William Ward Watkin began to look for a new football coach and director of athletics. The

84. *Football game, Rice* vs. *University of Arkansas (Thanksgiving Reunion), Rice Stadium, November 27, 1919.*

85. *Pep Parade preceding football game between Rice and Tulane, 1921.*

Thresher reported that the committee wanted a man with "considerable successful experience" to whom they could give virtually a free rein for two or three years.[29]

It did not take long for Watkin to find a candidate. John W. Heisman was looking for a new coaching job. Already famous, Heisman had coached championship football teams at Clemson, Auburn, and most notably the Georgia Institute of Technology. From there he had gone to Watkin's alma mater, the University of Pennsylvania; in 1924 he was at Washington and Jefferson College in Pennsylvania. Heisman was famous for his winning teams and also for inventing the forward pass, the hidden-ball play, the center snap, and the word "hike" for beginning a play. During a long talk with Watkin in February 1924 the coach announced his terms. He wanted to be in residence at Rice only for spring training and the football season, so that he could tend to his sporting goods firm in New York in the off-seasons; in spite of his absence, he would take general responsibility for all assistant coaches and teams as athletic director. He wanted a salary of $9,000 and a five-year contract to go with the position. Watkin thought that Heisman would soon withdraw from his New York business and become an "all year man" at Rice. In recommending his appointment, Watkin also pointed out that Heisman was willing to take $1,000 less than his present salary at Washington and Jefferson, which

86. *John W. Heisman, athletic director of the Rice Institute from 1924 to 1927.*

he wanted to leave because his "desire for discipline" was not being supported by the school.

Although they were somewhat "embarrassed" by the contract feature of Heisman's terms (the first contract offered a coach by the Institute) and by Heisman's age (he was fifty-five but looked forty-eight, according to Watkin), the trustees agreed to the coach's terms and desired salary. He was to be present at the Institute from September 1 through December 10 and from the beginning of March to approximately April 15 each year. In April of his first year at the Institute, Heisman proposed giving up all other work entirely and devoting himself solely to Rice athletics for

an additional compensation of $2,500 per year, but the board turned him down. The trustees did authorize Captain Baker to offer Heisman additional money to stay in Houston until after commencement exercises; it appears, however, that the arrangement fell through, because Heisman's salary never changed. Even at the part-time rate, the coach was making more than any of the professors. (Harold Wilson's salary, the highest on campus, was $7,500 in 1924 before he went to Scotland.)[31]

Coach Heisman hit Rice like a whirlwind in the spring of 1924. A charming man and a dynamic speaker (he had been a Shakespearean actor on the chautauqua circuit), he could hold an audience in the palm of his hand; he excelled at arousing enthusiasm for Rice sports. In addition to speaking, he wrote a *Thresher* column in the form of open letters to the students, telling them to publicize their school to prospective athletes and other students. His letters were pep talks full of words in capital letters: EVERYBODY was to SELL others on RICE and be a Rice BOOSTER.[32]

Back east during the summer of 1924, Heisman became embroiled in a situation that almost caused him trouble with the National Collegiate Athletic Association. He went to see a reporter for a New Jersey newspaper, and the story that followed left the impression that Heisman was "proselyting" among prospective students of New Jersey colleges. At that time the question of recruiting—how to do it, if it should be done at all, and if so, by whom—was very much unsettled. To President Alex C. Humphreys of the Stevens Institute of Technology, Heisman was poaching. Humphreys complained to the president of the NCAA, General Palmer E. Pierce, who wrote to Watkin and to Heisman. Watkin, in turn, wrote to Heisman asking for an explanation. He told the coach to clear up the situation with Pierce and Humphreys, remarking that he personally thought it would be "a great mistake" under the circumstances to bring any athletes from the Northeast to Rice. No matter how properly or honestly they should come, criticism would still follow.

Heisman saw Humphreys. Humphreys opposed athletic recruiting of any sort, so the conversation between the two men began with a direct conflict. They managed to settle the matter by agreeing to disagree, but Heisman did stop his recruiting activities in New Jersey.

The coach found Professor Watkin philosophically close to Humphreys. When he wrote to Watkin to explain the entire incident, the coach asked what Watkin had meant by saying that Heisman had made "a great mistake." Was the chairman of the Committee on Outdoor Sports speaking of a matter of principle or of university policy? Heisman thought it was proper in principle to bring boys down from the East, but what was the policy? What was the harm?

Watkin very much wanted to keep amateurism in athletics and not turn Rice's teams into semiprofessional ones. His ideas were probably not new to Heisman. Watkin thought that control of athletics should be in the hands of the faculty, without joint committees of alumni, undergraduates, and faculty such as some other schools had. He believed that athletic expenditures should be held to a minimum; there should be no extravagance, wasteful traveling, or "undesirable deviation" from a student's normal activities when he participated on a team. Scouting and recruiting were unadvisable, as were the scholarships for athletics; and student athletes should not be coddled with special courses or lenient grades. Watkin also believed that coaches should be members of the faculty and hold office for as long as possible. He knew that a football coach's salary was out of proportion with a professor's, but he expected the operation of the free market to bring those salaries down within a few years.[33]

Despite a summer of argument and a committee chairman with whom he did not completely agree, Heisman got off to a good start in his first season. The Owls won four and lost four football games, their victories including a defeat of the University of Texas by a score of 19–6, the first victory over Texas since 1917 and only the second in Rice history. The team finished the season tied with A&M for third place in the Southwest Conference. Part of the credit seems to be due to the consistent play-

ing of one of the two easterners whom Heisman had managed to lure to the Southwest, a big fullback named E. W. Herting, Jr.

Many faculty members believed with Watkin that athletes were, after all, students and entitled to no special academic treatment. But by the spring of 1925 it had become clear to the coach that Rice athletes had to have some help with their studies. Those who lived in the dormitories seemed to be the most prone to difficulties. The *Thresher* reported that of fifty-two athletes of "recognized worth" who lived on campus, twenty-three had either flunked out or gone on probation in the two preceding terms. Only five of the twenty-six who lived at home or elsewhere in Houston had failed. Heisman's remedy was to create an athletic dorm. The athletes took over part of East Hall and buckled down to study. There were rules—no liquor, study hours with confinement to rooms, no visiting for freshmen or those on probation during those hours—and student proctor-tutors to enforce them. The regimentation worked fairly well, and the athletes' grades rose; but the athletic dorm did not eliminate academic failures. The next fall Heisman exhorted women students to encourage Rice athletes to study and play well, and not to tempt them to stay out late and break his rules.[34]

In 1926 the Athletic Department hired Gaylord Johnson '21, who also had a Ph.D. in chemistry from Rice, to fill the newly created post of business manager for athletics. He held that position until 1940.[35]

More athletes might have been passing their courses as a result of the new dormitory arrangements, but the 1925 and 1926 football seasons were not improvements over the past. In 1925 the Owls won four, lost four, and tied one, thus ending up in seventh place in the conference with only one conference win. In 1926, although the full season record was the same as in 1925, they lost all four conference games and finished in the cellar. Heisman came in for much criticism; the *Thresher* asked, "What is wrong with Rice and her athletics?" The next year was even more dismal. Rice won two, lost six, and tied one, beating only Sam Houston and Baylor.[36]

Before the last game, which happened to be the contest with Baylor, Heisman was ready to resign. He had suffered enough criticism; he presented his terms to the board on November 21, 1927. On December 1 the trustees accepted his proposal for resignation, and on December 1 Heisman resigned, effective at once. The board canceled his contract and paid the rest of his salary for that year and a portion of the next. When asked why he resigned, Heisman would only say, "I will not discuss the reasons."[37] No one else would be formally named director of athletics until 1933.

For the rest of the decade, the Owl football team did little better under coaches Claude Rothgeb in 1928 or Jack Meagher in

1929 and 1930, although the team did beat arch-rival Texas in 1930 and again in 1931. As track coach, however, Rothgeb had reason to rejoice. The Institute had several conference track winners and record holders between 1924 and 1927—Fred Stancliff, William Smiley, and Nelson Greer—and the 1928 track team won the conference championship. Emmett Brunson (who was to be Rice's head track coach from 1934 to 1970), Claude Bracey, Ben Chitwood, and Walter Boone were the standouts. The golf team also did well, winning the conference title in 1929 and 1930 with lettermen Joe Greenwood, Forrest Lee Andrews, Reuben Albaugh, Carl Illig, Dan Smith, Jr., and Tommy Blake.

What to do with the athletic program and how to keep student athletes scholastically eligible became pressing problems after Heisman's resignation. Before William Ward Watkin resigned his chairmanship of the Committee on Outdoor Sports in January 1928, he made three suggestions. The first involved aiding Houston coaches to create a supply of good athletes, and the second was that alumni should encourage student athletes in other cities to consider attending Rice. His third suggestion was more innovative. To increase the number of freshman football recruits and to ensure their scholastic survival, Watkin proposed establishing a first-class preparatory school for scholastic and athletic training. Such a school could "in some manner" be directed in its educational and athletic policy by the

Institute and could produce a larger number of qualified athletes for the Rice athletic program. Watkin did not spell out any details for such a school, but he clearly thought that it was the only way to improve the athletes' scholastic performance, maintain a place in the Southwest Conference, and sustain the idea of amateurism in collegiate sports.[38]

The administration, trustees, and faculty decided on another solution. It is unclear exactly when the proposal was first made and who made it, but by December 1928 a joint report of the Committee on Honors Courses and Advanced Degrees, the Committee on Examinations and Standing, and the faculty members of the Committee on Outdoor Sports was presented to the entire faculty for consideration. It called for the establishment of a course in physical education and a Department of Physical Education.

Those in favor argued thus: although athletics in college should serve the purpose of giving athletic enjoyment and development to a maximum number of undergraduates, we have fallen far short of realizing that high purpose. We may deplore the attitude of many serious people who consider the victory or defeat of a Rice athletic team to be of great importance to the students, to the Institute, and to the community, but we cannot change this fact. Because we believe that athletic sports are an indispensable adjunct to academic life, we encourage all to participate. But the maintenance of an internal sys-

ANDREWS   BLAKE   ALBAUGH

Southwest Golf Champions 1930

Rice's golf team, under the leadership of Forest Lee Andrews, again proved that they knew their mashies in the annual tournament held at Houston this year by capturing both the individual and the team championships of the Southwest conference.

Joe Greenwood, one of the best collegiate golfers in the State, sank long putts from all corners of the green to cop the individual title while Greenwood, Blake, Albaugh, Andrews and Illig teamed to retain the team championship trophy last year by polling an aggregate score two shots below that of Texas University.

Although Reuben Albaugh, captain-elect, is the only letter man to return to the campus next year many veteran golfers will be on hand to take the place of those lost by graduation when spring rolls around. With Albaugh's brilliant playing and coaching to be relied on and Cole, McCarty, Dickey, Muller, Plath and other aspirants getting their form perfected, it is not too much to predict another championship team for next season.

ILLIG   *The Trophy*   GREENWOOD

87. *Golf team, 1930.* Clockwise: *Lee Andrews, Tommy Blake, Reuben Albaugh, Carl Illig, Jr., Joe Greenwood.*

tem seems impossible without external competition. Intercollegiate games have proved to be extremely expensive, and the Institute is losing $20,000 to $30,000 annually. At the same time we have been unable to hold an honorable place in the Southwest Conference, and we cannot maintain the interest of our own students, much less of the community or conference, unless we win more frequently. "We are not willing to go on as we have been, and we cannot abandon athletics." The way out appears to be a department of physical education to attract good athletes and a course leading to a degree of Bachelor of Science in physical education. In no way would Rice's high standards be lowered; admission would be open only to students whose first interest was to go to and through college. Furthermore, a degree in physical education would not affect the values or standards of Rice's other degrees in highly technical or intellectual subjects. Although by their very nature different, standards for the degree in physical education could be as high as those for other degrees.[39]

As presented to the faculty, the plan proposed that a course in physical education be established, with certain provisions. The number of new students admitted each year would be limited to 40 (over the regular quota of 400). The course would be open to any student seriously contemplating coaching as a career, and additional instruction would be provided in biology, English, business administration, and education so that students could obtain a teaching certificate along with the degree. Perhaps most important, funds for the new department would come from outside the existing endowment but through the trustees to preserve the Institute's freedom of action. Rice's very limited income would not support the creation of such a department without taking sorely needed funds from established departments, a move that would have alienated faculty members. The report recommended, therefore, that funds be raised from among Houston businessmen. Approximately $20,000 would be needed each year for the first five years. At the end of five years, the program was to be evaluated. The faculty vote was thirty-six for, fifteen against. Caldwell, McCants, Wilson, and Moraud were among those voting in favor, and Evans, Tsanoff, Altenburg, and Axson among those against.[40]

To raise money for the physical education program, the trustees first held a conference and then gave a dinner for certain Houston businessmen. Houstonians who contributed to the fund included Anderson-Clayton's chairman, Will L. Clayton; real estate and banking king Jesse H. Jones; lumber magnates J. W. Link and John H. Kirby; department store tycoon Simon Sakowitz; and Humble Oil founders Will Farish, Harry C. Wiess, and Walter W. Fondren. Baker of the Rice board joined in. There were a few influential men, such as Lamar Fleming, Jr., who declined to participate because they still thought that the main concern of a college should be to provide a scholarly education for "real students," not those whose chief purpose at college was athletics. However, Fleming recognized that he was "utterly out of step with current ideas in intercollegiate athletics."[41]

To head the new department, the Institute hired Harry Alexander Scott, who held a doctorate from Columbia University. Scott's title was "professor of physical education," and he received in salary about the same as the other full professors: $6,000 a year. His program was designed to prepare men for careers in physical education and coaching in high schools, colleges, and other organizations such as municipal recreation departments, but it did not stop there. The students also took biology, chemistry, education, economics, and business administration courses; they graduated with a state teacher's certificate, the competence to teach several courses in high school, and business knowledge. They would have their own 200-level English class, a chemistry course with a morning lab, and two special biology courses. Physical education students were excused from Math 100. How the program would affect Rice's ability on the football field and whether the school itself would be harmed (as William Ward Watkin seemed to fear) remained to be seen.[42]

Aspects of Student Life

A couple of new departments, the limitation on admissions, and curricular modifications were important to the Institute, but they did little to change the major aspects of student life in the 1920s. Nevertheless, some other changes did have an effect. Rice was still new, not even ten years old in 1920, and not many traditions had been solidified. Students were in the process of creating traditions and learning how to get along with the administration.

One of the best and longest-lasting changes took place in 1921, when a building that would be known as the "fireside of Rice" opened on Main Street across from the campus. It replaced a hut built from salvaged material and was under the auspices of the Episcopal Diocese of Texas. The original structure had been built through the initiative of the Reverend Harris Masterson, Jr., who wanted to minister to the Rice students in all their needs. In 1921 Mrs. James Autry donated $50,000 for a cultural, religious, and recreational center for the students in memory of her husband, Judge James L. Autry. The Institute's architects, Cram and Ferguson, designed the building, which was completed that fall. Autry House was open free of charge to all Institute faculty and student organizations and clubs. It included a canteen and cafeteria and was welcomed by students who had brought their lunches from home or had made do with what "The Owl," a little store nearby, provided. Stu-

88. *The laying of the cornerstone for Autry House, June 5, 1921. Left to right: William Ward Watkin, President Lovett, the Reverend Herbert L. Willett, the Reverend Harris Masterson, Dr. Peter Gray Sears.*

89. *Autry House, shortly after completion.*

dents made heavy use of the building for plays, meetings, Saturday night dances, and simple gatherings, especially for bridge games between classes. During the school year 1921–22, 260 organized meetings were held there and 18,000 lunches served. Many students remember with a great deal of fondness both the Reverend Mr. Masterson and Mrs. Eugene C. Blake, who served as matron for the place. An advisory board consisting of Mrs. Autry, Dr. Peter Gray Sears of Christ Church Cathedral, and President Lovett made policy decisions. Although Autry House did not cover its own expenses as had been planned, losses were made up through private contributions. The later construction of the adjoining Palmer Memorial Church, a gift of Mrs. Edwin L. Neville in memory of her brother Edward A. Palmer, gave students and faculty a nearby place to worship.[43]

The early twenties saw several Rice "firsts." "Rice's Honor"

made its first appearance in 1922 after the *Thresher* campaigned for a school song. Ben Mitchell put words to the Harvard "Marching Song" ("Our Director March" by John Philip Sousa), and at a pep rally in the mess hall, students liked that one the best of eight or so songs considered. The first May Fete was held in 1921, and even though the *Thresher* editor asked in 1922 what it was good for, the pageant became an annual event. That first year Queen Rosalie Hemphill and King Robert P. Williams reigned over a lavish spectacle with a court of honorees from each of the classes. After the Rice Dramatic Club was formed in the fall of 1921, the architecture and painting students decided to substitute another creative activity for the play they had usually produced. In February 1922 the Architectural Society held a costume ball, the first Archi-Arts of a long series of student-produced theme parties with

highly original costumes, design, and entertainment. On the literary side, *The Rice Owl*, a magazine for serious pieces as well as perfectly awful jokes, made its first appearance in 1922. In 1926 another literary magazine, the *Raven*, was also published; but it lasted only until the summer of 1927. *The Rice Owl* continued until 1938, then changed in 1939 to become an alumni magazine as well. It was published in that form until 1946.

In 1920 the Rice Engineering Society decided to repay the courtesies that companies in the area had shown the students, by inviting company representatives to come and see the work of the engineering, chemistry, and physics departments. The society wanted to set up demonstrations and create a show, which they called the Rice Engineering Show. Henry A. Tillett, a senior mechanical engineering student, asked President Lovett for permission to use university facilities and print a program for visitors. Lovett did not believe the show would attract much attention among Houstonians. He refused to give the society any financial aid for a program, but he did allow use of the grounds and buildings. Perhaps because of Lovett's pessimism, the students pitched in determinedly to sell advertisements for the program, and they raised enough money to print one thousand copies. Lovett wrote to about fifty industrial firms on behalf of the students, inviting spectators to attend the show; but until the day of the exposition, no one could predict the

90. *The first May Fete king and queen, Parks Williams and Rosalee Hemphill, with their attendants, Albert Guérard and Molly Tidden, May 10, 1921.*

91. *Stage sets for the first Archi-Arts Ball (Masque Español or Baile Español), February 3, 1922.*

turnout. Henry Tillett remembers looking anxiously out his dormitory window, only to find a number of school buses and cars and a line of visitors stretching from the Physics Building around to the Administration Building. Eventually some 10,000 Houstonians saw the show that year.

In the first show were only sixty-two exhibits, including a "bucking broncho," magnetic stunts, and nitroglycerin explosions. The Engineering Society decided in 1921 to make the show biennial, and to each succeeding production they added more exhibits. In 1922, there were X-rays, liquid air, and the Rice radio station (5YG), plus a coast defense searchlight from Fort Crockett in Galveston. Shows in the 1920s included "hooch tests" in the days of Prohibition, beating hearts of turtles and frogs, a radio-controlled car, a new automatic telephone switchboard on loan from Southwestern Bell (the first automatic board in Houston), the "den of the alchemist" (with chemistry students as the magicians), economic exhibits, and architectural drawings. More and more departments participated, and by 1930 there were 319 exhibits. The 1930s saw a television receiver, psychological tests, a paper-bladed friction saw, music broadcast over a light beam, an "oomph meter" to "see what you have a date with," and Woofus, a mechanical creature described as "an inhabitant of the planet Venus and . . . a gift . . . from the famous planet explorer, Buck Rogers."[44]

The first campus traffic regulations made their appearance in 1923. An average of 154 cars a day on campus made it necessary to bring some order to the roads and parking lots. Nonetheless, the usual way to get around was still by walking; President Lovett could be seen walking to campus from his home at the Plaza Hotel, with his bowler hat (straw boater in the summer) and bookstrap. Professors Heaps, Pound, McCants, and Tsanoff bicycled.[45]

Even before Coach Heisman stirred up the student body to boost Rice spirit, some of the students had whipped up their own enthusiastic support for athletic teams. The *Thresher* complained from time to time about the lack of spirit on campus and urged all to turn out for sports events. The cheering section at football games was led by male "yell leaders"; one *Thresher* editor, while praising the women students for wanting to be part of the school, thought it sounded better if they did not join the men in the organized cheers. Heisman's arrival raised school spirit considerably. In 1925 Sammy the Owl was resurrected for Rice's game with the Aggies, and the Rally Club was formed to help usher at events on campus, cheer for the teams, and be of service wherever its members could. Jack Glenn, Rice's premier cheerleader, was the first Rally Club president. No one could accuse the student body of lacking spirit after that year.[46]

Student concerns in the 1920s ranged from food to faculty to proper senior clothing. Meals in the Commons, often still called the "mess hall" (possibly for

The chorus says that you can't feather your nest chasing chickens.

Oily to bed
And oily to rise,
Makes politicians,
Wealthy and wise.

What mistakes people make. It's not whose running in these Spring elections, but whose running the Spring elections.

Co-education is alright as long as girls are not allowed to attend.

"She's in terrible shape," said the corset on being removed.

"That's well put," remarked the professional as he sank a twenty footer.

"HE'S GOT THE AXE ON ME," sighed the cherry tree as George cut loose with a full swing.

"What is the suit worth?"
"Fifty dollars."
"Alright, I'll take it on account."
"On account of what?"
"On account of my other being worn out."

"It's a ridiculous thing to rely upon," said the upper story as it looked upon the faulty girder.

"Let your countience be your guide," said the vote tabulator to his assistant.

Here is chronicled the best joke in this issue: The Houston Censor Board.

The frequency with which Rice men are seen walking the boulevard after dark is merely an indication that they like to exercise.

The office has adopted a new slogan for this University: "The Rice Institute founded for the advancement of letters, science, art and athletics."

"What are you doing?"
"Nothing."
"Why don't you quit?"
"I haven't started."

1: Did you kick me?
2: Hardly.
3: Sap! Answer me!

Page twenty-one

92–93. *Two pages from* The Rice Owl. 92. *April 1924.* 93. *December 1924.*

The RICE OWL

HOLDING HIS OWN

THE PHILOSOPHICAL LOVER

Is there another, my darling,
Who dares thy favor to crave?
Is there another, my darling,
Who causes thee to rave?

Is there one whose arms have taken,
Thy soft warm form to kiss?
And is my love forsaken
As I have fear it is?

And do your lips speak truly
In saying they've kissed but mine?
Does thy heart beat unduly?
Or does thy smile combine

Feelings of scorn and amusement,
As I press my ardurous plea;
When the blood in my veins is a torrent,
That is raging only for thee?

If so you may smile at my passion,
And with scorn your lips may curl.
If so . . . . I'll follow the fashion,
And get me another girl.

YE FOOTE BALLE BALLADE

Thanksgiven bin icomen in
Ye halfe backe pranceth alle arounde,
Y-ronneth in ye lyne betweene:
Eftsoons he falleth on ye grounde,
    And loudlye singeth cuccu

Ye referee doth calle a fowle,
A player straightwaie gripeth.
He smoteth him upon ye jowle,
And up the grounde y-wipeth:
    And loudlye singeth cuccu.

Cam: Is Fisher going to the lecture tonight?
Bert: Naw. Didn't you see him drink my bottle of Listerine?

Austin is in the state of Texas, is it not?
No—It's been in the state of coma since November first.

Page seventeen

more than one reason), had gone from bad to worse. In 1924 the manager resigned, the kitchen was overhauled, and the food improved a bit. After one food riot, the administration levied a fine of thirty-seven dollars on each diner, whether he had participated in the fight or not. That measure effectively put an end to such events.

More serious were losses from the faculty when Wilson, Guérard, Blayney, and Chandler left. The *Thresher* began to ask if the school was still up to standard, whether these professors could be replaced, and how the university planned to fill their shoes. The paper reported that President Lovett would say only that students should know that they were receiving better training at Rice than they could anywhere else, and that finding new faculty members took time. Lovett himself was traveling so much, representing the Institute at various academic functions, that the *Thresher* once reported in mock surprise that the president had actually been seen on campus.

As for dress, some seniors began to affect canes, wing collars, and derbies on certain days of the week.[47]

Hazing and Social Clubs

Connected with school spirit in some minds was the practice of hazing, which had been a part of student life since the first sophomore class met the second freshman class at the door of the Administration Building on regis-

41.   A Display of the Industrial Chemical Apparatus on Hand.

No experiments will be carried out with this as it is merely a display.

42.   This can be shown only at night and is known as the Milky Way. A solution of red phosphorus in Ether is made and the walls of the lab or a dark room are sprayed with it. The clothes of the persons present may also be sprayed without any harmful effects. The phosphorus gives a "spookish" effect.

43.   Last, but not least, the **"Chamber of Sighs."**

No advance information will be given out as to this exhibit. It must be seen to be appreciated. Everyone be there. It is perfectly safe.

CONTINUATION OF THE CIVIL ENGINEERING DISPLAY.

44.   Generation of Power by the Use of the Doble Water Wheel.

The water wheel receives its impulse from water supplied by the Power House, and drives this machine so as to generate power.

45.   Measurement of Water Flow by Use of Wiers.

By varying the head of water on the wier, the discharge is increased or decreased. This effect is shown by the discharge curve made for this wier. In this manner the flow over dams and spillways is determined.

46.   The Use of the Hydraulic Ram.

The ram receives its impulse from the velocity of the water flowing through the U-shaped pipe, and is made to pump water against a variable head. This piece of apparatus is used where a plentiful supply and natural source of water is available.

47.   Pulsometer.

This is a type of pump often used in construction work because it can be suspended by a rope to lower levels and controlled very easily from the surface. It will not operate against very high pressures but by operating two or more in series water can be raised from much lower levels.

94. Page from the first Rice Engineering Show program, 1920.

tration day in 1913. In the 1920s, freshmen had their faces painted green, had to wear special or peculiar clothing, and had to obey certain rules. (No freshman was to walk on the grass, for example.) Men were forced to push mothballs across the gravel walks with their noses and were subjected to swats with a broom or a paddle for infractions of the regulations. Hazing progressed through "Forestry 100"—where the freshmen were left to spend the night in Hermann Park—to brooming freshmen for outlandish reasons, to what appeared to some people to be simply gratuitous beatings. Before long, Rice gained a reputation for being the second worst hazing school in the state; Texas A&M was the first.

There were those on the faculty who thought that such a barbarous practice was distinctly out of place at an institution of higher learning. In 1919, after an episode involving five sophomores and the freshman class president, Dean Caldwell moved to stop hazing altogether because nothing serious had happened—yet. The classes met, supported Caldwell, and abolished hazing for the remainder of the school year 1918–19 and for the next year as well. However, abolition proved to be difficult to enforce; hazing had resumed by 1921.[48]

In January 1922 the Student Association passed rules to control the practice. Under this set of regulations, "individual, indiscriminate, physical hazing" was not allowed, and all hazing was to be strictly between freshmen and sophomores. Freshmen still had to follow certain customs and such rules as the sophomores decided in class meetings, and jurisdiction over violators was placed with the Hall Committee and the Student Council. The *Thresher* defined "indiscriminate hazing" as hazing without a cause, or in other words, beating a freshman just because he was a freshman. The editor was somewhat surprised that the Student Association had gone so far, but in March they went even further. A new hazing bill limited corporal punishment to the period between 6:30 in the morning and 8:00 at night and called for "discretion" in all hazing. Dissatisfaction on the part of either freshmen or sophomores was to be brought to the Hall Committee for redress.[49]

The new rules did not much mitigate rowdy behavior, and after a pitched battle in May between sophomores and freshmen (which involved freshman football players and members of the Alpha Rho club), the dean, the faculty, and the trustees stepped in. They used the occasion to abolish two aspects of student life that had been worrying them for some time. The first was hazing; the second was a trend among student social clubs to resemble fraternities and sororities. Lovett had opposed fraternity-like associations from the beginning, preferring instead that the residential halls themselves take over club functions and become similar to the English college system. The university's catalog emphasized that the campus was a

democratic one, with student organizations such as the Student Association, scholarly societies, and the YMCA and YWCA open to all. The new clubs were definitely not open to all, and there was a certain amount of dissatisfaction on campus with them, a discontent manifest in student elections and the operation of the Student Council. Caldwell reported that students and many alumni believed that the clubs interfered with the unity and democracy of Rice life. He urged their abolition before they became strongly entrenched. The dean also recommended that the Institute rid itself of hazing. He had hoped to extinguish it by a gradual process of persuasion and education but found that the process was entirely too slow and dangerous. Accordingly, the faculty met in June and passed resolutions against the two distasteful practices, and the trustees approved.[50]

On June 8, 1922, at a meeting with students in the physics amphitheater, the new policies were announced:

I. There shall be no social clubs, local, fraternity, or sorority.
II. There shall be no hazing.

Although current students would not be required to sign a pledge to honor these resolutions, all future matriculating students would. Stressing democracy and efficiency in student self-government and the character of the university, the statement called upon all members of Rice to observe the resolutions faithfully.[51]

There was one last night of hazing, set to end at midnight, and the sophomores made certain that the freshmen remembered the experience. Freshman roommates Fred Stancliff and Wilson La Rue tried to barricade themselves into 210 West Hall, but the sophomores managed to come in through the window at five minutes to twelve. At that point, Stancliff remembers, "all hell broke loose."[52]

When school opened the following autumn, Caldwell clarified the bans. To the board and the faculty, hazing meant physical punishment, not the wearing of special outfits or the other harmless customs that had become part of the system. Those traditions would be allowed to remain. Clubs were another matter. The literary societies, EBLS and PALS, could continue to meet. (There was already a social-club feeling about the societies; but presumably their "literary" purpose was still in operation, and they did raise money for scholarships.) The others were out; the administration wanted the Institute to be preeminently democratic, with undivided interests. Caldwell said that there were only four fundamental laws at Rice: reasonable quiet and order in the residential halls, no cheating, no hazing, and no clubs.[53]

For the most part, students accepted the club ban with good grace. Since literary societies were allowed, two men's societies—the Owl Debating Club and the Riceonian—were resurrected, and a new women's club, the Owen Wister Literary Society (OWLS), was formed. On the question of hazing, however, student reaction was mixed. On one hand, opposition to hazing had been growing, and class organizations had moved against the practice in previous years. On the other hand, some upperclassmen worried that freshman class spirit would suffer. Others resented interference from the administration; they thought that this was an instance in which administration interests and student interests differed. To foster freshman spirit, upperclassmen resolved to enforce observance of freshman "traditions," using social ostracism and expulsion from the Student Association as punishment for transgressions. Slimes, both men and women, were told to come in costume on certain days, and mothball races were once again held in the quadrangle. Sensing the moral backing of the administration, however, freshmen disobeyed and disregarded the rules. To enforce the regulations, sophomores had only two tools: ostracism or eviction from the dormitory. Ostracism was difficult to carry out, and suspension from the dormitory was almost the equivalent of a monetary fine. Nothing was settled during the first year of the ban on physical coercion, but the dean was satisfied with the result.[54]

In September 1923 "slime regulations" were published again for freshmen to follow, but enforcement remained difficult. In November the dean reported to the faculty that the hazing situation was satisfactory. That situa-

tion did not last long, because the following spring sophomores were once more battling freshmen as the Slime Ball approached. They also tried to kidnap the freshman class president. It appears that there was no formal action to curb the annual battles connected with the Slime Ball until Coach Heisman asked in 1926 for its cancellation because players' grades had declined during the uproar. The Student Council obliged and cancelled the freshman dance, but warfare was transferred to the Sophomore Ball when freshmen tried to kidnap the sophomore president. In 1927 freshmen received permission to reinstate their dance, on the condition that the Student Council draw up rules and police the affair; the freshman president

was once again fair game for kidnappers.[55]

Once the controversy over the dances diminished, the Slime Parade came under attack. In this parade, which ended in a pep rally at the Rice Hotel, sophomores herded freshmen down Main Street with the aid of brooms, belts, and other spurs to movement. In 1927 the trustees suggested to the president and dean that something be done to correct these "objectionable parades," and the following year they abolished the Slime Parade themselves. The *Thresher* supported their action, commenting that in spite of the pledge, sophomores still hazed freshmen in the old manner; the editor called for abolition of the "vicious forms" of hazing. During 1928

95. *The first Slime [Freshman] Nightshirt Parade, Fall 1921.*

and 1929, several students were expelled for hazing, and Caldwell optimistically stated that there would soon be no more hazing at the Institute. But hazing passed with the students into the 1930s.[56]

Alumni Activities and National Associations

By 1920 the trustees had conferred approximately 160 degrees on Rice students. That November at Thanksgiving homecoming activities, the former students organized into the Association of Rice Alumni. Their first president was Ervin Kalb '17. Alumni continued to meet at each homecoming, and their numbers grew as more students graduated each year. In 1929 the association began to collect funds for an alumni memorial building of offices and classrooms, to be dedicated to the memory of William Marsh Rice and to be located across the quadrangle from the Physics Building.[57]

One group of alumni who wanted to join a national organization found to their consternation that Rice did not meet its criteria. Although the Rice Institute was a provisional member of the American Association of University Women from 1922 to 1927 and Rice graduates were accepted as members during that period, the association refused regular membership to Rice and would not accept Rice graduates as members after that time. The Institute could not meet membership requirements for a certain number of women on the faculty and Board of Trustees, for a women's dormitory, for physical education for women, and for a dean of women with faculty rank.[58]

Although Rice could not satisfy AAUW requirements, it did obtain membership in two other organizations of national stature.

96. *Installation of Phi Beta Kappa, Beta Chapter of Texas, March 2, 1929.*

In 1927 a chapter of Phi Lambda Upsilon, an honorary chemistry fraternity, was founded on campus. More important to the president, perhaps, was affiliation with Phi Beta Kappa. Lovett began application for a charter for the second chapter in Texas (the University of Texas had Alpha Chapter) in 1921. At that time many of the organization's senators, who voted on membership, believed that the institution was too new; more time should be given for the development of its characteristics. In 1922 Oscar M. Voorhees, secretary of Phi Beta Kappa, wrote to Lovett,

There was no question in the minds of the Senate of the future of Rice Institute. There was a question as to whether with its changed ideals the present name is appropriate. Phi Beta Kappa has never entered any institution that does not bear the name of College or University. I presume this matter has had your consideration, and that developments in the future will follow the course that is consistent from the point of view of the Trustees and Faculty.

The organization had denied a charter to the Massachusetts Institute of Technology partly on the same grounds a few years earlier. However, even without changing its name, the Rice Institute was accepted for membership in 1928. Beta Chapter of Phi Beta Kappa was installed on March 1, 1929. Dr. Henry Osborn Taylor, an eminent medieval historian, delivered the inaugural address.

President Lovett left the 1920s worried about problems ranging from finances to hazing, but he could be content that a jury of Rice's scholarly peers considered the Institute good enough and broadly enough based to merit a chapter of Phi Beta Kappa. His aspirations to university status had borne fruit.[59]

CHAPTER 6

Survival through the Depression: The 1930s

Whether Rice would attain general recognition of the university status envisaged by President Lovett or fall to the rank of a primarily technical institute became almost an irrelevant issue in the 1930s. Survival was its main concern during the Great Depression. The controllers of Rice's destiny, the Board of Trustees, had changed somewhat over the years. From the 1912 board there remained Captain James Baker, President Lovett, William M. Rice, Jr., and Benjamin B. Rice. To these had been added John T. Scott in 1913 as Emanuel Raphael's successor. New in the 1920s were Edward A. Peden, chairman of Peden Iron and Steel, and cotton factor and wholesale grocer Alexander S. Cleveland, who replaced James E. McAshan and Cesar M. Lombardi in 1922. When Peden died in 1934, the board elected Humble Oil founder Robert L. Blaffer to succeed him. Under Baker's chairmanship, this board remained a conservative group of men, rightly worried

about the effect of the depression on Rice's income.

Until 1947 all members of the Board of Trustees were actively engaged in managing the business affairs of the Rice Institute and its endowment. The assistant secretary to the board handled investments on orders from the board and accounted to the board for all income and expenditures. The board as a whole made most of the decisions, both large and small, that involved money. The president of the university, on the other hand, was in charge of educational matters, which included preparation of each year's budget. The board approved that budget in detail, line by line, and no member of the university's administrative staff was authorized to approve any expenditure not specifically covered in the itemized budget. All revisions required board approval. The bursar on campus, J. T. McCants, was the purchasing agent, cashier, and supervisor of expenditures, as well as overseer of the auxil-

iary income-producing enterprises, such as dormitories. As the institution had grown, separate accounts for its various activities and needs had been added haphazardly to the original accounting structure. The result was that one person might handle several unrelated functions, or a department's account might be carried on the books of an office that was not the most efficient for supervising that particular activity. Some accounts were carried on the books of the Rice Institute, while others were independent of the president or even of the assistant secretary to the board. For example, the business manager of athletics came directly under the authority of the board and worked through channels that excluded the president and the assistant secretary, although the latter as comptroller of the Athletic Association could review its budget. The board faced the depression with a complex financial organization that had grown ad hoc with the Institute rather than having been planned for efficient management.[1]

A Move to Reduce Expenses

By March 1932 A. B. Cohn, assistant secretary to the board, was predicting dire consequences if expenditures were not reduced. He estimated that there would be a reduction in gross income from the endowment from $723,000 to $681,000 and that that amount would not be sufficient to cover both depreciation and budget expenditures. (As with a commercial enterprise, the board had established a depreciation reserve account that either served as a building fund or added to the endowment.) Furthermore, Cohn said, the bond market, in which the Institute had invested some $4 million, was unstable. Some South American bonds had defaulted on their interest payments of $167,500, and certain other bonds were especially weak. Securities continued to depreciate in value, and defaults on loans secured by real estate meant loss of interest income as well as additional obligations for Rice in the form of taxes on foreclosed property. Estimated shrinkage in the market value of the bonds and notes amounted to $978,000, a staggering sum in those days. In light of this bleak information, chairman Baker wrote to President Lovett, calling his attention to this situation and asking him to provide a statement of the economies and reductions in expenses that might be made without impairing educational efficiency. Baker also pointed out that some of the trustees were thinking of a "substantial reduction" in the number of students admitted and of reductions both in numbers of faculty and in the salaries paid them.[2]

When the proposed budget for 1932–33 reached the board, however, it was larger than that of the previous year, which had amounted to $592,000. The new budget called for expenditures of approximately $635,000, including construction of an addition to the Field House. Faced with rising costs and declining income, the board voted unanimously in Lovett's absence at its June 24, 1932, meeting to reduce all salaries by ten percent. The board's resolution pointed to the "distressing economic conditions existing throughout the world" as the reason and expressed the hope that those affected would accept the reduction "in a spirit of hearty cooperation with the purpose sought to be accomplished."[3]

Three days later the board met again, this time with Lovett present. He offered a suggestion from some members of the faculty that married men receiving less than $3,750 annually be exempted from the reduction. The trustees did not agree to exempt any members of the faculty completely from the austerity measures but did vote a reduction for these men of only five percent. Professor Wilson had suggested to President Lovett earlier that the faculty might cooperate more willingly in measures of econ-omy if they were given a clear picture of the financial situation of the Institute; possibly for that reason, Baker wrote a letter to Lovett explaining the need for the reductions. The tone of his letter indicates that it was designed for persons other than the president; it included a statement of revenues, expenses, and net income for the past ten years, even though Lovett was well aware of this information.[4]

The amended budget reduced expenditures by almost $147,000. Swept away were any appropriations for new construction and one-third of the amount normally allocated for new equipment and furniture. The library budget was cut by one-fourth and the Athletic Department by a third. Salaries were lowered the required percentages, and some assistantships and fellowships were eliminated entirely. The trustees approved a final budget of $488,000.[5]

Because of the agreement under which he had returned to Rice from Scotland, Harold A. Wilson's salary was considered separately from other faculty compensation. The Institute had guaranteed him $8,000 a year, and the trustees believed that they could not reduce that amount by unilateral action. When approached to cooperate with them, Wilson was quite prepared to do so, though in a manner somewhat different from what the trustees might have expected. He offered to contribute ten percent of his salary to the physics department, with the understanding that his salary would be paid in full and that no change would be made in his agreement with the Institute. The trustees agreed to his proposal.[6]

To reduce costs further, the trustees also moved to decrease the number of students. The Institute had enrolled a record number of 1,461 students for the year 1931–32, including a freshman class of 485. For 1932–33 the trustees declared that the total number of new students in all categories was to be held to 400 and that the number of out-of-state students newly admitted was not to exceed 25. The board considered a tuition charge for non-Texans but did not go beyond discussion of the idea. That fall only 403 freshmen were admitted; enrollment fell to 1,372 (930 men and 442 women).[7]

Costs were a critical factor in other board decisions regarding students. First, the registration fee assessed of all students was raised in 1932 from ten dollars to twenty-five dollars. Then in 1933, when vacancies in the residential halls rose to forty percent, Dean Caldwell and bursar John T. McCants devised a remedy that the board adopted. Every male student was required to spend at least one year in residence on campus. The board felt that this arrangement would promote the students' welfare, increase a feeling of solidarity in college life, and fill the halls. Each lease on a room would run the full academic year at a cost of ninety dollars for the year; henceforth no one would be allowed to move out at midterm. This regulation was to apply to Houstonians as well as to out-of-town students,

although financial hardship would be accepted as a valid reason to postpone the period of residence. Many men had moved out of the dorms in previous years when the Hall Committee cracked down on noise, while others moved out to evade distractions from study. The new plan set up a committee, which included the dean, "for the maintenance of conditions favorable to study." To promote those conditions even more forcefully, no radios were permitted except in the seniors' dining room. Jake Hess (for whom Rice's tennis stadium is named), chairman of the committee, said that the group would be very active because members would be paid for their work with free rent, and the only cost for dorm living would be board, about a dollar a day.[8] This arrangement was an attractive inducement for men to join the committee in depression times.

Another revenue-raising idea involved the Athletic Association, the Student Association, and a variety of events and organizations lumped together as "student activities." Until 1933 the Student Association had been a voluntary organization. Students who joined paid $18 per year in support of the Student Association, the Honor Council, and the student publications; for this payment they received free admission to all Rice athletic contests in Houston, the weekly *Thresher*, and the *Campanile*. In May 1933 the student body adopted a resolution favoring compulsory membership in the Student Association and a blan-

ket tax on each student. The Student Council requested that the trustees assess and levy the tax and provide for its collection. Captain Baker had already been considering such a fee as a way to increase athletic funds, so the trustees approved the tax, to be collected beginning the following fall. The blanket tax amounted to $8.40, with the Athletic Association receiving half, the *Campanile* $2.50, and various other publications and organizations lesser amounts.[9]

Additional Revenues

Rice's financial picture looked a bit brighter when Eugene L. Bender, a retired Houston businessman, builder, and lumberman, died in 1934 and left $200,000 to the Institute. This bequest came as a pleasant surprise to the Rice trustees, since Bender had had no official connection with the school in the past, although many Rice people had stayed at the Hotel Bender. The money would not be available until the will had been probated, and as a result the Institute did not actually receive the bequest until 1938. The trustees discussed using the money for a badly needed library, since the university owned more than 120,000 volumes but had no single location for them. However, the Bender bequest was not finally used until 1947, when it was spent to construct the Science Reading Room (now the Reference Room) of the new Fondren Library.[10]

Although income continued to fluctuate and economic conditions did not improve markedly, the trustees decided in 1936, at the urging of President Lovett, that faculty salaries should be restored to their former levels. From 1933 to 1936, the budget decreased every year. In 1934 net excess revenue after depreciation had reached a low point of $16,600, but by 1936 it had climbed to over $144,000. Only a little more than $21,000 was needed to restore the predepression salaries of the grateful faculty members. The new budget for 1936–37 amounted to $454,700.

More good news came in December 1936, when trustee William M. Rice, Jr., gave 10,000 shares of stock in the Reed Roller Bit Company to the endowment fund. The stock was estimated to have a value of $330,000 and to have an annual income of $8,000 to $12,000. This gift cheered James Baker considerably. "This will certainly make it a merry Christmas for Rice," he said in a newspaper interview. "It is primarily through the generosity of such men as Mr. Rice that we are able to look forward to the school's future with a great deal of pleasure and confidence."[12]

Two years later the Rice Institute received another substantial gift. This one was estimated to be $100,000 and was part of the estate of Arthur B. Cohn. Cohn had been secretary to the founder, William M. Rice, and then assistant secretary to the board and business manager for the Institute from its establishment until 1936. (In 1936 C. A. Dwyer became assistant secretary and business manager in Cohn's place.) Although very encouraging, such gifts were not enough to allow for real expansion, and in 1938 Baker again considered a tuition charge for out-of-state students. Once more, nothing came of the proposal.[13]

Changes in the Faculty

As there were some changes in membership on the board during the thirties, there were also changes in the administration and faculty. Dean Robert G. Caldwell left in 1933 to become ambassador to Portugal under President Franklin D. Roosevelt. At first Lee M. Sharrar, who had been instructor of economics and Caldwell's right-hand man, was made acting dean; but before classes started that fall President Lovett appointed Harry B. Weiser to be dean of the Institute. Weiser, a professor of chemistry, had been on the faculty since 1915 and was known for his work with colloids. Believing that "youngsters are inherently reasonable," Weiser anticipated few problems that could not be resolved through a better understanding of the students and their difficulties. In 1931 Sara Stratford, adviser to women from 1914 to 1931, died; her daughter, Mary Jane Torrens, class of 1918, took her place but stayed only through the spring and summer. In October 1931 Sarah Lane '19, assistant librarian, was named to the post, somewhat to her surprise. The

97. *Sarah Lane '19 was assistant librarian of the Institute and became the second adviser to women in 1931.*

administration operated as it always had, however; the new members made no significant changes.[14]

In fact, from the faculty point of view the Institute must have been rather quiet during the 1930s. Promotions were almost nonexistent, since there was little or no money for salary raises; some men remained assistant professors for years. For several faculty members, "the spirit of the whole institution was one of hand, Harold Wilson complained to Lovett about the infrequency of faculty meetings, which were being held only once a year to vote on candidates for graduation. He thought it might be desirable to hold four or five meetings a year and for Lovett to make some statement at the meetings about policy, future prospects, and the Institute's finances. "This is done in other universities," he wrote, "and I believe it is valuable because it promotes the idea among members of the faculty that they are a permanent part of the institution and that their cooperation in all matters pertaining to its welfare is regarded as of value. In many universities new schemes of organization, teaching, and athletics are being tried out and such matters might well be considered here. It seems desirable to do something to wake the place up a bit." His suggestions, however, do not seem to have been adopted.[15]

When salary cuts were announced in 1932, the news awakened the faculty, but not quite as Wilson had envisioned. It seems that no one except the department heads had known what any other faculty member made; when somehow the facts leaked out, some professors were upset at the inequities in compensation. It was rumored that the salary cut had convinced Griffith C. Evans, head of the mathematics department, to resign, because he thought the reduction showed that the board was not interested in building a university. In 1933 Evans accepted an offer from the University of California, Berke-

ley. Berkeley had been wooing Evans for years, as had Harvard and a number of other notable institutions, but he had remained at Rice. Whatever the real reason for Evans's departure in 1933, his leaving was a blow to the department. It was not until 1938 that Hubert Bray was promoted to professor and formally named chairman of the department, although he was in charge de facto from the time Evans left.[16]

Although some of the trustees wanted to reduce the number of faculty members as well as their salaries, President Lovett tried to keep as many people as he could. In 1934, however, he had to inform four instructors that their appointments would not be renewed because of the financial situation. Frederic W. Browne and Charles L. Browne, eight- and fourteen-year veteran teachers of architecture, along with Charles H. Dix, a five-year member of the mathematics faculty, and Joseph R. Shannon, a recent temporary appointment in economics, left the Institute that summer. For various reasons—other offers, the need for more money—some others left as well, so that the number of faculty members dropped from seventy-three in 1930 to sixty-five in 1934 to fifty-eight in 1938. After that the number climbed to sixty-four in 1940. In 1935 Rice lost another revered member of its faculty, but not for financial reasons. Much-loved English professor Stockton Axson died at the age of sixty-eight after a long illness.[17]

In spite of the depression, there were some additions to the fac-

ulty during the 1930s. Some of the new men had been hired before the salary cut, some replaced those who left, and a few came late in the decade specifically in response to the increased numbers of students who enrolled in engineering and because of increased accrediting requirements in that field. Among those who made their first appearance on the Institute faculty during the 1930s were Tom Bonner (for whom Bonner Nuclear Lab is named) in physics, Floyd E. Ulrich in math, George Holmes Richter in chemistry, Carl R. Wischmeyer in electrical engineering, Stayton Nunn in architecture, J. D. Thomas and Carroll Camden in English, Lynn M. Case and David M. Potter in history, and Joseph L. Battista in Spanish. Joseph I. Davies, who had been in the biology laboratory at Rice almost since the opening, received his Ph.D. in 1937 and in 1940 became an instructor in biology, beginning a legendary twenty-five-year career as one of the Institute's most flamboyant lecturers and inspiring teachers.

The Question of Tenure

Nonrenewal of appointments inevitably introduced the question of academic tenure. Since the founding of the university, no faculty member had been employed for any definite time longer than a year, except head football coaches like John W. Heisman, who had a five-year contract, and the two Englishmen Daniell and Huxley, who had been given three-year contracts early in the history of the Institute. In the absence of a formal system, faculty members seem to have assumed that as long as they did their jobs, their appointments would be continued. The custom followed at most institutions of higher learning was that the appointment of a full professor continued for life if the length of employment was not specifically stated, or for as long as the professor wished to remain at the institution and was competent to discharge his professional duties. This practice did not apply to assistant professors or instructors. A tacit assumption of tenure for full professors did not, however, appeal to the trustees, since it limited their freedom of action in reducing the number of faculty members, especially at the upper levels.

Aware of a difference of opinion regarding tenure, President Lovett wrote to several colleges and universities around the country in 1935 asking about their policies on the issue. Whatever their responses may have been, the trustees did not immediately state a formal position, probably because financial pressure had eased and they were able to restore salaries and allay anxieties concerning reductions in teaching staff. It was 1942 before the bylaws of the Institute's board were amended to state that all officers, faculty members, and employees were to be regarded as receiving annual appointments; no one was to be employed for a

period longer than twelve months without express authority from the board. It appears that no formal review procedure was established and that reappointment was usually automatic; nonetheless, the board had the express power to remove even full professors.[18]

Because members of the faculty met as a group so seldom and were not encouraged to discuss the university's situation when they did meet, curricular changes were few in the 1930s. The Department of Physical Education survived its five-year trial period and was continued; seventeen Bachelor of Science degrees in physical education were awarded at the 1933 commencement. In 1934 Dean Weiser raised the possibility of requiring a nineteen- or twenty-course schedule for the B.A. general curriculum instead of the eighteen-course schedule then required. Most 300- and 400-level courses seemed to require no more work than the average 100- and 200-level courses; and since there was a shortage of genuine "advanced" courses, Weiser thought it advisable to require another course from juniors and possibly from seniors. The policy was not changed, however, and it appears that the faculty never formally considered it. An innovation was added to the English requirements in 1937: a spelling test, which students had to pass in order to graduate.[19]

Some Memorable Professors

All was not gloom on campus in the 1930s, of course. Professors continued to have their idiosyncrasies. Edgar H. Altenburg liked to be greeted with applause when he appeared in "Bugs 100"; but during a snowfall in 1932, it was snowballs, not applause, that opened—and quickly closed—the class. During that same snowfall, John Slaughter postponed a scheduled sociology examination. He declared that he would not be coerced but that a student committee's kind request for cancellation, combined with the coldness of the amphitheater (doubtless because of snow left from the earlier bombardment in biology class), had convinced him to reschedule the exam for the following Monday.

Teachers continued to take roll before each class, although few resorted to opera glasses to read the numbers on the seats at the back of the physics amphitheater, as Claude Heaps did. L. V. Uhrig, civil engineering instructor, developed his own teaching device. In September he would give classes that had returned in a continuing subject the same examination that they had taken the previous June; some grades were rather embarrassing.

Frank Pattie employed a teaching practice that discomfited many students. His psychology class never knew when to expect true-false examinations. Seemingly designed to weed out those who thought that his class would be a snap, the questions were hypothetical, convoluted, and "strange." According to one victim, coins could be heard dropping throughout the amphitheater as students employed a time-honored method for decision in the face of ignorance. Pattie's demonstrations of the uses and art of hypnotism, however, made putting up with the exams worthwhile. The professor's admonitions of the dangers inherent in amateur experimentation seem to have been heeded; in one graphic exhibition of hypnotic suggestion for violence, the hypnotized person actually hit someone. In spite of the demonstrations, there were those who scoffed at hypnotism and spoke of the dubious value of this "so-called science."[20]

In 1934 a prominent Galvestonian complained to the island's League of Women Voters that their scheduled speaker, Rice's Radoslav Tsanoff, would be speaking "just plain communism, pure and simple." The philosophy professor laughed and declined to make a statement, saying only, "If anybody presumes to know the contents of an address not delivered, he is entitled to his opinion." The times had changed since Lyford Edwards had given his lecture in 1918, but the potential for another such affair arose when Heinrich Meyer of the German department wrote a letter to the *Houston Press* in 1938 defending recent German actions on the Continent. One reader objected privately to the board and the president, but no public issue

was made of the matter or of Meyer's views. That would come later.[21]

More Visiting Lecturers

As in earlier years, the Institute continued to bring prominent scholars to campus to speak. The 1930s saw such well-known figures as the mathematician and physicist T. Levi-Civita from the University of Rome, Samuel Eliot Morison, the prominent historian from Harvard, biologist Julian Huxley (then at the Royal Institute in London), and Carlos Delgado de Carvalho, a professor of sociology at the Colegio Pedro II in Rio de Janeiro and visiting Carnegie Professor at the Institute under the auspices of the Carnegie Endowment for International Peace. George Lyman Kittredge, internationally known as a leading authority on Chaucer, the English ballads, and Shakespeare, came after his retirement from Harvard to lecture and to visit his former student, Rice English professor Alan McKillop. McKillop told his students that Kittredge did not have a Ph.D. degree. After all, who was qualified to examine him?

The French Mission Nationale Française Cavalier de la Salle came to Houston in 1937 for the 250th anniversary of explorer La Salle's death in Texas. The members of the mission were René Maurier, Mme St. René Taillandier, Prince Achille Murat, Marcelle Tinagre, and Fortunat Strowski.

In 1938 James W. Rockwell founded the Rockwell lectureship in memory of his father, James M. Rockwell, a Houston lumberman. These lectures on religious subjects were inaugurated by Sir Robert Falconer, the former president of the University of Toronto.[22] They continue today.

Only a Few Building Projects

Straitened economic circumstances in the thirties meant that there was little construction on campus during that decade. There were additions to the Field House and new football stands at the stadium, but the only other large construction project was for scientific research. In 1937 Rice physicists began building a 2.5-million-volt atom bombardment machine to study the nucleus of the atom. The frame building constructed to house it had a heavy concrete floor and a concrete wall twelve inches thick to separate operators from the machine.[23]

One other construction project was completed during the decade. When William M. Rice, the founder, died, his remains had been cremated and the ashes kept in the trustees' vault. In 1922 a committee consisting of President Lovett, William M. Rice, Jr., and Benjamin B. Rice began to formulate plans for disposition of the ashes. This group of men decided on a monument to be situated in the middle of the academic quadrangle. The ashes would be placed in the monu-

98. *Unveiling of the statue of the founder, William Marsh Rice, June 8, 1930. Ralph Adams Cram, the commencement speaker that year, attended the unveiling* (right, with his hands in front of him).

ment, and above it would be a statue of the founder. To sculpt the likeness of William Marsh Rice, the board chose John Angel, a well-known artist. On May 22, 1930, in a fitting ceremony, the ashes, a certified copy of the certificate of cremation, and a statement that Rice was born in Massachusetts and had died at the age of eighty-four years, six months, and nine days were interred in the pedestal of the monument.[24]

Seldom is a statue installed on a college campus for long before it receives some indignity, and the founder's statue was no exception. Hazing had returned to the Rice campus by 1932—if indeed it had ever been missing—and the sophomores sent some freshmen out to "clean and shave" the statue. The Houston newspapers reported the story of the prank, whereupon a member of the Rice family took offense at what he called the disrespect shown the "tomb." The sophomores, the *Thresher*, and others denied knowing that the monument contained the founder's ashes, because there had been no publicity of the fact; in the furor that followed, sophomore president James II. Scott resigned his office. (Roberta Woods, vice-president of the class, assumed the office when Scott vacated it and became the first female class president in Institute history.) Being known as a tomb or not, the statue has not escaped the attention of other pranksters. Over the years, it has been subjected to innumerable paintings (by Aggies and others) and has sported Halloween pumpkins on its head and itinerant neckties around its neck.[25]

Hazing and Other Student Activities

Nor did hazing come to a halt because of this incident. Dean Weiser was inclined to permit the milder forms of hazing, which consisted of the traditional mothball race, painted freshmen, and slime-drawn water-cart rides. Slimes and "slimesses" had to wear certain costumes, including a beanie for everyone, a green tie and red suspenders for the men, and a pinafore for the women; and all freshmen had to follow certain rules about walking on the grass and showing proper respect for upperclassmen. The Slime Parade culminated downtown in the usual pep rally at the intersection of Main Street and Texas Avenue. Despite the no-hazing pledge and warnings by the dean, however, certain out-

lawed forms of the practice also continued. Broomings, Bayou 100 (tossing freshmen into the "Blue Danube"), Forestry 100, and the like went on as before, although with a little more circumspection. A freshman's broken ankle in 1939 caused the dean to reconsider the situation, and in 1940 Weiser banned hazing again. The Slime Parade was allowed to continue but without paint or pajamas, signs or costumes. The ban remained in effect through 1941; when World War II began almost all the men on campus either had been drafted or had joined the Naval ROTC, and hazing came to a halt for the duration.[26]

Hazing was not all that kept students busy in the 1930s; in fact, it was only a small part of life on campus. On the academic side, two national honor societies joined the already established chapters of Phi Beta Kappa and Phi Lambda Upsilon. In 1930 Pi Delta Phi, the honorary society for students of French, approved a chapter for Rice, and in 1938 a chapter of Tau Beta Pi was established for engineers. The engineers had had to operate their own organization (the Rice Engineophyte Society) for two years before the national Tau Beta Pi association granted them a charter.[27]

Extracurricular activities were numerous. The May Fete was still a popular spring occasion, but it erupted into controversy in 1933. Up to that time, only women had voted in the elections for queen and members of the court, and the literary so-

cieties had virtually controlled the outcome by bloc voting. A number of independents—women without literary affiliations—challenged the societies in the election of 1933 and elected about half the court. In the heat of the campaign, there was much rhetoric about the evil of exclusive clubs and the need for democracy. The *Houston Chronicle* even entered the fray with an editorial deploring the factionalism on campus. The result seems to have been that men were also allowed to vote for the May Fete court; after another challenge by independents in the class elections that year, the campus calmed down for a while.

In 1936 the May Fete again became the object of controversy when the queen elected was Bowe Davis Hewitt, a married woman who refused to resign her position on the grounds that the eligibility rules did not preclude married women. The Women's Council, in charge of the event, changed the rules for the next year. In 1940 a male student, J. P. Miller, ran for May Fete queen, stating that he was in the race because he was tired of having women invade all branches of business and competing with men. This time the rule that the queen must be a senior woman was in effect, and the Women's Council could reject Miller's nomination automatically. Contests between literary societies and independents continued at the polls, however, into the 1940s.[28]

Nineteen thirty-three must have been a vintage year for up-

99. *King Jim Nance crowning Mildred O'Riordan queen of the 1938 May Fete before an assembled court of class attendants.*

roars, for that fall the Dramatic Club precipitated another one. It chose the melodrama *Uncle Tom's Cabin* as its autumn production. In indignation, the local chapter of the United Daughters of the Confederacy protested vigorously against the production of a play that they labeled as "unfair to the South." The United Confederate Veterans joined in the protest, and after considerable publicity, the Dramatic Club decided to change its presentation to *Rose of the Southland, or, the Spirit of Robert E. Lee.*[29]

Aside from financial matters, the Institute seems to have changed little for students of the 1930s as compared to those of the 1920s. To be sure, there were a few differences. In 1937 Jean Miriam Slater '38 became the first woman to hold the chair of the Honor Council. In 1938 a larger cooperative store for books and supplies opened on the site of the old one, the third floor of the Administration Building. In 1937, after fourteen years of service, Lee Chatham resigned as director of the Institute band to devote more time to his business enterprises. Kit Reid '37, well known for his trumpet playing, took over Chatham's duties. Lee's Owls, the usual band for Saturday night dances, had relinquished their place to Pat Quinn's Rice Owls Orchestra in 1932. Jimmie Scott took over from Quinn, and Reid's Night (sometimes spelled Knight) Owls followed Scott. In 1939, after more than seventeen years of publication, *The Rice Owl*, campus humor magazine, merged with the *Rice Alumni News*. The new magazine was to include factual articles and alumni news as well as humorous pieces; the old *Owl* had come under attack several times for its "low literary standards." When the editor of the *Thresher* complained about the lack of school spirit in 1938, a student answered that undergraduates had become more serious than they were in the late 1920s. There were still the literary society functions, Saturday night dances, engineering labs, interminable bridge and poker games, student elections, cloister courses, and the inveterate Rice booster, gardener Tony Martino.[30]

Sometimes it appeared that the school administration worked hard to keep Rice from changing. From the opening in 1912, Rice students had always "dressed" to come to school, partly because people dressed more formally in general and partly because students had traditionally accepted the aura of gentility that was encouraged by President Lovett and many senior faculty members. In April 1936 sophomore William Josiah Goode showed up on campus in Bermuda shorts after the dean had already frowned on such apparel; a committee composed of Dean Weiser, bursar McCants, and registrar McCann told him that he would be allowed to finish the term but would not be readmitted in the fall. According to historian Andrew Forest Muir's account, the technical charge was insubordination; but Goode claimed that he had misunderstood the first warning. Weiser objected to the shorts, Goode said, because Rice wanted no new fads on campus.

Neither, it seemed, did it want a female cheerleader. When 1,000 of the 1,300 students signed a petition for one in 1939, the dean said that the odds were a thousand to one against the president's granting the request. Rice would not in fact have a woman as cheerleader until 1946.[31]

Athletics—The Golden Age

But even without a female yell leader and after a slow start, Rice athletic teams did well in the 1930s. Jack Meagher's football team had improved in 1932 so much that the conference championship was not out of reach for the next season. During February examinations in 1933, however, eight members of the varsity were suspended for violations of the Honor Code and thus were ineligible for the 1933 season. That fall the Owls won three games, lost eight, and placed last in the conference. In December the board and the Committee on Outdoor Sports reorganized the Athletic Department and released Meagher. In his place as both football and basketball head coach, they named Jimmy Kitts, who had been Rice's basketball coach for a year. Dr. H. O. Nicholas, who had been an instructor in chemistry, was made director of athletics, and Dr. Gaylord Johnson continued as business manager. It appears that Nicholas had very little to do with running the department and that Johnson continued to handle athletic matters just as he had since Heisman's tenure as coach. At the same time, Ernie Hjertberg, the coach for track, resigned, charging that the Committee on Outdoor Sports did not support his athletes the way it did the football and basketball teams.[32]

Hiring Kitts had been Johnson's idea. Johnson was responsible for arranging support, publicity, and direction for much of the Rice athletic program; in fact, without him the Institute's intercollegiate athletic efforts in the thirties would probably have been few and half-hearted. President Lovett wanted the students to have some athletic activities. However, he was not accustomed to the fact that collegiate athletics had become a business and did not see the links that could be forged between campus and town supporters. Accordingly, he was content to let the Committee on Outdoor Sports and the athletics business manager run the program. McCants had replaced Watkin as chairman of the committee, and to be sure, the bursar knew what was going on. For day-to-day matters as well as

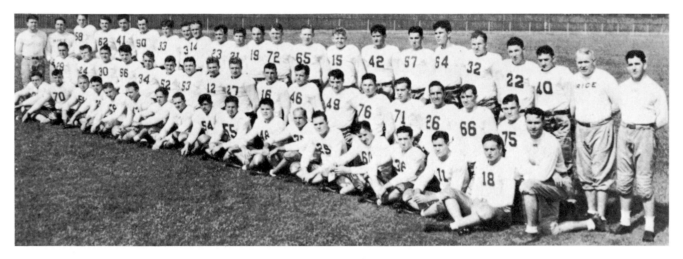

100. *Rice's 1937–38 Southwest Conference champion football team.*

larger concerns, though, Johnson was in charge. Johnson wanted to hire a high school coach with a good reputation. He reasoned that every high school coach believed he could coach successfully in college, if he were only given the opportunity. Johnson also thought that every other high school coach would send his best boys to that coach just to prove the first premise. So Rice hired Kitts from the Athens, Texas, high school as basketball coach in 1933, then made him football coach as well in 1934.[33]

With the suspended players back in action, Kitts's first season was a triumph. Rice boasted four All-Conference players that year: Leche Sylvester, Ralph Miller, and All-Americans Bill Wallace and John McCauley. At the Baylor game, which clinched the conference championship, President Lovett came to the locker room before the game to exhort the team to victory. John McCauley had left one of his shoes

behind, and Lovett used the opportunity to tell the story of Jason from Greek mythology, who was also missing a shoe at the beginning of his adventure. It is said that in the middle of the president's talk, one of the ends, Frank Steen, turned to captain Percy Arthur and asked, "Captain, who in the hell did Jason play for?"[34]

Rice won the Southwest Conference championship under Kitts in 1934 and again in 1937. In 1938 the Owls played their first Cotton Bowl game, beating Colorado 28–14. This game was the second played under the designation "the Cotton Bowl," which was at that time a private enterprise run by Dallas businessman J. Curtis Sanford. In that same year the conference contracted to play in the bowl game for three years. A group known as the Custodian Committee of the Cotton Bowl Game took it over in 1940, and that fall the conference faculty represen-

tatives approved the creation of the Cotton Bowl Athletic Association as an agency of the conference. Some have suggested that there was some opposition in conference schools to such an endeavor, but that through the combined efforts of Rice's Gaylord Johnson, James Stewart (director of the State Fair), and Dan Rogers of Texas Christian University, the opposition was overcome.[35]

With the addition of Eddie Dyer and Emmett Brunson (former Rice stars) to the coaching staff, and with the support of booster clubs made up of all sorts of Houstonians, the Rice athletic program took off. Johnson, Nicholas, the Committee on Outdoor Sports, and the coaches all worked for a balanced program, and the Institute reaped the rewards. Even with mediocre football teams, Rice beat Texas from 1934 to 1938. Kitts's 1935 basketball team tied for first place in the conference with Arkansas and

101. *A moment from a basketball game in 1935, the year when the Owls tied with two other universities for the conference championship.*

102. *E. Y. Steakley, a star from the 1938 track team, nosing out a victory.*

Southern Methodist. Buster Brannon, who was hired in 1939, coached the 1940 team to another championship with stars Frank Carswell and Bob Kinney. In track Brunson coached Fred Wolcott, the first man to hold world records for both high and low 220-yard hurdles. But that was not all. Brunson also coached Calvin Bell, Paul Sanders, Robert Fowler, and Joe Blagg to help win the conference in 1938 and 1939. After Jake and Wilbur Hess won tennis honors in the early thirties, Frank Guernsey and Dick Morris starred in 1938 and 1939. Golf was not left out, as the 1939 team of Ed Letscher, Harry Chrismann, Joe Finger, and Ed Seaman also won the conference championship. Veteran sportswriter Clark Nealon rightly calls the 1930s Rice's "golden era of athletics."[36]

It was clear by 1937 that, with strong community support for Rice teams, especially in football, the Rice Institute badly needed a new athletic stadium. The old bleachers held nine or ten thousand spectators, but thousands more wanted to come to the games. Because of the grim financial conditions, the trustees could not justify any construction out of Institute funds. When the alumni association, the R Association (made up of Rice lettermen), Gaylord Johnson, and J. T. McCants proposed that the old stadium be renovated, the trustees were perfectly willing to give the group a chance to raise money outside the campus, with the provision, of course, that the improved stadium remain the

103. *The 1938 tennis team.* Left to right: *Frank Guernsey, Joe Lucia, Ebbie Holden, Max Campbell. Guernsey was the outstanding player in the Southwest Conference.*

property of the Institute and under the direct control of the trustees. The money was raised, including $15,000 that the board donated from proceeds of the 1938 Cotton Bowl game; William Ward Watkin drew up plans, and the rehabilitated stadium soon held 30,000 screaming football fans.[37]

After a disappointing season in 1938 and a disastrous one in 1939, Jimmy Kitts was dismissed by the Committee on Outdoor Sports. In his place the board hired Jess Claiborne Neely, who had been coaching at Clemson Agricultural College. In Neely's first season, the Owls tied for third in the conference with the University of Texas (defeating Texas 13–0), and in 1941 they fell to fourth. Neely barely had time to build a team before World War II disrupted everyone's plans.[38]

The Distant Thunder of World Events

Rice was still its own little island during the 1930s. Only occasionally did the outside world seem to make any impression on the campus beyond student discussions in the dormitories or Autry House. Students writing in the *Thresher* made few comments about the depression or politics until the middle thirties, and then only in response to specific events. In 1935 a poll taken by the *Literary Digest* and the Association of College Editors revealed that Rice students opposed the League of Nations and wanted to stay out of war if one came, but that they favored universal conscription in time of war, along with government control of munitions and fighting if the United States were invaded.

In spring 1936 a satirical move-

ment begun at Princeton and calling itself the "Veterans of Future Wars" came to campus. Rice students who proclaimed themselves members of the organization called for their "1965 bonuses" to be paid immediately. At a rowdy meeting they elected officers, including lobbyists to represent the Rice chapter in Washington. Antagonistic students pelted the "future vets" with mud balls and interrupted them with catcalls. Although some genuine veterans' groups protested the existence of such an organization, Dean Weiser said he thought the protest movement was a farce; he took no action against the satirical group. After the rally, it appears that the students simply went back to their books or card games.[39]

When events brought Europe to the brink of war in 1939, the *Thresher* began to publish more

104. *The 1939 golf team. Ed Letscher and Joe Finger (lettermen) were co-captains.*

articles about the world outside the hedges. The actual declaration of war by Great Britain against Germany in September moved President Lovett in his matriculation address to call for strict observance of neutrality by the students; he urged them to "resolve to go forward with the business that brings you here as though there were no war, and thereby become better equipped to serve the country with all your might in peace and, if you must,

in war." Rice had its first casualty that September. Kurt von Johnson had been a student from 1929 until 1931, when his family moved back to their German homeland. Von Johnson became a lieutenant in the German army and died in the invasion of Poland.

In October 1939 the dean moved to abolish a new organization on campus, the Rice Progressive Party. The purpose of the party was to increase political in-

terest on campus, although the dean did not object to that. His reservations concerned other parties that might be organized in opposition and whether the party would remain true to its original purpose. Weiser thought that the best interests of the Institute would not be served through such organizations.[40]

By the end of the decade, the distant thunder of world events was moving ever closer to America and to the Rice Institute.

CHAPTER 7

A Decade of Change: The 1940s

The declaration of war against Japan and Germany by the United States had little immediate effect on the Rice campus. Seniors did not enlist in large numbers in December 1941, unlike their counterparts in April 1917; in fact, the *Thresher* advised students to stay in school and finish the year. Neither did the university administration try to make any schedule changes for the spring of 1942. In May 1941 the Navy had established an ROTC unit at Rice, and in September 107 freshmen and sophomores had been accepted into the voluntary program.[1] As a result, there was no need to impose a military structure on the entire campus, as the administration had done in 1917.

War Affects the Campus

In February 1942 the faculty proposed and the board accepted a plan to help seniors graduate be-fore entering the service. The academic year for engineers and architects would conclude early, and the date for commencement exercises was moved forward. For the school year 1942–43, senior classes in engineering and architecture were accelerated to finish by April 3, 1943. In addition, all students who held senior standing by the end of the spring term in 1942 were allowed to take two courses at approved summer schools, add one extra course to the regular senior schedule in the fall at Rice, and complete their graduation requirements in February 1943. Predental, prelaw, and premedical students who left to pursue professional degrees after their third year received bachelor's degrees from Rice after their professional graduation. Schedules for all other students remained the same as in previous years.[2]

To keep open the colleges and universities of the United States that would supply the military with officers and trained special-ists, the Army and Navy specified that some colleges have training programs that would be separate from their ROTC units. Some schools, like Rice, taught naval engineers; others, such as Texas A&M and Texas Technological College, taught army engineers and aviation cadets. Under these programs, men were picked by a branch of service and assigned to a campus for training. While in training, they were on active duty: they received pay, remained in uniform, and were governed by general military discipline. President Lovett was notified in March 1943 that Rice had been selected for the program; he was instructed to prepare for 530 trainees (342 engineering students designated "V-12" and 188 ROTC students).[3]

Although the Navy did not take over the school—the total student body remained about half civilian—at times it looked as if the sailors had. Navy men outnumbered civilian men by about two to one, and no civilian men were housed on campus. The residential halls were renovated and repaired, and two new classrooms for the Navy were constructed over the machine shop. Rice also went on the Navy's schedule, continuing classes year-round. The Navy prescribed the curriculum and general course outlines for its officer training and engineering courses and also set the calendar to consist of three sixteen-week terms beginning in July, November, and March. Under this accelerated schedule, commencement exercises were held at the end of each two-term segment beginning in February 1944 and lasting until March 1946. The thirty-third commencement in June 1946 put the Institute back on its normal prewar academic calendar.[4]

Navy men had to follow a military routine that included reveille at 6:00 A.M., drill, specified study time from 7:30 to 10:00 P.M., and taps at 10:30. However, they could also participate in any extracurricular activities that did not interfere with their courses or duties. They joined clubs, went to parties, played on both intramural and varsity teams, took part in the air-raid and blackout drills, and behaved pretty much as other Rice students did. Some of the V-12 men, however, were unprepared for college work, and their grades suffered. Six weeks after the start of the program, Wednesday night liberty was canceled, and the Second Battalion was ordered to remain on campus to work on their studies. The V-12 students were also handicapped in their gradua-

tion credits. The Navy sent them to Rice for six to eight terms, after which they went to Reserve Midshipmen's School or to another assignment, but without the full number of credits needed to meet Rice's graduation requirements. Dean G. H. Richter remembers that some of these men disliked the Institute while they were there and swore they would never come back; yet many did return after the war to earn their degrees.[5]

Although the campus was relatively quiet during the war, an off-campus incident resulted in the termination of an instructor's appointment. Heinrich K. E. M. Meyer, an instructor in German who had verbally defended his native Germany five years before, was found guilty in federal court of securing his United States citizenship by fraud. The court canceled his naturalization certificate in February 1943, and that same month the trustees released him from the faculty. Although the Fifth Circuit Court of Appeals reinstated Meyer's citizenship, he did not return to the Institute.[6]

With the cessation of hostilities, the Navy program in schools with only V-12 units came to a halt in November 1945. In those schools that had both V-12 and Naval ROTC units, as Rice did, the program continued until July 1946. At Rice twenty-one seniors who were still in the program received Bachelor of Science degrees in naval science in the June graduation ceremonies. The Naval ROTC program continued on a

peacetime basis thereafter at the Institute and was joined by a unit of the Army ROTC in the fall of 1951.[7]

Important Changes During the War Years

World War II was not the only momentous event that affected the Institute in the early 1940s. In April 1941 Captain James Baker asked two of his firm's lawyers to determine what legal proceedings would be necessary to permit the charging of tuition. Baker continued to be troubled by the school's financial situation, and when the alumni fund drive and appeals to Houstonians for support brought in only a small amount, the board chairman saw little chance of increasing income enough to cover ever-rising expenses without the relief that tuition might provide. His lawyers thought the court would permit tuition charges once the Institute had clearly demonstrated that the general object of the trust would be greatly hampered and in part defeated unless the change was made. Baker presented his firm's opinion to the board, recommending that the trustees test the question of tuition in court. The board in turn authorized him to proceed with the matter and notify them in advance of the filing of the suit. However, the suit was not filed because of subsequent events.[8]

May 1941 marked the fiftieth anniversary of the founding of the corporation, the William M. Rice Institute for the Advancement of Literature, Science and Art. The board held a special meeting on April 23 to vote to seek renewal of the charter, as was necessary under Texas law. The resolution to extend the charter for another fifty years was unanimously adopted and filed with the Secretary of State.[9]

On May 14, 1941, Edgar Odell Lovett resigned the presidency of the Rice Institute. Citing his age (seventy) as his reason, he asked to be relieved of the duties of the office that he had held since 1907, but he also offered to carry on until a successor could be found. He wished to retain his membership on the board. The trustees reluctantly accepted Lovett's resignation but were happy that he would stay until his successor assumed office. When the new president took over, Lovett would become president emeritus; of course he would continue as a trustee. Dr. Lovett and the board probably thought it would take a year or two to find a new president. Instead, it was to take five.[10]

On August 1, 1941, the man whom William Marsh Rice had designated chairman of the Board of Trustees, the only chairman the Institute had had, Captain James A. Baker, died at the age of eighty-five. He left his home, "The Oaks," to Rice for the trustees to use as they saw fit. If it was sold, the proceeds from the sale were to constitute a gift known as the "James A. Baker and Alice Graham Baker Bequest," to be used for scholarships and fellowships, prizes, or supplements to professors' sal-

aries. In 1942 the trustees chose to sell the home to the M. D. Anderson Foundation for $62,000 and establish four scholarships for undergraduates.[11]

One event, at least, ameliorated the financial situation. That fall, oil was discovered on the Rice lands in Louisiana that were part of the original endowment.[12]

Postwar Changes

In September 1946 the Rice Institute opened its doors on a purely civilian basis again, but it was not the old Institute of prewar days. Some extremely important changes had occurred at the highest levels, and more were to take place on the student level.

Changes began with the Board of Trustees. When Captain Baker died in 1941, William M. Rice, Jr., was elected chairman of the board. However, the trustees did not immediately name a successor to Baker's place. When they did not, the alumni association seized the opportunity to lobby for a Rice alumnus as trustee, an idea popular among the alumni since at least 1938. In that year the association president, I. M. Wilford, had sent the trustees an association resolution calling for alumni representation on the board. Baker, who confused the Association of Rice Alumni with the R Association in his letter, replied that the number of trustees was fixed, and since there no vacancies, the board was deferring further consideration on the request. He added, however, that the trust-

ees would be happy to confer with any committee that the alumni might form to discuss matters pertaining to "Public Relations, Athletics, or some kindred subject."[13]

In 1940 the Public Relations Committee of the alumni association met with the board. Consisting of the new association president Harvin C. Moore along with members J. Newton Rayzor, F. Fisher Reynolds, Carl M. Knapp, John Schuhmacher, and Henry Oliver, the committee requested again that the board seriously consider selecting an alumnus for the next vacant position. According to the board minutes, Baker stated "that it was his opinion, that should a vacancy occur on the Board, that the Trustees would be pleased to discuss with the Committee the selection of a new member of the Board, . . . that the Trustees and the Committee were working wholeheartedly in the interest of the Institute, and the Trustees will always be happy at all times to confer with the Committee in respect to all matters affecting the Institute." The minutes for the meeting ended with a statement of harmony and satisfaction in every particular, but appearances were deceiving. Trustee A. S. Cleveland later told his son-in-law, William A. Kirkland, that Baker was angry about such alumni "interference" in board affairs.[14]

By 1942, with the vacant board position still unfilled, the alumni association did not wait to be asked for advice. Its Executive Board, still under Moore's presidency, sent the trustees another resolution urging that an alumnus be selected for the position. They accompanied the resolution with a list of six candidates. Whether or not the trustees considered the alumni candidates is unknown, but in May they elected oilman Harry Clay Hanszen, who had attended the University of Chicago for two years.[15]

That year the board made its first venture into the oil business outside of the inherited Rice land in Louisiana. County Judge Roy Hofheinz, a Rice alumnus, had in his court the disposition of the estate of the late W. R. Davis. Davis's estate included half of the working interest in oil properties and other leases in the Rincon field in Starr County, Texas. Because of indebtedness amounting to approximately $5 million and the fifty percent tax on corporate profits, no corporation, including the Continental Oil Company (which owned the other half interest and operated the field), could afford to purchase the estate. The other lease properties comprised the Valley Pipe Line Company (which owned half of the pipeline), the Rincon Pipe Line Company, and half of the Brownsville Terminal.

Endeavoring to settle the estate, the judge sought a purchaser who would be exempt from the corporate tax. He decided that the Rice Institute would benefit best from ownership of the oil properties. He then approached George R. Brown of Brown & Root, who was a Rice alumnus, and Harry C. Wiess, one of the organizers of the Humble Oil

Company, to go before the Rice board with him and propose that the Institute purchase the properties. The first scheme of purchase called for a cash outlay of $547,000 by friends of Rice who would then give the properties, subject to the remaining indebtedness, to the Institute. The trustees, on advice of counsel, decided that such a plan would be acceptable under the charter, but the banks to whom the debts were owed insisted on a minimum of $1 million in cash before they would agree to such a purchase.

Everyone connected with the deal was confident of raising the first half million; they had planned to do that anyway. The other half million, however, would be more difficult. It would have to come from the Institute itself, even though its charter stated that the trustees were "expressly forbidden ever to permit any lien, encumbrance, debt or mortgage to be placed upon any of the property, or funds, belonging now, or that may hereafter belong to the said Institute; . . . that the entire property of the Institute shall always be kept free from debt."[16] The trustees nevertheless voted to make the investment in the oil field and supply the half million needed. So that no question could be raised about the propriety of their action, a suit was brought in district court against the attorney general for authorization of the investment. The court empowered the trustees to make the purchase with donated money and the Institute's funds and further autho-

rized them to make investments of a like kind and character in the future. The trustees could thereby diversify the Institute's investments, no longer limited to those types of first mortgage loans and bonds that had characterized the cautious investments of the Baker board. In addition, the court allowed the trustees to add to the endowment or treat as income the net proceeds from the Rincon investment.

Rice ultimately purchased 29/64 of the Davis interest in the Rincon field. Of the donations from friends of Rice, $200,000 was donated by Mr. and Mrs. George R. Brown, Mr. and Mrs. Herman Brown, Mr. and Mrs. W. S. Farish, Mr. and Mrs. S. P. Farish, Mr. and Mrs. Hugh R. Cullen, Mr. and Mrs. H. C. Wiess, and Mr. Harry C. Hanszen. The remaining $300,000 came from the M. D. Anderson Foundation with the understanding that the Institute would, with the profits from the investment, construct a library or other building in memory of Mr. Anderson (one of the four original partners in Anderson, Clayton), as soon as sufficient net oil revenues had been collected. The Rincon investment turned out to be extremely profitable. Debts owed to the banks were paid from profits by 1946, and by 1978 the Institute was some $35 million richer.[17]

In October 1942, while the board was still working on the Rincon purchase, trustee Robert Lee Blaffer died. To take his place, the board elected George R. Brown in January 1943. Brown

105. *The signing ceremony marking Rice's purchase of interest in the Rincon Oil Field, December 18, 1942.* Standing, left to right: *A. S. Cleveland, Tom Davis, C. A. Dwyer, Palmer Hutcheson, John Freeman, James E. Elkins, County Judge Roy Hofheinz, A. H. Fulbright, John Q. Weatherly, Harry Hanszen.* Seated: *James L. Shepherd, Jr., Benjamin Botts Rice, John T. Scott.*

was the first alumnus on the board, although he had not graduated from the Institute, having left to join the Marines in World War I and afterward having completed his college education at the Colorado School of Mines.

In July 1944 chairman William M. Rice, Jr., died after forty-five years on the board. Philanthropy must have run in the Rice family, for this William Marsh Rice also left the bulk of his estate, approximately $2 million, to the Institute. His successor as trustee was Harry C. Wiess, like Blaffer a Humble oilman, and like Brown one of the "friends of Rice" who had helped with the Rincon purchase. John T. Scott became chairman.[18]

By 1945 the board was ready to consider plans for the future of the Institute. The Rice alumni association's Executive Board, headed by Carl M. Knapp, had written the previous year to urge that the faculty, curriculum, and physical plant be improved; that the Board of Trustees determine what legal steps would be necessary in order to charge tuition; and that the board employ an person whose sole duty would be to raise money for the Institute. Also in that year Brown and Hanszen requested and received from President Lovett a three-page memorandum concerning the development of the Institute and early decisions regarding its educational program. Except for the information provided by Lovett, the board had only a vague picture of such matters as enrollment in the various disciplines, past university costs, and future needs.[19]

The Humble Oil and Refining Company, of which Wiess was president, had just completed a survey of its own history; and when Wiess became a trustee, he suggested that Rice do the same. With the W. M. Rice gift, the oil income from the Louisiana lands, and the future income from Rincon all to be invested, the board needed some idea of where the money was going and the direction in which the Institute should go. In February 1945 the trustees established three committees to work out a program. Wiess, B. B. Rice, Brown, and Lovett formed the Survey Committee, which was charged with an analysis of past developments, present status, and future outlook for the Institute along with its financial and educational affairs. On the Finance Committee for the purchase of securities were Brown, Hanszen, and Cleve-

land. The Loan Committee, which handled real estate loans, consisted of Scott, Rice, Cleveland, and Lovett.[20]

Under Wiess's direction, the survey covered a number of aspects of the university's experience from 1929 to 1943: enrollment by classes, gender, and division; degrees awarded; faculty and faculty compensation; educational expense per year and per student; income and expenditures; and financial resources. Some interesting information came to light in this survey. Rice was not simply the engineering school that many thought it was. Throughout the entire period, 49 percent of the students had been registered in the liberal arts school (which included the pure sciences and mathematics) and 33.7 percent in engineering and architecture. The remaining 17 percent were enrolled in physical education, premedical, and graduate programs. Engineering, however, was growing rapidly even before the advent of the Navy curriculum, with the proportion of men enrolled increasing from 36 percent in 1929 to 50 percent in 1941. Mechanical and chemical engineering accounted for the increase; civil and electrical engineering were in decline. Of the 3,421 degrees awarded from 1930 to 1943, 2,246 were Bachelor of Arts degrees, 959 Bachelor of Science, and 216 advanced degrees. While total enrollment had been kept at around 1,400 per year, the number of women had been decreasing, especially in the previous six years. During this time the number of faculty members

had declined from 73 to 55, although before the war started, there had been 64 faculty members. The decline in staff was mostly in mathematics, languages, and history, while the engineering faculty had increased in size. Faculty compensation had remained relatively constant through the fourteen years, at an average of $3,300 to $3,700 per year. The base rate of pay was $2,000 to $3,000 for instructors, $3,000 to $3,750 for assistant professors, and $3,500 to $8,000 for professors. In their preliminary survey report the committee remarked, "It is probable that the uniformity in salary rate and lack of advancement over a period of years had exerted an adverse influence on the faculty." Cost per student had decreased from $399 to 1929 to $332 in 1942 as the total annual operating expenses of the Institute had decreased in that period from $499,000 to $384,000. Income from investments had likewise decreased from $734,000 to $650,000.[21]

"It is the recommendation of this committee," the final report stated, "that Rice Institute continue the basic program that it has developed since 1912." The committee called for a well-rounded and balanced program in all fields, for expansion of the faculty, and for efforts to secure more financial support. Especially critical would be the selection of the next president of the Institute, who would have to administer the expanded activities and attract people of ability to the faculty. The financial outlook was optimistic. When the debt against Rincon was paid, Rice interest in the field was estimated to be worth at least $8 million on the basis of 3.5 percent interest. At that rate of return, the income available after providing for maintenance of capital would be about $280,000 a year, which was equal to more than 40 percent of the average annual income from all Institute investments from 1937 to 1943. The Rincon income, plus that from the W. M. Rice gift and from the Louisiana oil lands, would enable the Institute to increase its expenditures for educational purposes by more than 50 percent compared with the budget immediately before the war. For example, the committee estimated that $625,000 would be available for the school after 1947, compared with average yearly expenditures of $390,000 for the period 1938 to 1943. "This will make possible carrying out a number of improvements that will strengthen the Institute," the committee concluded.[22]

The Trustees' Long-Range Plan

One of the most momentous developments in the history of the Institute was the long-range plan that the Board of Trustees adopted in 1945. This ambitious program, perhaps more than any other, laid the groundwork for the Institute's metamorphosis from a school of mainly regional reputation to a university with national standing. The long-range plan would encompass aca-

demic objectives, an extensive building program, and expansion of the faculty and facilities, as well as a program of outreach into the community.

The foremost objective of the plan was academic development: the Institute would continue to provide especially good training for a limited number of students through a broad and sound basic program, to set a high standard of scholarship, and to provide leadership in higher education. The curriculum would also be well developed, with expansion in arts and letters, although the emphasis would remain on science and research. To help achieve these objectives, the trustees would look for aid from well-qualified individuals not directly connected with the board and would create committees for the various phases of the Institute's affairs staffed partly with these "outsiders." No longer would the board consist primarily of older men; provision would be made for the position of trustee emeritus after trustees had reached a certain age. The educational administrative hierarchy of president, deans, and other officers was to maintain a close relationship with faculty and students; written into the plan was the stipulation that administrative officers teach some classes.

The substantial building program included plans for a library, classrooms, laboratories, dormitories, and a house for the president. Concerning the faculty, the trustees wanted people of the highest ability and a lower ratio of students to faculty (ten

to one instead of the existing fifteen or twenty to one). To attract and maintain an illustrious faculty, the university would establish a salary scale competitive with other leading educational institutions.

As the faculty expanded, so would the curriculum, including diversified graduate and research work. For the latter, graduate fellowships and scholarships would be created. The program did not call for an enlarged student body, just a return to the prewar enrollment of about 1,400. It also did not specify how many graduate students there should be; from 1929 to 1943, the average number was 58. Careful selection would remain the rule for admission, in order to maintain high educational standards.

Finally, while the trustees recognized that current assets and income might be inadequate for full attainment of their goals, they were undertaking the program in the belief that the public would recognize the value of these objectives to the community, state, and nation and would help the Institute to complete its plans.[23]

Once the development plan had been formulated, and in some cases even before a particular segment had crystallized, the board started working toward its goals. By November Wiess could tell the Association of Rice Alumni that members of the faculty had been promoted and that salary adjustments had been made. Without waiting to conclude plans for financing, the trustees commissioned the local firm of Staub and Rather as architects for a library building, with William Ward Watkin as consultant. Preliminary estimates indicated that the cost of the building as envisioned would be over $1 million, and Wiess mentioned to alumni that the trustees would welcome and appreciate their support. Indeed, Wiess emphasized the need for their help for the realization of all the Institute's newly articulated goals.[24]

A President to Succeed Edgar O. Lovett

Selecting a new president took more time than choosing a library architect. Between 1941 and 1945, the board had considered at least twenty possible candidates, including Lee A. Du-Bridge, a physicist who took the presidency at the California Institute of Technology, William C. Devane, a dean at Yale University, and John C. Slater, a physics professor at the Massachusetts Institute of Technology. Of those mentioned, President Lovett was most interested in the two physicists and preferred getting "a young scholar on the way to a sound reputation." For various reasons, the wartime search had been unsuccessful. Many of the leading scientists had been engaged in war work, and none of the others had proved suitable.[25]

As the war wound down, and even before the preliminary survey was completed, the trustees discussed their search with the faculty. If alumni could help with financial matters, faculty could help with the selection of their next president. On April 10, 1945, the trustees gave a dinner for the faculty at Cohen House, at which John Scott addressed the question after explaining the financial prospects of the university and some improvements being contemplated. The trustees knew what they wanted in a president. "(1) He must be a man of excellent character, with an established reputation. (2) He should have had experience in teaching, the ability to lead and inspire confidence, and the personality to deal with people. (3) He should have a scientific training, but with a sufficiently broad background and attitude to give appreciation to all the needs of a well-balanced educational program."[26]

The trustees wanted the faculty to select a temporary committee of three members to be available to consult with them, to analyze the qualifications of the candidates, and to furnish information about them. So that there would be no misunderstanding, Scott also stated that the final choice was the responsibility of the board. "This is not the type of matter that can be handled by a majority vote, but it is one in which the best advice and counsel of all parties concerned needs to be taken into account," he said.[27]

Four days later the faculty met and elected three members for the committee. Alan McKillop would represent the humanities, George H. Richter the pure sciences, and Lewis B. Ryon the applied sciences. They agreed completely with the board's requirements for a president, adding their thoughts that the Institute would be best served also by a man "who has had a substantial part of his training and experience in a university having a comparable well-rounded program . . . , rather than by a man from an institution centered entirely about pure and applied science." They also wanted a president with "an interest in the practical problems of educational administration" and with demonstrated ability in handling the situations that arose in the daily life of a university.[28]

Harry Wiess, George Brown, and B. B. Rice made up the board committee that did the actual work of searching, but it was Wiess who traveled, interviewed, and gathered information on possible candidates. The trustees used every avenue they could to find their man. Old friends and new acquaintances suggested names, evaluated personalities, and offered advice. A query to the Navy produced an outstanding recommendation for one candidate, along with the admonition that, if Rice wanted him, he would be available only after V-J Day. The trustees had some excellent possibilities to consider, but it must have been frustrating to have men like Philip M. Morse of MIT and James Fisk of the Bell Laboratories take themselves out of the running.

Whenever a candidate said no, Wiess had a friend or acquaintance of the candidate sound him out a day or two later to be sure that his mind was really made up. One man to whom the trustees returned after he stated that he did not want to undertake an exclusively administrative job was William V. Houston (pronounced "how-ston") of the California Institute of Technology. A physicist, Dr. Houston had received unqualified recommendations but had been somewhat overshadowed, at least in Wiess's notes of his recruiting activities, by a couple of other candidates. By November 1945, however, when the trustees still had not found a president (and possibly because the faculty liked Houston), Wiess again approached the Californian, this time with an invitation to come to the campus. Regardless of whether it led to serious negotiations, Wiess told Houston, the visit would give the trustees a chance to consult with him about the presidential search. Houston seemed interested, but was still reluctant to leave research and teaching and become solely an administrator. Wiess thought that arrangements could be made for the president to have some time free from administrative duties.

Dr. and Mrs. Houston visited the campus in December, and the trustees were so impressed that they offered the physicist the position on December 8. Houston took two weeks to consider the offer and replied by phone that he was favorably inclined. Before making a final decision, however, he wanted to set forth his views on various matters so that he and the trustees would be sure they understood each other. They had mentioned moving the

business office of the Institute from the downtown office to the campus; Houston thought that highly desirable, since it was the president's duty in most institutions to prepare and present the budget to the trustees and then to exercise close scrutiny of the disbursal of funds. "Educational policy, as well as thrift, must determine the way in which the available income is used, for the way in which it is used determines the extent to which the institution is deserving of local and national support," he told the board. Houston questioned the appropriateness of a prominent football team in a university that wished to be known as an outstanding intellectual center. He thought he would be able to "get along with it," however, if the athletic program's enrollment were held to the existing size of about one hundred.

Those topics out of the way, Houston then concentrated on academic concerns. First, he intended to carry on research and teaching and wanted to be appointed professor of physics as well as president. Second, he wanted to continue developing the science and engineering programs, particularly physics, chemistry, and the engineering based on them, "somewhat to the exclusion of other fields." Principal expansion in graduate instruction and research should be in these areas, while other fields would concentrate on the undergraduate division. He expected to make additions to the faculty, not only with young teachers of initially low rank but also with two

or three men of distinction. Leaders in their fields would attract young instructors of the highest quality and make the Institute's objectives clear, but they would also be expensive, he warned. For the older faculty, Houston wanted to initiate a retirement plan providing for compulsory retirement at a definite age. Finally, to deal with the isolation of Rice from other intellectual centers, Houston proposed encouraging the faculty with some financial assistance to travel to scholarly meetings and to study elsewhere, and bringing in distinguished lecturers for periods of several weeks.

On December 31, 1945, the board expressed its accord with each of Dr. Houston's points. H. C. Wiess called Houston to tell him so, and Houston accepted the offer to become the second president of the Rice Institute. He planned to assume his duties on March 1, 1946, and seemed willing to accept Wiess's word "that while the situation regarding the athletic program at the Institute may not be ideal. . . it is basically sound and in excellent hands under Jess Neely." The terms of employment included a salary of $20,000 a year and a house still to be built.[29]

On January 4, 1946, the day after they announced the selection of a new president, the trustees met to make significant changes in their own organization. It was clear at the time of the announcement of the long-range program in July 1945 that all board members would have to devote long hours overseeing its completion and that it would be advantageous to the Institute if younger men replaced some of the older members. Not all of the older members wanted to give up their positions, but they capitulated to the majority opinion. Since the board did not want to cut itself off from its past experience, the reorganization included the creation of an emeritus position for trustees. Some members (Rice, Lovett, Scott, and Cleveland) could have retired at that time, but the other trustees asked that they stay on until a new president was selected. The beginning of the new year and Dr. Houston's acceptance of the presidency provided an appropriate opportunity for change.

First the bylaws of the Institute were amended to permit any trustee over the age of seventy to resign and be elected trustee emeritus. Trustees emeriti could attend all meetings, advise, and express their views, but they would have no vote. B. B. Rice, A. S. Cleveland, E. O. Lovett, and J. T. Scott then tendered their resignations, and in their places were elected Gus S. Wortham, William A. Kirkland, Frederick R. Lummis, M.D., and Lamar Fleming, Jr. Harry Hanszen was elected chairman. The new board then adopted a resolution of appreciation for the contributions of the retiring members. Rice had been on the board since 1901, Lovett since 1910, Scott since 1913, and Cleveland since 1922.

Of the new members, Wortham was president of the American General Insurance Company and had connections with other busi-

nesses as well; Kirkland, A. S. Cleveland's son-in-law, was a banker with the First National Bank of Houston; Lummis was physician-in-chief at Hermann Hospital and professor of clinical medicine at Baylor College of Medicine (the first academic besides Lovett to serve on the board); and Fleming was president of Anderson, Clayton & Co., whose founders had been generous supporters of the university in its early years.[30]

This new board was busy from the first, revamping investments for a higher yield, reorganizing accounting procedures to follow current methods for colleges, and helping the new president where it could. When debts on the Rincon property were paid off in 1947, total net assets of the Institute were more than $29 million. The trustees had received more good financial news before the 1947 accounting, however. In June 1946 Ella F. Fondren, widow of Humble oilman W. W. Fondren, contributed $1 million to the Institute for the construction of a library building. In October of that year, Harry Wiess gave Rice the income from 30,000 shares of Humble Oil stock for seventeen and one-half years, to be used for current operating expenses. Afterward, the stock was to go to his children. At the time of the donation, Rice hoped to receive about $1 million from Wiess's gift; the eventual sum was more than $4 million. The following March, James S. Abercrombie (an oilman and a founder of Cameron Iron Works), his wife Lillie, and their daughter Jose-

phine (Rice '46) gave $500,000 for an engineering laboratory building. The economic picture was bright indeed.[31]

President Houston Takes Office

Rice's new president arrived on campus in March 1946. William Vermillion Houston was born in Mt. Gilead, Ohio, on January 19, 1900. He attended Ohio State University for Bachelor of Arts and Bachelor of Science degrees in education and graduated in 1920 with membership in Phi Beta Kappa and Sigma Xi. He received a Master of Science degree from the University of Chicago in 1922 and returned to Ohio State for his doctorate, which he received in 1925. He had been a National Research Council fellow at the California Institute of Technology, a Guggenheim fellow, and a member of the faculty at Cal Tech since 1927, having been made full professor in 1931. He was the author of *Principles of Mathematical Physics* and many scientific articles, and during the war he had conducted research for the Office of Scientific Research, concentrating especially on antisubmarine devices and torpedo designs.[32]

Official inauguration ceremonies for Houston were held on April 10, 1947. This was the first presidential inauguration at Rice. Edgar Odell Lovett had never been formally inaugurated; the 1912 ceremonies that opened the school were formal ceremonies of dedication. Like those first cere-

106. *William Vermillion Houston, the second president of the Rice Institute.*

monies, the 1947 inaugural festivities were held outdoors, but this time in front of the Chemistry Building at eleven o'clock in the morning. They were kept simple and dignified. Again came the procession of delegates, including twenty-seven college presidents and various dignitaries from foreign institutions. Again the singing of "Veni Creator Spiritus" opened the solemnities, although "America" closed the program in place of the "One Hundredth Psalm." Karl T. Compton, president of the Massachusetts Institute of Technology, delivered an address entitled "Dynamic Education," and Harry C. Wiess as vice-chairman of the

trustees inducted Houston into the office of president. After the inauguration ceremony came lunch in the Commons in honor of the delegates, where Lee A. DuBridge, president of the California Institute of Technology, spoke.

Following an afternoon reception for the delegates at Cohen House, there was a dinner in honor of the new president and his wife. Addressing the group on behalf of the alumni was Carl M. Knapp, president of the Association of Rice Alumni, and on behalf of the people of Texas, Houston power broker Jesse H. Jones. Dr. Dixon Wecter, chairman of the Research Group at the

Huntington Library, then presented a paper entitled "The Lone Star and the Constellation." While not the marathon of the opening, it was a full day.[33]

Edgar Odell Lovett became president emeritus upon Houston's accession to the presidency, and in December 1947 the Administration Building was renamed "Lovett Hall" with the inscription, "He has reared a monument more lasting than brass." Lovett continued to occupy an office in the building, although he moved down from the top floor to a somewhat more accessible location on the third floor.[34]

Many people have said that William Vermillion Houston was the perfect man to follow Edgar Odell Lovett as president of the Rice Institute. Interested in the same scholastic qualities, Houston emphasized high standards, sound scholarship, and good teaching. "We aim to be a small university, small in total number of people and small in that we confine our efforts to restricted fields largely of the traditional university variety," he said. "We are firmly dedicated to the proposition that size and excellence are not synonymous. In fact, we believe that we pursue excellence better in a small institution than some can in institutions much larger. Private institutions can help to lead the way in the quality of education. This, I hope, the Rice Institute can do." While his own interest lay principally in science and its application to engineering, he also knew the value of humanistic studies. He wanted a balanced education for Rice

107. *Dedication ceremonies renaming the Administration Building "Lovett Hall," December 4, 1947.* Left to right: *Harry C. Wiess, Lamar Fleming, Jr., Harry Hanszen, President Emeritus Lovett, William A. Kirkland, George R. Brown, President Houston, Gus Wortham, Dr. Frederick Rice Lummis.*

students, both in introspective thought and the world of words and in material phenomena.[35]

President Houston must have been a pleasant surprise to the faculty when he took office. For years the Institute had run on the same track with few changes in procedure or personnel, espe-

cially in administration. To get things done on campus, one saw bursar McCants, registrar Mc-Cann, Dean Weiser, or architect Watkin. Seldom did a professor bother the president with day-to-day details or even have any contact with him, although the courtly Lovett enjoyed talking

with faculty members on those occasions when they did come to see him. Faculty meetings were few and far between, and no one seemed eager to bring up matters at them. The department heads ran their departments, the bursar, registrar, dean, architect, and president ran the Institute in a gentlemanly, low-key fashion, and that was that. Dr. Houston wanted a higher profile. During his first two weeks on campus, he visited as many faculty members in their offices as he could, seeking information and asking about problems. He wanted to know his faculty personally. He wanted them to take a more active role on campus.

At his first faculty meeting on March 16, Houston sketched his plans for the postwar Institute. He spoke of the need for students to have a balanced education, with the provision of a common core of basic training upon which to build specialties. The building program was under way, so relief was in sight for the overcrowded classrooms and offices. The size of the student body was to be held at 1,500 until the faculty was much larger than the existing number (about 60). Houston was particularly interested in graduate study and research; to increase graduate enrollment as quickly as possible, he had personally undertaken preparation and distribution of a graduate bulletin and poster indicating the availability of graduate fellowships. Since it took money to attract students of high quality and to compete with other graduate schools, Houston announced stipends available of up to $1,000, with remission of all fees.

Whatever the quality of students, or the number of buildings, or the victories of the football team, the academic standing and reputation of a university depended on its faculty. To meet the long-range program's goals,

the number of professors had to be increased. Houston asked the faculty for their assistance in nominating possible candidates and investigating suitable people. He did not expect this to be a quick or easy task, because certain special qualities were required. A faculty member had to be an outstanding scholar: a publishing scholar if in the humanities, involved in research if in science, recognized by others if in the engineering profession. He had to be an inspiring teacher and recognize that teaching was an important part of the profession. A faculty member had to be "cooperative and helpful" in the administration of the Institute. That meant serving on committees, since the new president wanted the faculty to take over certain quasi-administrative functions. Finally, a faculty member had to be a respected citizen of the community.[36]

To advise on appointments to the faculty committees, the faculty again elected Professors McKillop, Richter, and Ryon. These men formed the first Executive Committee along with the president and the dean. The purpose of the various committees was to deal with all matters pertaining to educational policy, administration, and student life. The president appointed the committees and delegated authority to them. Committees considered matters brought to them by faculty or students and applied rules and settled cases without referring details to the whole faculty for approval. New rules, policies, and precedents, however, did re-

quire such approval at regular faculty meetings, which were to be held twice a semester. Also, individual faculty members were specifically given the power to introduce new business outside the committee structure and to appeal committee decisions at faculty meetings.

A number of committees were appointed, most of them reorganizations of old committees. A few, however, were new: the Committee on Graduate Instruction with Dr. Houston as chairman until a dean of graduate studies was named; the Committee on the Library; and the Committee on Student Activities, which would be chaired by a new assistant dean for student activities, Hugh Scott Cameron, and which would include student members. The Navy Committee continued to operate as before, as did the Committee on Outdoor Sports, which was established in the Board of Trustees' bylaws.[37]

As had been obvious in negotiations for the presidency and in the establishment of committee policy, William V. Houston did not particularly care to run the school by himself. It has been said of him that he was never truly happy unless he was working in his laboratory, which he had installed next to his office on the second floor of Lovett Hall, close to the Physics Building. "Physics," he said, "is a hobby I've fortunately been able to pursue at full time all my life."

By 1949 Houston had developed his own inimitable style. Into one of the top drawers went almost everything that came across his desk. There it fermented for a week or two, sometimes longer. After a while, he would call in his assistant—a junior faculty member who helped with the busy work of the administration—and clean out his drawer. He told one of the assistants that he called the drawer "administration," and if he left things in there long enough, most of them settled themselves. What was left he divided between himself and the assistant. He used the same technique on the many questionnaires sent by various government agencies, professional organizations, and others. Houston detested questionnaires. He answered only the imperative ones, had the assistant handle some others, and left the rest to sit, maintaining that if one waited long enough, the inquirers would no longer need the information, anyway. Houston was never guilty of the vice of administering too much.[38]

Changes in the Curriculum and Admissions

The first task of the newly appointed Executive Committee was to consider the desirability of revising the undergraduate curriculum. Virtually untouched since its original formulation, the curriculum still did not provide for the modern concept of the "major" and required only four courses in each of the junior and senior years for the B.A. degree. To keep in step with developments at other major universities, to broaden the curriculum,

to give the students more experiences that would prepare them for the outside world and graduate schools, and possibly to extract more productive effort from the students, the Executive Committee decided to revise the curriculum. They presented a new plan to the faculty in July 1946. The new was quite a departure from the old, especially for the first two years of study, because the faculty wanted to emphasize basic subjects such as English, mathematics, history, and science, while at the same time deemphasizing early specialization. With this in mind, two main courses of study were created, academic and science-engineering, each having its own core of required subjects. When students were admitted, they usually leaned toward a tentative major, and that determined their division and their schedule for the first two years. The year-long courses were divided into three groups: Group A was languages and literature; B was history, social studies, philosophy, and education; C was mathematics and science. Under the old curriculum, Groups A and B had been combined.

First-year academic students were required to take Math 100, English 100, French or German, American or European history, and a choice of Physics 100, Chemistry 100, or Biology 100. Men were required to take physical training for one year; when the gymnasium was completed in 1951, the women also had compulsory physical training classes. Second-year students

took either Math 200 or 210 or a science; English or a general literature elective; a second year of the language they had begun in the first year; a Group B elective; and a free elective.

The science-engineering curriculum did not contain as many choices, and it added a sixth course to each year. The first-year student took Math 100, Physics 100, Chemistry 100, English 100, American or European history, and engineering drawing. The second-year student took 200-level courses in mathematics, chemistry, and physics, along with German 100, an English elective, and mechanical drawing. Premedical students and those intending to major in biology took Biology 100 instead of Physics 100. Although science-engineering students took Math 100 for three two-hour periods and academic students for three one-hour periods a week, the basic course was the same: trigonometry, analytic geometry, and elementary calculus. And it was still required for graduation.

For the third and fourth years of the academic program, a total of ten courses were required, at least one in each group in each year. This was later modified to two in each of Groups A and B and one in Group C, taken in any order. At least seven of the ten courses had to be advanced (numbered 300 or higher), and not fewer than three nor more than five could fall in the major field. In 1947 academic majors were offered in business administration and economics, English, history, modern languages, philosophy, and prelegal studies. In 1949 premedical studies could be taken as a major in either the academic or science-engineering program, and mathematics was listed in both courses of study in 1950.

For pure science and mathematics majors, the plan was not as flexible, but it did include a humanities elective each year. Otherwise the student took three courses in science (one outside the major field) in the third year, and two in the major during the fourth year. Another year of a foreign language, biology, and a free elective completed the ten required courses. Honors programs were available for both arts and science students, and each department offering them had its own formula for required courses.

Overall, the engineering curriculum was the most changed. Under the old curriculum engineers had taken mostly engineering courses, with only two humanities courses and some business administration and economics to leaven the mass of math, science, and engineering subjects. To broaden the curriculum with requirements in the humanities and to deepen work in the fundamental sciences, engineers now followed the scientific course of study for the first two years, then moved into the strictly engineering courses. One aspect of the engineering curriculum, however, did not change. Engineering majors had no choice of courses, except a humanities elective taken in the third or fourth year, depending on the branch of engi-

neering in which the student was enrolled.

The degree that engineering students received also changed. Up to that time, the Rice Institute had awarded a B.S. at the end of four years, and the degree of chemical, civil, electrical, or mechanical engineer at the end of five. The new curriculum called for a B.A. degree at the end of four years and a B.S. in a specific kind of engineering at the end of five.

Architects followed the academic first-year schedule with the addition of an architecture course. The remainder of their curriculum was virtually unchanged, as was the curriculum for physical education majors.

Almost all of the old courses at Rice were year-long and counted as one unit each, as they had from the beginning of the Institute. The new ones continued to be year-long, but under the new curriculum semester courses were to be counted instead of whole units. As before, students registered in the fall for the entire year. The faculty committee also called for daily attendance records for all freshman and sophomore classes on the premise that those classes were not "ready for freedom" in the matter of attendance. The spelling test required for graduation in 1937 was now a requirement for promotion and enrollment in courses in the junior year.

Although the new curriculum was introduced in July 1946 with the goal of instituting it the following September, the faculty

did not adopt it until April 1947. It was several years before students felt the effects of this curriculum.[39]

Another change took place for students in the fall of 1947: admission procedures were made more explicit and organized into a schedule. Four hundred was still the maximum number of entering freshmen, and fifteen the required number of high school credits, but the credits had been rearranged somewhat. The old system required three in English, two in algebra, one in plane geometry, two in history, and three in one foreign language or two in two foreign languages. One to three credits in science were recommended. Reflecting the times, as well as changes in high school curricula and the needs of the students, the new requirements called for four credits in English, two in algebra, one in plane geometry, one-half in trigonometry, at least two in social studies, two in a foreign language (preferably Latin), two in science (biology, chemistry, or physics), and one and one-half electives selected from a list of serious subjects ranging from botany to zoology. Seven of the sixteen subject categories of the electives were in science.

Personal and mental qualifications were the new requirements for admission. To prove himself or herself personally qualified, an applicant had to provide a health certificate from the family physician and letters of recommendation from teachers, and also to have a personal interview with a member of the Admissions Committee or the committee's representative. Mental qualifications were determined by grades in high school subjects, rank in the graduating class, and, if necessary, examinations given by the Institute. The majority of students were still admitted without entrance examinations on the basis of an outstanding high school record and satisfactory personal qualifications. Whereas previously students in the upper half of their high school classes were given preference, under the new system only those in the upper twenty-five percent were encouraged to apply, and they were not guaranteed admission without examination.

Applicants who did not have outstanding records but who were approved by the committee were given the chance to prove the adequacy of their preparation by taking entrance examinations in English and mathematics. The departments of English and mathematics wrote these tests, graded them, and ranked the grades to determine relative standings among the applicants. These results were confidential to the Admissions Committee; no applicant knew what his or her grade or rank was.

The committee established schedules for interviews and examinations in Houston and other Texas cities and set a deadline of March 1 for filling applications. Up to this time, the Institute had had no idea how many students would actually register in September, and the new plan sought to correct this logistical defect. A student had two weeks after the date on the notice of acceptance to signify in writing his or her intention of accepting admission and to send in a twenty-five-dollar registration fee. If the student did not appear to register in September and had not so notified the school before August 1, the payment was forfeited.[40]

There were also changes for graduate students, through the Committee on Graduate Instruction. No longer were a good undergraduate record and letters of recommendation sufficient for admission. Starting in 1947, the graduate studies committee "advised," although it did not absolutely require, candidates to take the Graduate Record Examination. The catalog stated that preference would be given to applicants with high scores on these tests. As for graduate degrees, a number of departments offered Master of Arts and Master of Science degrees, but the Ph.D. was available in 1947 only in biology, chemistry, mathematics, and physics. This limitation was soon changed as more teachers were hired.[41]

Changes in Faculty and Physical Plant

The hiring of new faculty members began just after Houston took office, and teachers returning from war duty further increased the numbers. Many came in with, or were elevated to, a rank new to Rice: associate professor. In 1946, 16 new faculty members and 4 veterans arrived; 21 more were added in 1947, and another 16 in 1948. In total number the faculty reached 100 in 1950. By that year the humanities, architecture, and science faculties had doubled from 1945 figures, and engineers had increased by more than one-third. Architecture hired James K. Dunaway and A. A. Leifeste, Jr., and welcomed James Morehead, Jr., home from the war. Biology saw the arrival of Roy V. Talmage and parasitologist Clark P. Read. John Kilpatrick and Edward S. Lewis joined the chemistry department, and chemical engineering added William W. Akers and Guy T. McBride. Other engineers included Paul E. Pfeiffer in electrical engineering and Hugh Scott Cameron and Alan J. Chapman in mechanical engineering. James R. Sims returned to civil engineering from the war. Physics added Gerald C. Phillips, J. R. Risser, and Charles F. Squire; philosophy acquired James Street Fulton. Hardin Craig, Jr., and Rice alumni Katherine Fischer Drew and William H. Masterson began teaching history. Mathematics welcomed Gerald R. Mac-Lane and Szolem Mandelbrojt, while economics added James B. Giles and John E. Hodges. And there were others.[42]

As there were arrivals, there were also departures. Rice inaugurated a retirement plan in 1946 that provided an option for retirement at age sixty and compulsory retirement at seventy. A pension plan was also established for those faculty members who had accumulated years of service before 1946. At the end of the school year in May 1947, two individuals who were campus fixtures retired—Harold A. Wilson with thirty-five years of service, and Alice Dean with thirty-three. Miss Dean went out in style; the board had finally given her the title "librarian" (not just "acting librarian") in 1946.[43]

Along with added faculty, more buildings were needed for offices, classrooms, labs, dormitories, and a library. The last was probably the most important, since Miss Dean had done an excellent job of collecting. By 1947 Rice's 150,000 library books could be found in nine library locations. The main library was on the second floor of Lovett Hall, with the history collection housed on the first floor and bound periodicals shelved in the basement. There were two libraries for chemistry in the Chemistry Building, and an architectural library as well; the physics library was in the Physics Building.

To plan for a new library, a Cooperative Committee on Library Buildings was formed in 1945 with representatives from many different university libraries; in addition, Rice sought special aid from John E. Burchard, director of libraries at MIT in 1946. Claude Heaps, professor of physics, was the first director of the library; he and his faculty committee knew fairly precisely what they wanted. The argument and sentiments were overwhelming for consolidating the scattered collections into one central library. The committee wanted open stacks, but they also anticipated the necessity for reverting to a "semi-closed" stack system in the event that the non-Rice public abused their open-stack privileges. (Under the terms of the Institute charter, the library was to be open to the public.) The faculty also wanted reading areas of adequate size with tables and chairs, small faculty studies (but no faculty offices) and student carrels within the stack area, and small rooms for seminars but not ordinary classrooms. To Burchard's suggestion that an outside specialist inventory the Rice holdings with an eye to pointing out gaps, the committee replied that the faculty was satisfied with the old system. They perceived that there were very few gaps in the holdings in use. The old acquisitions policy considered use as the ultimate criterion for book acquisition, and as a result Rice owned few rare books and in certain fields had only limited holdings. When the need arose, however, the board authorized special appropriations to meet the demands of the new curriculum.

One of the most controversial questions was the location of the library building. It was generally agreed that the building would be situated on the long central axis that passed through the Sallyport of Lovett Hall and the founder's statue, but how far beyond the statue? The architects wanted it on the site laid out in the original Cram and Ferguson plan, which would have put it where the soccer and band practice field is today, west of the present student center. Locating it there assumed that the school would grow tremendously and that future new buildings would be placed even farther from the main entrance. Proponents of this location spoke of the "enormous and significant vista." Most pragmatic faculty members, however, were more interested in how long it would take to walk from their offices to the library than in the view. Heaps's committee recommended the present location. They believed that that site would be central to the Institute for some time to come, possibly permanently. They thought that expansion to the west would probably be for men's housing, athletic buildings, or other auxiliary functions that would not place their main reliance on the library. The site would still provide a grand, more than adequate view.[44]

Even the generous million-dollar gift from Mrs. Fondren was not enough to cover the entire cost of the building as finally planned, so the trustees looked to other friends of the university for much of the remaining $785,000 needed. Part of the fund drive focused on alumni. Since 1928 the alumni association had been collecting money for a memorial building of offices and classrooms to be constructed across the quadrangle from the Physics Building. Because of the depression and the small number of Rice alumni, they had not collected enough for such a building; but in 1947 the association voted to earmark the accumulated funds (some $80,000) for construction of the library. The

108–110. *The construction of Fondren Library.* 108. *June 2, 1947.* 109. *April 1, 1948.* 110. *July 1, 1948.*

III

112

III–II3. The interior of the new Fondren Library. III. Circulation area, May 24, 1949. II2. Lecture Lounge, March 10, 1950. II3. Music and Arts Lounge, March 10, 1950.

Bender bequest was also added to the library fund.[45]

In December 1947 the cornerstone for Fondren Library was laid with the same silver trowel that the trustees had used to lay the cornerstone for the Administration Building in 1911. The trowel was then presented to Mrs. Fondren. The official opening came two years later during homecoming.[46]

Anderson Hall, a classroom and office building adjacent to the library on the Physics Building (north) side of the quadrangle, was the first structure completed in the postwar building program. Opening in 1947, the building was named in honor of M. D. Anderson, whose foundation had given $300,000 toward the purchase of the Rincon oil field with the proviso already noted that when debts were cleared from that transaction, the money be used for some such purpose.[47]

The Abercrombie Engineering Laboratory opened in November 1948. Located adjoining the Mechanical Laboratory Building, it was designed by the firm of Staub and Rather, architects for the library and Anderson Hall. William M. McVey, Rice '27, sculpted a mural for the entrance. A highly stylized figure (which McVey called "Uncle Jupe") represented "man's—the engineer's—transmission and storage of natural energy, symbolized by the sun, into power for a mechanical and industrial civilization." McVey used dynamos, power lines, oil tanks, and a refinery to designate the branches of engineering. The Houston chapter of the Architectural Institute of America selected the laboratory as the best nonresidential building erected and occupied in Houston during 1948.[48]

Expansion did not stop with these three structures. In 1949 a house for the president was finally constructed on campus, a house that had been discussed since at least 1912. The Houstons had a home. A new dormitory, badly needed to alleviate overcrowding, also went up in 1949 and was dedicated in 1950 as Wiess Hall in memory of trustee Harry C. Wiess, who had died in 1948.[49]

Plans for a new football stadium began as early as 1947, but it was several years before firm decisions were made. During that time, all sorts of proposals came up for consideration, involving people not only at the Institute, but also at the University of Houston and in city government, and private citizens as well. In 1948 there was much local enthusiasm for a 100,000-seat municipal stadium, in which both Rice and the University of Houston would have an interest. This idea was abandoned for a variety of reasons, including reluctance at both schools and lack of funding. Historically the Rice board had been averse to involving Institute money in projects that the Institute did not control. In November 1949 the trustees announced that Rice would build its own stadium.[50]

At first the trustees had toyed with the idea of remodeling the old stadium, but they decided after much discussion to build a new one. Seating capacity for the new stadium was first proposed to be 40,000, grew to 54,000, and was finally settled at 70,000. To raise as much of the cost (estimated at more than $2 million) as possible from sources outside the university, the trustees sold options on seats—$200 for each box seat and $100 for each grandstand seat, with previous season ticket holders and alumni having first choice. Trustee George Brown's Brown & Root Construction Company agreed to build the stadium at cost to save the time needed to advertise for bids; work began promptly in February for a target opening date of September 30, 1950. The final cost was $3,295,000. Construction on the stadium went on literally night and day, and the president began to receive letters from residents along Rice and University Boulevards complaining about the constant noise and confusion. American Federation of Labor pickets marched in front of the stadium to protest Brown & Root's open shop policy and the company's refusal to recognize the unions. At one point, Rice students who wanted the stadium picketed the pickets. As if that disruption were not enough, construction workers came upon an underground stream with a fairly rapid flow of water. It had to be diverted and routed through conduits, as did the old "Blue Danube," or Harris Gully, which meandered across what was to be the parking lot. Somehow in spite of the crises the stadium opened on time. It was designed purely for football with no cinder

114–116. Construction of Anderson Hall. 114. November 6, 1946. 115. July 1, 1947. 116. December 8, 1947.

117–119. *Construction of Abercrombie Laboratory.* 117. *Groundbreaking, July 1, 1947.* 118. *Aerial view of construction, December 2, 1947 (also shows Fondren Library construction and completed Anderson Hall).* 119. *July 1, 1948.*

120. *"Uncle Jupe," a sculpture by William M. McVey on the facade of Abercrombie Laboratory.*

track separating the field from the stands, and it had what Jess Neely called "just perfect turf." After the opening, the task of assigning seats to season ticket holders became problematic when some were not satisfied with their allotted locations. Naming the stadium stirred up more controversy. The trustees had intended originally to call it

Houston Stadium for the city, but that sounded like a municipally-owned stadium and seemed confusing. Neither were Rice students and alumni particularly happy to saddle their stadium with that name. The final decision to call it simply Rice Stadium met with almost universal agreement.[51]

As much as Rice needed new

classrooms, offices, dormitories, and a library, it needed a new Field House. The old one was falling down; conditions had reached the point where a telephone pole propped up a wall that was separating from the building. Coach Neely did not have to go outside to see if anyone was practicing on the field—he could just look through the crack in the wall. When prospective high school athletes came to visit, the last place they were shown was the Field House. In 1949, about the time the decision was made to build the new stadium, work was begun on a new gymnasium. The building included a basketball arena (the first one on the Rice campus), a swimming pool, squash and handball courts, offices for the Athletic Association and the physical education department, and facilities for women. Rice women could finally take physical training courses, and freshman women now had compulsory "P.T.," as did the men. The basketball court was named Autry Court in honor of Mrs. James L. Autry (donor of Autry House), whose daughter, Allie Autry Kelley, Rice '25, donated $250,000 toward the building. (In the 1920s, Mrs. Autry, a staunch supporter of Rice athletics, used to turn her house into a dispensary for bruised Owl players, and she traveled to Austin and College Station to cheer the teams.) The new Field House opened in 1951.[52]

121. *Interior view, Abercrombie Laboratory, September 1949.*

Student Concerns

Just as the campus changed physically in appearance, it was altered in many other ways for students during the 1940s. The war, of course, radically transformed the university. Student traditions of many years went by the wayside in the process. The May Fete was canceled; the *Thresher* was cut in size and gained its first full-time female editor when Marion Hargrove took over for her husband Jim; no speaker addressed commencement in 1942; and in a scrap drive Woofus, the mechanical monster from the Engineering Show, was zealously added to the pile of metal. The band dissolved for a while when Kit Reid went to war, but student volunteers started it again and carried on through the war. Senior rings were available in 1943, but the underside of the crest had to be hollow instcad of solid, to conserve metal for the war effort. The Engineering Society, known for shaved eyebrows, strange coiffures, and dead fish at initiation time, was disbanded after

some "unfortunate incidents" at onc of their welcoming ceremonies. No bonfires encouraged football players before the Aggie games, although the war did not stop the farmers from stealing Sammy in 1943. Corsages were banned for spring dances in 1945, because the Navy men said they had no money to buy flowers.[53]

These stringencies did not mean, however, that life at the Institute was dead. There was still plenty to do, including dances, athletic activities, club meetings, and cloister courses. As for schoolwork, the *Thresher* editor complained in 1945 about low grades and the decline of the old Rice standards. Grades were

122. *Construction of the new Rice Stadium, May 23, 1950.*
123. *The completed stadium, with athletic director Jess Neely in the foreground.*

falling, she noted, but "it is generally accepted that Rice is an easier school than it was before the war." The war usually got the blame, but the editor thought that poor grades were due to the students' habitual evasion of responsibility.[54]

When the war ended and President Lovett announced in the spring of 1946 that the university would return to the old schedule in September, everyone breathed a sigh of relief. By that time faculty and students alike needed a vacation from year-round classes. It did not take long for the Institute to return to normal the following fall. Students returning from the war picked up their studies where they had left off, in many cases under the same professor. In September 1945 the old practice of hazing had revived to include special slime clothing, the Slime Parade, and certain rules of slime conduct; persecution was to be verbal, not physical.[55] Tony Martino continued to entertain students at the bonfires with his tenuous grasp of the English language while he exhorted the team to victory. Literary society activities and social life resumed their hectic pace, while some students faced the old problem of how to fit all their extra-curricular doings into a day and still find some time for study.

The Rice that emerged from the war, however, was not the same as the Rice of old. A larger number of graduate students increased the total enrollment and altered the prewar ratio of graduates to undergraduates; by 1950 there were 150 graduate students. The new curriculum that was adopted in 1947 brought about change slowly and subtly, as those on the old curriculum graduated and each successive class came in under the new system. Another change was in the rules concerning scholastic probation—rules that were a source of increased pressure for the students. Under the new system, students who were failing in their first freshman semester were placed on probation instead of being dropped from school, and all students were henceforth allowed only two probations (a probation lasted one semester) during their academic careers, instead of the previous unlimited

number. A third probation meant automatic expulsion. A "special probation" at the discretion of the Committee on Examinations and Standing might also be granted. This probation, however, was extremely stringent, requiring no grade of less than III during the period of special probation and absolutely no academic difficulty thereafter.[56]

By 1949 approximately thirteen percent of all freshmen were failing in their first semester, and the faculty was concerned. Beginning in 1948, a committee known variously as the Committee on the Freshman Course and the Committee on Coordination of Freshmen, chaired first by Professor Heaps, began to investigate the problems that freshmen faced in adapting to Rice. Committee members interviewed all freshman students who had failed two or more subjects, and they found many causes for poor work, ranging from inadequate high school preparation to homesickness. Another step they took was to meet with the teaching assistants for courses that had many sections, in order to discuss their teaching methods. The graduate students suggested that one of the problems lay in the emphasis placed on research in their own studies. There was not much incentive for good teaching, they said, and they did not have adequate time to prepare for the classes they were teaching. The assistants also said that they wanted to meet with department heads and the faculty in charge of freshman sections to learn more about department policies, standards,

methods, and requirements. As a final measure in its investigation, the committee sent a questionnaire to members of the freshman class to determine whether certain courses were demanding more than their proper share of time. Analysis indicated that the average science-engineering freshman spent fifty-five hours a week in study, classes, and laboratory, while the representative academic student spent forty-four hours. The committee members thought that that was about the right amount of time, although perhaps the science-engineers were putting in a bit more than was desirable.

In its report, the committee speculated on the reasons why so many students were on probation. They listed the following possibilities: an inadequate selection process for admissions; poor teaching; a belief on the part of the faculty that awarding low grades indicated high standards; an actual raising of standards by the faculty, so that even able students could not make good grades. Even after they had studied admission procedures, however, the committee could not reach a judgment about the quality of freshmen, nor could they identify which of the possible causes accounted for the high failure rate. They considered administering aptitude tests to freshmen and issuing brief suggestions about how to study; they also discussed the question of more faculty-freshman communication and guidance, cautioned against a rigid curve grading system in any class, and

asked the faculty for further suggestions. Concerning a request that academic students have special sections of Math 100 and Physics 100 (the two courses that failed more freshmen than any others), Hubert Bray of mathematics and Claude Heaps of physics "maintained a somewhat intransigent attitude toward these proposals."[57]

The following year, the same committee sent out another questionnaire, this time surveying those on probation. When few replied, the committee again interviewed the students. Those who had replied to the questionnaire were more inclined to blame their failure on poor high school training than on any other cause. Of those whom the committee questioned personally, however, most appeared unable to do creditable work in a college such as Rice, "no matter how much help and advice is given them."

As in the previous year, the committee concentrated on the admissions process and on the quality of freshman students as the causes of so many freshman difficulties. The remedy for Rice's freshman "unsuccess" lay in obtaining a "higher type" of freshman to begin with, the committee concluded. That, however, depended on having a very large number of applicants from which to choose, and the number was declining in 1950. The Institute had competition from free state institutions, which gave well-recognized degrees without the amount of work that Rice required, and Rice had made no particular effort to publicize what it had to offer. Also, there were not many Rice alumni teaching in the public schools who might be able to influence better students to apply to the Institute. In addition, the postwar era was a prosperous one, when the absence of tuition was not as great an advantage as it once had been.

The committee was in a quandary. Administering tests such as those of the College Entrance Examination Board might aid in picking the best of the applicants. On the other hand, if Rice were compelled to accept almost any high school graduate who applied simply to keep the enrollment figures up, the tests would be moot. If the faculty abandoned a selective admissions process and high standards for freshmen, then Rice's traditional high standards for all students would fall, as well. "The time has come," the committee concluded, "when we must face the fact that efforts will have to be made to attract students to Rice."

"Under these circumstances," the committee wrote to the Committee on Examinations and Standing, "our Committee feels that the Institute can continue to maintain its high standards only if its attitude toward its freshmen is one of well-considered rather than of mechanistic legality. The student must be made to feel that he is getting more help, wiser instruction, more personal consideration, more exact understanding of his problems at Rice than he could get at any of those other universities that offer easier courses and more automatic

degrees than Rice offers." The committee then requested that the rules of special probation not be applied to freshmen who were readmitted after failing their first year. Examinations and Standing denied the request, maintaining that freshmen had a full year to make the adjustment to college and that readmission on special probation helped foster a favorable mental attitude in the student. Past experience showed that such readmitted students improved markedly.

In response to a report by the Committee on the Freshman Course, the faculty offered comments of their own. Hardin Craig drew attention to the "bedevilment of freshmen" and the bad effects to be expected from frequent extracurricular activities of doubtful value. When committee member Trenton Wann indicated that students were in favor of faculty guidance but wanted more extensive participation by the faculty, President Houston pointed out that such faculty involvement was an integral part of teaching. Admissions director McCann cautioned against rigid rules for uniformity in grading, but Edwin Wyatt was in favor of the curve. George Williams, another member of the committee, mentioned the difficulty of determining precise number grades in humanities courses and ventured the opinion that the large numbers of low grades might be indicative of poor teaching. The faculty minutes do not record any answer to his observation.

The committee made some efforts to help both students and

faculty. They sent the freshmen suggestions on how to study and solicited suggestions for teaching from both faculty and teaching assistants in the various departments. How the "unfit" got into Rice still needed an answer, but in the meantime the committee called for an active counseling program for freshmen and a rewritten section on probation in the *General Announcements*. According to some students, the section was so confusing that they had no idea that they were on probation until someone told them.

The problems of high failure rates and large percentages of students on probation did not go away, however, even when the number of applicants increased. It remained to be seen what effect these conditions, the new curriculum, and the admissions policy would have on students. The forlorn little figure studying for finals with a candle burning on his head made his first appearance in the *Thresher* in May 1949.[58] More than thirty years later, he is still resurrected at the end of every term.

Problems concerning the honor system resulted in a new constitution in 1948 and elicited much discussion. Faculty and students generally agreed that the system had been weakened during the war. According to a *Thresher* reporter, the honor system had worked well for thirty years until the advent of the Navy program on campus. The Navy's "outspoken refusal to believe in or promote an honor system" caused problems, he said. Whatever the reason, it was clear that students needed more explicit rules and procedures. The new constitution prohibited deliberate proctoring by the instructor; it allowed the student to leave the room during examinations solely for personal reasons, and arranged students in alternate rows and alternate seats for exams if possible. The pledge and signature were required on all examinations and whatever other work the instructor desired, as they had been from the beginning of the Institute. The constitution established a trial procedure and specified a minimum penalty of suspension for a semester plus the uncompleted portion of the semester in which the conviction was made.[59]

Student Activities in the 1940s

Not all the changes that took place were so serious or far-reaching. The first female cheerleader, Betty Jean "Foxie" Fox, was elected in 1946, thereby destroying a twenty-five-year-old tradition that yell leaders had to be male. Drum majorettes also joined the band in half-time shows. To replace the not-much-lamented *Owl*, a magazine called *RI* was published under the sponsorship of the English department and sought articles that would appeal to alumni, faculty, and the general public as well as to students. The first Rondelet replaced the May Fete and showed off a king and queen at the ball in 1947. The Senior Fol-

124. *The 1946 cheerleaders, including Betty Jean "Foxie" Fox, the first female yell leader at Rice.*

lies, a student-written play satirizing life at Rice and outside the campus, saw the light of day in 1949. In 1948 the alumni association opened a placement service for job-hunting students and graduates, thereby eliminating the need for professors to write more than one letter of recommendation per student.[60]

Campus clubs found that their activities came under the jurisdiction of the new assistant dean for student activities, Hugh S. Cameron, and his Committee on Student Activities. Cameron met with the clubs' officers to reiterate old policies and make some new ones. All clubs' books would be audited and their publications supervised; clubs had to bring their constitutions up to date, submit them to the dean, and formulate a calendar of club events. "The policy of the Dean of Student Activities," said Cameron, "is to have faith in the students, but once the students break that faith, they will never be given another chance."[61]

One set of organizations—the literary societies—survived the war in full strength. They were still the closest thing to sororities that were allowed on campus and had, if anything, become even more sorority-like and exclusive over the years. After much discussion of pseudo-aristocracy and democracy, a new society—the Sarah Lane Literary Society—was formed in 1947, named after the adviser to women. Expanding the number of women involved in the organizations appeared to put more flexibility into the system. Opening it up even more was the dean's proviso that in the future any ten women who wished to form a literary society be allowed to do so. After the Sarah Lane Literary Society was established, about half the women enrolled at Rice were members of a "lit."

In 1950 when Betty Rose Dowden (wife of English professor Wilfred Dowden) became adviser to women, she decided to combat the discrimination still being shown by the societies and enlisted Dr. and Mrs. Houston on her side. Although some members protested, four new literary societies were created: the Chaille Rice Literary Society, the Olga Keith Literary Society, the Mary Ellen Lovett Literary Society, and the Virginia Cleveland Literary Society. Any woman with satisfactory academic standing was eligible and was in fact guaranteed membership in a society, although it might not be the one she most wanted. Strict rules were drawn up for rush, and a complicated procedure was devised for final placement into the clubs. The two committees that had handled women students' issues and activities, the Literary Council and the Women's Council, were merged, with provision for one member to represent those women not affiliated with any literary society. Except for that one representative, independents continued to have no organized voice in women's activities on campus.[62]

The *Thresher* editor in 1950 did not care much for either the new system or the old one, saying that the literary societies had long been dedicated to the principle that it was a good thing to belong to a group that not everyone could belong to. Some of the students countered that they hoped for better representation, communication, and in general a stronger position for women on campus.

Although the organizations were criticized for their insensitivity in rushing, the resultant hurt feelings, and for the non-democratic environment they fostered, they served at least one important purpose. They brought together a scattered group of women, for whom very few facilities, and in some cases little encouragement, existed on campus.

Town students, both male and female, missed a great deal of college life and the education that accompanied it. The men had been somewhat better off in this respect after they had been required to spend at least one year in the dormitory, but that rule had not been repromulgated after World War II. For some town students, college was not very different from high school, except for the level of instruction. Through the 1940s, Rice was still primarily a man's school, with women enrolled. Although several women were listed as fellows and assistants in the instructional staff and students regarded them as faculty members, no woman became an assistant professor until the 1950s. Even Miss Dean, who taught Math 100 for years, was titled only a "fellow in mathematics," in addition to being acting librarian before 1946. The only woman to whom the female students could turn was the adviser to women, who was not a faculty member nor considered important enough to be listed as a member of the administration in the front of the catalog unil 1952. The literary societies helped fill some of the gaps.[63]

If the "lits" were not very literary, neither was the Rally Club much of a "service organization" by the postwar period. The club was as close to a fraternity as could be tolerated at Rice, with membership by invitation. It did perform whatever services the dean might require, such as parking cars at various campus functions, but the members do not seem strenuously to have searched out ways to help others. They were well known for their parties and for their initiation practices, reminiscent of the rites of the defunct Engineering Society.

Hazing, although stopped completely by the Navy takeover, was resurrected after the war. Like most other activities, it also changed, picked up a new name, and showed up in a different guise. Most of the old rules were revived in 1946, but the freshmen did not seem much interested in being hazed. The *Thresher* complained that there were few participants for the freshman shoe scramble during half time of the football game and claimed that the freshmen showed gross lack of sportsmanship. "Another such exhibition by the Freshmen or a continuation of the present attitude of them would make certain the present doubt as to their having qualities desired of students of Rice Institute," the editor stated.[64]

To remedy this appalling situation, a new program was instituted the next year under the name "guidance." Its purpose was to instill better school spirit and to assure freshmen of the opportunity to participate in all school activities. Traditional rules were in effect, ranging from wearing beanies and red suspenders, to attending pep rallies and games without dates, to not having haircuts until after Thanksgiving. Dorm slimes had special duties, involving cleaning the rooms of upperclassmen and running errands for them. Punishment for infractions of the rules could include standing at rigid attention, buttoning up shirts all the way to the neck, and wearing suspenders and ties every day. In charge of this program was a Guidance Committee of sophomores.[65]

This guidance program lasted about a year, until the *Thresher* and others began to complain and to ask questions. The editor thought that the announced program for 1948 was more fitting for fraternities, and he did not like forcing freshmen to parrot school history and other information as the Aggies did. Spirit should not be formalized, he said. "Rice student spirit, at its best," the editor maintained, "means an appreciation of individuality, the depreciation of 'masses.'" There was also the question of the Guidance Committee's authority and its source. The dean of student activities gave students the impression that he did not want to hear about any hazing; while he said that the Guidance Committee was responsible to him, he did not establish the committee or know of its legal right to exist. The Student Council disclaimed any knowledge of its establishment under the Student Association and set up another committee to investigate the program. However, their investigation found no serious objections to the guidance activities.

In May 1949, after much discussion on campus in Student Council meetings and in the *Thresher*, the Student Council offered the students a referendum on a bylaw that would establish a Guidance Committee and program. Both sides had a chance to put forth their views. On the one hand were those who approved hazing, including the physical type such as broomings. Those students claimed that it was the driving force in the guidance program, that it unified the class, brought the freshmen down off their high-school pedestals, was good practice for the "licks" a person had to take in life, that it was good to suffer once in a while, and that no permanent damage was done. On the other hand were those opposed not only to physical hazing but to any kind of extreme personal humiliation that might be involved in it. This side eschewed forced conformity and the psychological as well as physical effects of hazing. The Student Council passed a resolution condemning physical hazing and personal humiliation, although there was enough student sentiment to pass a bylaw establishing the Guidance Committee by a large majority. After more complaints about hazing the next fall, crude explosive devices were detonated in front of the house of two of the complainers, Raymond Lankford and Farrell Fulton. Finally, in the aftermath of this excess, the campus returned to normal. A certain amount of hazing went on as before, there was talk of the "voluntary" nature of guidance, and the Slime Parade and rules continued. Revived in 1948 or 1949 was the practice of kidnapping the sophomore class president before the sophomore dance, and the week before the party became known as Hell Week. Hell

Week soon had its own rules and regulations, but it would be a short-lived and tragic tradition.[66]

Hazing or no hazing, one of the rites of passage for freshmen was attendance at football games to yell for the team. Rice fans had much to cheer about in the 1940s. Coach Neely had barely had a chance to get settled into his position as head coach and athletic director before the war started and took most of his players into the armed forces. Practically the only player left from the 1941 team was Charles Malmberg, who, although 4-F because of his eyes, was still strong enough to become an All-Conference team choice in 1942. When the Navy took over the campus, however, they let their V-12 and ROTC students participate in the sports programs of the school, and Neely made up his teams with them. He remembers the next few years as some of the most interesting he ever knew. Those who showed up to play lacked outstanding ability, but they had interest, determination, and a lot of heart, and "they worked like Trojans," Neely said. The Southwest Conference played a full schedule, and with every school making up their teams with whomever happened to be there, the unexpected could happen and often did. In 1942 Texas beat Rice 58–0, and sportswriter Morris Frank asked assistant coach Joe Davis if he thought Neely would mind if Frank offered a comment that Rice would probably not entertain a bowl bid that year. Neely replied that he did not think

125. *Rice defeated Texas A&M in this 1946 football game, 27–10.*

126. *Another victory over A&M, 28–6 (1948).*

127. *Freshman track team, 1947–48.*

much of Frank's humor. The next year, however, with the same team against some of the same Texas players, the score was 7–0 with Rice on top. In 1944 in Austin the Owls won again, 7–6. Neely says that he probably got more satisfaction out of those two games than almost any others.

With players such as Weldon Humble, Carl Russ, J. W. Magee, Joe Watson, James "Froggy" Williams, Ralph Murphy, and Paul Giroski, Rice was a team to contend with in the postwar forties. In 1946, with many of the prewar players back on the field, Rice tied for first place in the conference with Arkansas and went on to the Orange Bowl. On New Year's Day 1947 the Owls defeated the Tennessee Vols 8–0. Once Rice was leading, Neely played very conservative football that day, and when some criticized the lack of excitement in the game, it is rumored that the Rice coach said that if they wanted to see a circus, they should have gone to Sarasota (where Ringling Brothers had their winter quarters). In 1949 Rice was ranked fifth in the nation, won the conference outright with a record of nine wins and one loss, and defeated North Carolina in the Cotton Bowl.[67]

In those years, tickets for Rice games in the old 38,000-seat stadium were at a premium, and scalpers were asking and getting as much as twenty dollars per ticket in 1948 for sellout games such as those against Texas and SMU. A drive against ticket scal-pers that year netted arrests of a San Antonio doctor, an Austin insurance man, an Austin golf pro, and three University of Texas students. The new stadium relieved the pressure. A Neely edict solved another very different problem. To protect the playing field from unnecessary wear, no hooved animals would be allowed on the Bermuda grass turf. That included Bevo, the University of Texas's steer mascot. However, neither the coach nor the university could solve the problem of fans who came over from Louisiana to see the Rice-LSU game. On their way home, many were stopped for speeding by officers of the Texas Department of Public Safety. They would often write Coach Neely to complain of this treatment and ask why Neely and Rice did not "educate" these patrolmen on behalf of the Louisiana boosters. Neely usually replied that he was sorry, but he had no jurisdiction over the police.[68]

Basketball teams also fared well through the 1940s, first under coach Buster Brannon (1939–1942) and then Joe Davis (1943–1949), winning the conference in 1940, 1942, 1943, 1944, 1945, and 1949. From 1941 to 1945, a Rice Owl was always on the All-American list. Bill Closs was named to the roster once, and Bob Kinney and Bill Henry both twice. The Rice track team continued to win individual conference championships with Fred Wolcott, Bill Cummins, Bill Christopher, Augie Erfurth, Harry Coffman, and Tobin Rote.

And tennis starred Bobby Curtis, Jack Rodgers, Chick Harris, and Jack Turpin.[69]

By 1950, the future for Rice looked very bright. The campus was expanding in both numbers of faculty members and numbers of buildings. The new president had steered through some much-needed reorganization of the administration, and the new curriculum was calculated to produce the kinds of students, occupations, and knowledge that the future would require. Although the primary emphasis was still in the sciences and engineering, the new curriculum called for expansion in the humanities. That expansion would bring the Institute ever closer to the ideal of Edgar Odell Lovett's 1912 vision:

Accordingly it is as a university that the Institute proposes to begin, a university of liberal and technical learning, where liberal studies may be studied liberally or technically, where technical subjects may be pursued either technically or liberally, where whatever of professional training is offered is to be based as far as possible on a broad general education.[70]

CHAPTER 8

A Decade of Growth: The 1950s

Much to their delight, the board announced in 1950 that most of the goals of the long-range program adopted in 1945 had been accomplished, five years ahead of schedule. The Institute had expanded the board, increased the number of faculty and provided raises in salary and benefits for them, added ninety-one semester courses to the curriculum, constructed a number of new buildings (including a library, a gymnasium, and a president's home on campus), and lowered the student-teacher ratio to twelve or thirteen to one. Realization of these aims did not mean that the trustees would rest on their laurels. The board wanted further improvement of the salary scale, an increase in faculty to reach and maintain a student-teacher ratio of ten to one, expansion in research activity, library development, more graduate and undergraduate scholarships, a higher enrollment (about 2,000), and more buildings to house and teach the larger

number of students and to provide research facilities for both faculty and students. Three million dollars in gifts had helped accomplish the goals set in 1945, but even more money was needed for the future.[1]

In 1951 estimated annual expenses for Rice amounted to more than $1.6 million, and by 1954 the university was spending more than $2 million a year. Most of the revenue came from income on investments; the rest came from student fees, research contracts, donations from alumni, and some income from restricted funds. By 1959 the Institute had more than $91.5 million in assets (including a physical plant valued at more than $28 million), income of more than $4.7 million, and expenditures of more than $4.3 million. In the decade from 1947–48 to 1958–59, the Rice Institute burgeoned from a small educational operation with a budget of approximately $1 million to a complicated business with a quadrupled budget. Contrary to

uninformed opinion, the university did not have excess money. The board still carefully watched all expenditures, as it had from James Baker's time, and it was looking for new sources of income and generous donors.[2]

Reorganizing the Board

Since at least 1947, board members had discussed increasing their own number and using help from outside. In September of that year, while discussing new accounting procedures and the relocation of the business office, board chairman Harry Hanszen had proposed that the Finance Committee be reorganized and enlarged. He suggested a committee of five or six, with three trustees and two or three outside members.[3] Harry Wiess picked some alumni to help on his Building Committee and also favored expanding the number of trustees, but the board took no formal action then. A year later it was clear that the board, especially its chairman, was overworked. Hanszen had been devoting almost full time to the Institute's affairs, and his neglected personal activities were demanding his attention to such an extent that he was considering resigning from the board. Harry Wiess had just died, and George Brown, looking after investments, had more work than one person could manage. In fact, the affairs of the Institute had become so complicated that the seven-man board could not handle them adequately as a committee of the whole or by separate committees made up only of trustees.

In a memorandum to the other members, Lamar Fleming proposed that board members delegate authority and responsibility to standing committees comprising both trustees and nontrustees. The innovation was not unattractive; mixed committees would enable the board to enlist the community's service for the Institute. Fleming suggested the Harvard plan, whereby trustees maintained legal ownership and responsibility as the charter dictated, but brought in others as members of the Board of Overseers (or officers with some other title) to sit with the trustees, vote equally with them, and serve on the various committees.[4]

In August 1949 the board acted. First the trustees asked J. Newton Rayzor to fill the vacancy created by Harry Wiess's death; after Rayzor accepted, they voted to expand to a fifteen-member Board of Governors. The new board consisted of the seven trustees, who still held legal ownership of the Institute, and eight governors, each of whom served a term of four years and was selected by a majority of the trustees. (The governors had no vote in their selection.) Terms were staggered so that every year two new governors were appointed, and the "term members" were ineligible for reappointment. When his term had expired, a governor became a governor adviser and continued to advise the university. The chairman of the Board of Trustees also chaired the Board of Governors, and committee chairmen were usually trustees. The first eight governors were Robert P. Doherty, Harmon Whittington, Walter L. Goldston, John S. Ivy, Herbert Allen, L. E. Garfield, Francis T. Fendley, and Robert H. Ray. The first committees established under the new plan were the Finance Committee, the Oil Committee, the Buildings and Grounds Committee, and the Alumni and Student Activity Committee.[5]

After George Brown became chairman of the board in February 1950 and John Ivy was named to Hanszen's place after the latter's death, membership of the Board of Trustees changed only twice from 1951 to 1963. Frederick R. Lummis retired in 1955 and Gus Wortham in 1961. To their places were named cotton expert Harmon Whittington and oilman Daniel R. Bullard, respectively.

One of the primary goals of the new board was to seek additional sources of funding for the Institute. To be sure, funds for special purposes had come to the school from various sources. In 1950 Sallie Shepherd Perkins donated funds to endow a school of music, but it was several years before the income from her gift grew sufficiently to maintain more than a lectureship and a few courses in music. Olga Keith Wiess endowed a chair of geology in memory of her husband Harry in 1952, and in 1954 she gave still more to construct a building with a laboratory for a department of geology. In 1953 trustee J. Newton Rayzor established a chair in philosophy and religious thought; Rayzor also wanted to see a chapel on campus. In the same year the Masterson family began the endowment of a chair of history in memory of Harris Masterson, Jr., the chaplain to Autry House. And in 1958 Mrs. Reginald Henry Hargrove donated funds for a chair of economics in memory of her husband, a Rice alumnus of the class of 1918.[6]

A New Emphasis on Fund Raising

Such donations as endowed chairs and bequests, like the part of the Hanszen estate that the Institute received, were always appreciated; but more money was necessary on a regular basis to fund continued expansion and to cover expenses of the enlarged educational program. It was clear that the university had to make a vigorous effort to attract donors and solicit funds from many sources if it was to continue to operate on its expanded scale. In 1953 the board began seriously to consider soliciting contributions. The Baker board had been reluctant to request funds outside of the Rice community because of possible strings attached to any donations; in contrast, the new board looked to thriving postwar Houston for aid.

In 1953 Harmon Whittington's Development Committee recommended a program to attract influential friends for Rice, and the board created the Rice Institute Associates in 1954. The purpose of this group was "to provide a channel for the free exchange of ideas between the students and teachers of the Institute and a group of representative citizens who have been influential in civic, cultural, and educational affairs of the region." Members would also advise the Institute on its development and help increase its service to the community. Membership in the Associates came by invitation, and some alumni who had worked for Rice's interests through the years were disappointed not to receive one. Newton Rayzor suggested forming a parallel group to be known as the Rice Alumni Associates, but the board decided instead to invite the alumni to join the group that was already constituted. The membership pledge was $10,000, paid at the rate of $1,000 per year.[7]

The Institute also turned to industry as a source of funds. In 1955 the board established the Rice Institute Research Sponsors and solicited support from selected companies at the rate of $10,000 per year for a three-year period. President Houston used this discretionary fund to train graduate students in research methods, to support new research, and to purchase research equipment. The program also provided business contacts and served to inform companies about the research being done on campus. Research Days, when representatives of the sponsors came to campus to see where their money was going, were great successes.[8]

Throughout the 1950s Rice also received various monetary grants. Companies began to support research and students in many more ways than through the Research Sponsors program, and Rice benefited from grants and scholarships from such companies as Union Carbide, Shell Oil, Superior Oil, DuPont, and Monsanto. The United States government also awarded funds for research and fellowships. Many private individuals and smaller firms established scholarships and fellowships as well, and by 1959 there were seventeen graduate fellowships and seventy-two undergraduate scholarships funded by these individuals and corporations (many of them multiple awards) and given out under Institute auspices. These totals do not include noninstitutional awards, such as the Atomic Energy Commission Fellowships, made directly to students by organizations outside the campus.[9]

One of the continuing goals of the board was to raise faculty salaries, and for that purpose in 1955 the Ford Foundation awarded two grants to the Institute, an Endowment Grant and an Accomplishment Grant. The Endowment Grant had to be invested and only its income used for salaries for a period of ten years, after which both principal and income were open to any educational use. The Accomplishment Grant could have been used directly, but the board voted to treat it as an endowment also. By 1957 the Ford Foundation had given the Institute more than $1 million under these grants, and Rice was better able to compete with other schools for good faculty.[10]

Growth in the Administration

Increased donations, programs, and grants helped to realize the board's goals, but an enlarged and more complicated Institute also meant that the administration had to expand to handle the increased load. Faculty committees could take some of the burden, but the administration itself grew slowly yet steadily.

A number of administrative changes took place in 1950. Dean Harry B. Weiser retired and returned to teaching chemistry, and in his place President Houston appointed Professor George Holmes Richter, Rice '26, another chemist. Hugh S. Cameron, dean of students, died suddenly during the summer, and Professor Guy T. McBride, a chemical engineer, became associate dean of students that fall. Why McBride was named associate dean and not dean, as Cameron had been, is something of a mystery, but his title is usually explained by the tradition that there should be only one dean at Rice, *the* dean of the Institute. When McBride left in 1958, James R. Sims became adviser to men, an office that despite its name retained the duties of a dean of students—disciplinarian of the campus. Sarah Lane left the office of adviser to women, which she had occupied since 1931, but remained on the library staff. That office saw a procession of occupants during the 1950s: Betty Rose Dowden (wife of Professor Wilfred Dowden of the English department), Clara Margaret Mohr Kotch (Rice '51), Paula Meredith Mosle (Rice '52), and Nancy Moore Eubank (Rice '55). There were also several assistants to the president during Houston's tenure: James Morehead, William H. Masterson, John Parish, and Thad Marsh.[11]

Three men who had become institutions at Rice left the university during the fifties. William Ward Watkin died in 1952, John T. McCants retired in 1953, and Samuel G. McCann retired in 1957. These three figures had probably done as much on campus as Edgar Odell Lovett had to keep Rice operating smoothly, and they were certainly known personally to many more students and teachers than any president could be. It took a number of people to replace them. Changes in the accounting system and movement of the busi-

ness office onto campus had altered greatly the duties of the bursar. No longer did he have independent control over all money spent and purchases made. The bursar's functions were distributed among several different sections. McCann had been both registrar and director of admissions. In 1953 he became director of admissions only, while J. D. Thomas was appointed acting registrar and Michael McEnany assistant registrar. In 1954 McEnany became registrar. James B. Giles became admissions director in 1957. Watkin had filled a number of posts, including chairman of the Committee on Outdoor Sports, curator of buildings, and, during the war, civil defense chairman, in addition to building the architecture department. His activities were split among a number of people.[12]

In 1953 a new position was created in the administration. The board and the president had been looking for someone to head the new geology department that Mrs. Wiess had established in honor of her late husband. They settled on Carey Croneis, who was at that time president of Beloit College in Beloit, Wisconsin. Croneis was to be both Harry Carothers Wiess Professor of Geology and provost of the Institute. As professor of geology, his duties were clear—teaching, continuing his research, and supervising and developing the new department. As provost, his responsibilities were vague. President Houston wrote Croneis that his duties would be worked out in practice and would concern

the interests of the Institute as a whole. Croneis would begin by serving on the Executive Committee and helping to improve Rice's public relations. It appears that chairing the Executive Committee and acting as goodwill ambassador for the Institute composed the greater part of the provost's duties; academic matters were handled by the dean and the president. A superb speaker, the popular Croneis represented the Institute very well.[13]

In place of the four men who had run the Institute under Edgar Odell Lovett, there were eleven listed as officers of administration in the 1956 *General Announcements*; they included an assistant to the registrar, the bursar, and the development assistant, in addition to the president, assistant to the president, provost, dean, associate dean, adviser to women, director of admissions, and registrar. While this may seem to be a significant increase and might imply a high degree of organization, that was not necessarily the case. Rice was still a highly personal institution where matters were handled directly without the intrusion of memoranda and complex organizational tables. In fact, when a faculty committee attempted in 1953–54 to answer a Carnegie Foundation questionnaire on higher education, it found making up a normal organizational chart practically impossible. There were no "channels" to speak of. Confusing though that might have been to outsiders, it worked for Rice at the time.[14]

In 1955 the duties of depart-

128. *Carey Croneis, at various times professor of geology, provost, acting president, and chancellor of Rice.*

the department. Houston also thought that it was desirable to rotate the chairmanship from time to time.[15]

New Faces on the Faculty

During the 1950s a number of faculty members made their first appearances on campus. In architecture David Parsons and Anderson Todd came, and in chemistry Ronald Sass and Richard B. Turner, while chemical engineering hired two Rice alumni, Sam H. Davis and Riki Kobayashi. John Merwin joined civil engineering, John H. Auden, economics, and John A. S. Adams, geology. Many will remember Jackson Cope, the poet and novelist James Dickey, Thad Marsh, and John B. Pickard from their English classes, and Andrew Muir, William Nelson, and Frank Vandiver in history. Franz Brotzen and James Wilhoit went to mechanical engineering and Konstantin Kolenda and Niels Nielsen to philosophy. Harold Rorschach and Calvin Class joined the physics department, as did Andrew Bryan, Rice '18, who returned from the business community to the campus.

In 1958 the *Journal of Southern History*, the scholarly publication of the Southern Historical Association, moved to Rice, and in 1960 the English department started a new quarterly, *Studies in English Literature: 1500–1900*, edited by Carroll Camden.[16]

Expansion of departments was a continuous activity in the 1950s, but it was by no means an explosion. About forty people

ment chairman were specifically stated and entered into the faculty minutes for the first time. These duties included the preparation of a departmental budget and recommendations for promotions. President Houston pointed out that the chairman had full responsibility for the department, but he who occupied the chair was not necessarily to be regarded as chief scholar within were added to the faculty from 1950 to 1959, with the numbers split fairly evenly among the humanities, the sciences, and engineering. The new element was an expansion in liberal arts. In 1951 the administration announced that the aim of the university was "to raise the liberal arts and humanities to the level of excellence and breadth of coverage now enjoyed by the sciences," and it set about developing a program to do so. The library's acquisition of new resources for the liberal arts also made possible more and better courses. Except for a single doctorate in history awarded in 1933, the only higher degrees in the humanities offered by the Institute had been master's degrees in history, English, philosophy, German, the Romance languages, and architecture. In 1951 Rice was able to offer doctoral programs in history and English. In 1954, to attract more students to the humanities, the Board of Governors established scholarships amounting to $300 each for fifteen freshmen in liberal arts.[17]

By 1959 the faculty was of such size and the departments of such complexity that two more administrative positions were created, with the dual purposes of further developing graduate programs and making the undergraduate departments more effective. William H. Masterson of the history department was named dean of humanities, and LeVan Griffis from the Borg-Warner Corporation became dean of engineering. Richter remained dean of the Institute. The duties of the new deanships included acquisition of new faculty, adjustment of salaries and academic ranks, and distribution of office space, laboratories, equipment, and the like; but the positions were not solely administrative. Houston expected these men to teach and carry on research as well.

Also in 1959, the Executive Committee was expanded and renamed the Faculty Council. This council was composed of the president, provost, dean of the Institute, deans of humanities and engineering, and six members elected by the faculty (two each from humanities, engineering, and science). The committee would continue to advise the president on matters of policy and curriculum. With these changes the administration began to respond to the more complicated institution that Rice had become.[18]

The 1950s Building Boom

More students and faculty needed more buildings, and Rice's building boom continued in the 1950s. The first of the new structures was opened in 1953; it housed a six-million-volt Van de Graaff accelerator. In 1963 this building was named in honor of Professor Tom Bonner, who died in 1961. It was built to the north of the physics amphitheater, across the street. Not long after that, plans were made for two laboratory buildings, an auditorium, a student center, and more dormitories.

The laboratory buildings, one for geology funded by a gift of $1 million from the daughters of the late Harry Wiess, and one for biology financed by a donation from the M. D. Anderson Foundation, were located on the western side of the secondary axis running north-south between the men's dormitories. That axis would terminate on the north with a new auditorium. In Hamman Hall, built with a gift from the George and Mary Josephine Hamman Foundation, the Institute finally gained a real stage for music, drama, meetings, and lectures. The new buildings opened in 1958 and 1959. Architect for all three was George F. Pierce, Jr., Rice '42, and his firm of Pierce and Pierce. For the stairwell of the Keith-Wiess Geological Laboratories, David Parsons, Rice's resident artist, created a metal mobile sculpture entitled *Universe*. For the walls of the biology building Parsons molded a number of bricks with intaglio designs representing the various phyla of animals.[19]

While the biology and geology laboratories were being built, across the street to the south of them a student center and chapel complex was under way. Trustee J. Newton Rayzor had been lobbying the board for a chapel since at least 1949. In 1953 he had suggested constructing some sort of multipurpose building to house a chapel and the Shepherd School of Music, and possibly the Houston Symphony Orchestra as well. Other board members agreed with Rayzor that a chapel was needed, but they thought that one structure would not be

129. *A view of Rice's Van de Graaff particle accelerator—the high voltage column, with the pressure tank removed.*

enough for the three activities. They decided that the chapel should be considered as a separate project.

In May 1954 Rayzor had pointed out again that a chapel was one of the most urgent needs on campus. Later that month, Dr. Houston reported on a meeting of a committee that was planning a memorial to the students and former students who had died in service to the country. He stated that, while no one favored a memorial monument by itself, there was much enthusiasm for a student union building dedicated to those lost. Representatives of the class of 1955, which had lost eleven of its members in a naval airplane crash in 1953, indicated a special interest in such a memorial. Further discussion, both of a chapel and student religious center and of a memorial student union, resulted in the merging of the two. The Rice Memorial Student Center was designed by Harvin C. Moore, Rice '27; its cornerstone dedicated the center as a memorial for "the students of Rice who have brought honor to the Institute through their contributions to the welfare of mankind and of those who have given their lives in the service of our country."[20]

Certain questions arose in connection with the planning of a chapel and a student union. The Institute, after all, had been "aggressively non-sectarian" (to quote Cram, Goodhue and Ferguson) from its inception, and the committee studying the center's proposed uses and the activities to be housed there had much to discuss. Their decisions were complicated by the need to determine exactly how the student union would be used, now that it was definite that a residential college system would replace the student dormitories (see pp. 170–187). The Committee on Student Housing that was studying the college system did not think that a bookstore, a cafeteria, and offices for student associations, publications, and alumni should be in the same building as a chapel. Even the structure's location and the possibility that such a center would distract attention from the colleges came under discussion. Eventually the center was placed in a line with the new biology and geology buildings. It took the form of a courtyard closed on three sides by the student center itself, a cloister with offices opening onto it, and the chapel. Located within the center were the campus store, Sammy's (the snack bar that replaced the small and very crowded Roost next to the old campus store in the basement of the library), various offices for student groups and alumni, and a large ballroom.[21] Funds came from Mr. and Mrs. J. Newton Rayzor, from the bookstore surplus, and from alumni.

Opening in 1958, the Rice Memorial Student Center was not an instant success but rather an instant failure. Students complained immediately: it was too far from normal activity areas, especially the dormitories and the library; it was too sterile (considering the state of the old Roost in the Fondren Library basement, anything merely clean

130. *The Keith-Wiess Geological Laboratory, April 14, 1958.*

131. *Construction of Hamman Hall, 1957.*

132. *Hamman Hall, a view of the nearly completed building, April 14, 1958.*

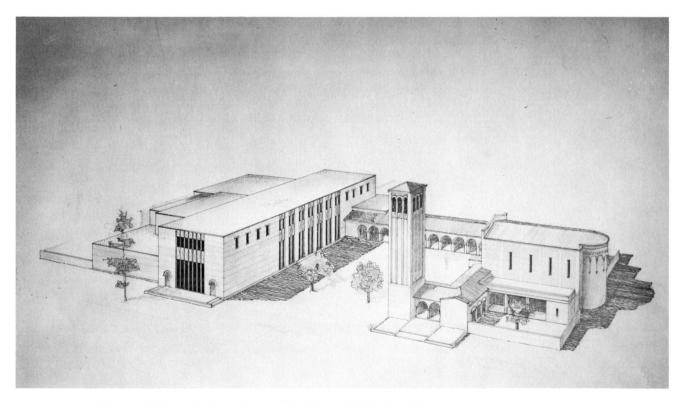

133. *Architect Harvin C. Moore's plans for the Rice Memorial Student Center.*

134. *Construction of the Rice Memorial Student Center.*

135. *Interior view of the bookstore in the student center shortly after it opened.*

would have looked sterile); there was nothing to do there and no one to see, and the addition of some Ping-Pong tables, a pool table, and a television set to the barren, concrete-floored basement did not attract many. The center did have its uses, though. Graduate students, faculty, and nonresident undergraduates often ate lunch and played bridge there, and various groups used the Grand Ballroom for dances and meetings. But the remote RMC did not supplant the Sallyport or the library lounge as the place on campus to meet people.[22]

Other small physical changes were made in 1957. Dr. Lovett's gravel walks were paved over with pebble concrete sidewalks, the roads were paved, and the traffic pattern changed drastically. Partly at the instigation of board governor J. T. Rather, Jr., the board decided to make the campus more conducive to walking than it had been. For a year or so before the asphalt was laid, barricades were erected across several roads through the middle of the campus to prevent automobile traffic. Many students protested the alteration of their familiar traffic routes, and from time to time someone would blow up one of the barricades with an explosive charge. By the time new landscaping was complete, the road running between the third entrance on Main Street and the Mechanical Laboratory had been blocked at its junction with the south part of the campus loop road. The academic quadrangle had also been closed to all vehicles, and the parking lots in front of the Mechanical Lab and Lovett Hall had been eliminated in favor of spacious lawns. Although new parking lots were opened, they were not sufficient; convenient parking places were soon at a premium, and some of those who did not like to walk took up bicycling.[23]

As badly needed as new classrooms and laboratories, perhaps more so, were renovated dormitories. With the exception of Wiess Hall, all of the dormitory buildings dated from the first days of the Institute and were in dilapidated condition. Doors had been kicked in and never repaired, walls needed new paint, electric wires hung haphazardly, bathrooms had out-of-date and often inoperative plumbing, and very little was clean. In addition, the dormitories were extremely overcrowded. Freshmen especially were crammed three to a room—usually a room that scarcely held two, that had only one closet, and that provided no study space at all. In 1952, 631 students occupied the space normally meant for 551. Students and faculty alike compared life in these communities to living in a zoo. The practice of hazing flourished, and any intellectual endeavor was considered by some to be strictly accidental. Nothing could have been further from Edgar Odell Lovett's concept of the Rice residential halls as gentlemen's clubs.[24]

The shabby physical condition of the dorms was due partly to student negligence and partly to Institute neglect. Once damage had been done to a room and not repaired, the successive inhabitants had felt little responsibility for careful treatment, so that the buildings deteriorated progressively. The deplorable housing situation was the culmination of several factors. Dormitories had been severely overcrowded before Wiess Hall was built in 1947; although the new dorm alleviated the strain somewhat, subsequent growth in enrollment had canceled out the gain. Furthermore, the new five-year engineering curriculum had added approximately fifty students a year to the dormitory load. Not only were more students being admitted, but a higher percentage were from out of town. The postwar growth of the University of Houston attracted many of the graduates from Houston high schools who in the past would have looked to Rice, thus relieving pressure on the Institute to act as the sole institution of higher learning for Houstonians. That, plus the actions of several groups connected with the Institute, including the faculty, encouraged young people from out of town and out of state to apply to Rice. Considering the pressure of dorm life, hazing, and the distractions of other extracurricular activities, it was no wonder that freshman grades suffered.[25]

Vitally interested in alleviating the dormitory situation were the associate dean of students, Guy T. McBride, and the chairman of the board, George R. Brown. In 1953 Brown stated that the most important project for the Development Committee was to increase dormitory facilities, and the board committees on grounds and buildings and on alumni and student activity met to investigate the construction of additional housing. McBride had talked to Dr. Lovett and read what Lovett had written in *The Book of the Opening* about the residential college system; he then wrote a memorandum to President Houston proposing that Rice embrace the college system to improve not only the physical conditions within the halls but the intellectual conditions as well.[26]

The Residential College System

Lovett had envisioned a system of residential colleges at Rice like the one Woodrow Wilson had planned for Princeton, which adapted the English residential college to American undergraduate life. Unlike the British models, colleges at the Institute would not have any fundamental educational responsibility; that belonged to the Institute itself. Instead, they would offer education of a more informal nature: intellectual stimulation, fellowship, competition, social activities, democratic self-government. By the 1950s several schools—Harvard University, Yale University, the California Institute of Technology, and a few others—had residential colleges, some quite different from the others, some with only subtle differences. The nature of Rice's system remained hazy.[27]

After a committee under the chairmanship of governor Herbert Allen had thoroughly studied the costs for new dormitory and dining facilities under a college system, the board adopted a program in September 1954. New dormitories for 225 men and 100 women would be constructed; the program stipulated that housing for 125 more men would be built, once there was sufficient demand. There was no rush to complete the scheme; the board wanted it to be carefully planned and executed. They expected completion with occupancy in 1956–57. As it turned out, planning and construction took every bit of the time allotted.[28]

To formulate a plan for the organization, administration, and supervision of the colleges, Dr. Houston appointed a faculty-student Committee on Student Housing with Dean McBride as chairman. It included faculty members from a number of departments, along with the adviser to women, representatives from the Student Council, and a new group, the Women's Hall Committee. J. Newton Rayzor attended several meetings and worked closely with the committee. Members of the board and of the committee traveled throughout the United States to visit schools with college systems. Of primary interest were those at the California Institute of Technology and Yale University, but the committee also visited such schools as Wellesley College, Radcliffe College, and Harvard University.[29]

Planning the colleges involved

elements from the elevated to the trivial, from discussions of what constituted a college and how to build "collegiate homes for human living" to the proper dress for the college lobby or breakfast. The committee reached some conclusions quickly. They decided that certain factors characterized a college: group living and dining, traditions, student government, continuity, a master in residence, group social affairs, and athletic and intellectual competition. Committee members also identified two "deficiencies" in the typical Rice undergraduate that they hoped the colleges would remedy: "a lack of a sense of social concern; not just a vague sympathy but rather an informed sense of responsibility in the spheres of community action, from the family unit to affairs of national global scope. . . [and] a deficiency in broad intellectual curiosity."[30]

In line with these observations, the committee decided that certain provisions should be built into the system. A large dining room and a lounge would allow student gatherings, especially for that most important reminder of the college's unity, the daily meal shared by all residents at one time. These implied buildings of a certain size and configuration. To place responsibility on the student wherever possible, a strong student government would be established in each college to initiate and maintain social and intellectual activities, competitions, and traditions, as well as to enforce discipline. The committee hoped to correct the other de-

ficiency noted in its report by encouraging increased intellectual contact with teachers outside the classroom; both married and unmarried faculty members would reside in the colleges. A study by the faculty Committee on Educational Inquiry had revealed that students thought contact with the faculty outside the classroom had usually proved unpleasant, although they still desired it. Perhaps natural informal interaction in a domestic environment would be more agreeable.

The committee had an ambitious program for the system. They wanted an atmosphere like that of Lovett's "gentlemen's club," a home away from home. They wanted to foster maturity in the students, as well as a sense of responsibility for the welfare of the group and the individual. They wanted to provide an environment conducive to discussion of ideas and suitable organization for the development of student leaders. They hoped that the colleges would make a positive contribution to the students' lives.[31]

In its basic deliberations on the college system, the committee originally considered establishing only four colleges (based on the four existing dormitories), and these were to be only for men. The planned women's dormitory had its own problems, but at the beginning of its study the committee concentrated on the men's facilities. That the Institute finally established a women's college at the same time is due largely to the efforts of trustee

J. Newton Rayzor and two successive advisers to women, Clara Margaret Mohr Kotch and Paula Meredith Mosle.[32] They convinced the others that if Rice was going to have a workable college system, the arrangement needed to apply to everyone on campus from the beginning.

The number of students residing in each college was fairly well determined by the existing dormitories. East, South, and West Halls housed 110 students and Wiess housed 220, so it was obvious from an architectural standpoint that college size should be some multiple of 110. The committee decided that 220 would be ideal, because that number was small enough to be responsive to a single master but large enough to include all types of students and thus maintain a democratic college and campus. (The committee wanted to avoid any semblance of exclusivity or a fraternity atmosphere about the colleges.) It finally recommended to the board a building program that provided for four colleges of 220 students each, using Wiess Hall as one and increasing the size of the other three. This total of 880 was 105 more than the initial board plan but within the eventual total number that the board had in mind. The committee was certain that the additional places would not go empty, as there was already considerable demand from town students to live in the dorms.[33]

Essential for the success of the system, the committee thought, were the master and his wife, because they would be the primary ones responsible for achieving the goals of social concern and intellectual curiosity. It was therefore important to choose the masters with great care; the committee recommended that they be chosen from the ranks of full professors. Although the committee originally thought that masters, faculty fellows, and student officers would handle disciplinary matters, the final report emphasized that masters were not to be thought of as disciplinarians. Fellows were left out of the process altogether. As in the first dormitories, the students themselves were to be responsible for discipline, though serious infractions would be dealt with, as they always had been, by the dean of students. The master retained overall responsibility for student life in his college, but his main duties were to counsel students, provide an example, and advise student committees. The committee further recommended that each master be provided with a house next to his college but physically separated from it.[34]

Other faculty members were to be associated with the colleges, either as residents or nonresidents. Called "fellows" at first, these people soon came to be known as "faculty associates." The committee saw the associates' function as stimulating intellectual and cultural interests and advising the students and master when asked to do so. They were to join a college by invitation from the master and college members, and the committee recommended that each college have at least fifteen non-resident and two to four resident associates.[35]

Most decisions could be made simply, but the committee spent a number of meetings discussing how a freshman would join a college. At first a separate dormitory was envisioned for freshmen, who would then join a college in their sophomore year after competition among the colleges for "desirable freshmen." Militating against this idea were the cost of such a facility in addition to the planned expansion of the colleges-to-be, and the fraternity-like atmosphere that such competition would engender. The committee investigated moving freshmen from one college to another during the year and allowing them to choose one at the end of that time, but the clear disadvantages in such upheavals soon shelved that proposition. Even inviting freshmen to dine at other colleges before they made their final decision seemed too much like fraternity rushing. Finally the committee decided to assign freshmen arbitrarily to the colleges upon admission, guaranteeing them the right to request one transfer (but no college could invite such a transfer). Masters and associates were to make the assignments after consulting the student college officers, taking care to distribute students by major and geographical section of the country to avoid any concentration in one college. An incoming freshman could ask for placement in a certain college, but he was not guaranteed that his request would be granted. In the placement system that was finally adopted, a new student was allowed to request the college in which a brother was enrolled, and two freshmen friends could request assignment together but could not designate a specific college. The committee was determined to provide a balanced environment in which individuals could find new friends from all geographical regions and from all academic fields.[36]

Although there was an early suggestion that town students have a college of their own centered around a student union, the committee decided in the end that all town students and transfers were to be assigned to colleges in the same manner that out-of-town students were. They would have all the rights, privileges, and responsibilities of resident college members, with a few exceptions concerning certain college offices. The committee also hoped that town students would eat meals at their colleges, especially on those special evenings designated as College Nights.[37]

Endeavoring to resolve as many details as possible for the colleges before they opened, the committee set up two subcommittees on student activities. One recommended appropriate social and sports activities and even told college officers to survey their members before formulating final plans. (The committee included a planning schedule for the first year.) The other subcommittee wrote a model college constitution, which established a representative government in a college Cabinet with executive, legisla-

tive, and judicial duties. The Cabinet was to meet regularly, supervise all the various college activities and committees, and control room assignments.[38]

If a college system was important for the men, it was equally important—perhaps more significant—for the women. From the beginning of the Institute, women had usually been left to find their own housing. They could often obtain lists of reputable boarding houses or rentable rooms from Mr. McCants' office or from the adviser to women, but otherwise they had to fend for themselves. Many boarded with the families of present or past Rice students, or lived at home. Partly because of these conditions, most women students at Rice were from Houston. In 1951 only 65 of the 300 women enrolled were from out of town.

That year the adviser to women, Betty Rose Dowden, recommended that the Institute convert some of its property into housing for female students. The Institute had bought a block of apartments on Banks Street in 1948, originally intending to provide housing facilities for faculty; postwar housing had not kept up with Houston's population growth, and new professors had found housing difficult during their first years at Rice. By 1951 the housing shortage had eased, and some of the Banks Street apartments were vacant; Mrs. Dowden wished to use them for women. The board agreed, and 60 young women moved into the apartments under the watchful of Margaret Dunn, the house-

mother. Curfews were established—the women had to be in by 11:30 P.M. on weekdays and 2:00 A.M. on Saturday nights—and neither liquor nor men were allowed in the apartments.

After the committee decided to include the proposed women's dormitory in the college system, the members realized that the number of women who desired housing would greatly exceed the number of spaces in the new dormitory. Paula Meredith Mosle, who was adviser to women in 1955, was authorized to find some additional temporary housing. She discovered that the Town and Country Apartments on HMC Street were willing to lease several units to the school. Clara Morrow was housemother for the accommodations there, from which a bus transported 50 women back and forth to classes. Security in both apartment houses left a great deal to be desired, and more than one mother must have wondered what she was leaving her daughter to after seeing the facilities. However, the women came back; and by 1955, 124 out-of-town women were among the 355 female students enrolled.[39]

In May 1955 the Committee on Student Housing presented its second interim report, this one on residence halls for women. For a number of reasons, the committee had not initially planned for a women's college. For one thing, only one residential unit was to be built, housing only 100 women. That meant that there could be no competition between colleges for members, as was originally planned for the men's

136. *The Banks Street apartments for Rice women.*

colleges. Since the dormitory would house only one-third of the female student population, the committee thought it impossible to define an absolute center of women's college life. The new dormitory would instead provide a sound basis for a residential campus system once more dormitories for women were built.

In the minds of the committee members, the existence of "strong female social organizations," the literary societies, also negated the need for immediate college facilities for women. While the committee, which was all male except for the incumbent adviser to women and Sarah Lane, was unwilling to let any hint of fraternities into the men's colleges, it is interesting that they ignored the societies' resemblance to so-

rorities, which could be as divisive among the women as fraternities among the men. Once the committee decided to assign freshmen arbitrarily to colleges, the first reason for excluding women from the college system was no longer valid; but the second impediment, the cost of building a dormitory for 220 women instead of the 100 authorized by the board, remained.

College or not, the creation of a women's residence hall necessitated answering other questions that had not arisen regarding the men's dormitories. First, its site had to be established. Some on the committee favored a location between the President's House and Abercrombie Laboratory; others recommended a spot between Cohen House and the Gate

Number 2 entrance off Main Street. The board decided instead to place the dormitory between the President's House and Sunset Boulevard. There was more space on that side of the campus for future expansion of facilities that would eventually house 440 women.

While it seemed to be taken for granted after McBride's original memorandum that each men's college would have a master, the motion that the women's halls also have a master and family living nearby was not introduced and passed until May 1955. In its interim report, the committee stated its strong belief in the importance of the master and his family to the women's hall environment; it also recommended that "an unmarried woman of faculty status" live in the women's dormitory. At that time, of course, the women's residence hall was not yet designated a college, and there was no unmarried woman of faculty status to serve as hall resident.[40] Such a woman would have to be hired first.

As early as February 1955 the committee agreed that accommodations for 200 women would be better than the 100 authorized. Women's applications were expected to increase, and the committee wished to preserve the existing ratio of men to women in the student body. But money was allotted for only one dormitory unit. In November 1955 Houston Endowment, Inc., gave the Institute funds for a women's dormitory to be known as the Mary Gibbs Jones College for Women, in honor of Mrs.

137. *Construction of Mary Gibbs Jones College, March 5, 1957.*

Jesse H. Jones. From that point on, women students had an equal place on the Rice campus.

Not long afterward, in July 1956, the board voted to name the men's colleges in honor of some of the Institute's major benefactors. East Hall became James A. Baker College, South Hall became Will Rice College (after William M. Rice, Jr.), and West Hall became Harry Clay Hanszen College. Wiess Hall had already been named for Harry C. Wiess.[41]

Dr. Houston finally appointed masters for the various colleges, and true to Rice tradition, none of them knew that the president had him in mind until Houston made the offer. The men chosen were William H. Masterson, professor of history, for Hanszen; James Street Fulton, professor of philosophy, for Will Rice; Roy V. Talmage, professor of biology, for Wiess; Carl R. Wischmeyer, associate professor of electrical engi-

neering, for Baker; and Calvin M. Class, associate professor of physics, for Jones. The new masters were at a disadvantage in that they had not taken part in any of the Committee on Student Housing's planning, but they had the committee's report. Although much of it seemed unrealistic to at least one master, the report was better than nothing.[42]

In March 1957, after room assignments, briefings, and elections, the students moved into their colleges. The administration had decided to inaugurate the system in the spring instead of waiting until fall, because construction had progressed so well. Certain shortages still existed, however, and the women in Jones Hall had almost no furniture for about six weeks.

Some rules and customs applied to all colleges, both men's and women's. No visitors of the opposite sex were allowed in the

rooms of any college except during Sunday Open House, and all colleges had a seated evening meal, served family style, with freshmen as waiters. In addition, the women were governed by some rules that applied only to them. They had strict requirements for dress in the Commons and lobbies; Rice was still a very dressy school for women. They also had a curfew. The hours established for the apartments, 11:30 P.M. weekdays and 2:00 A.M. on Saturday night, were retained. Restrictive though these hours seemed to some, they were quite liberal for the 1950s and for the state. (Most Texas colleges required their women students to be in much earlier.) Rice went from one extreme to another concerning women's housing rules. Earlier, no women lived on campus; soon a women could not live off campus outside her parents' home without the Institute's permission.

The introduction of the college system brought about a political revolution on campus. Until 1957 student affairs had been handled by the class organizations, but the classes clearly had little place in the colleges. When the *Campanile* announced in February 1958, during the first full year of the system, that students' pictures would appear with their colleges instead of their classes, protest resulted in a referendum in which the college arrangement won by a slim margin. Conflict between the Student Council and the Inter-College Council followed soon after, and again the college sys-

138. *A 1917 view of the Rice Institute dormitories, which became colleges in 1957.* Left to right: *Hanszen College (formerly West Hall), Will Rice College (South Hall), Baker College Commons (originally the dining area for all the dormitories), and Baker College (formerly East Hall).*

tem won. After a fierce campaign, students passed a new constitution for the Student Association that created a Student Senate composed mostly of college officers. The Senate comprised executive officers elected campus-wide, along with the freshman class president, the five college presidents, and two other representatives from each college. Class officers were still elected each year, but they had little to do beyond arranging a few social activities.[43]

Although the final report of the Committee on Student Housing stated specifically that masters were not to be thought of as disciplinarians, practice did not always conform to theory. College discipline was a gray area. Precedent laid the keeping of order first in the hands of the Hall Committee (now the college government) and then with the dean of students. The master's responsibility was vague. No one really knew what a master was supposed to do. When President Houston asked William H. Masterson to become master of Hans-

zen, the professor asked what a master did. "I don't really know," Houston replied, "whatever you find useful." The lack of clearly defined responsibilities sometimes resulted in conflict between a master and the dean of students (whatever his title). While James R. Sims was adviser to men, he considered anything that occurred outside a college to be his province, and anything inside the college to be the master's province. It appears that jurisdictions were not finally adjudicated until 1963, when a

139. *Wiess College, construction substantially completed, January 3, 1950.*

memorandum from President Pitzer to masters and deans delineated the responsibilities and interrelations of the masters, the dean of women, and the dean of students. For their internal order, the colleges developed their own judicial systems and in 1962–63 created an Inter-College Court to handle disputes between colleges.[44]

Including off-campus college members in the new organization proved to be difficult. At first there were many upperclassmen who were uninterested in their assigned colleges and who did not take part in their activities. An increase in college-sponsored social activities and a change in attitude as new students entered an established system helped somewhat, but the colleges did not find the key, if any existed, to attract and hold the interest of nonresident students.

A 1961 *Thresher* review of the college system after four years pointed out the lack of inter-college competition in academic endeavors. President Lovett's dream of debating societies never materialized. Hardly anyone paid attention to which college had the most scholarships, the best grade average, or the fewest students on probation. Any competition was usually athletic—or, as in the case of the Rondelet festivities, musical in the Song Fest and a combination of athletic and alcoholic in the Beer-Bike Race.[45]

Faculty associates found themselves in limbo, since their function and their relationship to the students had not yet been defined clearly. Although the designers of the college system intended for the interaction between students and associates to stimulate intellectual activity, some associates seemed to be as tongue-tied in talking to students as the students were in conversing with professors. At any rate, associates usually had only a social relationship with their colleges, a passive role rather than the active one envisioned.

Perhaps intellectual life in the colleges suffered because some students actively resisted it. Others were too tired from everything else they had to do to sit down at a table and discuss momentous issues, ideas, and ideology. Considering all the academic study required, many undoubtedly wanted a respite from brain work. Some did not wish to expose their ignorance in the presence of the associates, even in informal conversations. Besides (the argument ran), did stimulating intellectual discussions help you get a job?

Like students the world over, those at Rice liked to complain about their work load. Looked at even dispassionately, the academic requirements at Rice in the 1950s seemed designed to weed out the unfit. Fueled by anxiety among nonathletes about their own standing, resentment grew at the so-called double standard for athletes. Rumor had it that the athletes (mostly physical education majors, not those taking a "regular" schedule) had special help, special grading, and special courses, and that they did not measure up scholastically to other Rice students. Any differences in behavior or dress that

distinguished athletes from other students increased the rancor directed toward these supposedly privileged sportsmen. In a college where many were trying to establish traditions of "gracious living," the athletes seemed to be throwbacks to the old rowdy dormitory life when they showed up for Sunday dinner (a seated meal at which men were expected to wear coats and ties) flaunting wheat-colored jeans and T-shirts with their coats and ties. What really angered many students, however, was that the athletes seemed to have plenty of time to loaf, make noise, and enjoy themselves—another manifestation of the unfair system at Rice, they said.

By 1963 the colleges still had not measured up to the high hopes of some students and faculty. Although there were subtle differences among the men's colleges, none of them had a distinct individual personality, a fact that some on the *Thresher* staff deplored in a newspaper supplement on the college system. This was, no doubt, a result of the freshman placement system, in which a mix of types and majors was the goal. Comparison with the amenities of the houses at Harvard or the colleges at Yale also left the Rice system looking like a very poor cousin. For funds, the Rice colleges depended on a small fee collected from all the members; but that amount covered little more than the purchase of a television set or a Ping-Pong table. It was certainly not enough to finance construction of larger facilities, such as li-

braries, study rooms, and private dining rooms such as the Harvard and Yale houses had. In a statement on trends in the colleges in 1962, dean of students Sanford Higginbotham pointed out that students seemed not to feel a sense of responsibility for the colleges or real loyalty to them. He was disappointed that the colleges were primarily places of entertainment and had neglected their primary obligations to supply study facilities and opportunities for social and cultural growth. Higginbotham had observed many violations of the letter and the spirit of college and university regulations. In the six years since their establishment, the colleges had not yet become the focus of student social, athletic, and intellectual activities. In 1963 they still had to live up to their potential.[46]

Despite the defects that many alumni recall, the colleges made a number of positive contributions to life on campus. The new or renovated dormitories did much to improve living conditions on campus. College activities offered a chance to participate to many students who would not have been included or who would not have offered to help under the old system. The college governments attracted a type of candidate different from that for the old class offices and Student Council, and several masters professed to be surprised and delighted that the students proved they could run their own affairs without faculty guidance. College Nights brought in speakers whom students might not otherwise have had the chance to hear, and a program of seminars enabled students to discuss professional fields with Houston business and professional people. Even though the liaisons among college residents and associates were still tenuous, great strides had been made in faculty-student relationships compared to the days when a student described the Institute as "a cold place."[47]

The college system beneficially affected student life in another area as well: the treatment of the freshman class. Freshmen at Rice had always been harassed by sophomores, but during the 1950s the treatment of freshmen reached new lows, perhaps as a reflection of the less-than-civilized conditions in the dormitories. Although "guidance" was supposed to be different from hazing, and voluntary instead of compulsory, physical punishment continued, along with the requirement that freshmen wear beanies and run errands for upperclassmen; and Forestry 100 still flourished. Voluntarism vanished in the face of sophomore pressure on dormitory residents. Hell Week, in which the two classes tried to capture each other's president and vice-president, led to pitched battles in which some participants broke bones. In 1955 new rules were passed that decreed a milder Hell Week, with women being spectators instead of participants and men's activities restricted to the campus. Only the sophomore president was subject to kidnapping, instead of all the class officers and other students who

had also been abducted. The Slime Parade turned into what some termed "an orgy" in 1954; and although the sophomores protected the freshman women from smoochers in 1955, the parade could hardly be called tame. The next year, 1956, was the least restrained. In the Slime Parade, participants smashed in the door of Loew's State Theater; and after the Utah game, which the Owls won 27–0, forty or fifty freshmen mobbed a school bus carrying a high school band that had played at the game.

The incident that brought Hell Week to a halt resulted in the deaths of two sophomores, Bill Carroll and Karl Bailey, when they climbed the inside of the smokestack/campanile to put a tire on top and were overcome by carbon monoxide fumes. On February 5, 1957, Dean McBride informed the president of the Student Association that the administration was abolishing Hell Week, which had become "a quasi-legal brawl neither promoting the aims of the Institute nor satisfying the significant desires of the students." The tradition had become too dangerous to people, too disruptive of university life and education, and too divisive of the student body. The next fall, changes were also made in the Slime Parade. The line of march led to the Shamrock Hilton Hotel instead of downtown; participation was truly voluntary, and there was no physical hazing on the way.[48]

The inauguration of the college system changed "guidance" dramatically. The Sub-Committee

on Freshmen of the Committee on Student Housing had been unable to reconcile the various attitudes toward guidance and had not produced any recommendations, but the individual colleges soon worked out new practices. The most brutal forms of hazing disappeared in a few years—in some cases, immediately in the fall of 1957 when the freshmen entered the newly opened colleges. However, certain remnants persisted for a while. Freshmen still wore beanies, but now in the colors of their colleges instead of the traditional blue and gray. The Slime Parade continued as a pale reflection of its former self until 1964, when the colleges themselves abolished it. The greased pole event went on; freshmen tried to rescue a beanie from a pole in a sea of drilling mud, and if they were successful, the guidance period ended early. Bowing to Sammy at football games lasted until 1961, when the tradition broke down. In 1962 Hanszen, Wiess, and Baker Colleges reinstated the practice, but Will Rice did not. (Students still bow to Sammy in the 1980s.)

"Guidance" become "orientation," something quite different, during these years, as colleges welcomed their freshmen and tried to help them become acclimated to Rice, its people, the new college traditions, and Houston.[49]

Academic Difficulties

While the college system improved nonacademic life on campus considerably, it did not initially help much with academic matters. Those difficulties continued during the 1950s, as both faculty and students acknowledged—although they went about solving the problems in different ways and from very different perspectives.

Early in the decade the faculty began to study the effectiveness of the undergraduate departments. A Committee of Educational Inquiry was established during the 1952–53 school year to investigate undergraduate education. It took as its starting point a statement from the Carnegie Foundation for the Advancement of Teaching, which implied that colleges "drifted" into educational policies by yielding to pressures of the moment and thereafter followed the precedents set in haste. The drift had its origins in the fact that administrators could not devote sufficient time and attention to planning and policy matters, and the faculty did not. The committee thought that this criticism did not apply to Rice but decided to test its validity and see where the Institute stood.

Fortunately, the committee reported, the faculty generally agreed on the aims and purposes of the undergraduate program: providing the best possible opportunities for the development of "above-average minds," at the same time giving adequate atten-

tion to preprofessional training in certain areas. Indeed, these had been the goals since the founding of the university. There was, however, some difference of opinion about how successful the Institute had been in achieving those aims.

In theory, the common core curriculum introduced in 1947–48 provided all students with the opportunity to explore various fields and broaden their educational backgrounds before selecting their majors. The freshman and sophomore years offered basic studies in both humanities and sciences before the student decided on a specialty, and even in the last two years further required courses allowed only limited concentration in an academic field. In practice, the course requirements were not as rigid as they might have seemed. Changes had occurred before even one class had gone through the complete four-year program, as certain requirements were dropped for certain majors. For example, freshmen who expressed a desire to major in biology could bypass engineering drawing (even though biology was in the science-engineering division, which required the drafting course), and certain engineering students no longer took a second year of chemistry. The Committee of Educational Inquiry did not judge whether these changes were good or bad; that was a determination for the faculty to make. The committee was concerned instead with the motivation for these changes:

were they made to relieve localized pressures or to alter the basic philosophy behind the program?

The intent of the program—to provide a well-rounded education—was undermined by competing interests. Applicants were asked to specify a major, contrary to the plan's intent that a student should not choose a field of specialization until the end of the sophomore year. Students were, after all, admitted to each division on a quota system, which was defended because of the Institute's limited enrollment. The committee was asked whether this system was fair to the student and whether it ensured that Rice enrolled the most apt 400 applicants.

Major requirements and "strongly advised" electives competed with courses outside the students' specialties for slots in their schedules. Often their major departments "suggested" that particular electives be taken in the sophomore or junior years, leaving students no opportunity to satisfy their intellectual curiosity or to range very far afield from their majors. The choice of electives was narrowed considerably by course schedules; after registering for their required courses, students found their selection of electives limited to those that met during their remaining free periods.

True to the implications of the Carnegie Foundation's report, the Institute had "drifted" away from its educational policies, the committee decided. The drift was due to several reasons. First, the committee suggested, Rice's faculty did not really understand either the policies or the means of effecting them. Contributing to their confusion were the faculty's failure to discuss policies adequately before taking action, a general lack of information about committee and administrative decisions, and the fact that new faculty members were unfamiliar with the background of present policies and procedures. The committee ended its report by suggesting that the faculty reexamine the core curriculum, its implications, its applicability at Rice, and methods for retaining its desirable features.[50]

It appears, however, that the faculty never undertook a close study of the system and curriculum. In 1957 the Executive Committee appealed to the faculty to reaffirm the basic principle that students would not declare majors until the end of the second year, and the faculty so voted.

The Committee on the Freshman Course, still in existence in 1953, continued to wrestle with ever-present freshman difficulties. At least twenty percent of the first-year students were in scholastic trouble. They appeared to be bright and spent a reasonable amount of time on their studies. Counseling freshmen was doing no appreciable good, and the committee could reach no conclusion about the quality of instruction in freshman courses. Faculty members on the committee felt that something must be wrong with Rice's selec-

tion process. Certain facts were clear: academic students contributed disproportionately to the number of unsuccessful students; out-of-town students did also; and Math 100 was still the most difficult freshman course. However, no one had thought of a dependable method of raising freshman grades. The Committee of Educational Inquiry suggested that divisional, geographic, and gender quotas be abandoned; but their recommendation was not followed, and the Admissions Committee under S. G. McCann continued to apply quotas to the incoming freshman class.

One of the most worrisome problems was summer attrition of the most desirable prospective students. During 1954 approximately 130 of these withdrew, causing the Admissions Committee to turn to its waiting list—only to find that most of the prospects on the list had refused to wait for Rice's decision. McCann thought that replacements from further down the list were not as strong as those lost from the top. He wanted (and in 1955 received permission) to accept more candidates in the first round, expecting that a sufficient number would decline admission to keep the freshman class at the desired size. The top-rated applicants could thus be offered places before they made other plans. In a way, the problem of admitting only the best-qualified students solved itself during the 1950s, as the number of applicants rose. In 1950 the total number of applications considered was 713. In

1958 it was 2,100, and in 1962 it was 2,700. Rice finally had an abundance of applicants from which to choose, but the problem of keeping students in school remained.[51]

In 1955, still looking for a way to find perfect freshmen who could do the work required, the Admissions Committee made another change in its procedures: Rice's own entrance examination was replaced with the tests of the College Entrance Examination Board. The old exams had been used mainly to ascertain whether applicants were sufficiently prepared; the new ones were to be used not only for that purpose, but also to identify candidates of outstanding ability. The CEEB tests were not an absolute requirement for those who sought admission, but those who took them were given "marked preference" if they scored satisfactorily and fulfilled the other regular requirements. The Admissions Committee continued to emphasize that the primary considerations were the candidates' high school records, rank in their high school classes, and personal qualities. Still, the CEEB exams did provide a series of scores by which to evaluate prospects, and the Admissions Committee, deliberating long hours over its choices, appreciated help in making difficult decisions.[52]

Also in 1955 the faculty made an effort to help freshmen survive Math 100, by offering them a math review before school opened. (By 1956 other departments were asking to present sessions to acquaint students with fundamentals before scheduled orientation at the end of the week.) The mathematics department also changed the syllabus of Math 100; in 1956 the department dropped trigonometry, leaving the course to consist of analytic geometry and elementary calculus.

In 1958 freshman orientation was revised. The week before classes started, all freshmen were required to live on campus for four days. From eight o'clock until noon they took a class in trigonometry, and in the afternoon they studied math, read a book assigned by the English department, and took care of registration details. At the end of the week they were tested in math and wrote an essay. Whatever free time was left was filled with various quasi-social activities. The week could be a grueling one and, as it turned out, did not appreciably help the freshmen to succeed in either math or English. However, the practice continued until 1961.

One requirement was dropped in 1955, to the relief of poor spellers: the faculty abolished the spelling test that had been required to enter the junior year. Thereafter, passing any English course was assumed to represent proficiency in spelling.[53]

Investigations by two committees into the motives and methods of the university do not, however, seem to have answered some of the fundamental questions raised by the Committee of Educational Inquiry. Was Rice really providing the best possible opportunities for the development of above-average minds? Was the curriculum really achieving its stated goals?

In 1959 the dean of humanities could still ask what the purpose of the humanities division was. Was the undergraduate student to be "trained" for a professional career or given a "broader outlook" with more emphasis on the interrelation of courses? How were the courses to be interrelated and electives chosen—by the students, their major departments, or the Committee on Examinations and Standing? These questions could be applied to the science-engineering division as well. For more cross-fertilization of sciences and humanities, the dean thought that new humanities electives should be created to attract science and engineering students, and courses in scientific departments for non-science students ought to be established. Teaching techniques could be greatly improved in some instances, and the teaching of freshman courses by graduate students ought to be eliminated.[54]

A New Attitude Among Students

The faculty's discussions did not result in any real changes for the students, and the evident lack of change had an important effect on the outlook and general attitude of many. Alumni from earlier or later eras might scarcely recognize their alma mater as described by their counterparts from the watershed years of the 1950s.

Up to the mid-fifties, the predominant attitude of students toward Rice seems to have been great fondness. There were some people, often transfers from other colleges, who thought the Institute folk to be somewhat provincial and overawed with their own importance;[55] but the majority look back on their days at Rice as a time of opportunity, camaraderie, serious learning, and downright fun. They share a sense of closeness, loyalty, and fierce pride. Students were absolutely certain that they were receiving the best education available anywhere. Many can still remember every college yell, almost every member of their class, and every professor—with all their idiosyncrasies. Many alumni of the 1920s and 1930s unabashedly state, "I loved the place."

The new attitude was manifest in a bitter cynicism toward the university, the administration, the faculty, and even other students. The number of students who shared this altered viewpoint is difficult to determine, but it is clear from interviews and printed sources that it made its first appearance around 1952, when all four classes were enrolled in the new postwar curriculum; by 1956 it was widespread.

Several external factors as well as internal ones contributed to this cynicism. Pressure to succeed did a great deal to foster its development, and it started before a student was even accepted. Parents were ambitious for their children. A college diploma, especially from a university with the reputation of the Rice Institute, was considered a passport to success in the business world, and competition for the limited number of places in the best colleges became fierce. Admission depended on high school grades and College Board scores, and whole futures seemed to be decided by numbers alone.

Getting into college, however, was only the beginning. Once at Rice, students were faced with a new curriculum, which left little time for the broader aspects of a college education. It offered few electives and gave some students the feeling of being caught in a trap, subject to demands and procedures they thought they could do little or nothing to modify.

Many students saw a contradiction. On the one hand, Rice students were told, and they believed, that they were intellectually superior. They had achieved outstanding high school records, and they had succeeded over many applicants to be admitted. On the other hand, as they sat with their freshman class at matriculation, being congratulated on their superiority, they were told, "Look at the person on your left and on your right; one of you will not be here for graduation." When they started classes, their grades dropped for the first time in their lives, even though they felt that they were studying very hard. High school friends at other universities reported high grades

easily made, while Rice students worked considerably harder for no perceptible reward in grades. Then they were faced with explaining their low marks to their parents. The pressure to succeed was by no means unique to Rice, but added to the other factors, it increased the tension. To fail at Rice was devastating to some.[56]

Some students concluded that it was not their own fault that their grades were low; many placed the blame on the professors and their grading systems. As students examined the professors, with whom most had little or no contact outside the classroom, they isolated a number of factors that might explain their scholastic plight. Some professors seemed to hold students in low esteem, considering them to be necessary evils who encroached on valuable research time. These men were seen as careless and impatient teachers. Others, the students thought, were not as smart as their students, but their insecurity seemed to drive them to prove that they were, in fact, superior; it seemed that their method was to grade twice as hard as might have been appropriate. Some professors forced grades into a perfect bell curve, using them to rank the relative standing of students in a class, and not to reflect the worth of a student's work independently. Others gave extremely difficult tests over minutiae. Some seemed to think they would not be highly regarded unless they graded low, and others announced that they did not "believe" in giv-

ing Is. There were a few faculty members who seemed genuinely interested in the students and their education, but very few, the students thought.[57]

Because Rice charged no tuition, students saw themselves as being there on the administration's sufferance and consequently as being powerless. Any student request for changing the system seemed to meet with stony resistance, yet the administration could promulgate whatever arbitrary regulations it wanted.[58] (It should be remembered that in the 1950s, students everywhere were held to have few inherent "rights.") The apologia, "We hope this doesn't inconvenience you," accompanied announcements of administrative changes in regulations and became an ironic quotation, frequently applied. Some students put it into a simpler phrase: "They think they own us."[59]

The pressure and powerlessness were not all in the students' imagination. Dean Richter has said that the administration was determined to make the most of Rice's student potential and develop it to the highest possible level of achievement. The university in effect gave a scholarship to each student by charging no tuition, and it intended to get its money's worth. Students would be challenged to the utmost.[60]

In both student and faculty conversations a question arose concerning this challenge. Was Rice both a hard school and a good school, or only a hard one? In the view of at least one professor, there was a narrowly conceived education offered at Rice at that time that resulted in a heaviness and rigidity to the system. The joy of learning was absent. At the same time, however, that same professor and others complained that the students were intellectually docile and less enthusiastic about learning for its own sake.[61]

This debate went unresolved, but the problem of low grades remained. According to Dr. Kenneth Pitzer, the University of California, Berkeley, kept records of the grade-point averages of its transfer students. Transfer students from only a few colleges raised their averages at Berkeley; Rice students were among them.[62]

Some Rice faculty members recognized the harm that a difficult grading system could cause and tried to draw their colleagues' attention to the unfairness of a forced curve or extra-strict marking; but their arguments seemed to make little impression. One explanation advanced for the hard grading habits of some professors was that they had become accustomed to the single-minded, mature veterans who returned for their degrees after the war. The professors expected the same industry from the younger students, giving them lower grades when they were not as productive as the veterans had been. Such an explanation, however, does not take into account the new curriculum and new demands on both student and professor.[63]

Students reacted to the academic challenge in various ways.

Some accepted it, although they did not enjoy it, and made the "battle" into a game. These students often turned the system back on itself in a variety of ways, from splitting the chores for test-cramming, to choosing courses known to be easy (academic students had much more leeway here than engineers), to manipulating seating charts to appear present when they were actually absent. Others accepted the challenge by working all the time, becoming in the process what students called "grinds" or "weenies." These students often felt the pressure keenly and knew that worrying was a detriment to their performance, but they also knew that it was almost impossible to stop worrying. Worrying was built into the system. Some flunked out, but even that was done in individual ways. There were those who worked to the bitter end and failed anyway, and there were those who simply threw caution to the winds and enjoyed themselves before they had to leave.[64]

There were also some who refused to play the game and left for other colleges where the pressure was less and good hard work was rewarded more generously. An alumnus has remarked that he thought Rice was more a test of mental stability than of mental agility.[65] Reaction to the challenge created in a substantial number an "I hate Rice" feeling for the first time in the university's history.[66] Some students wanted to escape by graduating, showing the professors that the system could be beaten; they re-

solved never to come back and never, under any circumstances, to give money to the Institute. For some, the grind, the busy-work, the feeling that they were wasting their time in rote learning, were alleviated by a few very good teachers who truly challenged them to learn, to think, to reconsider old and new ideas, and to write clearly; a high grade earned from one of these professors was something to be prized.

One further aspect of the tension-filled situation should be mentioned. While "the system" created a great deal of pressure, the highly competitive Rice students created more of their own. One of the unanswerable questions, endlessly debated by students in the late 1950s and early 1960s, was whether Rice made students in its own image, or whether the students made Rice: that is, did Rice attract a distinctive type of person? Admissions certainly resulted in a homogeneous group, but it was also possible that Rice attracted applicants similar to the students who were already there.

In retrospect, many alumni of the fifties and early sixties have changed some of their negative opinions about Rice. Some found themselves quite well prepared for graduate schools; at the very least they knew how to study. Thinking back, some have realized that their perception of Rice's difficulty was artificial. The amount of study required of them had really not been as great as it had seemed at the time (except for the engineers). Some still cursed certain courses and professors for being a waste of time, but the good instructors helped temper their anger.[67]

One long-range effect of the change in attitude was the development of a special Rice sense of humor—self-deprecating, flippant, a bit morbid, somewhat misunderstood by the outside world—still in evidence today. It can be seen in some, but not all, of the half-time performances of the iconoclastic Marching Owl Band.[68]

As some changes in the curriculum (notably the creation of another Math 100 course called 101 for academic students, and an expanded selection of courses) "softened" the regulations; as new, younger professors joined the faculty; and as the college system civilized living conditions, the bitterest cynicism faded. Improved dormitory and academic conditions allowed students to look at the university with a clearer perspective. In the 1960s, they would not necessarily like every facet of the Rice experience, but the fundamental living and learning conditions seemed more humane.

A Lighter View of Campus Life

Of course, students did more than just study and complain during the fifties. There was hardly an atmosphere of perpetual gloom and doom, but rather quite the opposite. Students did their best to escape the

140. *Demonstration of radio and teletype at the Rice Exposition, 1954.*

pressure-cooker of classroom, laboratory, and carrel.

All sorts of activities still flourished on campus: the Dramatic Club, politics, literary societies, a reincarnated literary magazine, charity drives, and much else. The college system added more social events to the crowded schedule. Many notable speakers visited the campus, including General Dwight D. Eisenhower, at that time president of Columbia University; and the alumni continued to honor benefactors at homecoming. In 1957 the colleges first competed in the Beer-Bike Race as a part of the Rondelet festivities; in the early years of the race, the riders also did the drinking.

For a while the campus was absorbed in the mystery of what would happen next to Gertrude Stein. Mrs. Kenneth Dale Owen had given a bust of the author to the library as a memorial to trustee Robert Lee Blaffer, her father. The statue had not been in the library more than a few days when it disappeared, only to be found in a police station. On other occasions it was painted and otherwise adorned (at one point, catfish eyes were put in the eye sockets) before it was finally placed in the Music Room of the library.

The band, under the direction of Holmes McNeely, rose from what Dr. Houston called "an almost all-time low to what I

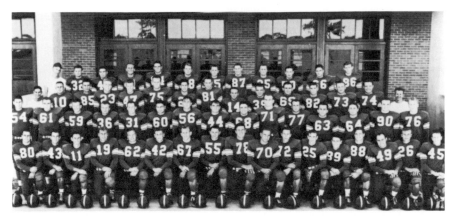

141

141–143. *Three Southwest Conference winners of the 1950s. 141. Football team, 1953–54. 142. Football team, 1957–58.*

think is a respectable organization for an institution of our size. It seems to me important," the president continued, "that we do not undertake to do the kind of thing that can be done by a very large organization and that we do not expect a large organization from a small student body. I do believe, however, that we can emphasize quality in the Band as

we do in other fields and that we have good reason to be satisfied."

Another kind of music was not so soothing to Rice's ear. Some Houston high school girls and some women students from the University of Houston came on campus several times, usually singing their school songs, and once, even more foolishly, Aggie songs. Rice men emptied the

dorms and surrounded the offending visitors, usually dousing the women with water and letting the air out of their tires. Several times the police came to rescue the women and had their tires flattened, too. Once Marvin Zindler, an intrepid reporter for the *Houston Press*, came to take pictures of the event, only to find himself cameraless, kidnapped for a while, and all wet besides. Of one of these encounters, a policeman said that the students were supposed to be educated but had acted like wild men, and he was happy that his son was a student at A&M.[69]

Sports, especially football, attracted the students' interest into the 1960s as Jess Neely and his teams continued to do well. Rice won the conference in 1953 and 1957, going to the Cotton Bowl, and went to other bowl games after the 1960 and 1961 seasons. The Owls beat Alabama in the 1954 Cotton Bowl, 28–6, but lost to Navy in 1958, 20–7, to Mississippi in the 1961 Sugar Bowl, 14–6, and to Kansas, 33–7, in the Bluebonnet Bowl. Victories over Texas and A&M during the fifties were satisfying to supporters, but especially pleasing was Rice's 1957 defeat of the Aggies, who were ranked first in the nation. Elated students revived the old custom of locking the campus for an undeclared school holiday after a big win.

Life was not without its exasperations for Coach Neely, however. Just when he thought the Owls had beat Army in the 1958 game, Army blocked a Rice field-goal attempt and then completed a long pass for a touchdown. The final score was Army 14, Rice 7. Neely said the worst thing that ever happened to him occurred during an Aggie game of this period. The Owls had scored 12 points, and time was getting short when the Aggies scored their first touchdown. Neely told his players, "There're 68,000 people here and every one of them knows that they're going to try an on-side kick. So stay right here on the 40-yard line, don't go back, just cover the kick." Despite the coach's order, somebody backed up, leaving a hole, and all the Aggies had to do was fall on the ball. A long pass resulted in another touchdown, and Rice went down to defeat.[70] The 1954 Cotton Bowl produced one of the most famous incidents in college football, when an Alabama player jumped off the bench to stop Dicky Maegle's unobstructed run for the goal line. But, as the coach said, Rice got a touchdown out of it, and it did not hurt Maegle.

Maegle was only one of the outstanding players that the Rice sports program produced during this period. In football the Owls boasted of such men as King Hill, Buddy Dial, brothers Rufus and Boyd King, mathematics student Frank Ryan, Kosse Johnson, John Hudson, Bill Howton, Richard Chapman, John Burrell, Rhodes scholar Robert Johnston, current Rice coach Ray Alborn, and Malcolm Walker. In basketball, Rice won the conference in 1954 with All-Conference players Gene Schwinger and Don Lance. The basketball team was coached by

143. *Basketball team, 1953–54 (co-champions).*

Don Suman from 1950 to 1959 and John Frankie from 1960 to 1963. Olympic gold medalist Fred Hansen and Warren Brattlof, Dale Moseley, Ed Red, Dale Spence, and Tobin Rote distinguished themselves in track, while the tennis team won conference titles with Ronnie Fisher, Art Foust, Jim Parker, and Fritz Schunck.[71]

The 1950s in Summary

During the 1950s the Rice Institute changed on several levels. It expanded in faculty, student body, and buildings. Graduate work and research also increased as the administration worked to attract outstanding and promising professors. The attitude of many students took on a new, bitter tinge, and the college system re-

arranged student housing, social activities, and politics. Almost all the changes of the fifties would pale by comparison with what was to come, but considering the period of stagnation in the depression years and the frantic war years in the forties, the fifties looked good indeed to those interested in the development of the Institute. By 1959 those people thought that Rice was ready to become what Edgar Odell Lovett had always wanted: a university in name as well as in fact.

CHAPTER 9

New Plans to Fit a New Name

Edgar Odell Lovett died in 1957 at the age of eighty-six. After his retirement in 1946, he had continued to come to the campus, to keep his eye on what he had built from an office on the third floor of the Administration Building, now named Lovett Hall. He had relaxed a bit during his years of retirement and had revealed a side of his personality that few had seen before. Professors now found him eager to talk about the Institute, and at a reception given by Dean Richter for retired faculty members, Lovett was the life of the party. Newcomers to the faculty often found that he knew their names and fields before they met him, and it was always difficult to get out of his office in less than thirty minutes when one dropped by to have a few words with him. As a board resolution said of him, he was "a rare combination of the dignified scholar and superb gentleman."[1]

Lovett had shepherded the Rice Institute through good and bad times. He had seen his hopes for a world-renowned university threatened by the financial problems of the 1920s and 1930s and had seen them rise again in the flush 1940s and 1950s. When he died, the humanities and social sciences at the Institute were finally beginning to move toward a balance with the other side of the campus, and the college system of which he had dreamed in 1912 was a reality. Lovett had called Rice a university from his first connection with it; his death prevented his seeing Rice called "university" in name.

Changing the Institute's Name

In December 1959 the Board of Governors met in special session to explore the possibility of changing the name of the Rice Institute. The term "institute" no longer conveyed the true scope of its educational program or its status in the academic world, and continued use of the name had caused confusion for some time among prospective students and faculty, not to mention the outside world. A consensus of board members agreed that a change in name would be desirable, but they decided to explore the attitudes of the alumni, faculty, and other interested groups before taking action.

Legally, it would not be difficult to effect a change in name. The 1891 charter stated that the Institute was to be known "by such a name as the said parties of the second part [the trustees], may in their judgment select." From the standpoint of public relations, however, the board wanted to be sure that the alumni were on its side, so it broke the news of its considerations in the January 1960 issue of *Sallyport*, the alumni publication.

In the article, the board outlined a number of reasons for its proposal. Confusion over the term "institute" (which was primarily used to describe a special-

purpose institution of noncollegi-
ate rank) was only one. Rice was
increasingly emphasizing undergraduate, graduate, and research
programs that marked a genuine
university, and it needed to assume its correct designation.
Strong evidence in Lovett's writings and in early faculty actions
showed that the institution was
conceived and launched from the
very beginning as a university. It
was proving difficult to attract
some potential faculty members,
especially in the humanities, because they thought the scope of
the Institute was limited; they
had usually heard of it as a college strongly oriented toward
science and engineering. Some
private donors, corporations, and
foundations, not knowing the Institute's program, would not contribute to a special-purpose institute, only to a university. Even
after an effort to build up the humanities, the Institute had found
it difficult to attract proper attention to that side of the Institute.
The trustees had also considered
the possibility of creating specialized institutes within the university. As long as the mother
institution bore the name "institute," confusion would reign and
it would be impossible to develop
interest in and financial support
for subsidiary institutes. Changing the name to Rice University
would make it possible for the
school to improve its national
and international standing and
would counter the assumption
that Rice was an institution of
narrow scope. Finally, the trustees said, more and better graduate students, especially in the

area of the humanities, would be
attracted to Rice if it were properly named.

For those who might not know
the connotations of the term
"university," articles in the same
issue of the *Sallyport* defined
the word: an institution of learning of the highest grade, with a
strong program of undergraduate
instruction; emphasis on the liberal arts; graduate work, including the conferral of doctoral
degrees; and significant research
activities. The *Sallyport* pointed
out that Rice met all of those
criteria and that other schools
such as Princeton and Harvard
had changed their names at various times. The president of the
alumni association, George Red
'25, advocated the change, as did
H. Malcolm Lovett '21, who was
a governor in 1959.

While faculty members saw
the possible change as advantageous to the Institute, some
alumni and students clung nos-
talgically to the old name. To a
Thresher poll the senior class
president responded, "Unless it is
necessary, it is regrettable"; but a
junior economics major thought
it was "an intelligent and long
overdue eradication of a funda-
mentally unwholesome condition." The *Dallas Morning News*
let it be known that its editor did
not approve of the change; but
despite sentiment and the Dallas
paper, the alumni expressed very
little opposition, and the state-
wide Executive Committee of
the alumni association voted
unanimously to recommend the
change of name. In March 1960
the board decided to proceed.

On April 6, 1960, the board
filed a petition for the name
change with the Secretary of
State's office in Austin and announced its action to the student
body in the *Thresher*. On July 1,
1960, The William M. Rice Institute for the Advancement of Letters, Science and Art became
William Marsh Rice University.[2]

A Change in Presidents

A heart attack caused Dr. Houston to go on leave for rest and
recuperation in August 1960, and
in September, when he found it
necessary to reduce his responsibilities and activity still further,
he resigned the presidency. In accord with Houston's suggestion,
the board voted to appoint him
chancellor, an honorary title without duties, and Distinguished
Professor of Physics because he
wanted to continue his teaching
and research. These designations
became effective February 1,
1961, at which time the board appointed Provost Carey Croneis to
be acting president. To find a new
president, J. Newton Rayzor's
Faculty, Student, and Alumni
Committee worked as a search
committee. A faculty committee
composed of Professors McKillop, Masterson, Griffis, Talmage,
Chapman, and McCann also
helped. The search did not take
long this time.[3]

Announcement of the appointment of a new president came at
commencement in June 1961.
After investigating several distinguished candidates, the board had
selected Kenneth Sanborn Pitzer

as Rice's third president. Pitzer, a forty-seven-year-old native of California, had received his B.S. in chemistry from the California Institute of Technology, where he had been in one of Houston's classes, and his Ph.D. from the University of California, Berkeley, where he had been a friend of Griffith Evans. He was a professor of chemistry at Berkeley when chosen by Rice and had also been director of research and chair of the General Advisory Committee of the Atomic Energy Commission. He was a member of both the National Academy of Sciences and the American Philosophical Society. Among his many awards were a Guggenheim fellowship, an American Chemical Society award, and the Alumnus of the Year award from the University of California Alumni Association. His major concerns in his field were the development of general principles for predicting chemical and physical properties of broad classes of substances, and he had published several books and articles. At the same commencement ceremony the board also announced that Croneis would become chancellor with administrative responsibilities and that Houston would be honorary chancellor.[4]

In many ways Rice was at a turning point when Pitzer took over the reins in 1961. Its reputation for academic excellence and for the high quality of its undergraduates had grown over the years to be a prime asset for attracting students and faculty, although the university's reputation continued to be stronger in science and engineering than in the humanities. The graduate school had strengthened under President Houston's leadership, but Rice still offered doctorates in only a few fields. The humanities especially needed to be augmented, and even the sciences needed more professors of national prominence in order for the university to gain high academic ranking.

As is true for all universities, the key to expansion on both graduate and undergraduate levels was money; as had so often been true in the past, the university was operating extremely close to the limit of its income. During the 1950s income had increased, but so had expenses. For the fiscal year ending June 30, 1952, income had been $1.8 million and expenses $1.7 million for the educational and general funds. For the year ending June 30, 1961, income had amounted to $5.2 million and expenditures to $4.6 million. Per student, the university had spent $1,060 in 1950; in 1960 instructional costs were up to $2,031, and by 1962 they were almost $2,400 per student. Raising funds was not easy, however, because Rice's old, unwarranted reputation for wealth discouraged donations.[5]

When the new president arrived, he already had some programs in mind to transform Rice into his conception of a leading university. He spoke of his ideas to the faculty, students, alumni, and other friends of Rice. For the graduate school, where his initial emphasis would be placed, Pitzer wanted a program of modest size but great distinction, staffed with outstanding teachers who were also eminent in research, in the humanities as well as science and engineering. He expected that the graduate school would double in size, from four hundred to about eight hundred students, but with more concern for quality than for mere quantity. He also proposed that undergraduate enrollment be increased.

Pitzer predicted that an upgraded faculty would benefit the undergraduate as well as the graduate program, as new departments would attract good students. The faculty was the key to a university's reputation; developing a strong faculty required attracting new people of high quality and scrutinizing those already employed. "Doing reasonably well will not be good enough at Rice," Pitzer warned the faculty. For evaluating faculty performance, he wanted an easily understood system, with clearly stated regular procedures for determining promotion and tenure.[6]

With these projects in mind, the new president began to put together a short-range plan with the help of an Academic Development Committee consisting of Alan Chapman (mechanical engineering), Gerald Phillips (physics), and Donald Mackenzie (languages). By the end of 1961, Pitzer presented a plan for the next five years. It assumed that graduate enrollment would double, with only a small increase in the number of undergraduates. More important to Pitzer than size was the quality of that graduate program; he characterized the

144. *Kenneth Sanborn Pitzer, Rice's third president.*

existing program as "at best second rate." "We have far to go," he stated, "before our graduate program attains the first quality standing that our undergraduate program has attained."

The short-range plan called for substantial development in certain fields, among them psychology, political science, biochemistry, and space science. There would be fifty-five additional faculty positions, of which twenty-five would be at a senior level at a cost of $750,000. The increase in numbers of professors would produce a student-teacher ratio of twelve to one for undergraduates and seven to one for graduate students. The cost of an additional ninety graduate fellowships would be $200,000; eighteen new secretaries and thirty-five technicians would produce a budget increase of $170,000. For the expanded programs, the library budget would need $200,000 more per year, while supplies, equipment, and overhead would cost $250,000.

Capital requirements included a new library or expansion of the existing one, costing $1.5 million; another $300,000 for special collections in new fields; new laboratory equipment not obtained through grants but costing Rice directly $500,000; building renovation for the Chemistry Building in the amount of $300,000; and $2 million for new laboratory buildings to provide 50,000 square feet. Altogether the short-range plan called for capital expenditures over a period of three to five years of $4.6 million and an increase in the an-

nual operating cost of $1.77 million over the existing budget. Pitzer urged that the money be sought as quickly as possible. He hoped to fund many of the capital items and professorships through special donations and endowments.

Pitzer also offered some thoughts on long-range plans for buildings and new academic programs. The first buildings to be constructed would house the architecture and fine arts departments, provide two additional undergraduate colleges (one for men and one for women), and create new housing units for single male graduate students and for married graduate students. As for new programs, Pitzer thought that Rice should consider establishing professional schools in law and business administration, as these seemed to fit the needs of Houston and Texas.[7]

None of Pitzer's plans could be achieved without money, of course. The board (especially Newton Rayzor's Faculty, Student, and Alumni Committee) began to study ways to raise the funds that would enable the program to proceed. New money was coming into the university, mostly in the form of grants from companies, foundations, and government agencies; but it was earmarked for specific purposes, not to be added to the endowment. The proximity of Rice University was an important element in the choice of the Houston area as the site of the National Aeronautics and Space Administration, and the university could expect substantial government aid and ben-

efits to the graduate programs in science and mathematics through its links with NASA. But that was still not enough. The university needed funds for all departments, especially general funds that the board could apply wherever needed. Gifts helped, like the one from John W. Cox '27, who gave the university the lease rights to the old Yankee Stadium in New York City. However, a university is a great consumer, and expansion made a long-term steady income necessary. It would be less difficult to manage the initial expansion than the ongoing maintenance of the larger program.[8]

The Move to Charge Tuition

Private colleges and universities usually raise some of their money by charging tuition, yet Rice's charter stated that the Institute was to be free. In 1941 the board had considered petitioning for a change in the charter to allow tuition fees, but the purchase of the Rincon oil field and some timely gifts had postponed the need to take action then. By 1960, however, it was becoming clear that costs were rising and would continue to rise and that the university had to investigate every possible source of income. Furthermore, the policy of not charging tuition was causing some problems in securing grants. Some foundations refused to give funds to a university that was not actively using all its resources (including tuition) to the fullest and that did not appear to be ambitiously striving for educational preeminence. An institution that had a reputation for wealth and seemed to be living comfortably and complacently on whatever money came its way gave the impression to foundations and corporations that their gifts might be used to better effect elsewhere. Rice's Board of Trustees had always felt that an image of mercenary eagerness was beneath its dignity. To rebut the arguments of grantors, however, the board had begun to consider the question of tuition as part of the overall financial situation in 1961, even before President Pitzer made his recommendations.[9]

By January 1962 Rayzor's committee was ready to recommend that the endowment be increased by $20 million and that the full board consider charging tuition. In February the committee recommended definite steps to be taken toward raising the funds for an expanded program: a study to determine how tuition would affect the numbers and quality of students, and a request that the university's attorneys determine what actions and information were necessary for the authority to charge tuition. With this information in hand, the board could decide how to proceed. In April the board further discussed introducing tuition step by step, beginning with the freshman class entering in September 1963. A scholarship system would accompany such a charge, and for this purpose they hoped to add $33 million (instead of $20 million) to the university's endowment by June 30, 1966. The board as a

whole approved the committee recommendations in principle and directed its attorneys to initiate the legal proceedings necessary to secure permission from the courts to charge tuition.[10]

Related but at the same time separate was racial discrimination in admissions. Here again loomed the charter, specifying that the school was intended for the white inhabitants of Texas. Although the Institute had admitted students of Asian descent for twenty years or more, there were still no black students on campus. Government research contracts included nondiscrimination clauses, and Rice's segregation policy, like its lack of tuition, was detrimental to fund raising. In May 1962 several board members thought that the board should not act unilaterally to integrate the school and that they should defer any move toward integration. After discussion, the board agreed that they should try to build favorable public sentiment for both tuition and integration. The lawyers reported in July that the Texas attorney general would cooperate with the university in legal action on both questions.

On September 16, 1962, the Board of Governors unanimously resolved to initiate legal action to obtain the authority to admit qualified students to the university without regard to race or color and to charge tuition. The resolution stated that while the indenture quoted in the charter imposed segregation on the school and limited the charging of tuition, it also left to the board

the right to set requirements for admission and the obligation to maintain good order and honor. The world had changed since 1891; complexity and costs had increased beyond any degree imaginable at that time, and customs, mores, and laws had also changed. For the university to continue to develop as an educational institution of the highest quality, as William Marsh Rice had desired, the university had to be free from the restrictive implications of the language of the charter.

A suit to amend the charter was filed in Judge Philip Peden's district court on February 21, 1963. After a challenge to the trustees' petition brought by alumni John B. Coffee and Val T. Billups, a jury considered the case in Judge William Holland's court and in February 1964 ruled in favor of the university. Judge Holland's ruling held that the university was then entitled to charge tuition and to admit students without regard to color. After an appeal by the challengers, the Texas Court of Civil Appeals in October 1966 affirmed the judgment rendered by the district court. Both judgments held that the restrictive provisions in the charter would prevent the achievement of Mr. Rice's main purpose, which was the establishment of an educational institution of the first class. Relatively certain of victory in the courts, the trustees and alumni began the $33 million campaign in the spring of 1965; by 1969 some $43 million had been raised.[11]

President Pitzer's Long-Range Plan

While the board was looking for ways to raise money, President Pitzer began constructing his long-range plan for the university. First the specific objectives of the $33 million campaign had to be spelled out. The Ford Foundation wanted more definite information before committing a proposed grant to the university, and Pitzer desired a current appraisal of his new institution. He also wanted the faculty's evaluation of long-term possibilities for the university.

In December 1962, Pitzer appointed an Academic Planning Committee composed initially of professors Edgar O. Edwards (economics), Thomas W. Leland (chemical engineering), Louis Mackey (philosophy), and Clark P. Read (biology). The committee was to prepare a plan for development, and it began work in January 1963 to chart a realistic course for the future, with the grand objective of making Rice into the major independent university "of a vast area." Pitzer's shorthand descriptions for his projected university were, in terms that a westerner could understand, "Stanford without a medical school" (since Baylor College of Medicine is across the street), and for an easterner, "Princeton with girls." Pitzer knew that his ideal might never be realized, but it would certainly provide a challenge. The committee was to consider such matters as optimum size of the student body and faculty, ratios of under-

graduate and graduate students to faculty, expansion of existing areas of study and introduction of new ones, costs, and priorities for development.

Before planning could begin, the committee needed basic guidelines concerning Rice's probable status in various areas. The president told the committee to assume that tuition and racial restrictions would be removed, that a large scholarship program would be instituted, that Rice would continue as a member of the Southwest Conference, that admission standards would remain high, that the college system would be retained, that the balance between general and specialized studies would be maintained, that space science and molecular biology would be developed, and that the emphasis on the scientific basis of engineering would continue. He also told the professors to plan for a balance between regional service and the broader service to Texas that a genuinely international institution would provide.

To help the committee, seven faculty subcommittees were appointed for various tasks. They studied virtually every academic area of the university: old and new departments, undergraduate and graduate education, research, relationships between the university and the world outside, and physical facilities. The committee reports did triple duty. They were incorporated in a self-study that Rice was obligated to prepare as part of the accrediting procedure for the Southern Association of Colleges and Schools

under the guidance of Chancellor Croneis. At the same time they were used in preparing requests for grants from various foundations and agencies. Their primary purpose, however, remained to aid the Academic Planning Committee in making its recommendations for the future.

In June 1963 the central committee reported on its progress. The members saw Rice's principal needs as more distinguished professors and good facilities, both as quickly as possible. The committee called for $5 million to be raised by the autumn of 1964, as well as new programs for research professors, visiting professors, and preceptors (young faculty members on contract for three years); an enlarged library; standard but flexible faculty teaching loads; increased research funds; and more liberal faculty salaries and fringe benefits to meet competition in the marketplace. For students, the committee spoke of more flexibility in the curriculum for the first two years, along with programs better tailored to student interests and needs and some interdisciplinary workshops at the senior level (but no specific interdisciplinary programs).

Several matters ought to be further discussed and studied, the committee thought. First, what exactly were the objectives of the undergraduate program in general? Was it to be an end in itself, or preparation for graduate work, or some combination? The committee cautioned that the paramount concern of any university was the education of human beings. Second, with respect to admissions, it appeared that as many as thirty-five percent of Rice students avoided standard requirements by participating in athletics, the band, or the Naval ROTC, or through personal status or influence. The committee suggested that the rate of failure of these special cases be determined. Third, the committee reiterated the long-felt need for a better student advisory system. Fourth, President Pitzer had specifically asked the committee to study the minimum practical size for a distinguished university. It reported that of those it had studied, Princeton was the smallest first-rate university; its student body was double the size of Rice's, but its faculty was three or four times as large. The committee's last recommendation was that professional schools be low in priority for the moment. The university's task would be difficult enough without adding another issue.[12]

The committee's final report was made public in the Ten Year Plan, published in 1964. Rice would expand on all levels. Ultimately (in 1975, according to the plan), the university was to have 4,000 undergraduate and graduate students and a faculty of 400. Students were to be selected for their high intellectual ability, motivation, and personal qualifications, and the professors were to be the ablest men and women that Rice could attract. The endowment would have to increase from the 1964 level of $81 million to about $93 million, and the annual budget would rise

from about $6 million to an expected $19 million. The $21 million building program was separate from the endowment and operating funds. It included new academic buildings, new residential colleges, improvements in existing structures, major purchases of laboratory equipment, and library acquisitions. The plan was extremely ambitious.[13]

From 1961 to 1963, before publication of the final plan, President Pitzer had seen that there was much to do. Administrative organization badly needed clarification and definition. The original Academic Development Committee had reported that faculty members were deeply disturbed by the administrative structure—or more precisely, by the lack of structure. In the past there had been no clear lines of authority, no administrative channels by which requests were made or decisions announced. A faculty member might take a matter to his department chairman, but he might just as readily go to the dean or for that matter directly to the president. In earlier days memoranda were not kept of queries or decisions, and departmental secretaries had appeared on the campus only in the 1950s. Pitzer instituted official lines of communication, and a number of policy statements defined responsibility for various administrative positions. One could still, however, bypass the formal channels and go straight to the top. Like his predecessors President Pitzer was interested in hearing directly from faculty and students.[14]

A slight reorganization of the administrative titles, functions, and personnel took place in 1961 and 1962. Sanford W. Higginbotham became dean of students, replacing James R. Sims, and the office was combined with that of assistant to the president. Catharine Hill Savage, who had received her B.A. from Rice in 1955 and was an advanced graduate student in the French department, became adviser to women in 1961 and was succeeded in 1962 by Alma L. Lowe, the first woman to hold the title "dean of women." Also in 1962, G. Holmes Richter, who had been the dean of the university, became dean of graduate studies, and the old office that had for so long been called simply "the dean" existed no more.[15]

The lack of a tenure policy mirrored the absence of administrative structure at Rice, and some faculty members had begun to lobby for definition in this area as well. Under President Lovett and on through William Houston's presidency, someone (possibly the president but probably the dean) usually told a new member of the faculty after a year or two (ordinarily two) whether his career at Rice was expected to be long or brief. If he was expected to remain, he received an annual notice of reappointment along with a statement of his next year's salary. In practice, faculty members, even assistant professors, assumed that they had tenure even though it had not formally been granted. The result of this procedure was clear: first-class people who might have stayed with the reward of tenure did not have the incentive to remain; mediocre professors who could not have passed a formal tenure review enjoyed a high degree of job security and were difficult to remove from the faculty. A period of two years was hardly enough time to judge the abilities of a new faculty member effectively, and if the decision makers guessed poorly, the university had to live with the mistake. Since the academic world was becoming more mobile, there was no reason to suppose that really outstanding professors would remain at Rice. Rice's ad hoc process seemed almost guaranteed to produce a second-rate faculty.

However, the system did have some positive aspects. New faculty members had time to develop professional competence and were spared the gnawing uncertainty of an untenured position. At other universities the scramble for tenure often led to petty personal rivalries, publication of trivia for the sake of publishing, and neglect of teaching to win a reputation for scholarship. As long as Rice was small, the university could minimize the disadvantages of its informal tenure system. As long as it developed slowly, strengthening only a few departments at a time, it could and often did leave its second- and third-rate people in place. If, however, Rice was to become a first-rate university in all fields, it could not afford to keep unproductive faculty or to continue without a formal mecha-

nism for evaluation that included clearly written procedures.

In 1960 the Rice chapter of the American Association of University Professors discussed the matter of tenure with acting president Croneis and the board. Reflecting the national trend toward tenure in higher education, Pitzer's first Academic Development Committee recommended a stated tenure policy as necessary to attract superior professors; early in 1962 the president submitted a tenure system for board approval. In January the board approved the system and in March confirmed the status (either with tenure or on a one- to three-year appointment) of all faculty members.[16]

Expansion of the faculty began even before the final plan was adopted. What had begun under President Houston continued during Carey Croneis's brief term as acting president and increased under Kenneth Pitzer. From about 130 in 1957, faculty numbers rose to over 150 in 1960 and to 183 (175 men, 8 women) in 1962. Additions to the ranks in the late 1950s and early 1960s included William Caudill in architecture, Edgar O. Edwards and Gaston Rimlinger in economics, Thomas Rabson in electrical engineering, Alan Grob and Walter Isle in English, and Frederic Wierum and James Wilhoit in mechanical engineering. Economics historian Louis Galambos, Bismarck and Roosevelt scholar Francis Loewenheim, southern historian Sanford W. Higginbotham, and Austrian specialist

R. John Rath joined history, while Jean-Claude DeBremaecker went to geology and Paul Donoho to physics. The cheerful Scot Donald Mackenzie came to teach classics; archaeologist Frank Hole and Japan scholar Edward Norbeck constituted the new department of anthropology; Alexander Dessler headed the space science department, the first such department in the country.

The board did not forget those outstanding professors now at the compulsory retirement age. Believing that some of these men could still be useful to Rice, the board, at Rayzor's suggestion, created the position of Trustee Distinguished Professor for certain honored faculty members, who would continue some teaching and research after official retirement. Each was limited to teaching six hours a semester. By 1963 Professors Chillman, Bray, McKillop, and Tsanoff had been chosen for this position.[17]

To be a university of national and international stature, Pitzer thought that Rice needed a more comprehensive curriculum; and as new teachers were hired, the course list expanded. The humanities and social sciences, unemphasized for so long, finally began to come into their own. New departments such as fine arts and the anthropology-sociology combination (sociology was transferred from its odd-fellow combination with economics and business administration), an expanded foreign language department, and new offerings in established departments strengthened the undergraduate level. By 1962 Rice offered doctorates in economics, German, and philosophy along with those previously established in history, English, and French. Curriculum additions in the sciences and engineering were mainly on the graduate level. Both humanities and the sciences benefited from a program for college teacher education assisted by the Ford Foundation. Under this program, designed to answer the national need for college teachers, a student was able to complete all requirements for the master's degree and be well on the way to a doctorate within five years of entering the university.

In 1960 and 1961 the campus received the good news that two more buildings would be constructed to house some of the academic expansion. In 1960 Mr. and Mrs. J. Newton Rayzor gave the university money for a new building for the humanities. Rayzor Hall was placed at right angles to the library, across the quadrangle from Anderson Hall. In 1962 Professor and Mrs. L. B. Ryon bequeathed their entire estate for a new engineering laboratory building. Ryon had been at Rice for forty-five years, having come as an instructor in civil engineering in 1917 and retired as a professor in 1958. The Ryon Laboratory site was to the west of the Mechanical Laboratory Building.[18]

145. *Rayzor Hall during construction, May 10, 1961.*

Further Changes in the Curriculum

Although there is little evidence that student opinion directly influenced curriculum changes, the cries of undergraduates did not go unheard. The faculty made small changes in the requirements to introduce a wider range of electives and greater flexibility. Groups A, B, and C were redefined to include the new offerings. In place of simply languages, literature, and music, the new Group A offered architecture, classics, English, fine arts, foreign languages, history, humanities, music, and philosophy. In place of history, social studies, philosophy, and education, Group B now had anthropology, economics and business administration, education, political science, psychology, and sociology. In addition to biology, chemistry, physics, mathematics, and geology, and in place of psychology, Group C included engineering and space science. The language requirement was changed to allow students to take whatever languages they liked. (In 1962–63 the foreign language department offered French, German, Spanish, Greek, Latin, and Russian in at least the 100 and 200 levels.) The nemesis of so many, Math 100, was split into Math 100 for science-engineers and

Math 101 for academic students in 1960; some third- and fourth-year engineering courses were changed to increase emphasis on the science underlying modern engineering; and the third-year science requirement was dropped for academic students of the class entering in 1962.

These redefinitions and additions did not really change the curriculum. Its basic premise was still to introduce breadth into each major program by means of outside electives or diversification requirements, and several of the old problems remained. There was still no agreement among the faculty about what specific courses constituted a "well-rounded" education. There was a general consensus that every student should be exposed to a variety of subjects within major divisions—that everyone should study some math, some history, and so forth. Exceptions to the requirements were still allowed, though, and some departments were still "strongly advising" their students to take certain electives closely related to the major. The *Self-Study* report pointed out these controversies and commented on the difficulty of assessing the effectiveness of the curriculum, but it made no recommendations for the future.

A perennial question, some faculty members thought, was how to treat athletes. The faculty perceived a conflict between academic and athletic interests in colleges and universities nationwide, and Rice was no exception. Some thought that the presence of the athletes and their separate

Department of Health and Physical Education lowered standards for the university as a whole. A vocal group rankled at the special consideration given to athletes at admission time and the rumored (but never substantiated) special academic consideration they received. While many faculty members recognized that the intellectual caliber of the students admitted under the athletic quota was constantly rising, that some Rice athletes in recent years had been outstanding scholars, and that more were able to carry a normal course load in addition to the demands of their sport, they still saw problems.

In 1960 a special faculty committee on the athletic curriculum began to study a new program for athletes. The committee recommended a new course of study toward a business administration degree. Called the commerce curriculum, the plan reasonably assumed that most college athletes would go into some form of business after graduation, not into coaching or teaching. This curriculum was placed before the whole faculty in 1961 and was vigorously debated. Those who objected to it claimed that it would depress academic standards in the interests of championship football, and they said that they thought football and a first-class university were incompatible. Those in favor of the plan advocated providing for students who were going to be on campus whether members of the faculty liked it or not (the board had just reaffirmed the university's commitment to

athletics in the Southwest Conference), and ridiculed the claim that one department or course of study could lower the standards of the entire university. The commerce curriculum passed the faculty by a vote of 67 to 51 on the first vote and 65 to 56 on the second.[19]

Admissions Procedures

Despite continual worries about the abilities of incoming freshmen, admission procedures changed little. Under director of admissions James B. Giles, who had assumed that position in 1957, the Admissions Committee retained its quota system, grouping students by science-engineering, academic, and architecture divisions. Physical education majors had always entered under a separate system. In the 1961–62 catalog, College Entrance Examination Board examinations were declared mandatory, and the quota system was mentioned specifically. There was a quota of sorts for women: the number of women in the academic curriculum was limited to the number of men admitted under that curriculum. On the other hand, there was no limit for the number of women admitted to science-engineering and architecture. Few women applied to those divisions, anyway. Whether Rice's single dormitory for women affected the number of non-Houston women admitted is unclear, but once the second women's college was built in 1966, the number of out-of-town women increased. One thing *was* clear: by 1960 Rice was no longer having difficulty attracting students.[20]

A continuing dilemma was the admission of out-of-state students. By limiting their number, Rice had to turn down some outstanding candidates, but the charter stated that the school was intended to educate residents of Houston and Texas. On the other hand, if Rice aspired to be more than a state or regional institution, it had to admit more of those it attracted from outside. Eventually the non-Texan enrollment was raised to thirty-five or forty percent, a figure that seemed to ensure admission of the most able students in both categories.[21]

The "Rice Myth"

By the early 1960s, incoming Rice undergraduates had heard quite a bit about the excellence of the school's standing. Rice's regional reputation remained high, and its research and scholarly achievements had gained some prominence nationally and internationally. Discussion about turning Rice into a first-rate university stimulated some students to consider their own situation, though their conclusions did not always match some of the glowing praise they were hearing. The school year 1960–61 seems to be the point at which students began to reexamine their own educational experiences at Rice; it was a year when several popular professors left. Their student supporters claimed that they were excellent teachers who challenged them to do more than memorize. An angry *Thresher* editorial in 1961 charged that Rice could not be one of the nation's finest schools, because its faculty contained too many people lacking in "academic vitality" and because dynamic newcomers often resigned to escape what some students saw as a stifling, provincial, closed-minded atmosphere. The idea that Rice was the "Harvard of the South" was a myth, the vociferous students claimed.

By 1962–63 corroboration and rebuttal for the existence of a "Rice myth" were coming from several directions, and the discussion widened to include all phases of undergraduate life. Students, particularly those in the academic division, criticized the grading system, the quality of instruction, the position of the humanities in relation to science and engineering (commonly called the "lag" of the humanities), the limited holdings of the library, and the merits of the college system. Grading and instruction seemed to be the focus of discussion, perhaps because it was in the classroom that the students confronted the system head-on.

Grades at Rice, the students claimed, were still overemphasized and maintained at artificially low levels, producing both apathy about learning and the phenomenon of "grade-grubbing" (the pursuit of grades instead of knowledge). Grade-grubbing had its roots early in the student's school career, as the result of pressure from parents and secondary schools; no one blamed solely the grading system at Rice, but its system certainly contributed. Furthermore, to the outside world, grades were earned on an absolute scale, and Rice students who were not at the top of their classes often faced unexpected difficulty getting into graduate and professional schools because of their records, even though they performed well on the Graduate Record Examinations.

Faculty members agreed with many of the student criticisms and began to say so in committee reports, *Thresher* articles, and communications with the president and deans. In the fall semester of 1961, grades were distributed as shown in Table 1. In the class of 1962, thirty-eight percent of the students were on probation at some time (twenty-one percent were on probation once and seventeen percent twice); and thirty-six percent of the class withdrew before graduation, twenty-seven percent voluntarily and nine percent involuntarily.[22]

Such a grade distribution was not anomalous with that of other selective institutions, such as the University of California, Berkeley, the University of Pennsylvania, the University of Chicago, or the Massachusetts Institute of Technology. However, it indicated to some professors that the overall grading standard at Rice was inconsistent with the high quality of the undergraduate student body. The Subcommittee on the Program on Undergraduate Instruction of the Academic Planning Committee commented

TABLE I
Distribution of Grades, Fall 1961

	I	II	III	IV	V	Number
100-level courses	9.5%	27.7%	39.6%	15.9%	7.3%	2,792
200-level courses	9.9	38.1	36.8	10.9	4.3	2,182
300-level courses	12.6	40.7	34.5	9.0	3.2	2,182
400-level courses	12.1	35.3	36.1	11.6	4.8	8,373

Figures do not include withdrawals or 35 "satisfactory" grades in 400-level courses. The total number of grades is in the last column, and percentages do not always total 100 percent.

in its progress report that the grading system appeared to be demoralizing many students; the committee members believed that many individual teachers and some departments were "indiscriminate" in awarding low grades. Donald Mackenzie wrote to President Pitzer: "The present system does, I believe, impair our effectiveness: the morale of our students is lowered, and they tend to become discouraged and dissatisfied, rather than encouraged to find the joy in learning which inspires true scholarship. High standards are created through excellence in instruction, not in low grades."[23]

Although the Committee on Examinations and Standing could find little conclusive evidence of irregularities or injustices in the grade distribution data, it recommended that all departments consider and discuss at length freshmen and sophomore courses especially. It encouraged faculty members to pay particular attention to grading, presentation, and content, taking into account the students' preparation, future objectives, and the work load. They should try to estimate the time needed for an average student to do all assignments adequately.

The most notorious course for failures was still Math 100, even without the academic students, who had moved over to Math 101. In 1961, 24.1 percent of Math 100 students made IVs and 19.8 percent made Vs. In 1963 the figures were 19.0 percent and 21.8 percent respectively. A defender for the mathematics department spoke in the *Thresher* of a "very difficult and demanding course" and claimed that part of the result was due to the "generally weak high school preparation" of most of the students. The next week a humanist asked how it could be that the students were unprepared, when 8 percent of the freshman class had scored above 130 on the National Merit Qualifying Test and when the class average on the mathematics aptitude section of the College Boards was 701 out of a possible 800 points. In 1964 the failure rates for Math 100 were still a high 13.9 percent IVs and

24.5 percent Vs; the *Self-Study* report stated, "Obviously this situation reflects an unrealistic grading standard, especially in view of the fact that Rice freshmen are selected on the basis of their promise in mathematics." The alarming failure rate was eliminated only by abolishing the requirement that every freshman take a form of Math 100.[24]

Discussion of the quality of instruction involved more than methods; it extended to the objectives, principles, and importance of undergraduate education in general and the place of undergraduate instruction in a university that emphasized research and graduate studies. Hearing announcements about the anticipated growth of the graduate school and reading about more and more research grants, some undergraduates became apprehensive about their position. They were not alone in their concern; faculty members had been discussing, in one form or another, the place and purpose of undergraduate instruction even before the Academic Planning Committee and its subcommittees were created.

The enduring question concerned the purpose of an undergraduate education: was it preparation for graduate study, or an end in itself for those going no further than a well-rounded B.A. degree? Most people felt that the solution should provide for both eventualities within the same basic curriculum. However, there were additional considerations.

A university has two purposes: production of new knowledge

through research and study, and production of knowledgeable graduates. Professors should be able to conduct research in their fields as well as teach. The problem was of course that twenty-four hours a day were simply not enough for one person to prepare lectures and teach, carry on research and writing, attend the numerous committee meetings by which the university ran itself, counsel students, and answer other personal demands. It was necessary to set priorities. In 1963 both the dean of humanities and the dean of engineering told the Academic Planning Committee that the university needed to emphasize teaching—to reward classroom proficiency and lighten the class load to allow more preparation time.

President Pitzer told a meeting of students that he believed a department should concentrate its best talent at the beginning levels, because "that's where the most souls are saved." Although professors and departments tried several different methods of rewards and types of organization over the ensuing years with varying degrees of success, the major problems—preparation time, evaluation of teaching, and rewards—remained. Students continued to complain and to cling to the few teachers whom they considered really inspiring as proof that they were not wasting their time.[25]

Student Activities

Although it was fashionable to be cynical towards Rice, most students still enjoyed the university experience in the early 1960s. With the advent of the college system and the building of a ballroom in the student center and an auditorium in Hamman Hall, many on-campus students found that they had little need to leave campus at all. They only had to make a quick trip to the nearby Village shopping area for articles unavailable on campus, or to eat on the days when the colleges did not serve food. Dances, plays, football games, visiting outside lecturers, and college functions could all now take place on campus.

The drinking age in Texas was still twenty-one at the time, and no alcohol was allowed on campus. The liquor laws drove many parties outside the hedges, but it was still possible to ignore the rest of the city for much of college life. Big dances such as Rondelet, the Senior Dance, the literary societies' formals, and other such events usually took place at a hotel or country club, but the Beer-Bike Race was run every spring on campus. No longer did the riders both drink and ride—that had proved entirely too dangerous—but teams of riders and drinkers practiced for months on their respective specialties. In 1961 the record for drinking twenty-four ounces of beer was 3.2 seconds, and for riding the loop road around the central campus it was 2 minutes and 8 seconds.

The administration brought

146. *Rondelet dance, 1962–63 school year.*

147. *Will Rice College Chorus, 1962–63.*

one student pastime to a halt for a while. In their disorganized warfare with members of other colleges, the men had refined water-bomb throwing (propelling balloons partially filled with water) by using slingshots made with surgical tubing, to the extent that one missile was capable of breaking a window. Being Rice students, they also calculated the muzzle velocity for these water cannons. The destruction caused by these skirmishes resulted in the banning of water fights and payment for repairs by the students.

"Rice's Honor," the school song, caused some argument in 1962. Many students and alumni did not think that a song that emphasized "fighting on" and that was sung to the same tune as many high school songs was appropriate for serious academic occasions. Although it had been used only infrequently, "The Rice Hymn," composed in 1947 by Rice alumni Louis Girard and Nealie Ross, was proposed as a substitute. In 1962 lyrics were written for Sibelius's "Finlandia," but neither anthem caught on and attempts to press for their use were dropped.

Students, faculty, and friends of Rice had the chance to see and hear a number of important speakers in the early 1960s. Two Presidents of the United States came to campus, Dwight D. Eisenhower in 1960 for a non-

148. *The visit of President Eisenhower to Rice, October 1960.*

149. *The visit of President Kennedy, September 1962. (© 1962, Aubrey Calvin)*

political address and John F. Kennedy in 1962 for a speech on space exploration. In 1962 and 1963 some of the most prominent scholars in the world spoke on the Rice campus. The 1962–63 academic year marked the fiftieth anniversary of the Institute's opening, and the semicentennial celebration rivaled the ceremonies of 1912.[26]

CHAPTER 10

Semicentennial

As in 1912, so it was in 1962. Again invitations went out to universities, colleges, and institutes, to learned and professional societies. The Board of Governors and the faculty of William Marsh Rice University would inaugurate the university's third president and celebrate its semicentennial with an academic festival on October 10, 11, and 12. Would the invited institution send a representative to attend the festivities? Again the replies came, this time from Oxford, Zurich, Toronto, Istanbul, Mexico City, and Taiwan, from the National Academy of the Lincei in Rome, the National Academy of Sciences, the American Geophysical Union, and the Institute of Aerospace Sciences, from Stanford, Columbia, Chicago, Notre Dame, Wellesley, and UCLA. Rice's fellow halls of learning were pleased to congratulate the university on its fiftieth anniversary and to send a delegate for the celebrations.

Planning for the semicentennial had begun in 1960. The committee that was placed in charge by the board had as its honorary chairman Professor Harold A. Wilson, a member of the original faculty. The cochairmen were governors H. Malcolm Lovett '21 and John D. Simpson '31; Chancellor Carey Croneis was the executive director. The committee planned an extensive celebration, not to be confined to only three days. It was to stretch throughout the school year, with special speakers, symposia, and other programs in each department of the university. And this time the students would not be left out.

There had been significant changes in Houston since the time of the first festival. It had grown from a small city to the largest in Texas, with a population of 950,000 in the city itself and 1,250,000 in the metropolitan area. The area was known throughout the United States and beyond for its petrochemical industries, its wealth, and the aerospace complex. Houston had several universities, many cul-

tural attractions, and international connections. It was no longer strange to see prominent philosophers, physicists, authors, artists, anthropologists, and chemists there.

In addition to the inauguration of the series of lectures, the ceremonies were to include presentations of Medals of Honor and Certificates of Merit to each of the speakers and to some of the university family. Hubert E. Bray, James H. Chillman, William V. Houston, Alan D. McKillop, Radoslav A. Tsanoff, and Harold A. Wilson were the Rice professors being honored. The guests who gave lectures included historian Arnold Toynbee of the British Royal Institute of International Affairs, speaking on the change in the United States' position and outlook as a world power; Brand Blanshard, professor emeritus of philosophy at Yale University, with a speech entitled "The Test of a University"; and chemical engineer Sakae Yagi from the University of Tokyo,

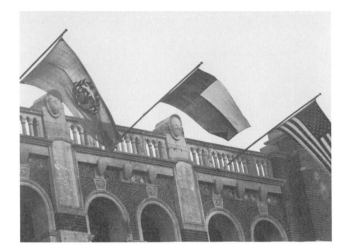

150–155. *Scenes from the semicentennial celebrations and the installation of President Pitzer.*

discussing Japanese problems in engineering education. Bertrand H. Bronson, professor of English literature at the University of California, Berkeley, spoke on English and American folk songs, and Sir George P. Thomson, a physicist from Cambridge University, traced the consequences of the last fifty years in physics. Architect John I. Reid discussed

design; Vladimir Prelog from the Swiss Federal Institute of Technology spoke on steric strain in organic chemistry; Allan Nevins, a historian from the Huntington Library, lectured on the relations between private and public universities; and Albert Szent-Györgyi, director of research at the Institute of Muscle Research at the Marine Biological Labora-

tory in Woods Hole, Massachusetts, surveyed the horizons of life sciences. Louis Landré from the University of Paris explored the cultural history of western Europe; Fritz Stüssi, a colleague of Prelog's at the Swiss Federal Institute of Technology, talked about structural engineering; Princeton economist Jacob Viner looked at the United States as

M.A. '27, Ph.D. '31, director of the Lamont Geological Observatory at Columbia University. Pollard addressed the alumni association dinner; honoree Keith Glennan, president of the Case Institute of Technology, spoke at President Pitzer's inaugural ceremonies; and nuclear chemist Glenn T. Seaborg, chairman of the United States Atomic Energy Commission, spoke at the Rice Associates' dinner.

As had the first festival, the semicentennial gathering defined objectives for Rice University. The opening celebration in 1912 had outlined aspirations and future plans and was designed to chart a distinguished course for the new Institute; the later festival looked to the past as well as to the future. The Semicentennial Committee expressed its purposes as follows:

To commemorate the first fifty years of Rice University; and to signalize the fulfillment of the dreams of William Marsh Rice, the founder—in which dreams there was envisaged the creation and development in Houston of an outstanding American institution for the advancement of letters, science and art; and, further, to re-create the international academic enthusiasm engendered by the significant ceremonies held at the opening of the University in the Fall of 1912.

To present to the world at large, as well as to scholars of every nation, plans and projects whose fruition, during the next half-century, will not only make secure the place of Rice University

a welfare state; and Henri M. Peyre, professor of French literature from Yale University, discussed a Frenchman's view of American education. Claude E. Shannon, a mathematician from the Massachusetts Institute of Technology, looked into the future of computers; another mathematician, Jean Leray from the Collège de France, dealt with a problem discussed in one of the 1912 lectures of Emile Borel; and anthropologist Margaret Mead talked of human capacity and potential.

Two Rice alumni were also honored: physicist William G. Pollard, M.A. '34, Ph.D. '35, executive director of the Oak Ridge Institute of Nuclear Studies, and William Maurice Ewing, B.A. '26, *in the forefront of the world's distinguished institutions of higher education, but also further increase the University's contributions to public enrichment through private endowment.*

To inspire among the friends of Rice, as well as in its Trustees, administration, faculty, students and alumni, a renewed aware-ness of the importance of both the research for truth and the dissemination of knowledge as exemplified by the record of the University during its first 50 years—and, further, to make plain to all citizens the rich op-portunities which in the next half-century will present them-selves for contributing to the progress and welfare of mankind through supporting an institu-tion pledged to the quest for ex-cellence in all its activities.[1]

These ceremonies, while filled with activities, did not demand the same stamina of the dele-gates and representatives as the first ones did. On Wednesday, Oc-tober 10, after lunch in the vari-ous college commons (honorees and delegates ate in a different college each of the three days), everyone gathered on the east side of Lovett Hall for the inau-gural ceremony, which had been postponed for a year to coincide with the semicentennial. A pro-cession made up of the senior class of 1963, the delegates, the Rice faculty, the Board of Trust-ees, and special honorees began the ceremonies.

The seniors entered first, dressed in black robes, and were seated behind the rows of dele-gates. The delegates, in contrast, wore the hues of their alma ma-ters—crimson, blue, gold—all the medieval colors from Old World and New World institu-tions. In place of mortarboards, many wore oddly shaped cha-peaux—tams, pillboxes, some-thing that looked like a French gendarme's cap. Surrounded by the flags, the solemn proces-sional music, and the partici-pants' regalia, one could easily imagine that he or she had been transported to a distant time and could savor one of the truly splendid ceremonial occasions that universities still celebrate.

After the crowd had sung the "Star Spangled Banner" and had heard the invocation and greet-ings from the students, the alumni, and the faculty, Dr. Houston presented the speaker, Keith Glennan, who delivered an address entitled "The Univer-sity in a World of Accelerating Change." The Rice University Chorus sang a song, and then Dr. Houston presented Dr. Pitzer to board chairman George R. Brown, who formally installed Kenneth Sanborn Pitzer as Rice's third president. Following the in-auguration were a reception at 4:30 P.M. in the Rice Memorial Student Center and a dinner for 1,220 at 7:30 that evening in the Crystal Ballroom of the Rice Hotel.

Only two things went wrong. It was extremely hot for October: at noon on the day of the inaugura-tion the temperature stood at ninety-five degrees. To relieve the discomfort of the formally robed participants, the next morning's speech by Arnold Toynbee and the presentation of medals to the honorees were moved downtown to the air-conditioned Music Hall, instead of being held on the Lovett Hall lawn as planned. The lectures that followed on campus were all in air-conditioned buildings. The second problem concerned the new president's voice. A viral in-fection attacked his throat and left him with almost no voice, but he still managed to be heard and was fully recovered in a few days.

Lectures morning and after-noon, lunch in the colleges' commons, and dinners at night completed the three days of fes-tivity. The Rice Hotel was the scene of all the dinners: the in-augural banquet, the Rice Asso-ciates' dinner for the visiting scholars, and the homecoming dinner of the alumni association.

On Saturday the alumni laid their yearly wreath at William Marsh Rice's monument. Follow-ing a practice that President Houston had begun at his inaugu-ration, Pitzer had placed a second wreath on the steps of the monu-ment before joining the pro-cession to his inauguration the day before. At 10:30 Saturday morning the new president pre-sided at the dedication of Rayzor Hall. The alumni attended a brunch and later a showing of the alumni semicentennial film *Golden Years*, the work of Mr. and Mrs. Shad Graham (Ruth McLain '28) and Grace Leake Watts '22. Festivities ended that night at the football game, which the Owls lost to the University of Oregon, 31–12.

The semicentennial celebration continued throughout the year, as departments and colleges held their own festivals with additional distinguished participants. The history department discussed theory in American politics, the idea of the South, and perspectives in medieval history. Physics looked at fast neutron physics; the geology department held symposia on natural radiation in the environment and on the earth sciences; and psychology contrasted behaviorism and phenomenology. Biology held a symposium on delayed implantation and anthropology studied prehistoric people in the New World, while economics discussed the nation's objectives in that field. The English department organized two symposia, one with essays on Restoration and eighteenth-century literature in honor of Alan McKillop, and the other with critical and historical essays. The architects looked at the people's architects, and Jones College held its own gathering focused on the role of the educated woman.[2]

One regret might have saddened participants in the celebration: Edgar Odell Lovett did not live to see Rice's fiftieth year. More than anyone else, except the founder, he was responsible for the idea of Rice, what the university stood for, what it hoped to be. Lovett had been with Rice since its inception. He had seen his dreams for a university interrupted in the hard economic times of the 1920s and the 1930s,

and he had seen them revive in the 1940s. His Institute was a small place, with an excellent reputation for scholarly standards, for its graduates, and for some of its faculty members. At first its reputation was concentrated in Texas and the South. At the same time, the Institute had friends at some of the most prestigious universities both in the United States and abroad, mainly because of Lovett's wide acquaintance, his continuing travels, the faculty he had attracted, and the accomplishments of Rice graduates. The academic world was much smaller in those days. Transportation was slow, Rice was far from the centers of learning on the east and west coasts, and scholars in the East had difficulty thinking that distinguished universities could be found west of the Appalachians or south of the Ohio River. Many people, including some applicants for faculty positions, hardly knew where Houston was. Without money for expansion, the Institute could do little but try to maintain its position.

As with most universities, the progress of Rice has been tied to its finances. The Baker board members are much to be praised for establishing the university as they did. Their reluctance to raise additional funds in the 1920s may have stemmed from provisions in the charter placing full responsibility for the Institute in their hands and forbidding them to go into debt, and from the fear that donations would often have unwarranted strings attached. The proscription

against debt made the cautious businessmen only more conservative in their financial dealings. To such men the oil business in the 1920s and 1930s looked like dangerous speculation, and they were hampered by Texas law, which apparently prohibited trustees from investing in equities. Furthermore, at that time Texas was a place for self-made men, without the tradition of community giving and with an aversion toward fund raising. Although Rice did not grow as it might have had more funds been available, the Institute survived the Great Depression while many other schools did not. In this case the board's conservative fiscal management proved to be the right course to follow.

Through it all, President Edgar Odell Lovett pressed on. He was able to attract and hold such professors of sterling repute as McKillop, Lear, Hartsook, Wilson, Tsanoff, and Weiser. Of course, he had help. It is impossible to imagine Rice without McCann, McCants, and Watkin, and the contributions of these men are legion. When Lovett relinquished his beloved Institute to a new president and a new board in 1946, he could justly be proud. Its reputation for excellence was intact, its potential sound. The Institute had produced, and continues to produce, eminent graduates, including prominent scientists, literary figures, businesspeople, teaching scholars, and public servants at the state and national levels.

The history of the Rice Institute has also been closely related to the city of Houston. When the city began to grow in size, wealth, importance, and reputation, so did Rice. After World War II many people learned more about both the city and the Institute. After the war, thanks to the Board of Governors, their investments and contributions, and the new president, William Vermillion Houston, Rice was at last able to begin the expansion that President Lovett had wanted so much in 1920. Emphasis was still on the sciences, but the humanities had begun to grow with the strong encouragement of President Houston and the endorsement of the board. With its dominant scientific and engineering reputation, however, the Institute still had trouble convincing the academic and outside worlds that it was not the "Rice Institute of Technology." Changing its name to Rice University in 1960 helped to alter the misconception. But it was not until the humanities had strong and well-known undergraduate programs to match those in science, and the faculty had exceptional teachers at all levels, that Rice was to become a university in the complete sense.

Kenneth Sanborn Pitzer hoped to complete the task set by his predecessors, and in 1963 the world was full of promise. Some students were disgruntled, but they were constructively pointing out important concerns and weaknesses that they felt needed consideration. Although several of the semicentennial speakers discussed the problems inherent in the vast enlargement of scientific and technological knowledge and wondered about human ability to to cope with the new realities, the academic festival was invigorating and exciting. The university was expanding at a rapid pace, there were plans for numerous improvements, money was coming in from many grants and gifts, and the first fundraising drive in Rice history was about to start. Everyone could look forward with anticipation and enthusiasm to the next half century.

NOTES

Chapter 1

1. One hundred fifty-two organizations sent delegates to the opening. *The Book of the Opening of the Rice Institute*, 1; J. T. McCants, "Some Information Concerning the Rice Institute," Woodson Research Center. The center will be cited hereafter as WRC. The information on the opening ceremonies has come from *The Book of the Opening* and the McCants manuscript unless otherwise noted.

2. The city directory estimate of Houston's population in 1912 was 109,594, based on a "name count" of 60,411 individuals and the number reported for their families.

3. *Houston Post*, October 12, 1912.

4. Julian Huxley, "Texas and Academe," p. 54; *Book of the Opening*, 1:41–44; Julian Huxley, *Memories*, pp. 94–95; photographic file, WRC.

5. McCants, "Rice Institute," p. 75; Harry Marshall Bulbrook, "Odyssey of a Freshman—1912," manuscript copy in possession of the Rice Historical Commission.

6. Huxley, *Memories*, p. 95.

7. *Houston Post*, October 14, 1912.

8. Bulbrook, "Odyssey."

9. *Houston Post*, October 10, 11, 12, 13, 1912; photographic file, WRC.

10. It is interesting to note that few provisions of any kind were made for the students, and there was no one to represent them at the convocation. Hattie Lel Red '16 heard some of the lectures from the bal-

cony over the Faculty Chamber and remembers being much impressed by the people who were there. Hattie Lel Red, June 28, 1977.

Chapter 2

1. For a complete biography of the founder, see Andrew Forest Muir, *William Marsh Rice and His Institute*.

2. Muir, *William Marsh Rice*, pp. 104–9.

3. Ibid., p. 109; J. T. McCants, "Some Information Concerning the Rice Institute," p. 13.

4. James A. Baker, Jr., "Reminiscences of the Founder," pp. 127–44; McCants, "Rice Institute," p. 81.

5. McCants, "Rice Institute," pp. 82–83.

6. William M. Rice, Jr., had the idea of electing his brother Joseph to the board in 1901; but Raphael said that the board could not do that, since Joseph did not live in Houston and the charter said that the trustees must reside in the city. The exception had been made in the case of the original trustees because that was what the founder had wanted. James Baker concurred with Raphael, so the position remained open. William M. Rice, Jr., to E. Raphael, April 13, 1901, Letters addressed to Secretary E. Raphael, 1891–1907, WRC (cited hereafter as Raphael Letters); Raphael to Rice, Jr., April 17, 1901, Raphael Letters; James A. Baker, Jr.,

to Raphael, April 27, 1901, Raphael Letters; Ellis A. David and Edwin H. Grobe, comps. and eds., *New Encyclopedia of Texas*.

7. *Charter of the William M. Rice Institute for the Advancement of Literature, Science and Art*, WRC.

8. McCants, "Rice Institute," pp. 13, 14; Minutes of the Board of Trustees, William M. Rice Institute, Treasurer's Office (cited hereafter as Board Minutes), April 27, 1910. Prior to the early 1940s, there were no Texas statutes governing investments by trustees. However, there were laws of "guardianship," which prohibited guardians from investing in stocks. Trustees generally assumed that they were governed by these statutes, and the Rice board was no exception; therefore, they limited their investments of the Rice endowment to bonds, liens, etc. In the early 1940s, some trustees went to court and received permission to invest in equities. Later the Texas Trust Act was passed, further freeing trustees to invest their trusts in the stock market. H. Malcolm Lovett, oral communication, January 15, 1982.

9. The charter stated that the Institute would be open to white inhabitants; the indenture within the charter said "open to all."

10. *Charter of the Institute.*

11. Muir, *William Marsh Rice*, pp. 53–55.

12. Raphael and McAshan to "Dear Sir" [recipient unknown], January 10,

1907, Raphael Letters; bylaws in Board Minutes, August 4, 1905.

13. Raphael to the Board of Trustees, December 28, 1906, in Board Minutes, January 8, 1907; H. H. Harrington to Raphael, July 23, 1906, Raphael Letters.

14. J. N. Anderson to Baker & Botts, February 26, 1906, Raphael Letters; D. F. Houston to Raphael, January 25, 1906, Raphael Letters; A. R. Hill to Rice Institute, October 18, 1905, Raphael Letters; Board Minutes, January 8, 1907.

15. Raphael and McAshan to "Dear Sir," January 10, 1907, Raphael Letters.

16. D. F. Houston to Raphael, January 11, 1907; J. E. Pursons to Rice Institute, January 15, 1907, both in Raphael Letters.

17. Collection Index, No. 2, Raphael Letters; Board Minutes, February 20, 1907.

18. Raphael and McAshan to Board of Trustees, February 18, 1907, Raphael Letters; Board Minutes, February 20, 1907.

19. D. F. Houston to Raphael, January 11, 1907, Raphael Letters; Board Minutes, February 20, 1907.

20. A. R. Hill to Raphael, March 3, 1907, Raphael Letters; H. McClanahan to Raphael, March 3 [1907?], Raphael Letters; Board Minutes, February 29, 1907, March 20, 1907.

21. Statement by Edgar Odell Lovett, July 19, 1944, in Presidents' Papers, Edgar Odell Lovett, Office Records, WRC.

22. Ibid.

23. Ibid.; Lovett to Rice, Jr., December 18, 1907, copy in possession of H. Malcolm Lovett.

24. Statement by Edgar Odell Lovett, July 19, 1944, in Presidents' Papers, Lovett, Office Records.

25. Hill to Raphael, March 25, 1907, April 4, 1907, Raphael Letters.

Hill said that there were other fields that on the whole offered greater attractions.

26. Collection Index, No. 2, Raphael Letters; Raphael and McAshan to the president and the Board of Trustees, February 18, 1907, Raphael Letters; Houston Post, April 15, 1907.

27. Board Minutes, November 20, 1907.

28. Board Minutes, December 18, 1907.

29. Baker to Lovett, December 19, 1907, copy in possession of H. Malcolm Lovett. The same letter is also in Edgar Odell Lovett, Personal Papers, Correspondence, Lovett-Trustees, WRC, and in Raphael Letters.

30. Raphael to Lovett, December 21, 1907, copy in possession of H. Malcolm Lovett.

31. Ibid.

32. Board Minutes, December 28, 1907; Raphael to Lovett, December 29, 1907, Raphael Letters.

33. Lovett to Raphael, January 2, 1907 [1908], Lovett, Personal Papers, Wilson Correspondence; Board Minutes, January 22, 1908.

34. William V. Houston, "Edgar Odell Lovett," pp. 137–40; Lovett to J. F. Downey, May 12, 1897; J. M. Page to Downey, May 12, 1897; O. Stone to Leavenworth, April 3, 1897, April 15, 1897; Alexander Ziwet to Leavenworth, May 5, 1897, all in Presidents' Papers, Lovett, Miscellaneous Correspondence.

35. W. Wilson to Lovett, Lovett, Personal Papers, Wilson Correspondence; Andrew Forest Muir, "Rice's Future Mapped in Early 1900s"; Lovett to Wilson, January 3, 1908, copy in possession of H. Malcolm Lovett.

36. Board Minutes, March 11, 1908; "Recommendations," n.d., copy in possession of H. Malcolm Lovett.

37. Clippings, n.d., with Weems to

Lovett, n.d. [1908?], Lovett, Personal Papers, Correspondence, Lovett-Trustees.

38. Board Minutes, May 6, 1908, June 10, 1908; Lovett's Travel Journal, Presidents' Papers, Lovett.

39. Lovett's Travel Journal, Presidents' Papers, Lovett; Lovett to Raphael, August 12, 1908, November 27, 1907, January 31, 1909, March 14, 1909, published in Dallas News, Lovett, Personal Papers, Unarranged; Lovett to Raphael, September 5, 1908, October 15, 1908, November 17, 1908, December 21, 1908, March 14, 1909, March 25, 1909, Lovett, Personal Papers, Unarranged, and Correspondence, Lovett-Trustees; Board Minutes, April 28, 1909.

40. Lovett to Raphael, August 12, 1908, September 5, 1908, March 14, 1909, March 25, 1909, Lovett, Personal Papers, Correspondence, Lovett-Trustees.

41. Edgar Odell Lovett, "Historical Sketch of Rice Institute, A Gift to Texas Youth"; idem, "Early Decisions in the Development of the Rice Institute," n.d., both in Presidents' Papers, Lovett, Office Records.

42. University and college histories and studies of higher education that I consulted included: John S. Brubacher and Willis Rudy, Higher Education in Transition; Nicholas Murray Butler, Across the Busy Years; Horace Coon, Columbia; C. H. Cramer, Case Western Reserve; Ernest Earnest, Academic Procession; Orrin L. Elliott, Stanford University; Hugh Hawkins, Pioneer; Brooks M. Kelley, Yale; Samuel Eliot Morison, The Development of Harvard University Since the Inauguration of President Eliot; George Wilson Pierson, Yale College: An Educational History; idem, Yale: The University College; Frederick Rudolph, The American College and University; George P. Schmidt, The

Liberal Arts College; Laurence R. Veysey, *The Emergence of the American University*; and Thomas Jefferson Wertenbaker, *Princeton*.

43. Lovett, "Historical Sketch"; idem, "Early Decisions."

44. Board Minutes, May 10, 1909, July 15, 1909, August 4, 1909; Lovett, "Historical Sketch."

45. Board Minutes, July 15, 1909.

46. Board Minutes, April 10, 1907, April 24, 1907, June 24, 1908, April 7, 1909; McCants, "Rice Institute," pp. 16–24.

47. McCants, "Rice Institute," pp. 23–26.

48. Ralph Adams Cram, *My Life in Architecture*, pp. 124–28; *Thresher*, February 20, 1963.

49. Cram to Lovett, August 30, 1909, in Presidents' Papers, Lovett, Lovett-Watkin Correspondence.

50. Lovett to Charles W. Eliot, September 27, 1910, Presidents' Papers, Lovett, Lovett-Watkin Correspondence.

51. Board Minutes, November 30, 1909, December 1, 1909; Lovett to Cram, Goodhue and Ferguson (CG&F), December 16, 1909, Presidents' Papers, Lovett, Lovett-Watkin Correspondence.

52. Lovett to CG&F, January 13, 1910; CG&F to Lovett, January 14, 1910, both in Presidents' Papers, Lovett, Lovett-Watkin Correspondence.

53. Lovett to CG&F, January 13, 1910, February 4, 1910, March 11, 1910; CG&F to Lovett, January 14, 1910, January 28, 1910, March 17, 1910, all in Presidents' Papers, Lovett, Lovett-Watkin Correspondence.

54. CG&F to Lovett, January 18, 1910, January 19, 1910; Lovett to CG&F, February 4, 1910, all in Presidents' Papers, Lovett, Lovett-Watkin Correspondence; Lovett, "Historical Sketch."

55. Board Minutes, April 27, 1910, June 27, 1910, September 16, 1910;

"The Rice Institute, A Memorandum of Information Prepared for the Senate and National Council of Phi Beta Kappa" (1921), pp. 5, 6, in Presidents' Papers, Lovett, Department Records.

56. Pamphlet entitled "The Rice Institute"; William Ward Watkin, "Architectural Development of the William Marsh Rice Institute," pp. 110–12.

57. Pamphlet entitled "The Rice Institute"; Watkin, "Architectural Development," pp. 110–12. Cram, *My Life*, pp. 126–27; Julian Huxley, "Texas and Academe," pp. 61–62.

58. *Thresher*, November 12, 1937; Hubert E. Bray, June 18, 1976, September 30, 1976.

59. Muir, "Rice's Future."

60. *The Book of the Opening of the Rice Institute*, 1:175–76; la Rose to Lovett, Presidents' Papers, Lovett, Planning of the Institute; Lovett to la Rose, December 14, 1910, ibid.; Lovett to J. T. McCants, December 14, 1910, Lovett, Personal Papers, Early, Math.

61. Lovett to McCants, February 4, 1912 [1911?], Lovett, Personal Papers, Early, Math; Lovett to Lombardi, February 24, 1911, Presidents' Papers, Lovett, Opening of the Institute, Lovett Correspondence; Board Minutes, March 1, 1911.

62. Loose clippings in envelope, Lovett, Personal Papers, Unarranged.

63. Board Minutes, May 31, 1912.

Chapter 3

1. Board Minutes, October 8, 1908.

2. H. A. Wilson to Lovett, March 22, 1912, Presidents' Papers, Lovett, Miscellaneous Correspondence.

3. P. V. Bevan to Lovett, February 26, 1912, April 20, 1912, Presidents' Papers, Lovett, Planning of the Institute.

4. Bevan to Lovett, February 26,

1912, Presidents' Papers, Lovett, Planning of the Institute; Wilson to Lovett, March 22, 1912, Presidents' Papers, Lovett, Planning of the Institute and Miscellaneous Correspondence; Board Minutes, May 31, 1912, June 5, 1912, June 12, 1912, July 11, 1913; Samuel Eliot Morison, *The Development of Harvard University Since the Inauguration of President Eliot*, p. lxi; H. Malcolm Lovett, July 27, 1981.

5. Wilson to Lovett, March 22, 1912, Presidents' Papers, Lovett, Miscellaneous Correspondence; G. C. Evans to Lovett, February 28, 1912, Presidents' Papers, Lovett, Planning of the Institute.

6. Evans to Lovett, February 17, 1912, March 3, 1912; Maxime Bocher to Lovett, March 4, 1912; William F. Osgood to Lovett, March 4, 1914, all in Presidents' Papers, Lovett, Planning of the Institute.

7. Board Minutes, May 2, 1912.

8. A. S. Cleveland to Lovett, August 16, 1941, Presidents' Papers, Lovett, Office Records, Trustees; Lovett to Baker, June 13, 1935, Presidents' Papers, Lovett, Office Records, Trustees; *Thresher*, November 12, 1937; *Houston Post*, September 27, 1912; *Houston Chronicle*, September 26, 1912.

9. *The Rice Institute Preliminary Announcements*, 1915. The catalog for the university has varied in title and publication over the years. From 1912 to 1924, it was called the *Preliminary Announcements*; from 1925 to 1950, *Announcements*; and from then on, *General Announcements*. From 1947 to 1954, it was published as part of the *Rice Institute Pamphlet*. Between 1950 and 1960, the annual catalog alternated between the general announcements issue and the graduate announcements issue. In the notes to this book, the catalog will be cited here-

after as *Announcements.*

10. Sarah Lane, October 20, 1975.

11. J. T. McCants, "Some Information Concerning the Rice Institute," pp. 88–90; Harry Bulbrook, October 28, 1977; Hattie Lel Red, June 28, 1977; Helen Batjer, August 10, 1976; J. W. Wilkinson to Board of Trustees, January 4, 1913, Presidents' Papers, Lovett, Office Records.

12. Hattie Lel Red, January 23, 1976; *Campanile,* 1916.

13. Draft article, "Coeducation in the Colleges," dated September 17, 1929, for *Gargoyle,* in Lovett, Personal Papers, Speeches. The copy has two endings. In the first Lovett said he would endow a women's college if he were in a position to endow an undergraduate college. The second said he would endow a college restricted to men or women for a hundred years; and if he endowed a women's college, he would make it subject to such academic organization as Harvard or Oxford.

14. Hattie Lel Red, June 28, 1977.

15. *Houston Chronicle,* July 24, 1915; William H. Wilson to Lovett, July 31, 1915, Lovett, Personal Papers, 1911–1957; Lovett to W. H. Wilson, August 31, 1915, Lovett, Personal Papers, 1911–1957. The *Chronicle* article spoke in the name of the founder, William Marsh Rice, and claimed to know what he wanted for women; it was not what they were getting at the Institute. W. F. Edwards to Baker, April 5, 1915, May 20, 1915, with Baker to Lovett, May 21, 1915, Lovett, Personal Papers, Unarranged.

16. Mrs. Harold Wilson, "Rambling Reminiscences of Early Days at Rice by a Septuagenarian," WRC; Hattie Lel Red, January 23, 1976; Board Minutes, September 29, 1915.

17. Harry Bulbrook, October 28, 1977; idem, "Odyssey of a Freshman—1912."

18. Lovett to Board of Trustees, January 30, 1918, Dean of Students, Cameron file, WRC; speech at student meeting, September 28, 1920, Lovett, Personal Papers, Speeches; Florence McAllister Jameson, February 3, 1978; *The Book of the Opening of the Rice Institute,* 1:164.

19. *Announcements,* 1915; *Thresher,* December 15, 1916; Bulbrook, "Odyssey."

20. Hattie Lel Red, June 28, 1977.

21. *Campanile,* 1916; *Thresher,* December 15, 1916.

22. Isaac Sanders, note on Rice University Historical Commission, vol. 1, no. 1, in possession of the commission; Henry A. Tillett, December 23, 1975; Bulbrook, "Odyssey"; H. Malcolm Lovett, May 19, 1976.

23. After participating in 1915, the Institute took a leave of absence in 1916 and rejoined the conference in December 1917.

24. *Houston Post,* October 10, 1912; *Football '77: Southwest Conference Roster and Record Book,* pp. 5, 64.

25. *Thresher,* February 15, 1917; Debbie Davies, "Rice has been trading knocks with the distinguished Texas A&M University for 63 years," pp. 10–11; *Basketball '78: The 1978 Southwest Conference Roster and Record Book,* pp. 24–29; *Southwest Conference 1978 Spring Sports Media Guide,* pp. 24–36.

26. Wilson to Lovett, February 28, 1913, March 2, 1913, March 31, 1913, June 13, 1913, Presidents' Papers, Lovett, Miscellaneous Correspondence.

27. Clipping from the *Daily Princetonian,* August 10, 1913, in Presidents' Papers, Lovett, Office Records; Lovett to John R. Effinger, April 24, 1920, Presidents' Papers, Lovett, Department Records.

28. Board Minutes, July 11, 1913; Wilson to Lovett, March 2, 1913, Presidents' Papers, Lovett, Mis-

cellaneous Correspondence, "The Development of the Rice Institute," typescript, in Lovett to George R. Brown, July 20, 1944, Presidents' Papers, Lovett, Office Records, Trustees.

29. Ortrud Much, oral communication, March 24, 1982.

30. Weiser wrote in August asking for a job and was hired for the fall, but it unclear how many hopeful applicants did this and were successful. Apparently Lovett, the dean, and various department chairmen relied on recommendations from friends and well-known men in the various fields to fill most vacancies in the faculty ranks. Weiser to Lovett, August 11, 1915, Lovett, Personal Papers, 1911–1957.

31. Andrew Forest Muir, "Rice's Future Mapped in Early 1900s."

32. Belle Heaps, February 17, 1978; Florence McAllister Jameson, February 3, 1978; Hattie Lel Red, June 28, 1978; Huxley and Hughes to Lovett, August 13, 1914, Presidents' Papers, Lovett, Miscellaneous Correspondence; Huxley to Lovett, November 5, 1914, Lovett, Personal Papers; Julian Huxley, *Memories,* pp. 99–100.

33. Board Minutes, January 10, 1917; Tony Martino, vertical file, WRC; Mrs. Jess Neely, oral communication, October 10, 1977; notes from Eula Goss Wintermann, July 24, 1979.

34. Board Minutes, May 30, 1916, June 1, 1910.

35. Address by Lovett on H. A. Wilson, June 2, 1950; Wilson to Lovett, March 2, 1913, March 31, 1913, all in Presidents' Papers, Lovett, Miscellaneous Correspondence.

36. Faculty Minutes, June 5, 1914; *Announcements,* 1915, pp. 21–22.

37. Faculty Minutes, June 5, 1914; *Announcements,* 1915, pp. 21–24.

38. *Announcements,* 1915, pp. 53–54.

39. George Wilson Pierson, *Yale College: An Educational History*, pp. 202, 258–66, 317–18, 329–33, 428–31; idem, *Yale: The University College*, pp. 198–205.

40. *Announcements*, 1917, pp. 33–34; Huxley, *Memories*, p. 99.

41. Faculty Minutes, Early Committee Lists.

42. Faculty Minutes, June 5, 1914; Blayney to Lovett, June 1914, Presidents' Papers, Lovett, Miscellaneous Correspondence.

43. Bulbrook, "Odyssey"; Hattie Lel Red, January 24, 1976; Faculty Minutes, January 7, 1915; *Announcements*, 1915, p. 24.

44. Faculty Minutes, February 3, 1916, April 13, 1916, April 27, 1916, March 1, 1917, June 5, 1919.

45. Recommendations from Committee on Examinations and Standing and Committee on Schedule and Courses of Study, October 1916, in Presidents' Papers, Lovett, Office Records; Faculty Minutes, November 23, 1916, January 10, 1918, February 21, 1918; Blayney to Lovett, June 1914, Presidents' Papers, Lovett, Miscellaneous Correspondence.

46. Lovett to T. J. J. See, October 17, 1911, Presidents' Papers, Lovett, Opening of the Institute.

47. Alice Dean, vertical file, WRC; Sarah Lane, October 20, 1975, July 1, 1977. It appears that in 1915, at least, the question of a librarian came up. Evans wrote Lovett that perhaps he, Evans, should ask at Columbia and other schools for "a reliable and capable man, trained in the history of science, who would be willing to enter the library at an instructor's salary, with the hope of eventually becoming the librarian." Lovett's reply is lost, but if such a search was begun, it never produced a candidate. Evans to Lovett, August 5, 1915, Presidents' Papers, Lovett, Planning of the Institute.

48. Board Minutes, July 11, 1913, November 18, 1914, November 17, 1915, July 10, 1920; Library Appropriations, 1916–1917, Faculty Minutes.

49. Sarah Lane, October 20, 1975, July 1, 1977.

50. Edgar Odell Lovett, "The Meaning of the New Institution," 51.

51. *Rice Institute Pamphlet* 5, no. 1 (January 1918), 3.

52. Lovett, "Historical Sketch"; *Announcements*, 1918, pp. 87–88.

53. Ibid.

54. Commencement, vertical file, WRC.

55. Faculty Minutes, February 18, 1915, March 30, 1916; W. F. Edwards to Baker, April 5, 1915, May 20, 1915, with Baker to Lovett, May 29, 1915, Lovett, Personal Papers, Unarranged. Edwards was an older faculty member and had been president of the University of Washington. He seems to have thought that he was to establish the chemistry department, but other sources indicate that Lovett was still looking for a chemistry professor. Edwards had the rank of lecturer. Edwards wrote some bitter letters to James A. Baker, Jr., but he evidently did not receive satisfacion. The quarrel between Lovett and Edwards seems to have been personal as well as professional and ended with Edwards leaving the faculty in 1915. Whether he resigned or was fired is unclear, but he considered himself "dismissed." If he had wished to stay, however, it would appear that he chose a difficult way to do so, since in his last letters he did not hesitate to take the board to task for not doing what he saw as their duty: to get rid of Lovett.

56. Guérard to Lovett, January 21, 1918, Presidents' Papers, Lovett, Office Records, Trustees.

57. H. O. Murfee to Lovett, July 21, 1909, Presidents' Papers, Lovett, Planning of the Institute; A. L. Hughes to Lovett, July 23, 1916, Lovett, Personal Papers.

58. F. Carrington Weems to Lovett, January 7, 1926; Lovett to Weems, January 26, 1926, both in Lovett, Personal Papers.

Chapter 4

1. Hughes to Lovett, September 1, 1914, Lovett, Personal Papers; *Thresher*, March 11, 1916, October 18, 1916, December 15, 1916, February 1, 1917.

2. There was the proviso that the faculty members on war duty be in condition physically and mentally to perform their faculty duties in order to return to the faculty. Board Minutes, April 30, 1917, July 11, 1917.

3. Andrew Forest Muir, "Rice's Future Mapped in Early 1900s"; H. Malcolm Lovett, March 29, 1978.

4. *Rice Institute Pamphlet* 6, supplement (1919). The entire supplement is devoted to those who served in the war.

5. [Lovett] to General Scott, April 19, 1917, Presidents' Papers, Lovett, Office Records, World War I, *Announcements*, 1917, pp. 56–57.

6. *Thresher*, September 29, 1917.

7. *Thresher*, October 27, 1917; *Campanile*, 1918; H. Malcolm Lovett, March 29, 1978; Sarah Lane, July 1, 1977; Florence McAllister Jameson, February 3, 1978.

8. Sarah Lane, July 1, 1977; Florence McAllister Jameson, February 3, 1978; Hattie Lel Red, January 23, 1976, June 28, 1977.

9. *Thresher*, September 29, 1917.

10. *Tape*, January 19, 1918; *Thresher*, December 14, 1917, February 2, 1918.

11. *Tape*, January 19, 1918.

12. *Thresher*, December 14, 1917.

13. *Thresher*, January 19, 1918.

14. *Tape*, January 19, 1918.

15. *Thresher*, February 2, 1918.

16. Ibid.

17. Ibid., February 16, 1918.

18. Ibid.; Helen Batjer, August 10, 1976.

19. Rice was not alone in suffering the wrong man for the job. At Yale the retired army captain who took over the ROTC proved likewise unable to handle his assignment, and school morale sagged. George Wilson Pierson, *Yale College: An Educational History*, pp. 444, 459–71.

20. *Thresher*, February 2, 1918; [Lovett] to President Maclaurin, August 7, 1918, Presidents' Papers, Lovett, Office Records, World War I; ROTC regulations, ibid.; Abstract of General Order Number 49, ibid.; Graustein affidavit, 1919, Presidents' Papers, Lovett, Department Records; *Tape*, January 19, 1918.

22. *Thresher*, February 16, 1918.

23. Ibid., February 15, 1917, March 1, 1917, March 24, 1917, February 2, 1918, April 20, 1918, May 25, 1918.

24. Faculty Minutes, April 25, 1918.

25. Student Association Constitution, *Thresher*, February 6, 1919, May 25, 1919; File with constitutions for the Women's Council in Dean of Students, Cameron.

26. "Three Gifts to the Rice Institute, announced by the Trustees at the third Commencement Convocation," *Rice Institute Pamphlet* 5, no. 3 (July 1918), 153–58.

27. Pierson, *Yale College*, pp. 444–46, 473–74; Charles F. Thwing, *The American Colleges and Universities in the Great War*, pp. 56–58; SATC, vertical file, WRC.

28. *Thresher*, February 6, 1919; McCants to Lovett, August 30, 1918; McCann to Lovett, August 17, 1918, both in Presidents' Papers, Lovett, Office Records, World War I; SATC, vertical file, WRC.

29. Caldwell to Robert E. Vinson, October 24, 1918; Commissioner Rees to Lovett, November 26, 1918, both in Presidents' Papers, Lovett,

Office Records, World War I; Pierson, *Yale College*, pp. 444–45, 473–74; SATC, vertical file, WRC.

30. Faculty Minutes, November 19, 1918, December 5, 1918; Committee on Education and Special Training to A. H. Wheeler, January 3, 1919, Presidents' Papers, Lovett, Office Records, World War I; *Thresher*, February 6, 1919.

31. Axson to Baker, June 24, 1918, Presidents' Papers, Lovett, Office Records, Trustees; Hawes to Lovett, January 3, 1919, Presidents' Papers, Lovett, Department Records.

32. Board Minutes, December 31, 1918, February 26, 1919; Wheeler to Cohn, January 11, 1919; Lovett to Cohn, February 27, 1919, both in Presidents' Papers, Lovett, Office Records, Trustees; Floyd Seward Lear, "History and the Humanities in Our Earlier Years," 5.

33. Caldwell to Lovett, July 16, 1929, July 17, 1932, Lovett, Personal Papers, Unarranged; Board Minutes, July 14, 1919.

34. Newspaper clippings on Huxley lectures, Presidents' Papers, Lovett, Miscellaneous Correspondence; *Houston Chronicle*, May 22, 1916; Baker to Lovett, February 15, 1918; D. K. Cason to Baker, February 5, 1918, both in Presidents' Papers, Lovett, Office Records, Trustees.

35. [?] to Board of Trustees, March 11, 1918, Presidents' Papers, Lovett, Office Records.

36. Most of the information for this episode comes from the Lyford P. Edwards file in the vertical file, WRC. This file consists of newspaper clippings from several papers with the *Houston Post* and the *Houston Chronicle* predominant, dating from May 14, 1919, to June 22, 1919. Other sources are "To the Public" [the trustees' statement; n.d.], Presidents' Papers, Lovett, Office Records; Lyford P. Edwards to Jerome Davis, November 17, 1931, Presidents' Pa-

pers, Lovett, Office Records; Resolution on Academic Freedom, Faculty Minutes, May 26, 1919; Muir, "Rice's Future"; *Thresher*, May 22, 1919.

Chapter 5

1. Elisha D. Embree and Thomas B. Eaton, *The Flying Owls: Rice Institute from the Air*.

2. *Thresher*, October 22, 1920, September 22, 1922, October 12, 1923; Faculty Minutes, October 6, 1921; Weiser to Lovett, January 7, 1920, Presidents' Papers, Lovett, Department Records; Chandler to Lovett, January 29, 1923, ibid.

3. Faculty Minutes, June 5, 1919, February 12, 1920, March 11, 1920, April 8, 1920, June 4, 1921.

4. Faculty Minutes, May 17, 1923; *Thresher*, October 12, 1923.

5. Faculty Minutes, November 8, 1923, November 22, 1923; Board Minutes, March 5, 1924.

6. Board Minutes, March 5, 1924; Notice to the Faculty, November 21, [1924], Presidents' Papers, Lovett, Office Records; Faculty Minutes, November 8, 1923, November 22, 1923.

7. *Thresher*, September 21, 1926; "Suggestions regarding the matter of admissions to the Rice Institute," from S. G. McCann, May 28, 1927, Presidents' Papers, Lovett, Office Records; Board Minutes, June 18, 1927.

8. Caldwell to Lovett, December 8, 1927, Presidents' Papers, Lovett, Office Records.

9. Caldwell to Lovett, December 19, 1927, ibid.

10. Caldwell to Lovett, May 4, 1928, ibid.

11. Ibid.

12. Hughes to Lovett, June 25, 1919, Presidents' Papers, Lovett, Department Records; Wilson to Lovett, March 26, 1920, ibid.; Lovett to Wil-

son, July 17, 1919, April 3, 1920, ibid.; Lovett to various university presidents, April 3, 1920, and replies, ibid.; Board Minutes, July 24, 1918, May 21, 1919, July 14, 1919, May 22, 1920, July 10, 1920, May 18, 1921.

13. Board Minutes, July 10, 1920, June 27, 1923, July 23, 1924, July 1, 1925, June 22, 1926, June 18, 1929.

14. Lovett to Baker, April 2, 1923, Lovett, Personal Papers.

15. *Houston Post*, February 15, 1924, May 7, 1924.

16. *Houston Chronicle*, June 9, 1924; clipping with no paper given, dated June 10, 1924, both in Presidents' Papers, Lovett, Office Records, Commencement; *Houston Post*, December 12, 1924.

17. *Thresher*, September 21, 1926, November 25, 1926; *Houston Post*, December 31, 1929, September 30, 1930; Lovett to D. S. Jordan, May 9, 1929, Presidents' Papers, Lovett, Office Records, Trustees. The registrar of Stanford replied that all that was necessary to charge tuition was an enabling act of the California legislature. *Houston Chronicle*, December 30, 1928; *Houston Press*, April 1, 1929; Slaughter to Baker, June 19, 1929, Presidents' Papers, Lovett, Office Records, Trustees; Baker to Slaughter, June 20, 1929, ibid.; Board Minutes, May 20, 1929; Will Hogg to George S. Cohen, June 26, 1929, Lovett, Personal Papers.

18. Chandler to Lovett, November 28, 1933, Presidents' Papers, Lovett, Department Records; McCants to Lovett, September 30, 1924, ibid.; Wilson to Lovett, June 3, 1924, ibid.; C. W. Heaps to Lovett, July 5, 1924, ibid.; Lovett to W. S. Farish, June 6, 1924, Lovett, Personal Papers; Faculty Minutes, June 7, 1924; *Thresher*, October 3, 1924, October 30, 1925, April 11, 1924.

19. Wilson to Lovett, February 11, 1925, February 15, 1925, March 2, 1925, Lovett, Personal Papers, Unar-

ranged; Lovett to Wilson, March 24, 1925, ibid.; Baker to McCants, February 12, 1925, ibid.; Board Minutes, March 20, 1925; Wilson to Lovett, April 10, 1925, Presidents' Papers, Lovett, Department Records; W. S. Farish to Lovett, March 23, 1925, ibid.; Chandler to Lovett, May 5, 1926, ibid.; Altenburg to Lovett, August 16, 1924, ibid.

20. As president of the Institute, Lovett received a salary of $12,000 in 1920, which was raised to $16,000 in 1921. This was very high for the South and higher than all the colleges studied by the registrar of Georgetown College in 1925. "Salary Study by the Registrar of Georgetown College," 1925, in Presidents' Papers, Lovett, Office Records. Board Minutes, January 8, 1926, June 21, 1928.

21. Weiser to Lovett, March 26, 1927, Presidents' Papers, Lovett, Department Records; Evans to Lovett, January 14, 1929, Lovett, Personal Papers, Unarranged; Watkin to Lovett, May 27, 1929, ibid.

22. Altenburg to Lovett, August 16, 1924, Presidents' Papers, Lovett, Department Records; *Thresher*, April 3, 1925.

23. *Houston Chronicle*, April 22, 1929, April 29, 1929. Miss Dean was apparently never appointed as the *Chronicle* recommended.

24. Faculty Minutes, January 15, 1920; James U. Teague, June 29, 1977; John Parish, September 28, 1977.

25. Board Minutes, March 21, 1927; Lovett, speech to Faculty Club, October 1, 1931, Lovett, Personal Papers, Speeches; *Thresher*, January 22, 1920, March 25, 1927, November 24, 1927.

26. Faculty Minutes, March 6, 1919, May 28, 1919, February 24, 1921, May 5, 1921, March 25, 1921, January 12, 1922, February 23, 1922, November 20, 1922, June 10, 1922,

May 7, 1925, June 6, 1925, February 11, 1926, April 15, 1926, January 13, 1928, February 13, 1928, June 6, 1928; *Thresher*, May 15, 1925; *Announcements*, 1927, pp. 38–39, 45–48.

27. Faculty Minutes, November 4, 1920, June 2, 1926, June 5, 1926, June 4, 1927; *Thresher*, April 29, 1927; *Announcements*, 1926, p. 52–53; 1927, pp. 55–56.

28. Faculty Minutes, April 3, 1919, November 18, 1920, December 2, 1920, February 24, 1921; *Thresher*, February 27, 1919, March 6, 1919, October 29, 1920, January 7, 1921, October 21, 1927; H. K. Humphrey to [?], November 1, 1927, Presidents' Papers, Lovett, Office Records.

29. Lindsey, Dyer, Hinckley, and DePrato were in track and field sports, and Underwood and Dyer again were consensus All-Conference in football. *Football '77: Southwest Conference Roster and Record Book*, pp. 61–69; *Basketball '78: The 1978 Southwest Conference Roster and Record Book*, pp. 24–29; *Southwest Conference 1978 Spring Sports Media Guide*, pp. 24–36; Watkin to Lovett, December 9, 1923, Presidents' Papers, Lovett, Office Records; *Thresher*, December 14, 1923. There is some evidence that President Lovett was about to ask for Arbuckle's resignation, but whether he did is unclear. At any rate, Arbuckle did resign. Lovett to Arbuckle, November 28, 1923, marked "Not sent," Presidents' Papers, Lovett, Office Records.

30. Watkin to Lovett, January 29, 1924, January 30, 1924, February 3, 1924, February 6, 1924, Presidents' Papers, Lovett, Office Records; Watkin to Lovett, February 3, 1924, William Ward Watkin Papers, WRC.

31. McCants to Watkin, February 7, 1924, Presidents' Papers, Lovett, Office Records; Board Minutes, February 12, 1924, April 2, 1924; April 25, 1924.

32. *Thresher*, February 19, 1924, March 28, 1924, April 11, 1924, April 18, 1924, May 3, 1924, May 10, 1924, September 18, 1924; Hubert E. Bray, June 18, 1976; Gaylord and Louise Johnson, February 20, 1978; Jack Agness, "All About the Heisman," *Houston Post*, December 4, 1977.

33. Alex C. Humphreys to Palmer E. Pierce, June 18, 1924; Pierce to Heisman, July 7, 1924; Watkin to Heisman, July 11, 1924; Heisman to Watkin, July 15, 1924, July 16, 1924; Pierce to Watkin, July 16, 1924; Humphreys to Watkin, July 17, 1924; Heisman to Lovett, July 18, 1924; Watkin to Frank W. Nicholson, November 4, 1924, all in Presidents' Papers, Lovett, Office Records.

34. *Thresher*, April 3, 1925, April 10, 1925, May 1, 1925, October 9, 1925. Heisman also did not like the idea of female cheerleaders; *Thresher*, November 7, 1924. East Hall, before Heisman appropriated it, had been *the* place for seniors and "big men on campus" to live. Dean G. Holmes Richter, who was one of the tutors for the athletes, remarked that he did not know how Heisman managed to get hold of that building. G. Holmes Richter, July 5, 1977.

35. Gaylord and Louise Johnson, February 20, 1978.

36. *Thresher*, January 21, 1927; *Football '77*, p. 64.

37. Heisman Terms, November 21, 1927, Presidents' Papers, Lovett, Office Records; Lovett to Heisman, December 1, 1927, ibid.; Heisman to Lovett, December 2, 1927, ibid.; Board Minutes, December 9, 1927; *Thresher*, December 9, 1927; Gaylord and Louise Johnson, February 20, 1978.

38. Watkin to Baker, December 5, 1927, Presidents' Papers, Lovett, Office Records.

39. Baker to Lamar Fleming, Jr., February 20, 1929, Presidents' Papers, Lovett, Office Records, Trust-

ees; "Note on the Proposed Course in Physical Education," from H. A. Wilson, December 4, 192[8?], Presidents' Papers, Lovett, Office Records.

40. Faculty Minutes, December 13, 1928.

41. Board Minutes, February 27, 1929; Fleming to Baker, February 15, 1929, March 6, 1929, Presidents' Papers, Lovett, Office Records, Trustees.

42. *Announcements*, 1930, pp. 95–99; Watkin to Lovett, January 16, 1929, January 17, 1929, Presidents' Papers, Lovett, Department Records.

43. Harris Masterson, Jr., to Lovett, September 30, 1921, Autry-Masterson, Lovett Papers, WRC; *Thresher*, September 30, 1921, October 23, 1947; Autry House, vertical file, WRC.

44. Henry A. Tillett, December 23, 1975; Programs for the Rice Institute Engineering Show, WRC; *Thresher*, May 13, 1920, February 4, 1921, April 23, 1926.

45. *Thresher*, November 5, 1920, November 19, 1920, October 6, 1922, November 7, 1930, May 6, 1921, May 12, 1922, February 8, 1924; *Campanile*, 1922. The pageant for the first May Fete presented the poem from the opening, "Texas, A Democratic Ode." Article on Archi-Arts from *Pencil Points* (March 1922), in Watkin Papers; *Thresher*, November 11, 1921, October 19, 1923.

46. *Thresher*, October 22, 1920, April 8, 1921, November 3, 1922, September 25, 1925, October 16, 1925, October 23, 1925; Andrew Forest Muir, "Rice's Future Mapped in Early 1900s."

47. *Thresher*, January 26, 1923, October 19, 1923, November 2, 1923, September 18, 1924, February 15, 1924, September 26, 1924, October 17, 1924, October 24, 1924, October 31, 1924, November 27, 1924, February 27, 1925.

48. *Thresher*, March 27, 1919;

Houston Chronicle, March 29, 1929.

49. Constitution of the Student Association, 1922, in Dean of Students File, Cameron; *Thresher*, January 13, 1922, March 10, 1922.

50. Caldwell to Lovett, May 6, 1922, Faculty Minutes, Early Committee Lists, December 2, 1920, June 5, 1922; *Thresher*, March 2, 1962; Fred J. Stancliff, September 28, 1977; "Statement read to the students of Rice at a called meeting held in the Physics Amphitheatre at twelve-fifteen O'Clock, Thursday, June Eighth," June 8, 1922, Presidents' Papers, Lovett, Office Records. The clubs that were abolished can be seen in the *Campanile*, 1922. They were the Tattlers, Blue Moon, Hoots, Sigma Beta, Idlers, Alpha Rho, Samurai, and the Ku Klux Klan. The Toilers had disbanded themselves in May "in the interest of Rice Institute." *Thresher*, May 26, 1922.

51. "Statement read to the students," June 8, 1922, Presidents' Papers, Lovett, Office Records.

52. Fred J. Stancliff, oral communication, March 28, 1979.

53. *Thresher*, September 15, 1922.

54. *Thresher*, September 15, 1922, October 13, 1922, October 20, 1922, November 28, 1930; Faculty Minutes, October 19, 1922, January 18, 1923.

55. *Thresher*, September 21, 1923, September 28, 1923, February 23, 1924, January 22, 1926, April 16, 1926, March 25, 1927, April 15, 1927; Faculty Minutes, November 8, 1924.

56. Board Minutes, October 5, 1927; *Thresher*, May 18, 1928, October 12, 1928, November 9, 1928, January 11, 1929, November 8, 1929, November 28, 1930.

57. *Thresher*, November 25, 1920, December 3, 1920, November 22, 1929.

58. Ella Lonn to Lovett, April 7, 1922; Pamphlet, AAUW, 1925; Mary

S. Torrens, Report of AAUW Conference, April 1926; Lonn to Lovett, March 8, 1927; Lovett to Mrs. Leata Mercer, April 14, 1930; Mary H. Smith to Edwina Wiess, November 4, 1936; Wheeler to Wiess, November 30, 1936; Wheeler to Mrs. Don Kimmel, November 14, 1945, all in Presidents' Papers, Lovett, Office Records.

59. Oscar M. Voorhees to Lovett, December 30, 1921, September 26, 1922, Presidents' Papers, Lovett, Office Records; John J. McGill to Lovett, May 23, 1927, ibid.; *Thresher*, October 5, 1928, January 25, 1929, March 1, 1929, March 8, 1929, March 21, 1930.

Chapter 6

1. Outline of a System of Accounts, Budgets, and Reports for the Board of Trustees, May 30, 1947, Budget File, Comptroller's Office.

2. Baker to Lovett, March 26, 1932, Lovett, Personal Papers, Unarranged; Cohn to Baker, March 25, 1932, ibid.; Board Minutes, May 25, 1932.

3. Board Minutes, June 24, 1931, June 2, 1932.

4. Board Minutes, June 5, 1932, June 8, 1932; Wilson to Lovett, April 4, 1932, Presidents' Papers, Lovett, Department Records; Baker to Lovett, June 6, 1932, Presidents' Papers, Lovett, Office Records, Trustees.

5. Board Minutes, June 29, 1932.

6. Wilson to Lovett, June 9, 1932, Lovett, Personal Papers, Unarranged; Board Minutes, June 29, 1932.

7. Board Minutes, June 1, 1932, August 24, 1932; Report on William M. Rice Institute for the Advancement of Literature, Science and Art, prepared for the Board of Trustees by the Survey Committee, May 7, 1945, Presidents' Papers, Lovett, Office Records, Trustees (cited hereafter as Survey Committee Report).

8. Board Minutes, April 11, 1933;

Houston Chronicle, April 12, 1933, April 13, 1933, September 8, 1933; *Thresher*, April 14, 1933; Baker to Trustees, April 3, 1933, Presidents' Papers, Lovett, Office Records. Board was provided for the students at cost, and the price fluctuated from month to month. The initial cost was $1.05 in 1931; it dropped to 94¢ in 1933, rose to 98¢ in 1934, and to $1.00 in 1936. Rooms had previously cost from $78 to $115 in 1932, depending on the size of the room and the number of roommates. The new plan charged everyone a flat rate of $90. *Announcements*, 1931, 1932, 1933, 1934, 1935, 1936.

9. Baker to Lovett, February 24, 1933, Presidents' Papers, Lovett, Office Records; Board Minutes, May 26, 1933.

10. *Houston Chronicle*, December 3, 1934, December 6, 1934, December 7, 1934, July 28, 1938, July 29, 1938; *Thresher*, December 7, 1934; Board Minutes, May 18, 1939, December 19, 1934.

11. Baker to Lovett, June 4, 1936, Presidents' Papers, Lovett, Office Records, Trustees; Weiser to Lovett, August 9, 1936, Presidents' Papers, Lovett, Department Records; Board Minutes, June 3, 1936; Faculty Minutes, June 6, 1936.

12. *Houston Chronicle*, December 23, 1936, January 8, 1937.

13. Board Minutes, December 24, 1936; *Houston Chronicle*, December 23, 1936, January 8, 1937; *Thresher*, September 15, 1938; Baker to Lovett, October 19, 1938, Presidents' Papers, Lovett, Office Records, Trustees.

14. *Houston Chronicle*, July 14, 1933, July 30, 1933, September 11, 1933, October 11, 1931; *Thresher*, March 6, 1931, March 20, 1931; Sarah Lane, August 10, 1976.

15. Hubert E. Bray, June 18, 1976; Wilson to Lovett, June 9, 1932, Lovett, Personal Papers, Unarranged.

16. J. D. Thomas, July 13, 1977;

Carroll Camden, September 20, 1977; Evans to Lovett, October 12, 1933, Presidents' Papers, Department Records; Board Minutes, October 18, 1933; *Houston Chronicle*, October 27, 1933.

17. Watkin to F. Browne, February 1, 1934, Watkin Papers; Survey Committee Report, March 8, 1945, Presidents' Papers, Lovett, Office Records, Trustees; *Thresher*, March 1, 1935; Faculty Minutes, April 15, 1935.

18. Board Minutes, April 20, 1938, August 4, 1905, February 25, 1942; Lovett to Nicholas Murray Butler, October 29, 1935, Presidents' Papers, Lovett, Office Records, Trustees.

19. Scott to Lovett, December 14, 1933, Presidents' Papers, Lovett, Department Records; Weiser to Lovett, July 28, 1934, ibid.; *Houston Chronicle*, June 4, 1933, November 28, 1937.

20. *Thresher*, January 17, 1936; *Houston Chronicle*, March 11, 1932; A. C. Lederer to Rice University Historical Commission, May 10, 1978, in possession of the commission; Eula Goss Wintermann, July 24, 1978.

21. Baker to Lovett, April 26, 1938, Presidents' Papers, Lovett, Office Records, Trustees; Lawrence Sochat to Baker, April 22, 1938, ibid.; H. Meyer to Editor, *Houston Press*, n.d., clipping, ibid.; Lovett to Baker, June 20, 1938, ibid.; *Thresher*, April 29, 1938.

22. Baker to James W. Rockwell, October 6, 1937, in Board Minutes, October 13, 1927; *Thresher*, January 22, 1937; André Bourgeois, November 28, 1977.

23. *Thresher*, October 22, 1937.

24. Board Minutes, May 24, 1922, November 28, 1928, May 28, 1930.

25. *Thresher*, October 28, 1932, November 4, 1932; *Houston Chronicle*, November 4, 1932, November 10, 1932, March 20, 1934.

26. *Thresher*, November 28, 1930,

September 15, 1932, October 7, 1932, September 13, 1934, September 19, 1940, September 27, 1940, October 4, 1940, October 17, 1940, October 10, 1941, October 2, 1942; *Houston Chronicle*, September 14, 1933, September 27, 1933, October 24, 1933, September 11, 1934, September 19, 1935, September 24, 1936; newspaper clippings with no papers named, dated September 16, 1938, October 1, 1938, September 14, 1939, September 19, 1940, September 24, 1940, October 5, 1940, September 18, 1941, September 27, 1941, from a collection of newspaper clippings made by Dr. Floyd S. Lear and given to the Woodson Research Center by the Rice University Historical Commission, cited hereafter as Lear clippings.

27. *Thresher*, April 11, 1930, October 28, 1938; Pound to Lovett, April 9, 1938, Presidents' Papers, Lovett, Department Records.

28. *Thresher*, March 17, 1933, March 6, 1936, March 13, 1936; Baker to Lovett, March 30, 1933, Presidents' Papers, Lovett, Office Records; *Houston Chronicle*, April 28, 1933, May 4, 1933, May 7, 1933; Lear clippings, March 7, 1940.

29. *Houston Chronicle*, October 27, 1933, October 28, 1933, October 29, 1933, October 30, 1933, November 9, 1933, November 10, 1933, November 27, 1933, November 28, 1933; *Houston Post*, November 8, 1933; *Thresher*, November 3, 1933, November 10, 1933, November 24, 1933; J. D. Thomas, July 13, 1977.

30. Cooperative store indenture in Board Minutes, May 31, 1938; Hanszen to A. H. Fulbright, August 26, 1947, Presidents' Papers, Houston, Office Records; Fulbright to Hanszen, September 2, 1947, ibid.; *Thresher*, May 11, 1937, May 23, 1937, October 4, 1938, February 17, 1939.

31. Andrew Forest Muir, "Rice's

Future Mapped in Early 1900s"; *Thresher*, April 24, 1936; Lear clippings, May 28, 1939.

32. *Houston Chronicle*, February 10, 1933, February 12, 1933, November 30, 1933, December 9, 1933, December 10, 1933; *Houston Post*, February 10, 1933, February 11, 1933; *Thresher*, February 17, 1933, December 15, 1933.

33. Gaylord and Louise Johnson, February 20, 1978; Clark Nealon, February 2, 1978.

34. Clark Nealon, February 2, 1978.

35. Board Minutes, October 5, 1938; Clark Nealon, February 2, 1978; *Football '77: Southwest Conference Roster and Record Book*, p. 14.

36. *Football '77*, pp. 60–65; *Southwest Conference 1978 Spring Sports Media Guide*, pp. 24–36, 73–74, 84; *Basketball '78: The 1978 Southwest Conference Roster and Record Book*, pp. 26–29, 76–77; *Houston Chronicle*, March 5, 1934, March 6, 1940, March 20, 1934, April 8, 1934, August 21, 1934.

37. Board Minutes, December 15, 1937, January 26, 1938, March 30, 1938; Clark Nealon, February 2, 1978; *Houston Chronicle*, April 27, 1938.

38. *Houston Post*, December 15, 1939; *Thresher*, January 12, 1940; *Football '77*, pp. 60–65.

39. *Thresher*, February 15, 1935, February 23, 1935, March 1936.

40. *Thresher*, March 3, 1939, September 14, 1939, September 29, 1939, October 14, 1941; *Houston Chronicle*, October 17, 1941.

Chapter 7

1. Naval ROTC, vertical file, WRC; *Thresher*, September 18, 1941, December 12, 1941, December 20,

1941. It appears that the administration had applied for an Army ROTC unit in 1940. Lovett said that the unit had been approved by the War Department, but it was never established before the war. *Thresher*, September 27, 1940.

2. The provision for dental, law, and medical students remained in effect only for the war years. Faculty Minutes, February 5, 1942; Board Minutes, February 4, 1942.

3. L. E. Denfeld to Lovett, March 11, 1943, Presidents' Papers, Lovett, Office Records, World War II; "Manual for the Operation of a Navy V-12 Unit," *Navy V-12 Bulletin*, no. 22 (June 18, 1943), ibid.; Board Minutes, March 17, 1943; Naval ROTC, vertical file, WRC.

4. *Thresher*, April 9, 1943; L. E. Denfeld to Lovett, March 11, 1943, Presidents' Papers, Lovett, Office Records, World War II; Board Minutes, April 7, 1943; "The Navy College Training Program—V-12, Curricula Schedules," Presidents' Papers, Lovett, Office Records, Navy.

5. *Thresher*, July 8, 1943, August 19, 1943, September 9, 1943, April 9, 1943; "The Navy College Training Program—V-12, Curricula Schedules," Presidents' Papers, Lovett, Office Records, Navy; "V-12 and NROTC Routine," ibid.; *Campanile*, 1944, vols. 1 and 2; Naval ROTC, vertical file, WRC; George Holmes Richter, July 5, 1977; *Houston Chronicle*, June 25, 1943.

6. Andrew Forest Muir, "Rice's Future Mapped in Early 1900s"; Board Minutes, March 3, 1943; Lovett to Meyer, February 25, 1943, Presidents' Papers, Lovett, Department Records; *Thresher*, April 20, 1944.

7. *Announcements*, 1947, pp. 129–35; 1952, pp. 187–90; Report to the President from the Registrar, 1946, 1947, Registrar's Office Files.

8. Board Minutes, April 16, 1941; *Houston Post*, November 23, 1940,

November 24, 1940; *Houston Chronicle*, November 23, 1940.

9. Board Minutes, April 23, 1941.

10. Board Minutes, May 14, 1941; *Houston Post*, May 18, 1941, May 20, 1941; *Houston Chronicle*, May 18, 1941, May 20, 1941.

11. Board Minutes, August 13, 1941, October 8, 1941, May 6, 1942; *Thresher*, September 18, 1941; *Houston Chronicle*, August 14, 1942, June 2, 1942.

12. *Houston Chronicle*, December 28, 1941, October 15, 1941.

13. Board Minutes, August 6, 1941, November 9, 1938, December 7, 1938.

14. Board Minutes, January 9, 1940, March 20, 1940; William A. Kirkland, July 19, 1977.

15. Board Minutes, February 11, 1942, May 6, 1942, February 1, 1951.

16. *Charter of the William M. Rice Institute for the Advancement of Literature, Science and Art*, WRC.

17. Board Minutes, October 7, 1942, November 9, 1942, November 18, 1942, November 28, 1942, December 18, 1942; Auditor's Report as of June 30, 1943, Presidents' Papers, Lovett, Fiscal Records; H. Malcolm Lovett, June 27, 1977; *Thresher*, December 4, 1942; *Houston Chronicle*, November 24, 1942, December 18, 1942, December 19, 1942, January 1, 1943, January 16, 1944, April 5, 1944.

18. Board Minutes, July 6, 1944, September 17, 1948; *Houston Chronicle*, March 22, 1935, July 6, 1944; *Thresher*, December 9, 1955.

19. Carl M. Knapp to Board of Trustees, May 30, 1944, Presidents' Papers, Lovett, Office Records; Lovett to Brown, July 20, 1944, Presidents' Papers, Lovett, Office Records, Trustees.

20. Board Minutes, February 28, 1945; Lovett speech on the naming of Wiess Hall, March 25, 1950, Lovett, Personal Papers, Speeches.

21. Survey Committee Report, May 7, 1945.

22. Ibid.; "Rice Looks Forward," speech by H. C. Wiess, in Wiess to Scott, November 8, 1945, Presidents' Papers, Lovett, Office Records, Trustees.

23. Board Minutes, July 30, 1945.

24. Board Minutes, October 11, 1945; "Rice Looks Forward," speech by Wiess, in Wiess to Scott, November 8, 1945, Presidents' Papers, Lovett, Office Records, Trustees.

25. Board Minutes, April 8, 1942; Lovett to W. M. Rice, Jr., November 19, 1942, Lovett, Personal Papers, Correspondence; Lovett to Cleveland, February 22, 1944, Presidents' Papers, Lovett, Office Records, Trustees; Cleveland to Lovett, June 14, 1944, ibid.; Wiess to W. K. Lewis, March 31, 1945, ibid.

26. Survey Committee Report, May 7, 1945.

27. Remarks of J. T. Scott, April 10, 1945, in Faculty Minutes, April 14, 1945.

28. Faculty Minutes, April 14, 1945; Preliminary report submitted to the Trustees of the Rice Institute by the Committee selected by the Faculty for consultation on the choice of a new President, April 25, 1945, Treasurer's Office Correspondence, Retirement of Dr. Lovett and Selection of a new President, Treasurer's Office; George Holmes Richter, July 5, 1977, March 9, 1978.

29. Wiess left notes of his meetings and phone calls during his travels, and without these notes it would have been very difficult to trace the hiring process. Very little correspondence with the candidates or their supporters survives. Notes and other enclosures from Wiess are with Weiss to Members of the Board, June 9, 1945, Presidents' Papers, Lovett, Office Records, Trustees; Wiess to Scott, June 12, 1945, ibid.; Wiess to Members of the Board, June 15, 1945, ibid.; Wiess to Members of the Board,

July 13, 1945, ibid.; Wiess to Members of the Board, November 20, 1945, ibid. Other sources for this section are Faculty Minutes, April 14, 1945; Board Minutes, April 11, 1945, January 4, 1946; McKillop, Richter, and Ryon to Trustees, April 25, 1945, Treasurer's Office Correspondence, Retirement of Dr. Lovett and Selection of a new President; Wiess to W. K. Lewis, March 31, 1945, Presidents' Papers, Lovett, Office Records, Trustees; George Holmes Richter, July 5, 1977, March 9, 1978.

30. Board Minutes, January 4, 1946; Press Release, January 4, 1946, Treasurer's Office Correspondence, Retirement of Dr. Lovett and Selection of a new President; H. Malcolm Lovett, May 19, 1976, June 27, 1977, March 29, 1978; William A. Kirkland, July 19, 1977.

31. Board Minutes, June 27, 1946, May 21, 1947, July 28, 1947; Hanszen to Trustees, August 6, 1947, Presidents' Papers, Houston, Office Records, Board Minutes; Hanszen to Trustees, August 26, 1947, ibid.; Report of Committee on the System of Accounts, Budgets and Reports, June 2, 1947, ibid.; Report of Committee on the System of Accounts, Budgets, and Reports, May 30, 1947, Outline of System, Budget File, Comptroller's Office; Kirkland to Samuel L. Fuller, March 19, 1947, in possession of the Rice University Historical Commission; Shamblin to Trustees, May 4, 1964, ibid.; *Houston Chronicle*, November 13, 1946, March 5, 1947; *Thresher*, November 7, 1946, March 6, 1947.

32. Sketches from *American Men of Science* and *Who's Who in America* in Wiess to Scott, June 12, 1945, Presidents' Papers, Lovett, Office Records, Trustees; *Thresher*, April 10, 1947.

33. *Thresher*, April 10, 1947.

34. Muir, "Rice's Future"; Board Minutes, December 4, 1947.

35. Muir, "Rice's Future"; Houston's address to the faculty, March 16, 1946, in Faculty Minutes, March 16, 1946.

36. Houston's address to the faculty, March 16, 1946, in Faculty Minutes, March 16, 1946.

37. Faculty Minutes, March 16, 1946.

38. The assistants to the president were James C. Morehead, William H. Masterson, John E. Parish, Thad Marsh, and Sanford W. Higginbotham. *Thresher*, April 10, 1947; James C. Morehead, April 6, 1978; William H. Masterson, October 11, 1977; George Holmes Richter, July 5, 1977, March 9, 1978.

39. Faculty Minutes, April 15, 1946, June 28, 1946, October 15, 1946, November 6, 1946, April 23, 1947, April 18, 1949; Minutes for the Committee on Examinations and Standing, May 5, 1948, Undergraduate Dean's Office; *Houston Chronicle*, December 2, 1946, August 14, 1947; *Announcements*, 1946, pp. 51–60, 106–7, 109–16, 131–33; 1947, pp. 19–30, 44–52; 1949, pp. 57–67; 1950, pp. 61–74; George Holmes Richter, July 5, 1977, March 9, 1978.

40. Faculty Minutes, November 6, 1946; *Thresher*, December 5, 1946; *Announcements*, 1940, pp. 37–42; 1947, pp. 19–27.

41. *Announcements*, 1947, pp. 26–27.

42. Board Minutes, April 4, 1946, May 8, 1946, May 29, 1946, March 6, 1947, October 30, 1947; *Thresher*, October 3, 1946; *Houston Chronicle*, September 18, 1947, September 12, 1948.

43. *Thresher*, March 22, 1947, May 22, 1947; Board Minutes, April 4, 1946; *Houston Chronicle*, November 21, 1946.

44. *Thresher*, October 9, 1947; Cooperative Committee on Library Buildings, Report, April 27–28, 1945, Presidents' Papers, Lovett, Office Records; John E. Burchard to Trustees, January 1, 1946, ibid.; Heaps to Burchard, January 7, 1946, ibid.

45. Board Minutes, March 11, 1946, May 6, 1946, October 30, 1947, December 3, 1947, December 4, 1947; Hanszen to Trustees, April 29, 1947, Presidents' Papers, Houston, Office Records, Board Minutes; *Houston Chronicle*, November 8, 1947, June 29, 1946.

46. *Thresher*, December 18, 1947; *Houston Chronicle*, December 22, 1947, November 21, 1948, August 15, 1949, October 30, 1949.

47. Board Minutes, October 30, 1947; *Houston Chronicle*, March 12, 1946.

48. Program for the opening of Abercrombie Laboratory, November 20, 1948, Presidents' Papers, Houston, Office Records, Abercrombie; McVey to Rather, November 13, 1948, ibid.; Maurice J. Sullivan to Hanszen, April 7, 1947, ibid.; *Thresher*, February 12, 1949. McVey also did the sculptures for the San Jacinto Monument.

49. The Houstons had been provided a house to live in until the house on campus was completed. *Houston Chronicle*, July 20, 1949; *Thresher*, February 9, 1949, March 24, 1950; *Announcements*, 1950, pp. 7–8, 42; 1952, pp. 7–8, 44–45.

50. Burchard to Wiess, October 9, 1947, Presidents' Papers, Houston, Office Records, Stadium; Burchard to Wiess, November 6, 1947, ibid.; *Houston Chronicle*, December 2, 1948–February 12, 1949, May 6, 1949, February 15–July 12, 1949, November 15–18, 1949, November 20, 1949, November 23–December 4, 1949; Board Minutes, January 9, 1948, November 17, 1949, December 30, 1949.

51. Board Minutes, January 9, 1948, November 17, 1949, December 30, 1949, October 25, 1951; Jess Neely, October 10, 1977; *Thresher*, January 13, 1950, September 15, 1950; *Houston Chronicle*, November 20, 1949, November 23, 1949, December 4, 1949, December 30, 1949, April 5, 1950, October 24, 1951.

52. Jess Neely, October 10, 1977; *Houston Chronicle*, August 31, 1949, November 5, 1949, December 3, 1950, November 5, 1950; *Announcements*, 1950, pp. 7–8.

53. *Thresher*, January 16, 1954, February 27, 1942, May 15, 1942, October 16, 1942, December 18, 1942, February 19, 1943, November 18, 1943, November 26, 1943, January 4, 1945, May 3, 1945, May 23, 1945; *Campanile*, 1944.

54. *Thresher*, May 17, 1945.

55. *Thresher*, September 20, 1945.

56. *Announcements*, 1941, pp. 52–55; 1948, pp. 64–67; *Houston Chronicle*, February 29, 1948; Report to the President from the Registrar [1948–49?], Registrar's Office.

57. Report to the Faculty from the Committee on the Coordination of Freshmen (also called Committee on the Freshman Course), in Faculty Minutes, June 1, 1950; Minutes, Committee on the Freshman Course, November 15, 1948, January 17, 1949, January 20, 1949, WRC.

58. Minutes, Committee on the Freshman Course, March 6, 1950, April 8, 1950, April 17, 1950; Committee report in Faculty Minutes, June 1, 1950; Faculty Minutes, April 11, 1950; G. Williams to Committee on Examinations and Standing, marked received March 30, 1950, with Minutes of the Committee on Examinations and Standing, April 10, 1950, Undergraduate Dean's Office; Committee on Examinations and Standing to Committee on the Freshman Course, April 10, 1950, ibid.; *Thresher*, May 18, 1949.

59. Faculty Minutes, February 13, 1948, April 23, 1947; *Thresher*, March 25, 1948, April 29, 1948, March 25, 1948.

60. *Thresher*, October 31, 1946, February 13, 1947, March 6, 1947, December 11, 1948, December 9, 1949; Faculty Minutes, November 11, 1948.

61. *Thresher*, May 2, 1946.

62. *Thresher*, April 17, 1947, February 17, 1950, May 12, 1950; Nancy Moore Eubank, February 22, 1978; Clara Mohr Kotch, February 10, 1978; Paula Meredith Mosle, September 7, 1978.

63. *Thresher*, April 17, 1947, February 17, 1950, May 12, 1950; Paula Meredith Mosle, September 7, 1978; Clara Mohr Kotch, February 10, 1978.

64. *Thresher*, September 20, 1945, October 3, 1946, October 24, 1946.

65. *Thresher*, October 2, 1947.

66. *Thresher*, September 22, 1948, September 25, 1948, October 2, 1948, October 9, 1948, April 30, 1949, May 7, 1949, May 14, 1949, September 30, 1949, October 7, 1949, January 13, 1956; *Houston Chronicle*, September 30, 1949, October 26, 1949, October 30, 1949, March 15, 1950, March 16, 1950, March 17, 1950; Raymond L. Lankford, January 30, 1978.

67. Jess Neely, October 10, 1977; Virgil C. Eikenberg, February 9, 1978; *Football '77: Southwest Conference Roster and Record Book*, pp. 62–69.

68. *Houston Chronicle*, October 21, 1948, October 24, 1948; Jess Neely, October 10, 1977.

69. *Basketball '78: The 1978 Southwest Conference Roster and Record Book*, pp. 24–29, 68–70; *Southwest Conference 1978 Spring Sports Media Guide*, pp. 24–36, 73–74.

70. *The Book of the Opening*, 1:177.

Chapter 8

1. *Thresher*, September 22, 1950; *Houston Chronicle*, February 26, 1950, December 31, 1950; *Houston Post*, February 26, 1950.

2. Board Minutes, May 2, 1951, May 5, 1954, September 30, 1959, April 22, 1953.

3. Hanszen to Board of Trustees, September 5, 1947, Presidents' Papers, Houston, Office Records.

4. Fleming to Trustees, September 15, 1948, Presidents' Papers, Pitzer, On Campus, 1961–1963; William A. Kirkland, July 19, 1977.

5. Board Minutes, August 5, 1949, September 23, 1949, May 27, 1953; *Houston Chronicle*, September 8, 1949; William A. Kirkland, July 19, 1977; James U. Teague, June 29, 1977; Herbert Allen, September 27, 1977.

6. The donor's stipulation that the music school be housed in a building in the style of early colonial Virginian architecture was a small source of worry but was somehow finally settled. Board Minutes, November 24, 1950, February 1, 1951, March 8, 1951, May 2, 1951, January 24, 1952, December 1, 1954, April 22, 1953; *Houston Chronicle*, September 18, 1950, December 5, 1950, January 6, 1952, June 1, 1958; *Houston Post*, December 5, 1950, June 6, 1962.

7. Board Minutes, February 4, 1953, September 23, 1953, May 5, 1954; *Announcements*, 1956, p. 4. The pledge is now $15,000, payable over a period of ten years.

8. Board Minutes, February 23, 1955; Faculty Minutes, November 22, 1955; The President's Discretionary Research Fund, August 24, 1960, Presidents' Papers, Houston, Departments.

9. *Houston Chronicle*, September 5, 1950, February 8, 1953, March 22, 1954, May 31, 1956, March 30, 1957, June 8, 1956, November 18, 1958, January 6, 1959, April 24, 1959, May 31, 1959, June 4, 1959; *Houston Post*, May 12, 1957; *Announcements*, 1959, pp. 38–43; 1960, pp. 62–66.

10. Board Minutes, July 25, 1956; Houston to Robert M. Hutchins, February 28, 1951, Presidents' Papers, Houston, Office Records; Ford Foundation College Grants Advisory Committee Questionnaire, ibid.; Houston to Joseph M. McDaniel, Jr., June 24, 1957, ibid.; Survey of Salaries, ibid.; *Thresher*, December 16, 1955; *Houston Chronicle*, June 24, 1957.

11. Board Minutes, August 28, 1950; *Thresher*, September 15, 1950, September 18, 1952, September 16, 1955, April 6, 1951.

12. *Thresher*, May 15, 1953, May 10, 1957; Faculty Minutes, October 30, 1953.

13. Board Minutes, June 15, 1953, June 24, 1953; Houston to Croneis, June 18, 1953, Presidents' Papers, Houston, Departments; George Holmes Richter, March 9, 1978; William H. Masterson, October 11, 1977.

14. Faculty Minutes, May 30, 1953; Michael V. McEnany, September 1, 1977.

15. Faculty Minutes, April 21, 1955.

16. Board Minutes, May 7, 1958, July 30, 1958; *Thresher*, September 11, 1958; *Houston Post*, February 12, 1960; *Houston Chronicle*, February 12, 1960.

17. *Houston Post*, December 21, 1951; *Houston Chronicle*, January 4, 1951, October 9, 1954; William H. Masterson to T. M. Greene, April 21, 1954, Presidents' Papers, Houston, Office Records; Board Minutes, September 29, 1954.

18. Board Minutes, June 23, 1959; *Thresher*, September 19, 1959; *Houston Chronicle*, July 26, 1959; Houston to Griffis, May 8, 1959, Presidents' Papers, Pitzer, On Campus,

1961–1963; Faculty Minutes, October 19, 1959.

19. *Announcements*, 1956, p. 92; *Houston Post*, July 15, 1951, April 13, 1956, February 10, 1957; *Houston Chronicle*, October 14, 1951, December 12, 1954, August 28, 1955, September 23, 1956, February 19, 1957, April 4, 1958, June 3, 1960; *Thresher*, February 27, 1953; Tom Bonner, vertical file, WRC; Biology Building, vertical file, WRC; Geology Building, vertical file, WRC.

20. Board Minutes, March 25, 1953, May 5, 1954, May 26, 1954, December 15, 1949, June 29, 1955, July 26, 1955; Nielsen and McBride to Houston, [August 1955?], Presidents' Papers, Houston, Office Records; Press release, ibid.; Minutes of meeting of an informal committee on the Student Religious Center, July 13, 1955, ibid.; *Houston Post*, November 1, 1955.

21. Board Minutes, June 29, 1955, September 28, 1955; McBride to Porter Butts, July 27, 1954, November 8, 1954, Presidents' Papers, Houston, Office Records; Minutes of informal committee on Student Religious Center, July 13, 1955, ibid.; *Houston Post*, November 1, 1955, October 26, 1958, February 29, 1956; *Thresher*, November 4, 1955; *Houston Chronicle*, November 4, 1955, October 26, 1958.

22. *Thresher*, November 6, 1963.

23. *Houston Chronicle*, September 1, 1957; Nancy Moore Eubank, February 22, 1978; George R. Brown, July 14, 1977.

24. Guy T. McBride, October 24, 1977; *Thresher*, May 28, 1962; Committee on Student Housing Minutes, November 22, 1954, Committee on Student Housing, vertical file, WRC; Committee on Student Housing, "New Dimensions in Student Life, Reports of the Committee on Student Housing," September 1, 1956, bound volume of reports in Fondren

Library, Rice University, Houston, Texas, 1–5. The Committee on Student Housing will be cited hereafter as CSH.

25. Guy T. McBride, October 24, 1977; "New Dimensions," 5–6.

26. Board Minutes, May 27, 1953, June 24, 1953; Guy T. McBride, October 24, 1977; "New Dimensions," 1–15.

27. *The Book of the Opening*, 1:164–70.

28. Board Minutes, September 29, 1954, August 25, 1954.

29. "New Dimensions," 17–22; Faculty Minutes, October 26, 1954; Guy T. McBride, October 24, 1977; Clara Mohr Kotch, February 10, 1978; Board Minutes, March 30, 1955; Houston to A. Whitney Griswold, February 15, 1955, Presidents' Papers, Houston, Office Records; Houston to L. A. DuBridge, February 15, 1955, ibid.

30. Report to the faculty by the CSH, Faculty Minutes, April 21, 1955.

31. CSH Minutes, November 22, 1954, November 29, 1954; "New Dimensions," 22–25; Faculty Minutes, April 21, 1955.

32. "New Dimensions," 32; Paula Meredith Mosle, September 7, 1978.

33. "New Dimensions," 26–27; Faculty Minutes, April 21, 1955; CSH Minutes, February 7, 1955, April 1, 1955.

34. "New Dimensions," 14, 27–28, 53–55.

35. "New Dimensions," 14, 27–28, 54–57.

36. "New Dimensions," 13–14, 24–25, 45–48; CSH Minutes, November 29, 1954, January 10, 1955, January 17, 1955.

37. "New Dimensions," 37–41.

38. "New Dimensions," 67–76.

39. After Mrs. Dunn retired, Daisy Coe became housemother along with Mrs. Morrow. Paula Meredith Mosle, September 7, 1978; Dowden and

McBride to Houston, May 2, 1951, Presidents' Papers, Houston, Office Records; Meredith to Houston, May 22, 1957, ibid.; *Houston Chronicle*, July 12, 1948, May 20, 1951; Board Minutes, March 28, 1956, July 25, 1956; *Thresher*, September 28, 1951; Clara Mohr Kotch, February 10, 1978.

40. "New Dimensions," 28–33; CSH Minutes, February 9, 1955, April 1, 1955, May 6, 1955, May 16, 1955; Paula Meredith Mosle, September 7, 1978; Board Minutes, June 29, 1955.

41. Board Minutes, November 30, 1955, June 27, 1956, July 25, 1956; *Houston Chronicle*, November 17, 1955; CSH Minutes, February 9, 1955; McBride to Houston, February 15, 1955, Presidents' Papers, Houston, Office Records; Will Rice College, vertical file, WRC.

42. Calvin M. Class, January 20, 1978; James Street Fulton, September 30, 1977; William H. Masterson, October 11, 1977; Paula Meredith Mosle, September 7, 1978; Guy T. McBride, October 24, 1977.

43. *Thresher*, March 13, 1963.

44. Paula Meredith Mosle, September 7, 1978; William H. Masterson, October 11, 1977; James Street Fulton, September 30, 1977; James R. Sims, January 18, 1978; Calvin M. Class, January 20, 1978; Responsibilities and Interrelations of the College Masters, the Dean of Women, and the Dean of Students, April 11, 1963, Presidents' Papers, Pitzer, On Campus, 1961–1963; *Thresher*, March 13, 1963.

45. *Thresher*, April 21, 1961.

46. *Thresher*, April 21, 1961, March 13, 1963; Statement on Trends in the Colleges from Higginbotham, January 24, 1962, Presidents' Papers, Pitzer, On Campus, 1961–1963; Paul Burka, September 12, 1978; James B. Giles, September 6, 1978; James Street Fulton, Septem-

ber 30, 1977.

47. William H. Masterson, October 11, 1977; James Street Fulton, September 30, 1977; Calvin M. Class, January 20, 1978; James R. Sims, January 18, 1978; *Thresher*, April 21, 1961, March 13, 1963.

48. *Houston Post*, October 10, 1956; *Thresher*, October 8, 1952, March 4, 1955, October 7, 1955, October 14, 1955, February 24, 1956, February 17, 1956, October 12, 1956, November 9, 1956, February 8, 1957, October 25, 1957, February 22, 1957; *Houston Chronicle*, October 10, 1956, November 4, 1956; McBride to Jack Holland, February 5, 1957, Presidents' Papers, Houston, Office Records; McBride to Houston, October 10, 1957, ibid.; Faculty Minutes, May 10, 1957; Paula Meredith Mosle, September 7, 1978; Nancy Moore Eubank, February 22, 1978; Jacquelin Collins, September 9, 1978.

49. *Thresher*, October 31, 1962, December 3, 1964; *Houston Chronicle*, October 14, 1959; "New Dimensions," 48.

50. Mike V. McEnany to Houston, May 28, 1953, Presidents' Papers, Houston, Office Records; Report to the Executive Committee from the Committee of Educational Inquiry, May 1953, ibid.; Faculty Minutes, March 30, 1953.

51. Oral communication, Mrs. Douglas Dunlap, Admissions Office, Rice University; Annual Report to the President, Registrar's Office.

52. Report of the Committee on the Freshman Course, October 1953, with the papers given to the Rice Historical Commission by J. D. Thomas. The commission then gave the papers to the WRC. McCann to Houston, March 29, 1955, Presidents' Papers, Houston, Office Records; Statement of revised admission requirements and procedures, 1955–1956, ibid.; Faculty Minutes, October 26, 1954, May 10, 1957, June 2, 1955;

oral communication, Mrs. Douglas Dunlap; Annual Reports to the President, Registrar's Office. The Committee on the Freshman Course was abolished in 1955, and a new committee was appointed to study the problem of providing better opportunities for contact between students and faculty.

53. Faculty Minutes, April 21, 1955, February 17, 1956, May 10, 1957, May 29, 1958; *Thresher*, May 5, 1961.

54. Proposals for the Humanities Division, in Masterson to Houston, September 23, 1959, Presidents' Papers, Pitzer, On Campus, 1961–1963.

55. Louise Johnson, February 20, 1978.

56. James B. Giles, September 6, 1978; Frank E. Vandiver, April 3, 1978, April 25, 1978; George H. Richter, July 5, 1977, March 9, 1978; Paula Meredith Mosle, September 7, 1978; Paul Burka, September 12, 1978; and informal conversations with Hugh Rice Kelly, Molly Kelly, Myra Bahme, Patricia Teed, Mary Fae McKay, Mary Margaret Hill, Katherine Drew, S. W. Higginbotham, Caroline Reynolds, and Sam Stewart.

57. Paul Burka, September 12, 1978; James B. Giles, September 6, 1978; Frank E. Vandiver, April 3, 1978, April 25, 1978; Calvin Class, January 20, 1978; Jacquelin Collins, September 9, 1978; Paula Meredith Mosle, September 7, 1978; and informal conversations with those cited in note 56.

58. Some remember a cartoon from the period that showed a student, dripping blood, walking down the sidewalk in front of the Physics Building, with an enormous sword of the old Roman style stuck in his back. Two other students are watching, and one says to the other, "I think he just asked to change a course." James B. Giles, September 6, 1978.

59. James B. Giles, September 6, 1978; Paul Burka, September 12, 1978; Jacquelin Collins, September 9, 1978.

60. George H. Richter, March 9, 1978.

61. Calvin M. Class, January 20, 1978; Frank E. Vandiver, April 3, 1978, April 25, 1978; James B. Giles, September 6, 1978.

62. Kenneth S. Pitzer, October 26, 1977.

63. Report of the Committee on the Freshman Course, October 1953, WRC; Report to the Executive Committee from the Committee of Educational Inquiry, May 1953; Presidents' Papers, Houston, Office Records; Mike V. McEnany to Houston, May 28, 1953, ibid.; Kenneth S. Pitzer, October 26, 1977; James B. Giles, September 6, 1978; Jacquelin Collins, September 9, 1978; Collins to Meiners, December 14, 1978, in possession of the commission.

64. Paul Burka, September 12, 1978; Jacquelin Collins, September 9, 1978; and informal conversations with Myra Bahme, Caroline Reynolds, Sam Stewart, and Hugh Rice Kelly.

65. Paul Burka, September 12, 1978.

66. Jacquelin Collins, September 9, 1978; James B. Giles, September 6, 1978; George H. Richter, July 5, 1977, March 9, 1978; and informal conversations with S. W. Higginbotham, William H. Masterson, Hugh Rice Kelly, Jacquelin Collins, and Frank E. Vandiver.

67. Paul Burka, September 12, 1978; George H. Richter, March 9, 1978; Paula Meredith Mosle, September 7, 1978; and informal conversations with Myra Bahme, Frank Vandiver, Hugh Rice Kelly, Jacquelin Collins, Patricia Teed, and Mary Fae McKay.

68. Other sources for this section are Finis E. Cowan, March 16, 1978;

William P. Hobby, July 28, 1977;
Nancy Moore Eubank, February 22,
1978; Chalmers M. Hudspeth, July
19, 1978; James Street Fulton, September 30, 1977; James R. Sims, January 18, 1978; John E. Parish,
September 28, 1977; Houston to W.
E. Allen, February 1, 1955, Presidents' Papers, Houston, Office
Records.

69. *Houston Chronicle*, October
28, 1950, November 9, 1950; January
11, 1954, November 10, 1950, April
27, 1951, May 14, 1955, May 22,
1953, November 19, 1954; *Thresher*,
November 10, 1950, February 23,
1951, April 12, 1957, May 3, 1957,
December 11, 1959; *Houston Post*,
May 14, 1955, November 19, 1955,
December 21, 1955; Jacquelin Collins, September 9, 1978; Gertrude
Stein, vertical file, WRC; Houston to
F. Talbott Wilson, September 4, 1953,
Presidents' Papers, Houston, Office
Records; Report of the Food Committee, 1950–1951, Presidents' Papers,
Pitzer, On Campus, 1961–1963. The
bust of Gertrude Stein was the work
of sculptor Jacques Lipchitz.

70. Jess Neely, October 10, 1977.

71. Jess Neely, October 10, 1977;
*Football '77: Southwest Conference
Roster and Record Book*, pp. 61–69,
157–204; *Basketball '78: The 1978
Southwest Conference Roster and
Record Book*, pp. 24–29, 82–88;
*Southwest Conference 1978 Spring
Sports Media Guide*, pp. 24–36,
73–76.

Chapter 9

1. Board Minutes, September 25,
1957; George Holmes Richter, July 5,
1977; Guy T. McBride, October 24,
1977.

2. Board Minutes, December 16,
1959, March 30, 1960, June 29, 1960;
Sallyport 16 (January 1960); *Thresher*,
January 16, 1960, February 26, 1960,

April 6, 1960, April 9, 1960; Houston
to Rice Associates, February 2, 1960,
Presidents' Papers, Pitzer, On Campus, 1961–1963; *Houston Chronicle*,
January 9, 1960, January 10, 1960,
April 7, 1960, April 8, 1960, April 9,
1960; *Houston Post*, January 10,
1960, January 18, 1960; H. Malcolm
Lovett, June 27, 1977.

3. Board Minutes, September 19,
1960, January 25, 1961; Houston to
Faculty, July 27, 1960, Presidents'
Papers, Pitzer, On Campus, 1961–
1963; Faculty Minutes, January 30,
1961, February 20, 1961; *Thresher*,
September 10, 1960, October 28,
1960, September 23, 1960.

4. Board Minutes, April 26, 1961,
May 31, 1961; Mrs. J. Newton Rayzor, February 8, 1978; Kenneth S. Pitzer, vertical file, WRC.

5. Board Minutes, October 2, 1952,
September 28, 1960, September 27,
1961, March 28, 1962; *Thresher*, October 3, 1961; *Houston Post*, April
17, 1960; Masterson to Croneis, June
7, 1961, Presidents' Papers, Pitzer,
On Campus, 1961–1963.

6. Faculty Minutes, September 28,
1961; Pitzer to J. Wallace Sterling,
August 31, 1962, Presidents' Papers,
Pitzer, On Campus, 1961–1963;
"Call to the Semifrontier," *Time*, No-
vember 24, 1961, clipping in Presi-
dents' Papers, Pitzer, On Campus,
1961–1963; "The Third President
Looks at Rice," *Rice Alumni Maga-
zine* 1 (March 1963), 5–9; *Houston
Chronicle*, July 6, 1961; *Thresher*,
September 15, 1961.

7. Pitzer to Board, January 25,
1962, Presidents' Papers, Pitzer, On
Campus, 1961–1963; Report of the
Academic Planning Committee to
the President, December 8, 1961,
ibid.; *Houston Chronicle*, December
21, 1961, December 22, 1961, clippings in Presidents' Papers, Pitzer,
On Campus, 1961–1963.

8. *Houston Chronicle*, February 4,
1960, February 21, 1960, April 4,

1960, May 15, 1960, July 24, 1960,
January 3, 1961, March 9, 1961, April
21, 1961, August 25, 1961, September 19, 1961, September 24, 1961,
December 14, 1961, December 21,
1961, December 27, 1961, January 7,
1962, January 18, 1962, March 23,
1962, April 4, 1962, April 8, 1962,
April 12, 1962, May 29, 1962, June
22, 1962, July 19, 1962, August 23,
1962, October 8, 1962; *Houston Post*,
June 19, 1962; *Houston Post*, n.d.,
clipping in Presidents' Papers, Pitzer,
On Campus, 1961–1963; Board Minutes, August 23, 1961, October 25,
1961; *Thresher*, September 19, 1962.

9. *Houston Chronicle*, February 10,
1961, March 19, 1961, November 19,
1961; Kenneth S. Pitzer, October 26,
1977; Report of joint meeting of
members of the faculty and of the
Board of Governors, November 15,
1960, Presidents' Papers, Houston,
Office Records; Board Minutes, May
23, 1962, September 27, 1961.

10. Board Minutes, January 31,
1962, February 28, 1962, April 25,
1962, September 27, 1961; Chancellor Croneis thought that $20 million
was much too small a sum. He suggested to Rayzor that at least $75
million was needed and that it would
only be the beginning. The $20 mil-
lion would be helpful, but he thought
the board should be told "quite
plainly" that even $75 million would
prove to be entirely inadequate. Croneis to Rayzor, February 27, 1962,
Presidents' Papers, Pitzer, On Campus, 1961–1963.

11. Board Minutes, September 27,
1961, May 23, 1962, July 25, 1962,
September 26, 1962, February 27,
1963; Faculty Minutes, June 1, 1962;
H. Malcolm Lovett, June 27, 1977,
March 29, 1978; Kenneth S. Pitzer,
October 26, 1978; *Thresher*, February
27, 1963, February 12, 1964, February
13, 1964, February 19, 1964, February
26, 1964, March 11, 1964; *Houston
Post*, February 22, 1963; $33 Million

Campaign Newsletter, WRC.

12. Kenneth S. Pitzer, October 26, 1978; Notes written in Pitzer's hand, n.d., in Presidents' Papers, Pitzer, On Campus, 1961–1963; "The Academic Planning Committee: Purpose and Program," n.d., but stamped March 6, 1963, ibid.; Academic Planning Committee Minutes, January 4, 1963, February 11, 1963, April 29, 1963, May 7, 1963, ibid.; Progress Report of Academic Planning Committee, June 4, 1963, ibid.; *Self-Study of William Marsh Rice University,* October 1, 1964, pp. xii–xx; Faculty Minutes, March 12, 1963.

13. *Self-Study,* pp. 4–6; *Thresher,* October 15, 1964. The General and Educational Budget for 1978 amounted to $25 million.

14. *Self-Study,* pp. 9–11; Faculty Minutes, September 28, 1961; Memo on role of the Dean of Students, n.d., Presidents' Papers, Pitzer, On Campus, 1961–1963; Policy for Masters, Dean of Women, Dean of Students, April 11, 1963, ibid.; Kenneth S. Pitzer, October 26, 1978; Frank E. Vandiver, April 3, 1978; Report of Academic Development Committee, December 8, 1961, Presidents' Papers, Pitzer, On Campus, 1961–1963.

15. Faculty Minutes, April 16, 1962; *Thresher,* May 12, 1961, September 15, 1961, April 13, 1962.

16. Board Minutes, January 31, 1962, March 28, 1962; Donald Mackenzie to Masterson, May 1, 1961, Presidents' Papers, Pitzer, On Campus, 1961–1963; Pitzer to Department Chairmen, March 9, 1962, ibid.; Report of Academic Development Committee, December 8, 1961, ibid.; Kenneth S. Pitzer, October 26, 1978; Frank E. Vandiver, April 3, 1978.

17. Board Minutes, November 30, 1961, May 29, 1963; *Thresher,* February 10, 1961.

18. Board Minutes, February 24, 1960; *Thresher,*

February 26, 1960, December 16, 1961; *Houston Post,* February 26, 1960; *Houston Chronicle,* February 26, 1960, December 10, 1961.

19. *Announcements,* 1958, pp. 69–81; 1961, pp. 37–46; 1962, pp. 36–46; Faculty Minutes, January 30, 1961, February 20, 1961, April 24, 1961; *Self-Study,* pp. 70–74; *Thresher,* February 26, 1960, April 29, 1960, September 16, 1960, April 28, 1961; *Houston Chronicle,* July 24, 1960, September 11, 1960, February 24, 1961, April 1, 1962; Notes and minutes on meeting of division of the humanities, March 29, 1960, Presidents' Papers, Pitzer, On Campus, 1961–1963; Croneis to Mackenzie, February 4, 1961, Presidents' Papers, Houston, Departments; Jess Neely, October 10, 1977; Hubert E. Bray, June 18, 1976, September 30, 1976.

20. James B. Giles, September 6, 1978; *Announcements,* 1961, p. 33; Admissions policy, n.d., Presidents' Papers, Pitzer, On Campus, 1961–1963; *Thresher,* March 4, 1960, May 11, 1962, September 19, 1962; *Houston Chronicle,* September 6, 1960.

21. James B. Giles, September 6, 1978; Kenneth S. Pitzer, October 26, 1977; Admissions policy, n.d., Presidents' Papers, Pitzer, On Campus, 1961–1963.

22. "Distribution of Grades in Selected Institutions, Spring 1961," Presidents' Papers, Pitzer, On Campus, 1961–1963.

23. Mackenzie to Pitzer, February 25, 1963, Presidents' Papers, Pitzer, On Campus, 1961–1963.

24. *Thresher,* May 5, 1961, May 12, 1961, February 6, 1963, February 13, 1963, March 13, 1963, September 24, 1964; "Distribution of Grades in Selected Institutions, Spring 1961," ibid.; Subcommittee on Program of Undergraduate Instruction to Academic Planning Committee, n.d., ibid.; Committee on Examinations

and Standing to Pitzer, March 5, 1963, in Minutes of the Committee on Examinations and Standing; *Self-Study,* pp. 48–49, 76–78; James B. Giles, September 6, 1978; Paul Burka, September 12, 1978.

25. Joint Meeting of Members of the Faculty and of the Board of Governors, November 15, 1960, Presidents' Papers, Houston, Office Records; Subcommittee on Program of Undergraduate Instruction to Academic Planning Committee, n.d., Presidents' Papers, Pitzer, On Campus, 1961–1963; Academic Planning Committee Minutes, April 29, 1963, May 7, 1963, ibid.; *Thresher,* September 19, 1962, March 13, 1963, February 13, 1963, September 18, 1963, September 24, 1964, October 1, 1964; *Houston Post,* May 12, 1963; *Self-Study,* pp. 48–49.

26. *Thresher,* November 10, 1961, September 19, 1962, October 24, 1962, November 28, 1962, October 8, 1964; *Houston Post,* October 22, 1960, April 29, 1961, September 6, 1962, December 6, 1962; *Houston Chronicle,* September 8, 1960, September 25, 1960, May 10, 1961, September 7, 1962, December 6, 1962, December 13, 1962; Chalmers Hudspeth, July 19, 1978.

Chapter 10

1. *The Inauguration of Kenneth Sanborn Pitzer and Semicentennial Ceremonies at William Marsh Rice University, October 10–13, 1962* (Houston: Rice University, 1963), pp. 23–25.

2. Semicentennial, vertical file, WRC; *Inauguration of Pitzer,* passim; *Man, Science, Learning, and Education, the Semicentennial Lectures at Rice University* (Houston: Rice University, 1963), passim.

BIBLIOGRAPHY

Manuscripts

Rice University, Houston, Texas
  Comptroller's Office, Allen Center
    Budget file
  Registrar's Office, Lovett Hall
    Report to the President from the
    Registrar, 1912–1964
  Treasurer's Office, Allen Center
    Office Correspondence
    Minutes of the Board of Trustees
  Undergraduate Dean's Office,
  Lovett Hall
    Minutes of the Committee on
    Examinations and Standing,
    1946–1964
  Woodson Research Center,
  Fondren Library
    *Charter of the William M. Rice
    Institute for the Advancement
    of Literature, Science and Art,
    Houston, Texas* [1891]
  Committee on the Freshman
  Course file
  Dean of Students, Hugh S.
  Cameron file
  Letters Addressed to Secretary
  E. Raphael
  Presidents' Papers: Edgar Odell
  Lovett
  Presidents' Papers: William
  Vermillion Houston
  Presidents' Papers: Kenneth
  Sanborn Pitzer
  Photographic file
  Vertical file
  $33 Million Campaign
  Newsletter
  Rice Institute Engineering Show
  Programs

William Ward Watkin Papers
McCants, John T. "Some
Information Concerning the
Rice Institute"
Wilson, Mrs. Harold. "Rambling
Reminiscences of Early Days at
Rice by a Septuagenarian"
Bulbrook, Harry Marshall.
"Odyssey of a Freshman—1912"

Books and Journal Articles

Baker, James A., Jr. "Reminiscences
of the Founder." *Rice Institute
Pamphlet* 18, no. 3 (July 1931):
127–44.
*Basketball '78: The 1978 Southwest
Conference Roster and Record
Book.* N.p.: Southwest Conference,
1977.
*The Book of the Opening of the Rice
Institute.* 3 vols. Houston: Rice
Institute, 1915.
Butler, Nicholas Murray. *Across the
Busy Years: Recollections and
Reflections.* 2 vols. New York:
C. Scribner's Sons, 1939, 1940.
Coon, Horace. *Columbia: Colossus
on the Hudson.* New York: E. P.
Dutton & Co., Inc., 1947.
Cram, Ralph Adams. *My Life in
Architecture.* Boston: Little, Brown
& Co., 1936.
Cramer, Clarence H. *Case Western
Reserve: A History of the
University, 1826–1976.* Boston:
Little, Brown & Co., 1976.
Davies, Debbie. "Rice has been
trading knocks with the

distinguished Texas A&M
University for 63 years and all
we've got to show for it are a few
bruises—and many memories.
That's no joke." *Sallyport* 32, no. 2
(November 15, 1976):10–11.
Davis, Ellis A. and Grobe, Edwin H.,
comps. and eds. *The New
Encyclopedia of Texas.* Dallas:
Texas Development Bureau, n.d.
[ca. 1926].
Earnest, Ernest. *Academic
Procession: An Informal History of
the American College, 1636 to
1953.* Indianapolis: Bobbs-Merrill
Co., Inc., 1953.
Elliott, Orrin Leslie. *Stanford
University: The First Twenty-five
Years.* Stanford, Ca.: Stanford
University Press, 1937.
Embree, Elisha D. and Eaton,
Thomas B. *The Flying Owls: Rice
Institute from the Air.* N.p., 1921.
Copy in WRC.
*Football '77: Southwest Conference
Roster and Record Book.* N.p.:
Southwest Conference, 1977.
General Announcements. Houston:
Rice Institute (University),
1915–1964.
Hawkins, Hugh. *Pioneer: A History
of the Johns Hopkins University,
1874–1889.* Ithaca, N. Y.: Cornell
University Press, 1960.
Houston, William V. "Edgar Odell
Lovett." *Yearbook of the American
Philosophical Society* (1957):
137–40.
Huxley, Julian. *Memories.* 2 vols.
London: George Allen & Unwin,

238 Bibliography

Publishers, Ltd., 1970, 1973.
──────────. "Texas and Academe." *Cornhill Magazine* 118 (July 1918):53–65.
Jourdain, Philip E. B. "A New American University." *Rice Institute Pamphlet* 5 (October 1918):209–14.
Kelley, Brooks M. *Yale: A History.* New Haven, Conn.: Yale University Press, 1974.
Lear, Floyd S. "History and the Humanities in Our Earlier Years." *Flyleaf* 15, no. 1 (October 1964:2–17; 15, no. 2 (January 1965):1–11.
Lovett, Edgar O. "Some Relations of the University." *Rice Institute Pamphlet* 5 (October 1918): 191–94.
──────────. "Historical Sketch of Rice Institute, A Gift to Texas Youth."
Houston Post Annual Industrial Number, November 17, 1920.
Morison, Samuel Eliot, ed. *The Development of Harvard University Since the Inauguration of President Eliot, 1869–1929.* Cambridge, Mass.: Harvard University Press, 1930.
Muir, Andrew F. "Rice's Future Mapped in Early 1900s." *Houston Post*, October 7, 1962.
──────────. *William Marsh Rice and His Institute.* Edited by Sylvia Stallings Morris. *Rice University Studies* 58, no. 2 (Spring 1972). Reprint. Houston: Rice University, 1972.
Pierson, George Wilson. *Yale College: An Educational History, 1871–1921.* New Haven, Conn.: Yale University Press, 1952.
──────────. *Yale: The University College, 1921–1937.* New Haven, Conn.: Yale University Press, 1955.
Ramsay, William. "The Functions of a University." *Rice Institute*

Pamphlet 5 (October 1918): 225–38.
The Rice Institute. N.p.: DeVinne Press, n.d. Known as the DeVinne Pamphlet. Copy in WRC.
Rudolph, Frederick. *The American College and University: A History.* New York: Alfred A. Knopf, Inc., 1962.
Schmidt, George P. *The Liberal Arts College: A Chapter in American Cultural History.* New Brunswick, N. J.: Rutgers University Press, 1957.
Self-Study of William Marsh Rice University. Houston: Rice University, 1964.
Southwest Conference 1978 Spring Sports Media Guide. N.p.: Southwest Conference, 1978.
Thwing, Charles Franklin. *The American Colleges and Universities in the Great War, 1914–1919: A History.* New York: The Macmillan Company, 1920.
Veysey, Laurence R. *The Emergence of the American University.* Chicago: University of Chicago Press, 1965.
Watkin, William Ward. "Architectural Development of the William M. Rice Institute, Houston, Texas." *Southern Architectural Review* 1 (November 1910):110–12.
Wertenbaker, Thomas Jefferson. *Princeton, 1746-1896.* Princeton, N. J.: Princeton University Press, 1946.

Newspapers

Houston Chronicle
Houston Post (also known as *Houston Daily Post* and *Houston Post Dispatch*)
Houston Press

Interviews

Allen, Herbert, September 27, 1977
Batjer, Helen, August 10, 1976
Battista, Joseph L., March 8, 1978
Bourgeois, Andre, November 28, 1977
Bray, Gertrude, January 22, 1976
Bray, Hubert E., June 18, 1976, September 30, 1976
Brown, George R., July 14, 1977
Bulbrook, Harry M., October 28, 1977
Burka, Paul, September 12, 1978
Camden, Carroll, September 20, 1977
Chapman, Allen, September 30, 1977
Class, Calvin M., January 20, 1978
Collins, Jacquelin, September 9, 1978
Cowan, Finis E., March 16, 1978
Davis, Joe W., February 21, 1978
Dwyer, C. A., July 26, 1977
Eikenberg, C. Virgil, February 9, 1978
Emison, Sam and Mary Frances, September 21, 1977
Erfurth, August, September 20, 1977
Eubank, Nancy Moore, February 22, 1978
Filson, Martha, February 19, 1976
Fuermann, George, August 5, 1977
Fulton, James Street, September 30, 1977
Gallegley, Joseph J., October 26, 1976
Giles, James B., September 6, 1978
Hartsook, Arthur J., July 21, 1977
Heaps, Belle, February 17, 1978
Hobby, William P., July 28, 1977
Hudspeth, Chalmers, July 19, 1978
Jameson, Florence McAllister, February 3, 1978
Johnson, Gaylord and Louise, February 20, 1978, March 27, 1978
Johnson, Marguerite, August 5, 1977
Kirkland, William A., July 19, 1977
Kotch, Clara Margaret Mohr, February 10, 1978
Lane, Sarah, October 20, 1975, July 1, 1977
Lankford, Raymond L., January 30, 1978

Lovett, H. Malcolm, May 19, 1976, June 27, 1977, March 29, 1978, July 27, 1981

McBride, Guy T., October 24, 1977

McEnany, Michael V., September 1, 1977

Masterson, William H., October 11, 1977

Morehead, James C., April 6, 1978

Mosle, Paula Meredith, September 7, 1978

Nealon, Clark, February 2, 1978

Neely, Jess C., October 10, 1977

Nunn, Stayton, April 5, 1978

Parish, John, September 28, 1977

Pitzer, Kenneth Sanborn, October 26, 1977

Rayzor, Eugenia, February 8, 1978

Red, Hattie Lel, January 23, 1976, June 28, 1977

Reynolds, Walter M., September 19, 1977

Richter, G. Holmes, July 5, 1977, March 9, 1978

Sanders, Isaac, July 27, 1976

Shelton, Fred V., September 29, 1977

Shimek, Joe and Evelyn, September 22, 1977

Sims, James R., January 18, 1978

Stancliff, Fred, September 28, 1977

Teague, James U., June 29, 1977

Thomas, J. D., July 13, 1977

Tillett, Henry A., December 23, 1976

Vandiver, Frank E., April 3, 1978, April 25, 1978

Waples, Margaret A., February 24, 1976

Whitmore, William, January 19, 1978

INDEX